Breaking Open The Boxes

100 Quadrants For Wisdom and Success in Life

Andrew Munro and Robert Bolton

Copyright © Andrew Munro & Robert Bolton 2024

The Authors assert the moral right to be identified as the authors of this work.

ISBN: 9798340246028

All rights reserved. No part of this publication may be reproduced, stored in a retrieval system, or transmitted in any form or by any means, electronic, mechanical, photocopying, recording or otherwise, without the prior permission of the authors.

This book is sold subject to the condition that it shall not, by way of trade or otherwise, be lent, resold, hired out or otherwise circulated without the author's prior consent in any form of binding or cover other than that in which it is published and without a similar condition including this condition being imposed on the subsequent purchaser.

About the Authors

Andrew Munro (MA Hons, C Psychol)

His business career began with a psychometric test consulting firm. Working on a variety of client assignments was hugely enjoyable, but after a while, it became obvious that selection testing was only one piece of a much bigger jigsaw of business success. He moved into corporate life with a financial services company in a series of roles that included assessment, performance management, career development, talent and succession planning. This experience indicated that organisational life was even more complex than he thought, and that his previous solution - introduce psychometric testing for better selection - was a fairly limited response to the challenges business face. Sustainable business success depends on the inter-play of multiple factors. It was a progressive boss - the co-author - who broadened his perspective with systems thinking.

It also became clear that organisations do like to complicate and why simplicity is critical. Andrew moved back into consulting, working with a range of clients over the last twenty years on a variety of talent management and organisational change assignments. He is the author of several books, recently, Personality Testing in Employee Selection, and co-author with Masoud Golshani-Shirazi of A To Z And Back Again: Adventures and Misadventures in Talent Management.

He is the lead Director of Talent World Consulting; and can be contacted at andrew@amazureconsulting.com.

Robert Bolton (MSc, MA, ARPS)

Robert started business life as a management trainee for a retailer, moving into the people and organisation space. From retailing, Robert went to local government and then an NGO. His career advanced rapidly when he joined a well-known financial services organisation in the UK, with the good timing to work with some outstandingly talented individuals. He also had the misfortune at one point to manage Andrew.

Robert gained an MSc and an MA, and in the process, recognised the power of systems thinking: an approach to solving complex, messy and sometimes wicked organisation problems. Systems thinking has been his one ring to rule them all, and invaluable in his career as a management consultant with KPMG.

Along the way, he was awarded HR Consultant of the Year by the Management Consultancy Association. His clients have included government, telecoms, oil and gas, and the chemical sectors, and nearly always a joy to work with. More recently, Robert coordinated the global People and Change communities across KPMG to lead on new solutions and thought leadership on people consulting and Human Resources, including KPMG's Future of HR report. Contact rpbrpb@mac.com.

He is also building a reputation as a fine art minimalist photographer. See www.quietlandscapes.net

Acknowledgements

Many individuals - friends, colleagues and clients - have shaped this book - most who probably don't know they did. However, from exploratory conversations about the initial concept through to suggestions for new grids and feedback on draft versions, several people kept this project on track.

Stand out advisors include:

Duncan Armitage, David Bannister, Paul Barrett, Rory Bolton, Nick Cowley, Masoud Golshani-Shirazi, Ann Hartley, Kate Holt, Tom Kennie, Stephen McCafferty, Lis McCormick, Simon Parrett, Tim Payne, Katie Tayler, Nikola Tosic, Sharon Toye, Dominic Ward. And all at the Talent World Consulting network.

And key thinkers whose ideas underpin much of this book:

Baltasar Gracián and The Art of Worldly Wisdom
Ray Dalio's Principles
Iain McGilchrist's, The Master and His Emissary
Roberrt Greene, and The Laws of Human Nature
Shane Parrish at the Farnam Street blog
Marshall Goldsmith, and his array of writings, specifically, What Got You Here, Won't Get You There
Peter Bevelin's Seeking Wisdom: From Darwin to Munger
Michael Mauboussin, and The Success Equation
Peter Senge's The Fifth Discipline, and Peter Checkland
Venkatesh Rao at Ribbon Farm
James O'Brien, both his books and his LBC radio show
Oliver Burkeman, and his articles on personal development
Dave Trott; his blog and books
Rory Sutherland and Alchemy
Marcus du Sautoy, Thinking Better: The Art of the Shortcut
Max Gunther, How to Get Lucky
Elliott Jaques on requisite organisation and stratified systems theory
Will Storr, The Science of a Story

Reviews

Andrew Munro and Robert Bolton take a fresh approach to the 4 box grid. They combine theory and practicality in a highly readable format. The kind of book to keep at hand to help thinking through life's challenges. **Kate Holt, Partner, People Consulting, KPMG**

A lively and fascinating journey to understand the many challenges we all face - personally and in business - with invaluable insight into tactics and actions. An essential read to make sense of a messy world. **David Bannister, Director, Scotwork International**

Breaking Open the Boxes offers fresh insights into the value of the classic 2 x 2 matrix. This helicopter perspective and multiple lens is novel, and well worth exploring. **Dr Tom Kennie, Director, Ranmore Consulting**

Finally, a book that I can pick up and quickly make sense of with its clarity and logic. Munro and Bolton have a knack of using new perspectives to bring engaging insights to everyday life and business scenarios. This book helps me rethink, challenge and change. **Ann Hartley, Head of Assessment, Penna Consulting**

An immensely practical and thought provoking book which is a must for Organisational Development. The authors provide powerful tools for practitioners and consultants. **Stephen McCafferty, former Group Head of Talent, Performance, Learning and Development, European Investment Bank**

Andrew and Robert take a fresh approach to the classic 4-box grid. At times quite quirky but always relevant and thought provoking, with grids that use engaging metaphors. This book will make you think and arm you with what you need to apply the grids in the real world. **Mark Williamson, Partner and Head of People Consulting, KPMG, UK**

This set my mind running. How grids can be used across many different disciplines and circumstances. **Alastair Taylor, Former CEO of the Institute of Agricultural Engineers**

An essential book for anyone interested in organisational dynamics. The authors share their extensive experience and insights to explore critical scenarios. A book that practitioners will return to again and again. **Dominic Ward, Senior Capability Consultant, Scottish Power**

Quadrants that bust our assumptions about how we operate in the world opening up new possibilities for leading ourselves for success. **Sharon Toye, Founder Partner, Leadership Mindset Partners**

I've always had a love-hate relationship with 4 box grids, but the authors have found a way to breathe new life into them. Their wry commentary mixed with decades of rich experience, show that these simple tools can actually be a window into complex and subtle organisational topics. Insightful and valuable for work and beyond. **Tim Payne, Partner, KPMG**

In this highly readable book, the authors provide a range of grids that form an Ordinance Survey map of kinds. They encourage us to be thoroughly and precisely curious about the diverse paths tracking through the problematic landscapes of everyday life - personal and professional - and offer us a way of choosing the most appropriate one. **Simon Parrett, Psychotherapist and Educationalist**

Contents

Overview 1
Who Should Read this Book 3
How to Read this Book 5
How Crazy is it Getting: VUCA, BANI, RUPT or TUNA? 7
Cognitive Biases and Heuristics 11
A Brief History of the Quadrant 13
The Criteria of a Good Grid 17

Ten By Ten 25

Personal Mastery	Working Through Others	Managing The Business
Self Management & Life Success	Interpersonal Relationships & Skills	Communication, Influence, Negotiation & Conflict
		Strategic Analysis & Planning
Problem Solving & Decision Making	Leadership & Management	Culture & Change Management
		Financial Analysis & Risk Management
Implementation, Project Management & Doing Stuff		Technology & the Future Work Force

Self Management and Life Success 27
Do We Expect too Much from Life? 29
Do We Know What We Want? 33
What is the Fine Line Between Success and Failure? 37
Do We Feel Lucky Today? 41

Why Our Attitudes to Time Matter... 45
Do We Know our Real Strengths?.. 49
How to Achieve and Sustain Success... 53
Which Habits are We Building?.. 57
How Should We Set Goals? 61
How Can We Best Manage the Difficulties of Life? 65

Problem Solving and Decision Making.. 69
Which Problems are Best Avoided 71
Why Do Intelligent People Do Daft Stuff? 75
Why Didn't the Dog Bark? 79
Which Sources of Information Can We Trust?................................... 83
Should We Mistrust the Experts?.. 87
How to Explain Mystery... 91
Is it Ethical?... 95
How to Decide How to Decide 99
How to Optimise our Decisions 103
What is the Focus of Innovation?.. 107

Implementation, Project Management and Doing Stuff............. 111
Have We Got our Priorities Right?.. 113
How Far are We Prepared to Go?.. 117
Is Resistance Futile?... 121
Do We Have - or Even Need - A Plan? 125
Is There an Easy Way to Project Success? 129
Are We in Control of the Project? 133
How Do We Manage Project Heist? 137
Are We Playing Project Chicken?.. 141
Can We Become More Productive?.. 145
Is it Possible to Idle Productively?.. 149

Interpersonal Relationships and Skills 153
Why Connections Matter 155
Are We Pleasing or Pushing? 159
Who is ok? 163
How Do We Build Trust? 167
Are We Gaining or Losing? 171
Are We too Popular? 175
Who is Kidding Who? 179
What is the Destructive Dynamic of Relationships? 183
How to Find a Partner in Life 187
Will this Relationship Survive? 191

Communication, Influence, Negotiation and Conflict 195
Is our Firm Communicating with Impact? 197
Are our Meetings Productive? 201
Are We Boring? 205
Why Arguments Rarely End Well 209
Can We Improve the Chances of Winning an Argument? 213
Can We Resolve Conflict? 217
What is our Negotiational Style? 221
Are our Negotiational Tactics Working for Us? 225
Do We Present with Impact? 229
Are We Having a Big Conversation? 233

Leadership and Mangement 237
Are We for Real? 239
What Kind of Leader Do We Want? 243
Why is Strategic Leadership so Difficult? 247
Are We in Leadership Flow? 251
Who is in our Team? 255

Are We at Risk of Group Think?.. 259
How Do We Gain Promotion? 263
Who Should We Promote? 267
Who Should We Demote? 271
What Leadership Legacy Will We Leave? 275

Culture and Change Management 279
Are the Firm's Values of Much Value?... 281
How Much Change is Possible? 285
Are Silos an Inescapable Fact of Organisational Life? 289
Does our Culture Reflect our Operating Model?........................... 293
Is the Organisation Inclusive?.. 297
Will this Organisation Change Last? 301
Are our Employees Afraid to Speak Up? 305
Is our Company for Real? 309
What is Holding Back Organisational Innovation? 313
Are our Incentive Systems Working for Us? 317

Strategic Analysis and Planing... 321
Why Business Success is Elusive.. 323
Can We Predict the Strategic Future? 327
Does our Strategy Need a Strategy?.. 331
Which Strategic Scenario Do We Face?... 335
What Information Will the Board Act on?..................................... 339
Will our Organisation Survive? 343
Is the Lord in the Castle? 347
What is on the Breakfast Table?.. 351
Is the Senior Team Having the Right Conversation?..................... 355
Will this Acquisition Succeed?... 359

Financial Analysis and Risk Management 363
Can We Achieve Cost Savings? 365
Does the Firm Have a Black Hole? 369
How is the Business Performing? 373
Are We Covering Up? 377
Will our Prospects Become Profitable Clients? 381
Should We Outsource? 385
What Do We Value Most in Supplier Relationships? 389
Which Consultancies Should We Avoid? 393
How Do our Attitudes to Money Affect our Lives? 397
Which Investment Opportunities are Best Avoided? 401

Technology and Future Workforce 405
Why are We not Working Less? 407
What are the Building Blocks of an Organisation? 411
What Will the Future Workforce Look Like? 415
Does Hybrid Working Work? 419
Will a Robot Do my Job? 423
Can We Thrive in a Digital World? 427
Is Technology Now Part of the Problem? 431
How Should We Invest in Business Technology? 435
Should We Welcome Generative AI? 439
Can We Believe the Chatbot? 443

How to Break Open The Boxes 447
Four Ways of Looking at the World 449
Top Down or Bottom Up Wisdom 453
Know the Scope of the Problem and the Solutions 455
Breaking Out of the Boxes: Left and Right Brain 459
Think 461

Talk 464
Do 467
Grid 101 and Beyond 470
Final Thoughts 472

Appendix 1: Your Attentional Mode 475

OVERVIEW

You don't have to know everything. A few really big ideas carry most of the freight. **Charlie Munger**

Charlie Munger was the advisory side-kick of Warren Buffett who runs the investment vehicle Berkshire Hathaway. $100 invested in its stock in 1965 is now worth $2.42 million. This money invested in the S & P 500 would be worth only about $22,400.

Charlie Munger's philosophy: *we can't know everything. And we don't need to know everything. But some issues we do need to know.* A few big ideas will give us insight into what we do need to know about the important stuff for personal, professional and business success.

Whenever I mention the idea of the shortcut, people invariably think I am trying to cheat somehow. The word short cuts sounds like you could be cutting corners. I'm after the correct path to get to the correct solution. I'm not interested in a shoddy approximation to the answer. I want complete understanding, but without unnecessary hard work. **Marcus du Sautoy**

The 100 grids in this book are thinking tools to navigate through the range of the tests and trials we encounter in life to:

- gain traction into the key factors behind the wicked problems of life.
- recognise when a quick good enough decision will satisfice, or when we need to rethink options to optimise our plans.
- trigger a debate within ourselves to check we are engaging with the relevant issues and not fooling ourselves.
- explore problems in workshops as part of strategic planning and team building activity.
- open up conversations with our family, friends and colleagues as we grapple with the messiness of life.

The book is structured around some really big ideas.

Who should read this book

If only we could have two lives: the first in which to make one's mistakes. The second in which to profit by them. **DH Lawrence**

This book should be read by those who want to live life the *easier* way. There is rarely an easy way, but sometimes we make life much more difficult than it should be. This collection of quadrants - which includes the quirky and idiosyncratic - has been consolidated to cut through the confusing complexity of information overload, extravagant hype and often absurd and wrong-headed advice.

Tell my why. Why do we make it so hard? **Steve Gibbons Band**

Specifically, the book is intended for:

Next generation business leaders who participate in a range of training and educational programmes at management colleges and business schools. This book provides a tool kit - not just intellectual but intuitive - for an informed view of the personal, professional and organisational challenges they have to overcome in their careers.

Facilitators of workshops and programmes who want fresh insights to share with their participants. Each grid provides the basis for a half-day event for discussion, debate and action planning. References with additional resource are included for each grid.

Management consultants applying frameworks and methodologies for their clients to open up new perspectives about the challenges they encounter. This is set of perspectives stimulates debate about the problems they are experiencing - or don't even recognise those they are confronting - to work through the trade-offs of different solutions.

Executive coaches and mentors. Here the issues are often much more personal. What specifically is working or not working for the individual right now? Often the boundaries of business, professional and personal life are fuzzy. These grids - well positioned and timed -

have the potential for the AHA moment when a client identifies the problems and choices they are grappling with.

How to read this book

I kept always two books in my pocket, one to read, one to write in. **Robert Louis Stevenson**

This is not a book to be read from cover to cover. We anticipate three approaches:

1. As a dip in and dip out book. One reviewer recommended this as a book for the toilet. Harsh. But the point is well made. Look at the listing of contents. Does one question capture your interest when you have a few reflective minutes? It will trigger your thinking - whether you agree or disagree with the analysis. We suggest you keep returning to the book for fresh insights. It will be a useful resource in your journey through life. Review the conclusions, and identify how a shift in approach requires both left and right brain thinking.

2. When faced with a particular life challenge. Check the list of 100 grids. Do any of the questions resonate? Life is a series of problems which can be framed as opportunities or threats. There is always an upside and a downside of the options. Use the quadrants to gain a sense of perspective to identify a response that optimises the upside.

Books are mirrors: You only see in them what you already have inside you. **Carlos Ruiz**

3. Preparing for an assignment. It may be an initial client meeting, a proposal, a presentation or pulling together content for a workshop or programme. Which of the 100 grids will ignite a debate to address the key issues that challenge others to rethink and reframe the issues? Which quadrant will open up a conversation to build a relationship? And use the grids of Think, Talk and Do in the conclusion to identify ways of breaking out the boxes that often constrain us.

If one cannot enjoy reading a book over and over again, there is no use in reading it at all. **Oscar Wilde**

See this collection as a field book to navigate the territory of work and life.

How crazy is it getting: VUCA, BANI, RUPT OR TUNA?

We are told we live in a world of VUCA. In this world we can expect:

- **Volatility**: change is rapid and unpredictable in its nature and extent.
- **Uncertainty**: if the present is unclear, the future is fuzzier.
- **Complexity**: many different, interconnected factors come into play, all with the potential to cause chaos and confusion.
- **Ambiguity**: there is a lack of clarity about the situations we face.[1]

More than any other time in history, mankind faces a crossroads. One path leads to despair and utter hopelessness. The other, to total extinction. Let us pray we have the wisdom to choose correctly. **Woody Allen**

VUCA was first used by the United States Army War College following the 9/11 terrorist attacks of 2001. It was then adopted as a marketing slogan to drum up business for the change management industry. This is the grouping of thought leaders whose sense of history extends as far back as yesterday's newspaper headline. But if VUCA hasn't terrified us enough, the thought leaders go on to propose we are also entering the worlds of:

- **BANI**: Brittle, Anxious, Nonlinear and Incomprehensible.
- **RUPT**: Rapid, Unpredictable, Paradoxical, and Tangled.
- Or even more frighteningly, **TUNA**: Turbulent, Unpredictable Uncertainty, Novelty and Ambiguity.[2]

We now face a battle of acronyms, summarised as *Hey it's crazy out there*[3] to remind us why we should be un-cheerful.[4]

Management theory books and disaster films have something in common. Both confront the prospect of the near-total destruction of life as we know it. **Matthew Stewart**[5]

Only occasionally does a commentator remind us that this is no different to the world of previous generations. History has had no shortage of times of change and disruption.[6] VUCA and the associated acronyms are over-played in the hype of the consulting script: we are all heading to hell in a handcart.

Nonetheless - as always throughout history - we need mental maps to make sense of the world. Without these cognitive frameworks, we cannot understand complexity, make informed judgements and decisions, or implement practical action plans.

Maps by their very nature are discarded when a new and better one comes along. Even their name suggests this, which means Latin for napkin. **Ray Talson**

Charlie Munger made the distinction between the experienced decision maker and the novice. The difference? An experienced decision maker is not necessarily more intelligent. But they do know how to use their intelligence to access **a wider and deeper set of mental** models.

Wider indicates the ability to draw on a range of frameworks from different disciplines.
Deeper reflects the power of these mental models to explain and predict the important stuff.

Shrewd observers and actors in life recognise the tension between generalised principles that offer a universal truth and the specific tactics demanded within a given situation. They also know how to apply these general principles within a specific context.[7]

Generalised principles are incorporated within proverbs along the lines of *look before you leap*. Wise counsel to remind us of the need for careful deliberation and caution before making a major decision. An unthinking acceptance of this advice may also result in missing an unexpected opportunity. Here, *those who hesitate are lost* provides better guidance. *If at first you don't succeed, try try again* was popularised by the story of Robert the Bruce, the Scottish warlord hiding in a cave as he observed a spider attempting to spin its web. Alternatively, d*on't beat your head against a brick wall* reminds us the folly of unthinking persistence when our talents and energies could be deployed more productively elsewhere. Or as WC Fields put it: *If at first you don't succeed, try, try again. Then quit. There's no point in being a damn fool about it.*[8]

Almost every wise saying has an opposite one, no less wise, to balance it. **George Santayana**

Our mental mapping of reality informs judgement of which tactics to deploy where and when. Some models are cul de sacs, others roundabouts, and others are genuine short cuts. The wisest are those which combine intellect and intuition.

An intuition is neither caprice nor a sixth sense but a form of unconscious intelligence. **Gerd Gigerenzer**

The best models are working theories which understand cause and consequence within context to integrate:

- **Simplicity** and ease of understanding. We get it quickly.
- **Accuracy** and the theories that explain and predict events. It works for us.
- **Generalisability** that can be applied across the broad sweep of situations we face. We can assume it will work again.

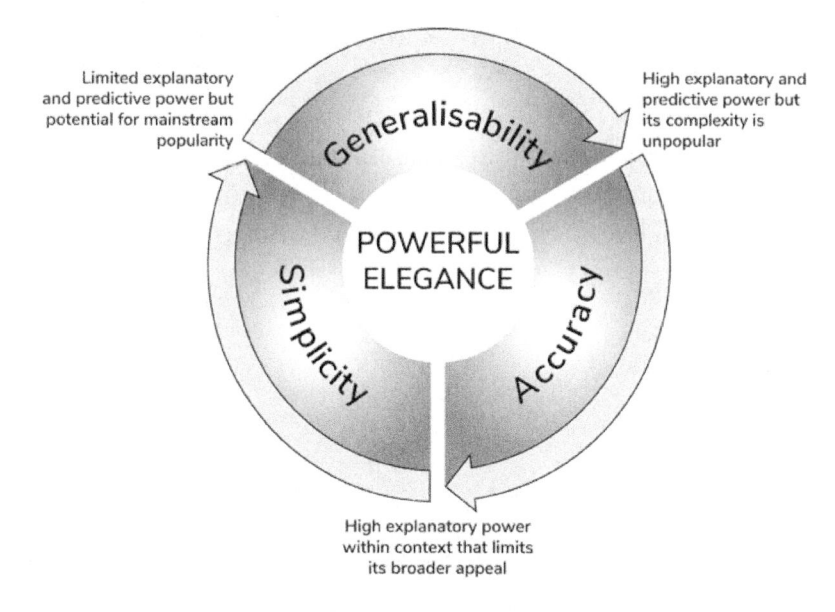

Limited explanatory and predictive power but potential for mainstream popularity

High explanatory and predictive power but its complexity is unpopular

POWERFUL ELEGANCE

Generalisability
Simplicity
Accuracy

High explanatory power within context that limits its broader appeal

Simple and generalisable theories have limited explanatory power or predictive potential, but are easy to access and understand. This gives them mainstream popularity. Accurate and generalisable theories have high explanatory and predictive power. Their complexity however makes them unpopular and are rarely taken up in the mainstream. Simple and accurate theories have high explanatory and predictive accuracy but only work within a specific context, limiting a broader appeal.

Simplicity, accuracy and generalisability is **perfect elegance**; easy to understand, powerful to explain and predict events and with broad application. Few theories however possess this perfect elegance. It helps therefore if we take a multi-disciplinary approach rather than rely on any one thing.

People are experience rich but theory poor. **Malcolm Gladwell**

What are our theories of success in, for example:

- **Business**. Why do some firms achieve growth and sustainable profitability? And others disappear from the landscape? What explains organisational decline and failure?
- **Career and financial success.** Why do some individuals get better performance appraisals and progress rapidly to take on bigger roles of responsibility? Why do some people make more money than others? Why do some individuals achieve financial security whilst their equally high earning peers don't?
- **Relationships**. What attracts us to some people but not others? Why are some relationships effortless and enjoyable and others difficult? What are the factors of a rewarding and happy long-term relationship?

Cognitive biases and heuristics

How does grid thinking help us build better theories of how the world works?

Intelligent decision making entails knowing what tool to use for what problem. **Gerd Gigerenzer**

Our cognitive biases - the story goes - limit our judgement and decision making. Over 300 at the last count.[9] Popularised by Daniel Kahneman in his best-selling book, Thinking Fast And Slow, the suggestion is that by and large, we are irrational idiots. Kahneman points to any number of errors we make in problem solving. As it turns out, many of these errors are an outcome of experimental artefacts identified in a psychology laboratory rather than a genuine reflection of judgement and decision making in the real world.[10]

Nonetheless, this sentiment persists. We make bad judgements and poor decisions because of these biases. How we manage to get out of bed in the morning and make progress during the day given these shortcomings is quite extraordinary. But we do. As Kahneman's rival, Gerd Gigerenzer, points out, without these biases we could not function in the real world.

There is strong evidence that intuitions are based on simple, smart rules that take into account only some of the available information. **Gerd Gigerenzer**[11]

It would be a strange world without these cognitive biases. Our brains evolved with mental software to cope. In the savannah of our evolutionary origins more than 100,000 years ago, speed and the emotional impulse of intuition were key to our survival, not the calm deliberation of logic.

Buster Benson proposes that there is a reason for every cognitive bias: to save our brains time or energy. *Look at them by the problem they're trying to solve. It becomes a lot easier to understand why they exist, how they're useful, and the trade-offs, and resulting mental errors, that they introduce.*

Benson groups the cognitive biases around four cognitive problems that we encounter.

- **too much information**: this avoids information overload; our brains filter out tons of inputs to focus on what appears to be the most useful.
- **not enough meaning**: we fill in the gaps with what we already know or with what seems right.
- **need to act fast**: this makes decisions even when there's ambiguity.
- **what should we remember**: we can't remember every piece of information that comes into our brains; we pick and choose.

Few readers of this book live on the savannah. Our mental software is ill adapted to modern life. But the appeal to rational thinking as a road map to success is misguided. It has been tried and doesn't work. Gigerenzer suggests we need better heuristics - a tool box of problem solving methods - to manage uncertainty and risk for better judgement and decision making.

We organise much of our lives around reassuring ourselves about the accuracy of the hallucinated model world inside our skulls. **William Storr**

A brief history of the quadrant

In a cave in Lascaux in the Dordogne region of France, along with other paintings that record the challenges of Paleo life, one of our ancestors scribbled a two by two grid. It mapped risk vs reward for the community to check the geography of the next hunting expedition. This account is highly unlikely.

The first well known 2 by 2 grid probably goes back to 1954. In a speech given by US President Eisenhower, he quotes an unnamed university president: *I have two kinds of problems, the urgent and the important. The urgent are not important, and the important are never urgent.*

The **Eisenhower Matrix** organises tasks by urgency and importance to prioritise activity for personal effectiveness. Urgency and importance, at first sight, seem fairly similar concepts. They are different. Failing to make the distinction explains poor time management and low productivity. Urgent tasks require immediate attention. The task must be done now and if not, there are clear consequences if they are not completed within the timeline. Urgent tasks can't be avoided. Delays can only create stress. Important tasks may not require immediate attention, but these tasks are critical to the achievement of long-term objectives. They may not be urgent right now. But it doesn't mean they don't matter.

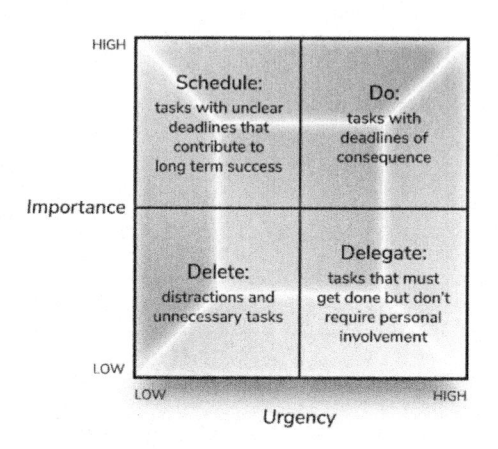

	LOW Urgency	HIGH Urgency
HIGH Importance	**Schedule:** tasks with unclear deadlines that contribute to long term success	**Do:** tasks with deadlines of consequence
LOW Importance	**Delete:** distractions and unnecessary tasks	**Delegate:** tasks that must get done but don't require personal involvement

Then the popularity of the **Boston Consulting Group Matrix**. Developed in the 1970s and much loved by strategy consultants as a business analytical tool. It provides a quick snapshot into an organisation's business portfolio. The consulting snake began to eat its own tail when SWOT analysis was applied to the BCG Matrix, and found more weaknesses than strengths.[12]

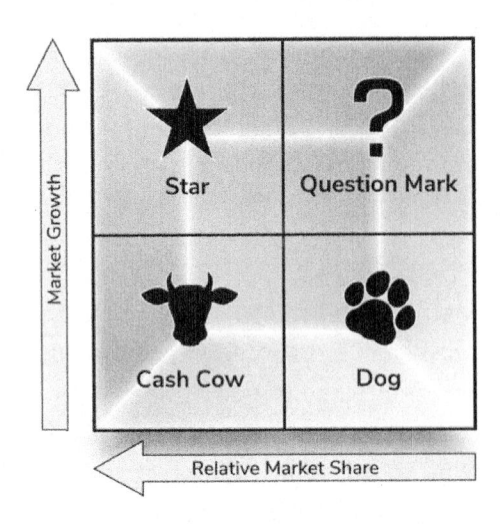

Another grid. The **Gartner Magic Quadrant** gained traction from organisations in the review of options for the purchase of technology.

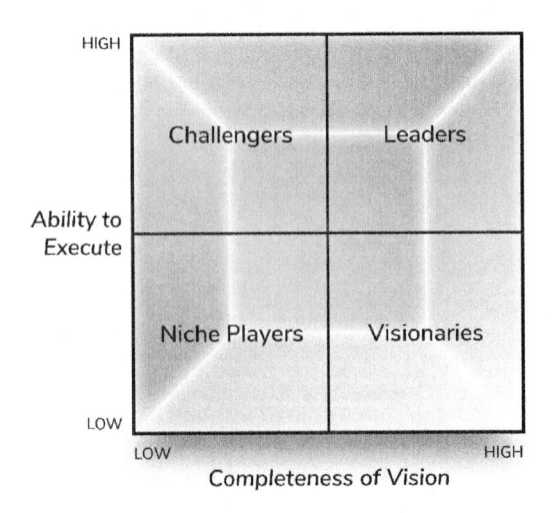

This quadrant plots technology vendors within a matrix based on completeness of vision and ability to execute. Each vendor is placed into one of four boxes: Leaders, Challengers, Visionaries, and Niche Players. Ironically the Magic Quadrant is now the focus of criticism for its *proprietary and almost secretive methodology. In fact, they've been sued twice. Gartner is falling prey to what so many companies do over time - complacency and an inability, or unwillingness, to evolve. It isn't agile. It isn't measuring itself by some of the same criteria it's using to evaluate technology providers.*[13]

The criteria of a good grid

Twenty years ago, in his foreword to The Power of the 2 X 2 Matrix, Joseph Gilmore proposed that the matrix *represents the most notable analytical tool ever to emerge in business management.* More recently, Venkatesh Rao argues: *the quadrant diagram has achieved the status of an intellectual farce, providing mediocre consultants a picturesque path for their descent into madness.*[14]

Which is it? It depends. Quadrants designed with thought and imagination highlight issues for insight and action. Badly designed grids are meaningless and confusing.

Differentiation. An example of where grids don't work, and the well-known mapping of performance by potential. This framework is extensively used by organisations in talent reviews to take stock of bench-strength as part of a succession planning exercise. Often displayed as a 9 box grid rather than as quadrants, it has the virtue of simplicity. Hence its appeal.

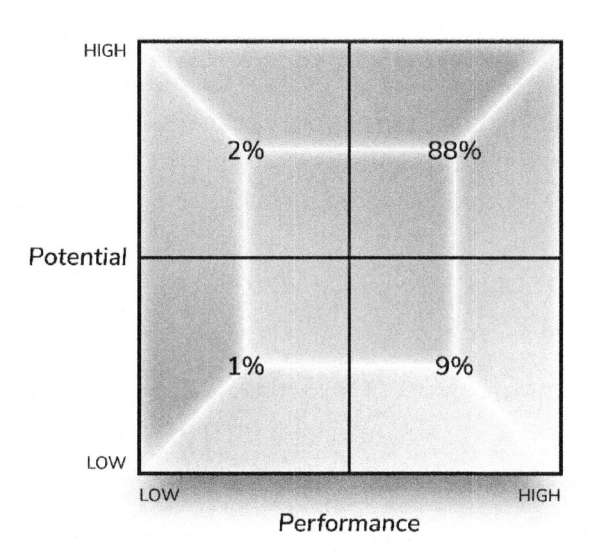

	Performance LOW	Performance HIGH
Potential HIGH	2%	88%
Potential LOW	1%	9%

The frequencies indicate that in this grid - adapted from a Roffey Park research report - simple becomes simplistic and useless. It may reflect an organisational reluctance or inability to discriminate levels of performance, or difficulties in the evaluation of potential. After all, potential is a vague concept. Potential for what? Anything and everything? Potential to advance to which level, over which time scale? Whatever the reason, this is an undifferentiated quadrant lacking insight, particularly when individual names are plotted within the four boxes.[15]

Independence of the axes. The most likely reason for the shortcomings of this grid is that the performance and potential axes are highly interdependent. Those rating their people rely on the evaluation of performance today to make judgements of potential tomorrow. The halo effect: evaluations on one attribute shape judgements on others.[16] If the two variables we select for the X and Y axes are highly correlated, we shouldn't anticipate much insight from the four boxes.

Memorability of the labels. As a rule of thumb, when the four boxes of the grid cannot be labelled with descriptive insight, the grid is probably not working. This is not to say that labelling is easy. A truly outstanding grid requires a combination of informed judgement and creative flair. It is no accident that the Boston Consulting Group Matrix - the mapping of market growth by market share - became popular. It was not, as it turned out, a particularly useful business analytical tool. But the Dogs, Problem Children, Cash Cows and Stars of the framework gained attention because of the vocabulary. In this book, most of the labelling we think is coherent and thought provoking. For other quadrants, the terminology is more idiosyncratic. This is the fun of a quadrant.

The so what factor. Without an actionable insight, we are looking at words as an exercise in evaluation. These quadrants lack the understanding that results in next steps and action.

If people see your diagram and instantly feel a sense of relief and recognition, it means you are articulating and clarifying something they've already subconsciously noticed. **Venkatesh Rao**

Good grids make us stop and think. We have captured something important to gain a better appreciation of the issues. Great grids also stimulate a thought process about the implications and responses. An example we use in debrief discussions with leaders. The two dimensions are:

Context. The dynamics of the working environment. What is helping or hindering a leader? The scores range from low, extremely challenging to high, extremely supportive.

Impact. An index of leadership effectiveness and how it is perceived by different colleagues.

	Low Context	High Context
High Effectiveness	Managing in the Face of Adversity	Optimising the Opportunity to Deliver
Low Effectiveness	Overwhelmed by the Challenge	Failing to Exploit an Advantageous Situation

Four patterns emerge.

Overwhelmed by the Challenge. The box in which difficult circumstances makes it tough for leaders to operate effectively. Colleagues indicate that the individual is not having the kind of impact that they expect. This is uncomfortable feedback - in the short-term. This feedback should trigger critical conversations to move in a positive direction to manage the situation to develop greater effectiveness.

Managing in the Face of Adversity. Despite working within a challenging environment in which several dynamics constrain performance, the feedback from colleagues is positive. Colleagues recognise the difficulties that have to be overcome - and factor this into their evaluation. Or identify a leadership style and skill set displayed within the tough challenges of the role.

Failing to Exploit an Advantageous Situation. Troublesome feedback. Colleagues ask difficult questions of the leader's effectiveness. There is a tail wind working in the individual's favour, with the potential to make leadership life relatively straightforward. It may be that colleagues have unrealistic expectations of what is possible. Or, typically, this is a wakeup call for the leader to revisit their approach and the dynamics of their different relationships.

Optimising the Opportunity to Deliver. Individuals who operate within a supportive environment with enabling factors to make a positive impact. Colleagues identify mainly leadership strengths with few gaps and recognise a significant contribution. This is highly energising feedback to encourage a greater contribution.

Choosing when grid thinking will work. The quartet has limitations.[17] It relies on a **binary distinction** of low or high. In reality, most variables run on a continuum with no defined cut off point. The four permutations of boxes within the quadrant are caricatures. Quadrants can become crude representations of reality that lack nuance and subtlety.

The engineering model of the lunar surface actually used for Surveyor design was developed after a study of all the theories and information available. Fortunately, this model was prepared by engineers who were not emotionally involved in the generation of scientific theories, and the resulting landing system requirements were remarkably accurate. **Oran Nicks on NASA's lunar and planetary programs**

Yes, the quadrant is reductionistic. Nonetheless, just because we can't explain everything in a quadrant, it doesn't mean we can't explain anything. Take personality as an example. We struggle to understand the uniqueness of an individual's temperament and character. Does this mean we can't understand anything about behaviour?

It is no coincidence that one of the world's best-selling personality profiling tools emerged from a two by two grid. Developed in the 1920s by the maverick William Marston - also the creator of Wonder Woman - DISC was based on two dimensions. A quadrant mapped four themes: *Dominance is characterised by actively using force to overcome resistance in the environment. Inducement involves using charm to deal with obstacles. Submission is a warm and voluntary acceptance of the need to fulfil a request. Compliance represents fearful adjustment to a superior force.*[18]

The more important reservation. **Not every phenomenon lends itself to two variables**. Sometimes, three or more variables compete and contrast to explain context, causes and consequences. The quadrant system breaks down and other forms of analysis and visualisation are more appropriate.

But two by two grids represent working models to summarise complex phenomena[19] and give us a starting point. George Box pointed out: *All models are wrong, but some are less wrong than others.* He also commented that *statisticians, like artists, have the bad habit of falling in love their models.* Our models become barriers to understanding and insight when we see the map as reality.

A map is not the territory it represents, but, if correct, it has a similar structure to the territory, which accounts for its usefulness. **Alfred Korzybski**[20]

However if a quadrant triggers thinking into the complexity within the interplay of key dimensions, it achieves its purpose as a tool for better judgement.

NOTES

1. Managing in a VUCA World; https://www.mindtools.com/asnydwg/managing-in-a-vuca-world

2. VUCA, BANI, RUPT OR TUNA; https://www.vuca-world.org/vuca-bani-rupt-tuna/

3. Hey, it's crazy out there, Nathan Bennett and G. James Lemoine, Harvard Business Review, 2014

4. The juice of a carrot, the smile of a parrot, Reasons To Be Cheerful Pt 3, Ian Drury and the Blockheads; https://youtu.be/ClMNXogXnvE

5. The Management Myth; https://www.theatlantic.com/magazine/archive/2006/06/the-management-myth/304883/

6. Wasting away in the VUCA World; https://gagandeep.org/2016/09/17/wasting-away-in-the-vuca-world/

7. For example, Murphy's Law: Whatever can go wrong, will go wrong. An extreme variation: If anything can possibly go wrong, it will, and at the worst possible time. Unwritten Laws, Hugh Rawson

8. Contradictory proverbs; https://www.derekchristensen.com/15-pairs-of-contradictory-proverbs/#:~:text=Next%20time%20you%20find%20yourself,succeed%2C%20try%2C%20try%20again

9. Buster Benson and cognitive biases; https://medium.com/unexpected-leadership/buster-bensons-cognitive-bias-cheat-sheet-453e75eb9fa8

10. Left Brain, Right Stuff, Phil Rosenzweig
The Irrational Agent, Steve Sailer; https://www.takimag.com/article/the_irrational_agent/

11. Gerd Gigerenzer's Rationality for Mortals: How People Cope with Uncertainty, Jason Collins; https://www.jasoncollins.blog/posts/gerd-gigerenzers-rationality-for-mortals-how-people-cope-with-uncertainty

12. Shortcomings or Limitations of BCG Matrix; https://bcgmatrixanalysis.com/shortcomings-or-limitations-of-bcg-matrix/

13. Is the Gartner Magic Quadrant Obsolete? https://www.technewsworld.com/story/is-the-gartner-magic-quadrant-obsolete-86789.html

14. How to Draw and Judge Quadrant Diagrams; https://www.ribbonfarm.com/2009/04/20/how-to-draw-and-judge-quadrant-diagrams/

15. A Little Less Plotting And A Lot More Conversation Please; https://talentworldconsulting.com/wp-content/uploads/2023/08/A-Little-Less-Plotting-Talent-Reviews.pdf

16. The halo effect, and other managerial delusions; https://www.mckinsey.com/capabilities/strategy-and-corporate-finance/our-insights/the-halo-effect-and-other-managerial-delusions

17. Criticisms of the two by two grid; http://www.ribbonfarm.com/2009/04/20/how-to-draw-and-judge-quadrant-diagrams/

18. DISC based personality assessment. The history, current status, and the fascinating life of William Marston; https://talentworldconsulting.com/wp-content/uploads/2023/08/DISCPastAndPresentAndWilliamMarston.pdf

19. How to summarise the complexity of life using 2 X 2 grids; http://www.ribbonfarm.com/2015/02/25/the-mother-of-all-2x2s/

20. Korzybski, a Polish-American scientist and philosopher, articulated this idea in 1931 at a presentation to the American Association for the Advancement of Science. It became a foundational concept in his field known as general semantics. The statement highlights the difference between a representation of reality and reality itself, emphasizing that models or descriptions of the world are not the world itself. It's a reminder of the limitations and abstractions of maps, models, and symbols when trying to capture the complexity of the real world.

TEN BY TEN

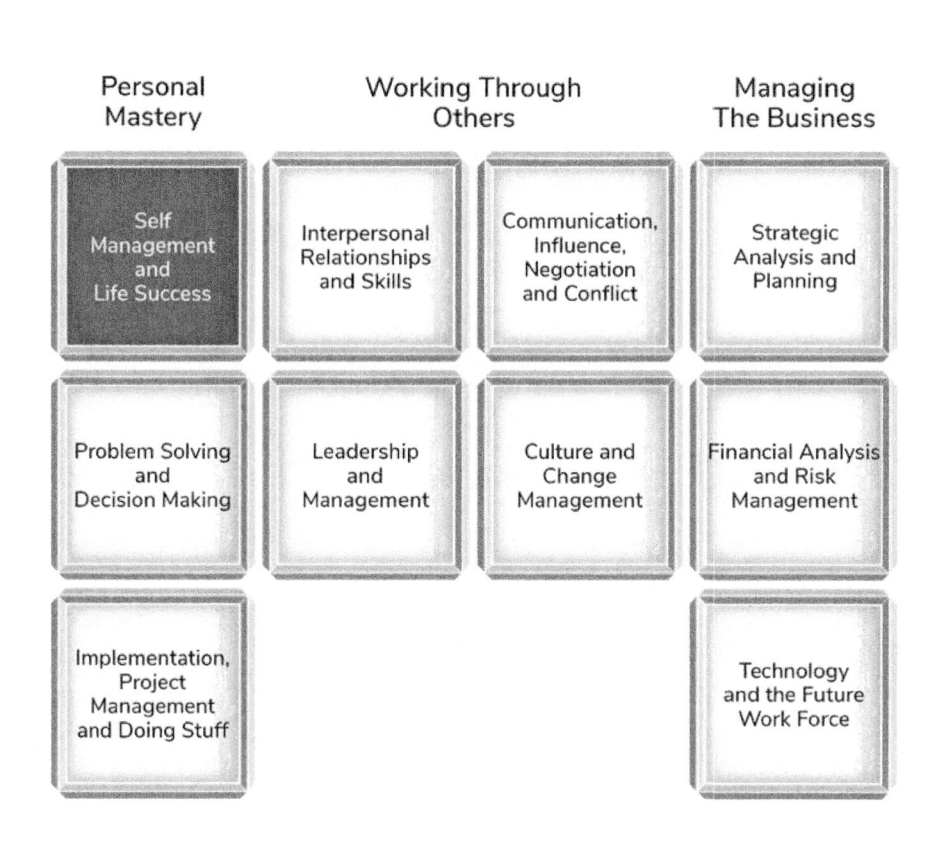

Personal Mastery	Working Through Others		Managing The Business
Self Management and Life Success	Interpersonal Relationships and Skills	Communication, Influence, Negotiation and Conflict	Strategic Analysis and Planning
Problem Solving and Decision Making	Leadership and Management	Culture and Change Management	Financial Analysis and Risk Management
Implementation, Project Management and Doing Stuff			Technology and the Future Work Force

Do we expect too much from life?

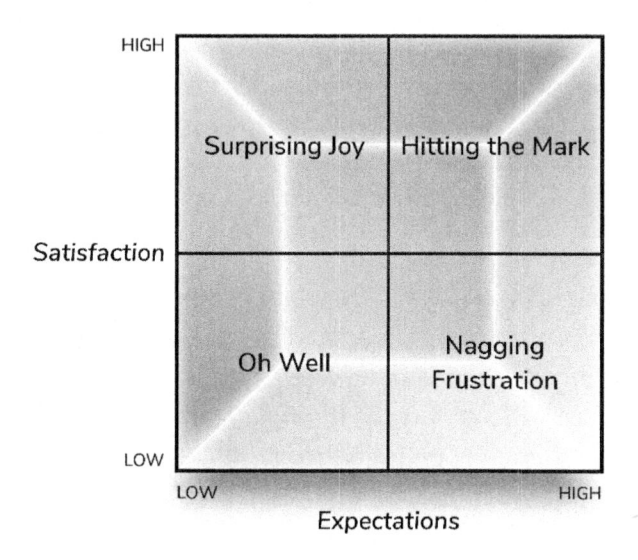

	Low Expectations	High Expectations
High Satisfaction	Surprising Joy	Hitting the Mark
Low Satisfaction	Oh Well	Nagging Frustration

Nothing defines humans better than their willingness to do irrational things in the pursuit of phenomenally unlikely payoffs. **Scott Adams**

Is there a recipe for happiness? The psychoanalyst Sigmund Freud did not think so. *The intention that humankind should be happy is not included in the plan of Creation.* His job was to turn *neurotic misery into ordinary unhappiness.* Others are less gloomy. The happiness project, boosted by the pseudo-science from the positive psychology movement, has never been happier.[1]

There are two tragedies in life. One is not to get your heart's desire. The other is to get it. **George Bernard Shaw**

This quadrant identifies the factors at play that account for relative happiness or unhappiness in life.

Expectations. This dimension responds to the key question of life: can I be happy? At the low end of expectations, we have a modest claim on life. At the other, we are entitled to believe that life should provide us with an engaging and rewarding experience.

Satisfaction. Do we feel that life is paying us well? In a state of dissatisfaction, we feel robbed. Something is not working. We are not finding much pleasure or joy in life. In high satisfaction, we think the world is rewarding us well, and we are content.

As long as you are aiming at happiness, you cannot obtain it. The more you make it a target, the more you miss the target. **Viktor Frankl**

Four life outlooks emerge.

Oh Well. This reflects low levels of expectation and satisfaction. A philosophical stance in which - since we didn't expect much from life in the first place - we should not be too disappointed with the current state of affairs. Life is turning out as well as could be expected. Much mocked by the aspirational tone of the media which sells the dream of fulfilment, this stance is criticised for its dull tedium. Conversely, this is a stoical strategy to play a poor hand.

Each success only buys an admission ticket to a more difficult problem. **Henry Kissinger**

Surprising Joy. When low expectation meets high satisfaction, life becomes an enjoyable adventure. Not much was asked of life, but through any combination of luck and hard work, life has delivered beyond our initial hopes. At best, the outlook of Joe Walsh's *life's been good to me so far*. So far. The hazard: this happiness shifts quickly to a life style of entitlement.

Before we set our hearts too much on anything, let us examine how happy are those who already possess it. **Duc de La Rochefoucauld**

Nagging Frustration. Expectations are high, but life has not delivered on our ambitions and we experience disappointment.[2] In this scenario, there are two strategies. One is to rethink our expectations and accept the uncomfortable advice of Quentin Crisp: *if at first you don't succeed, failure may be your style.* An emotionally difficult exercise, it brings our expectations in line with our life situation. The second response: shift tactics to close the gap by finding greater levels of life satisfaction.

If no mistake have you made, yet losing you are, a different game you should play. **Yoda**

Hitting The Mark. The stars align in the box of life fulfilment and reward. Our ambitions are achieved and life happiness is secured. Some accept this good fortune to recognise that the future course of life will be a continual balance between expectation and satisfaction. Others rest on their laurels assuming that current good fortune will ensure sustained happiness. And for others, **enough is never enough** and expectations are raised again to the extent that happiness will never be achieved.

The perfection of wisdom, and the end of true philosophy is to proportion our wants to our possessions, our ambitions to our capacities. We will then be a happy and a virtuous people. **Mark Twain**

SO WHAT?

He got what he wanted but lost what he had. **Little Richard speaking of Elvis Presley**

This quadrant presents two competing positions in life. For Baltasar Gracian[3]: *it is wise to aim high so as to hit your mark, but not so high that you miss your mission at the beginning of your life.* In contrast, Michelangelo proposes the *greatest danger for most of us is not that our aim is too high and we miss it, but that it is too low and we can reach it.*

The choice: shift our expectations or work out a way to fulfil these expectations.

NOTES

1. Is positive psychology all it's cracked up to be? https://www.vox.com/the-highlight/2019/11/13/20955328/positive-psychology-martin-seligman-happiness-religion-secularism
Bright-Sided: How Positive Thinking Is Undermining America, Barbara Ehrenreich
The Pursuit of Happiness: Why are we driving ourselves crazy and how can we stop? Ruth Whippman

2. *Is it possible, he thinks, that nothing true and important has been seen, recognised or said? Yes, it is possible.* Rainer Maria Rilke
The Soul-Expanding Value of Difficulty;
https://www.themarginalian.org/2015/03/10/rilke-letters-to-a-young-poet-sadness/

3. The Art of Worldly Wisdom, Balthasar Gracian; https://sacred-texts.com/eso/aww/index.htm

Do we know what we want?

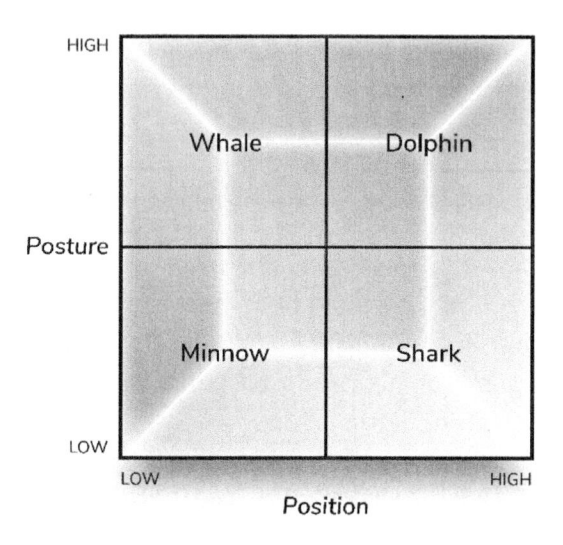

He was one of those people who possess almost every gift, except the gift of the power to use them. **Charles Kingsley**

Shane Parrish in Clear Thinking[1] makes the point that to achieve results, we must, firstly, create the space to think. Secondly, use this space to translate our thoughts into action. This grid is based on two dimensions.

Position. This represents the hand we play, known only to ourselves. Life shuffles the cards. For some, this looks like a losing hand with limited options. For others, luck provides a formidable set of cards for a winnable game.

Posture. This is how we appear to the world. Low, and we convey an impression of being overwhelmed by events and a victim of circumstance. High, we project power and influence. Here, others think we have a strong hand.

Anyone looks like a genius when they're in a good position, and even the smartest person looks like an idiot when they're in a bad one. **Shane Parrish**

Four scenarios emerge.

Minnow. A weak position and a low posture. For the minnow, the life strategy is largely that of survival. This accepts the limitations of the current situation. It adopts tactics to keep a low profile and avoid any potential challenge from others. If life is a poker game, the minnow is quick to fold.

Life is too long to play bad cards. **Frank Di Elsi**

Whale. A weak position is accompanied with a strong posture. This strategy optimises the blow hole of an impressive spout that is eye catching and imposing to others. For the most part, the whale is an imposter in the game of life, reliant on social confidence to bluff its way through events. Impression management goes a long way in life.

What's true of the poker game is true of life. Most people are suckers and don't realise it. **Michael Faust**

Shark. A strong position but with a low posture. The shark maintains a low profile and utilises a strategy of stealth to advance its objectives. No need to talk to impress. Only to act and do. Others often fail to identify the threat of the shark.

The game of life is not so much in holding a good hand as playing a poor hand well. **HT Leslie**

Dolphin. This life stance combines a strong position with a positive posture. It is an impressive performance in full display. This is life lived within a range of options evident to others to command respect which in turn opens up further options for greater success.

Spend each day trying to be a little wiser than you were when you woke up. Discharge your duties faithfully and well. Systematically you get ahead, but not necessarily in fast spurts. Nevertheless, you build discipline by preparing for fast spurts. Slug it out one inch at a time, day by day. At the end of the day - if you live long enough - most people get what they deserve. **Charlie Munger**

SO WHAT?

What a lot of people miss is that ordinary moments determine your position, and your position determines your options. **Shane Parrish**

Self reflection helps understand our position. As does feedback from others to recognise how our posture is perceived by others. The deployment of shrewd tactics helps us optimise both our position and posture.[2]

NOTES

1. Clear Thinking, Shane Parrish

2. The Laws of Human Nature, Robert Greene

What is the fine line between success and failure?

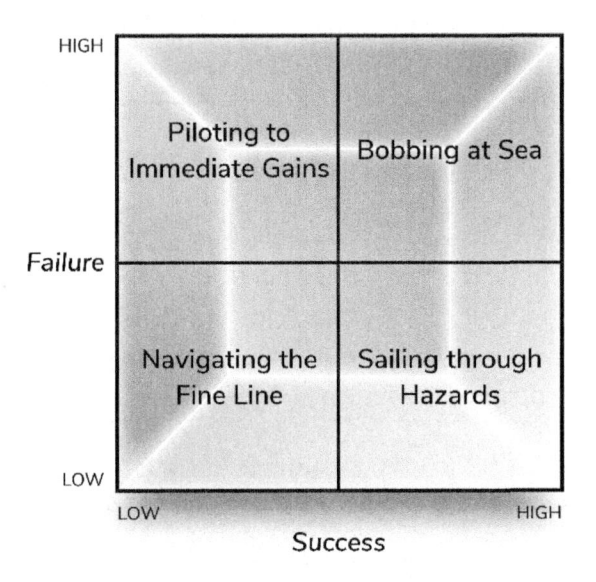

```
           Failure/Success Matrix
HIGH  ┌─────────────────┬─────────────────┐
      │                 │                 │
      │   Piloting to   │  Bobbing at Sea │
      │ Immediate Gains │                 │
      │                 │                 │
Failure├─────────────────┼─────────────────┤
      │                 │                 │
      │ Navigating the  │ Sailing through │
      │   Fine Line     │    Hazards      │
      │                 │                 │
LOW   └─────────────────┴─────────────────┘
       LOW                            HIGH
                   Success
```

If you can meet with Triumph and Disaster. And treat those two impostors just the same. **Rudyard Kipling**

FedEx began operations in April 1973, and quickly grew. However, rising fuel costs eventually caught up with the young company, putting FedEx millions of dollars in debt. Investors declined to give FedEx more money. Bankruptcy was a distinct possibility. On his way home, CEO Fred Smith took a detour to Las Vegas and won $27,000 playing blackjack, which he wired back to FedEx. Smith said: *the $27,000 wasn't decisive, but it was an omen that things would get better Smith said.*[1]

From the sublime to the ridiculous there is only one step. **Napoleon**[2]

Our mental models of success and failure are often based on very different assumptions of cause and consequence. For some, success is the result of a meritocracy. Talent and hard work is deserving of the outcome. Failure, on the other hand, is the fate of the feckless; a grouping unable or unwilling to achieve much and can be predicted to lose out in life.

Is this so? To paraphrase Malcolm Gladwell, success is an outcome of history and geography - to be born at the right time in the right place.[3] This quadrant is based on the fine line between success and failure. It highlights the dynamics of the near and the far in success and failure.

There is a fine line between fishing and just standing on the shore like an idiot. **Steven Wright**

Success. This outcome runs the spectrum of near to far. In near, success is almost within our grasp; we are close to our ambitions. In contrast, the far is distant; there is only a possibility of achievement at some vague point in the future.

Failure. There is the prospect we fail. At one end of this spectrum, failure is highly likely and predicted to happen very soon. At the other end, a faraway prospect that is unimaginable.

Once you believe that you are infallible, that success will automatically lead to more success and that you have got it made, reality will be sure to give you a rude wake-up call. **Felix Dennis**

Four life outlooks are identified.

Navigating the Fine Line. The paradox in which success and failure are both imminent. This is life lived on the margin of reward and risk. One judgement call can trigger either exceptional success or devastating failure. At best, a cool head makes the correct decision for success. Alternatively, luck determines the outcomes.

The line between failure and success is so fine that we scarcely know when we pass it; so fine that we are often on the line and do not know it. **Elbert Hubbard**

Piloting to Immediate Gains. Success is near and failure is distant. A happy scenario in which our talents and efforts migrate to success in the short-term. In this scenario, intelligence and boldness recognise and exploit the opportunity. Only hesitation, an uncertainty about possible failure hold us back. In a counter-factual, this is the beginnings of disaster when short-term hubris[4] plunders the present to ignore warnings of future calamity.

One day you're cock of the walk, the next day you're a feather duster. **Piers Morgan**

Sailing through Hazards. Life presents us with the prospect of near failure but we retain the possibility of distant success. We have to hold our nerve to overcome pressing difficulties and maintain a vision of long-term triumph over adversity. This is the narrative of drama; the hero escapes their current predicament. Sometimes however life doesn't know the plot we have told ourselves. We find ourselves in a losing situation. The immediacy of pending problems undermines any ideal of future success.

It is hard to distinguish between the concentration needed for success and the narrowness that guarantees irrelevance. **Jagdish Sheth**

Bobbing at Sea. This is the realisation that both success and failure are far off. There is no immediate risk. But neither is there much prospect of reward. This stance of low commitment may be based on an evolving strategy, working out priorities to decide a focus for the future. Conversely, a disengagement from life's challenges to retreat into a zone of mediocre comfort.[5]

SO WHAT?

He was a visionary or a fool. I have found the line perilously thin myself. **Khaled Hosseini**

It is the fine line that makes life an adventure, the hope of success and the prospect of failure and the uncertainties of future reward and success.[5]

NOTES

1. How Fred Smith rescued FedEx from bankruptcy by playing blackjack in Las Vegas; https://www.foxbusiness.com/money/fred-smith-fedex-blackjack-winning-formula

2. This is a variation of the observation of Thomas Paine: *the sublime and the ridiculous are often so nearly related, that it is difficult to class them separately. One step above the sublime makes the ridiculous; and one step above the ridiculous makes the sublime again.*

3. Malcolm Gladwell in Outliers. *To build a better world we need to replace the patchwork of lucky breaks and arbitrary advantages that today determine success - the fortunate birth dates and the happy accidents of history - with a society that provides opportunities for all.*

4. Hubris: The Silent Killer of Business; https://www.proactiveinsights.com/blog/hubris-silent-killer-business/

5. Face Your Fear: The Knowledge Project Ep. 183, Paul Assaiante; https://fs.blog/knowledge-project-podcast/paul-assaiante/

Do we feel lucky today?

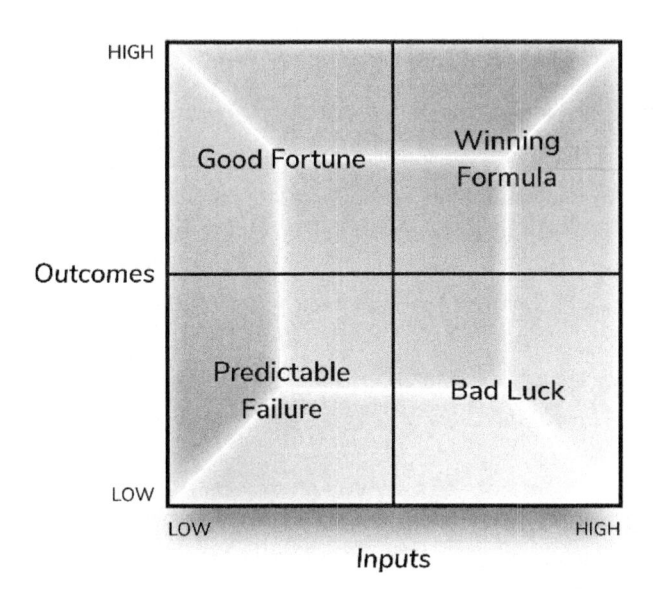

[A 2x2 matrix chart with Outcomes (Low to High) on the y-axis and Inputs (Low to High) on the x-axis. Top-left: Good Fortune. Top-right: Winning Formula. Bottom-left: Predictable Failure. Bottom-right: Bad Luck.]

You've gotta ask yourself a question: "Do I feel lucky?" Well, do ya, punk? **Clint Eastwood**

Karl Weick recounts the story of a group of Swiss soldiers. On a training exercise, it got lost in a blizzard in the Alps. After several days of anxiety, one soldier realised he had a map of the region. The group followed the map and made its way back to safety. At base camp, the commanding officer asked: how did you find your way back? The soldiers explained: we had a map. The officer checked the map: you found a map all right, but it's not of the Alps. It is of the Pyrenees.

Don't try to make a mathematics problem with yourself in the centre and everything coming out equal. When you are good, bad things can still happen. And if you are bad, you can still be lucky. **Barbara Kingsolver, The Poisonwood Bible**

If there was a direct correlation between process and results, life would be simple. Locate the right inputs and follow a consistent sequence to translate these inputs into positive outcomes. This becomes a winning formula. But life is not straightforward. Every outcome represents a mix of skill and luck.[1]

Bad outcomes don't always mean that managers made mistakes. And good outcomes don't always mean they acted brilliantly. **Phil Rosenzweig**

The balance varies across different life activities. Luck however makes success messy. If a positive outcome is achieved with a bad process, is this the happy circumstance of good luck? Or maybe the bad process was not so bad after all. If results are not achieved with a good process, is that the vagaries of bad luck? Or maybe we need to rethink the process.[2]

Luck shuffles the cards how and when she will. Let each person know their luck as well as their talents for on this depends whether they lose or win. **Balthasar Gracian**

This quadrant maps out the interplay of two dimensions.

Inputs. This represents the mix of knowledge, skill and effort to integrate and deploy within a process. At one end of the range, inputs are limited by a lack of talent and motivation. At the other end, an array of skills is deployed with sustained effort.

Outcomes. This reflects the range of results from the application of the process. It ranges from the low of disappointing failure, to the high of exceptional success.

You want to go into a game where you're very likely to win without having any unusual luck. **Charlie Munger**

Four stances are highlighted.

Predictable Failure. A combination of low inputs and bad outcomes. If this pattern is repeated over time, the process needs a rethink. It may be that much has been invested in the inputs and process. The temptation is to assume luck will change. This is the poker strategy of staying in a losing game in the hope that things will turn around. They rarely do.

It's no good crying over spilt milk, because all the forces of the universe were bent on spilling it. **Somerset Maugham**

Good Fortune. Low inputs give rise to positive outcomes. Luck comes to our rescue to transform low skill and effort into positive results. Human nature attributes this happy circumstance to our personal brilliance. We repeat the same formula until our luck runs out. Much time and energy can be wasted without a reappraisal of our results and a rethink of our inputs.

The average millionaire is only the average dishwasher dressed in a new suit. **George Orwell**

Bad Luck. A frustrating position. A repertoire of skill and energy is deployed within a process that delivers poor outcomes. It is tempting to give in at this point and move to a new set of tactics within a different process. Alternatively, if the game is to be played over the long-haul, we persist with the original position.

I think we consider too much the good luck of the early bird and not enough the bad luck of the early worm. **Franklin D Roosevelt**

Winning Formula. Bullseye. The arrow of inputs hits the target of outcomes. The process is working to deliver results. All good. The hazard is now one of complacency. The conviction that what works today will continue to work in future is reinforced. Sustained success requires a combination of experimentation and continual improvement to keep refining the process and apply feedback systems to track progress and shifts in outcome.

The important question is not whether you will fail, but when, and above all, what happens next. **Ed Smith**

SO WHAT?

Beware of advice about successful people and their methods. For starters, no two situations are alike. Your dreams of creating a dry-cleaning empire won't be helped by knowing that Thomas Edison liked to take naps. **Scott Adams**

Humility avoids the delusion that our success is a consequence of our innate brilliance and hard work. Empathy recognises that others' failure may be less about them, and more a result of the contingencies and vagaries of life events they have experienced.

I played so perfect; I couldn't play more perfect. **Phil Hellmuth after losing in the World Series of Poker**

Above all, we need the reality check of feedback to track the inputs and process we are deploying for improved outcomes.

NOTES

1. The Success Equation, Michael Mauboussin; https://eversightwealth.com/book-summary-of-the-success-equation/

2. *Hard science gives sensational results with a horribly boring process; philosophy gives boring results with a sensational process; literature gives sensational results with a sensational process; and economics gives boring results with a boring process.* Nassim Taleb

Why our attitudes to time matter

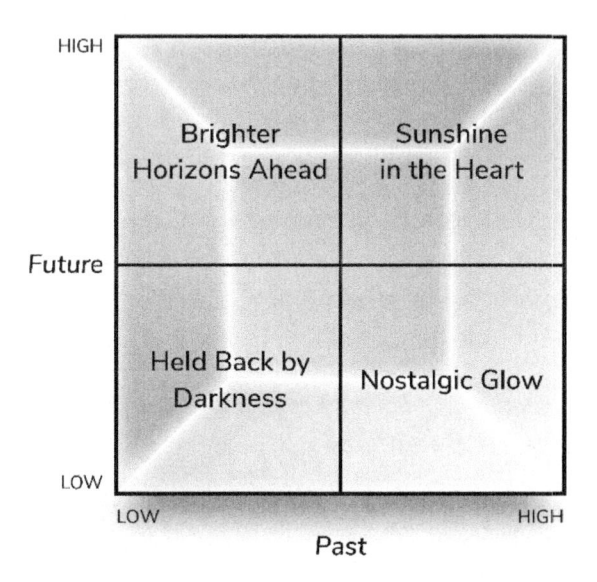

```
         HIGH
              ┌─────────────┬─────────────┐
              │             │             │
              │   Brighter  │   Sunshine  │
              │ Horizons    │  in the     │
              │   Ahead     │   Heart     │
              │             │             │
  Future      ├─────────────┼─────────────┤
              │             │             │
              │  Held Back  │  Nostalgic  │
              │  by         │    Glow     │
              │  Darkness   │             │
              │             │             │
         LOW  └─────────────┴─────────────┘
              LOW                      HIGH
                        Past
```

Decisions taken today are driven by our visions of tomorrow and based on what we learned yesterday. **Bruce Lloyd**[1]

How we think about our past, present and future has a major impact on life outcomes - our job satisfaction, career progression and long-term life success. We focus on the management of time. The more important question is how we manage our minds. How we think about yesterday, today and tomorrow matters. The feelings we have about our past, how we view the present, and anticipate our future are important indicators of our well-being and success in life.

Time it was and what a time it was it was. A time of innocence a time of confidences. **Bookends, Simon & Garfunkel**

This quadrant is based on two dimensions.

Past. This looks back on previous life events. At one end, the past was a negative place, a space associated with bad memories. At the other, a highly positive experience of happy emotions.

Future. What stance do we adopt when we look ahead? A pessimistic outlook in which trouble can be expected? Or, an optimism to anticipate delightful times?

Thinking about the future can be so pleasurable that sometimes we'd rather think about it than get there. **Daniel Gilbert**

Four time frames are highlighted.

Held Back by Darkness. This summarises a negative past and pessimistic future. For any number of reasons, there is a resentment of what happened and no expectation of better happenings in the future. This is a troublesome outlook to constrain life in the present.

One must always maintain one's connection to the past and yet ceaselessly pull away from it. **Gaston Bachelard**

Brighter Horizons Ahead. The past has been negative, but the future is viewed with optimism. A life outlook to move on in the expectation of better days ahead. Despite previous difficulties, there is the prospect of reinvention for a different future.

You can't go back and change the beginning but you can start where you are and change the ending. **CS Lewis**

Nostalgic Glow. A positive past but a pessimistic future, and the sense that the best has been rather than yet to come. Here there is a longing to relive the better times and a fear of what the future might hold. Yesterday's fond memories - and attachments - may hold back the possibility of a different tomorrow.

The stories that you tell about your past shape your future. **Eric Ransdell**

Sunshine in the Heart. The past has been a positive experience and these memories are brought forward in anticipation of an even brighter future. This is a confident stance. Life has been good with the prospect it will get even better.

Enjoying the future begins with learning to enjoy the present. **Daniel Siddins**

SO WHAT?

We should all be concerned about the future because we will have to spend the rest of our lives there. **Charles Kettering**

It matters where we live. Is it in the past, present or future? It can be caught up by looking back either with resentment of what went wrong, and what might have been. Or a nostalgia to rediscover a past that has long gone? Or, shaped by a future that is fantasy of what might be possible? Or a dread in which the worst scenario is imagined. Our present is now.

It's easy to carry the past as a burden instead of a school. It's easy to let it overwhelm you instead of educate you. **Jim Rohn**

NOTES

1. Now It's About Time, Andrew Munro; https://www.amazon.com/Now-its-about-time-Andrew/dp/1447607767

Do we know our real strengths?

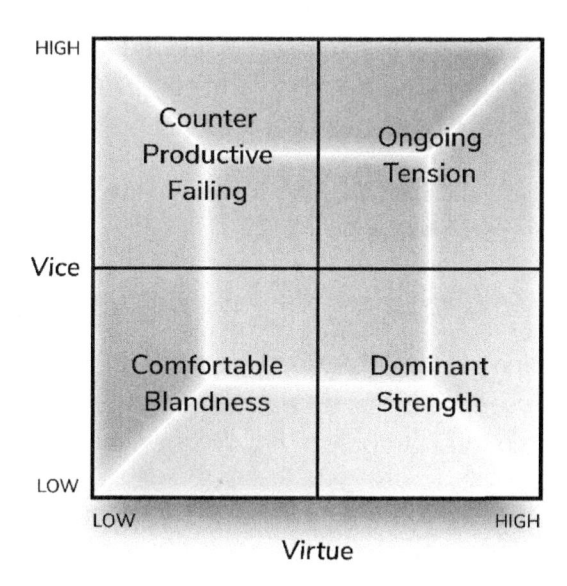

	Low Virtue	High Virtue
High Vice	Counter Productive Failing	Ongoing Tension
Low Vice	Comfortable Blandness	Dominant Strength

The problem with people who have no vices is that generally you can be pretty sure they're going to have some pretty annoying virtues. **Elizabeth Taylor**

Conventional practice in assessment and development assumes that strengths and limitations are different. This identifies strengths as personal and professional assets to be built on and deployed for greater success. Any highlighted limitations are gaps and liabilities that undermine our effectiveness and progression.

What if the virtues of our strengths are linked closely to the vices of our limitations?

I find that the best virtue I have has in it some tincture of vice. **Michel de Montaigne**

This quadrant is based on two dimensions.

Virtue. The positive attributes and qualities expressed as our strengths. Absence, that end of the spectrum in which a specific virtue is less evident to others. Presence, the active display of a positive trait that features prominently in our behaviour and conduct.

Vice. A theme to reflect those behaviours with a determinantal impact on ourselves, and in turn upon others. If absent, this vice is not evident within our behaviour. When present, a negative behavioural pattern is recognised by others as a dysfunctional characteristic.

Be careful when you cast out your demons that you don't throw away the best of yourself. **Friedrich Nietzsche**

This interplay of virtue and vice creates four permutations.

Comfortable Blandness. Virtue and vice are both absent. There is no single distinguishing stamp of character. It is a configuration that won't get us into much trouble in life. Neither will it feature much in exceptional success.

It's not bad, but it's not good either. **Steven Magee**

Counter Productive Failing. The absence of a virtue is associated with the presence of a vice. This is life potentially constrained by a failing that limits other virtues. It is the weakest link in the chain to undermine our overall efforts. The law of multiplication applies. Any strengths are wiped out by the negative of limiting factors.[1]

We have met the enemy and it is us. **Walt Kelly**

Dominant Strength. The presence of a virtue intersects with the absence of a vice. This represents an important asset in life to provide opportunity for advancement and success. Alternatively, the over-deployed talent that limits versatility to adapt to different life circumstances.[2]

Absolute virtue is as sure to kill a person as absolute vice is, let alone the dullness of it and the pomposities of it. **Samuel Beckett**

Ongoing Tension. Both vice and virtue are present. This is a strength with the potential to trigger our downfall. Courage, for example, is no longer an outstanding virtue if it becomes the vice of recklessness.

Conversely, it can be the expression of a vice that others interpret as a virtue. Our arrogance, for example, is perceived by others as a positive that appeals.

A single redeeming quality in a black sheep wins greater esteem than all virtues in honest people. **Harry Flashman**

SO WHAT?

The nature of a virtue is that a vice is almost always hidden inside. **Mary Loftus**

Our virtues are closely linked to our vices. Aristotle's Golden Mean[3] points to moderation, and the absence of excess. This isn't moderation as mediocrity or blandness. This is moderation to walk the tight rope and balance the competing tensions of different attributes and operating styles. The optimal life philosophy is knowing when little is way too little and much is far too much.

It is a revenge the devil sometimes takes upon the virtuous, that he entraps them by the force of the very passion they have suppressed and think themselves superior to. **George Santayana**

NOTES

1. The Lollapalooza Effect works both ways. Multiplying strengths for exceptional impact or a scenario in which strengths are wiped out by a zero. Berkshire Hathaway, assessment and rethinking talent management;
https://talentworldconsulting.com/wp-content/uploads/2023/08/The-Lollapalooza-Effect-Charlie-Munger-Talent-Assessment.pdf

2. Is strengths based development weakening your talent pipeline?
https://talentworldconsulting.com/wp-content/uploads/2023/09/Rethinking-Strengths-Based-Development.pdf

3. The stoics coined the term *antakolouthia* to highlight that no virtue is a virtue by itself. True virtue requires the balancing of opposites;
https://hbr.org/2010/11/redefining-greatness-its-compl

How to achieve and sustain success

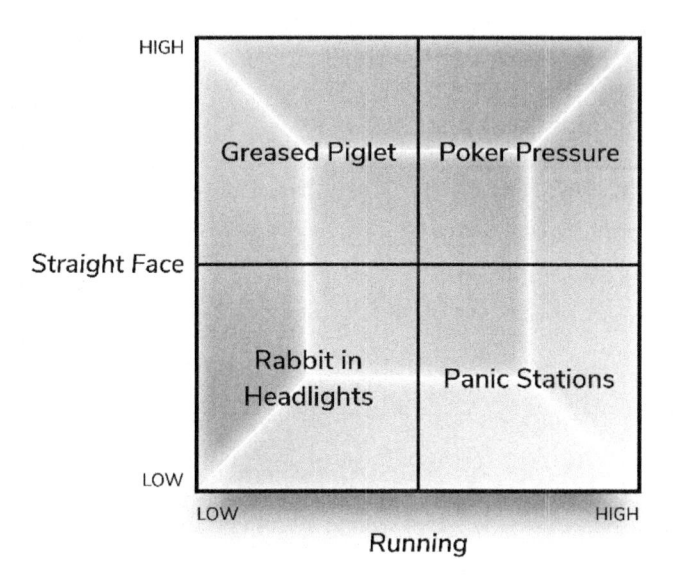

	Straight Face	
HIGH	Greased Piglet	Poker Pressure
LOW	Rabbit in Headlights	Panic Stations
	LOW — Running — HIGH	

If half the art of survival is running, the other half is keeping a straight face. **Harry Flashman, George Macdonald Fraser**

Harry Flashman is the cowardly anti-hero of the George Macdonald Fraser historical novels, inspired by the bully of Tom Brown's School Days. Macdonald Fraser records Flashman's military adventures during the Victorian era - *a scoundrel, a liar, a cheat, a thief, a coward - and, oh yes, a toady.* Despite his own lack of principle and courage, Flashman is an astute observer of human nature, in particular of its follies and failings.

Don't look back. Something might be gaining on you. **Leroy Satchel Paige**

The Flashman Law of Survival hinges on two dimensions.

Running. This is the speed at which the game is played. At the low end of the range, slow gets found out and caught. At the other end, fast stays ahead of potential trouble.

Straight Face.[1] This theme is the Brass Neck factor. At the low end of the spectrum, an openness to disclose feelings and intentions and to acknowledge limitations. At the high end, a complete lack of embarrassment or contrition[2] even when confronted by the most obvious mistakes and misdeeds.

This gives rise to four orientations.

Rabbit in Headlights. Slow running without a straight face is the shame when confronted with transgressions and no defence. The appeal of this grouping lies in the honesty of *mea culpa*. In a cynical world, it is a stance that is punished.

Greased Piglet.[3] This is slow running but with a straight face when questioned and challenged about any shortcomings. This is the full on brass neck to deny any involvement in misunderstandings and mishaps. Here it can be difficult to overcome the shamelessness of outright denial.

Let's say you arrest three guys for the same killing, Special Agent Kujan tells his colleagues. You put them all in jail overnight. The next morning, whoever's sleeping is your man. **The Usual Suspects**

Panic Stations. Fast running without a straight face represents those who keep on the move knowing if are found out, they are in trouble. Speed is critical for this group to stay ahead of indefensible past actions. This tactic is often accompanied by appeals to others' sympathy for a predicament not of their making.

On the keyboard of life, always keep one finger on the escape key. **Scott Adams**

Poker Pressure. This is the Flashman strategy of fast running and a straight face. A life game played at pace to stay ahead of events in combination with a high level of emotional composure. Everything is under control. Hazardous for organisations when its leaders adopt this stance.[4]

If you're skating on thin ice, you might as well dance. **Anita Shreve**

SO WHAT?

The secret to my success is that I bit off more than I could chew and chewed as fast as I could. **Paul Hogan**

At a personal level, the Flashman factor is a common tactic for rapid career progression as individuals zig zag through a series of roles, leaving chaos behind them. For organisations, this lack of accountability represents a significant problem.

NOTES

1. A variation: Thick Face, Black Heart: The Warrior Philosophy for Conquering the Challenges of Business and Life, Chin-Ning Chu; https://www.goodreads.com/review/show/785780052

2. When you're 18, you worry about what everybody is thinking of you; when you're 40, you don't give a damm what anybody thinks of you; when you're 60, you realise nobody's been thinking about you at all. Daniel Amen

3. Greased piglet: a person who is very proficient at slipping out of tight situations, used by David Cameron in reference to disgraced former Prime Minister Boris Johnson.

4. There is no shortage of brass neck CEOs who, despite a track record of failure, manage to smell of roses. Why It's About Time; https://talentworldconsulting.com/wp-content/uploads/2023/08/Its-About-Leadership-Time.pdf

Which habits are we building?

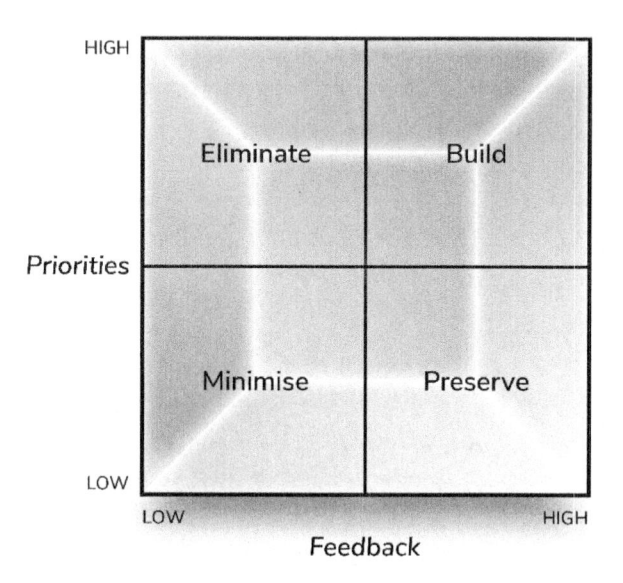

```
         HIGH
              ┌─────────────┬─────────────┐
              │             │             │
              │  Eliminate  │    Build    │
              │             │             │
Priorities    ├─────────────┼─────────────┤
              │             │             │
              │   Minimise  │   Preserve  │
              │             │             │
         LOW  └─────────────┴─────────────┘
              LOW                      HIGH
                        Feedback
```

Successful people form the habit of doing what failures don't like to do. **Earl Nightingale**

The personal development movement has been dominated by the philosophy of *dream the impossible*. Tony Robbins - Awaken The Giant Within - has been the most vocal advocate.[1]

This is like having the Universe as your catalogue and you flip through it and you go, Wow, I'd like to have this experience and I'd like to have this product. It's you placing your order with the Universe. **Joe Vitalie, The Secret**

Alternatively, *dreams will get you nowhere, but a good kick in the pants will take you a long way*. Positive psychology is now floundering. Exaggerated claims ran way ahead of evidence.[2] The sentiment has shifted to a more grounded approach that sees personal change through the small gains of replacing bad habits with good habits.[3]

This grid adapted from Marshall Goldsmith[4] highlights two dimensions.

Feedback. The signal of what is going well or not so well. At the low end, *do less of* is the message to stop. At the high end, *do more of* is the encouragement of positive impact to build on what is working.

Priorities. This is the theme of importance. Some issues matter much more than others. A low priority for personal change requires no immediate response. A high priority is the recognition that this issue needs to be addressed with urgency.

Am I willing at this time to make the investment required to make a positive difference on this topic? **Marshall Goldsmith**

Against these two themes, four development responses are highlighted.

Minimise. *If I'm a 1, can I live with this fact, or at least ensure the 1 of my inputs doesn't become a 1 of my outcomes?* Tough feedback but not a priority. It can also be the acceptance that some our vices will never become virtues. The most effective strategy is to minimise the impact of these shortcomings. This self-awareness recognises, for example, the warning signs of stress levels bringing out a natural tendency to impatience, with the savvy to manage the situation when it will negatively affect others.

Eliminate. *If I'm a 1, what do I need to do to at least move to a 5?* Challenging feedback and a higher priority to respond. This is the type of change often made with some reluctance. After all, some of these habits may have served us well in the past. It is also the change that can come with some difficulty; these habits may be an integral part of our identity.

Chains of habit are too light to be felt until they are too heavy to be broken. **Warren Buffett**

Preserve. *If I'm a 7, how can I keep it a 7?* This is the arena to maintain and reinforce established positive patterns that are working well for us. The focus here is less: what do we need to acquire, and more what do we need to do to ensure we don't lose a productive habit.

Build. *If I'm a 7, what do I need to do to become a 9?* It's working well but not well enough. This is the kind of change that may require a rethink of personal identity to identify a new me and put in place a different pattern of behaviours based on new habits.

It's very hard to stop doing things you're used to doing. You almost have to dismantle yourself and scatter it all around and then put a blindfold on and put it back together so that you avoid old habits. **Tom Waits**

SO WHAT?

There's just one way to radically change your behaviour; radically change your environment. ***BJ Fogg***[5]

The hoopla of a motivational workshop that promises easy personal transformation through ambitious thoughts and big dreams is nothing more than a dream. It doesn't happen. A more grounded approach is realism through implementation intentions, small wins and tiny habits through check-lists and score cards to review progress to identify any setbacks and maintain focus.

It also helps to conduct regular reviews with key colleagues and stakeholders, and draw on a support system.[6]

NOTES

1. Historically, this outlook goes back Napoleon Hill and his 1937 book Think and Grow Rich: You become what you think about. *Tragically, this was true, and later in life, Hill confessed: I had spent the better portion of my life in chasing a rainbow. I had begun to place myself in the category of charlatans who offers a remedy of failure which they, themselves, cannot successfully apply.*

2. The critiques and criticisms of positive psychology: A systematic review; https://www.tandfonline.com/doi/full/10.1080/17439760.2023.2178956

3. Why Goal Setting Doesn't Work; https://www.psychologytoday.com/blog/wired-success/201407/why-goalsetting-doesnt-work
Why Setting Goals Could Wreck Your Life;
http://www.fastcompany.com/3002763/why-setting-goals-could-wreckyour-life
Teresa Amabile and Steve Kramer, 2011, "Small Wins and Feeling Good"; Harvard Business Review; https://hbr.org/2011/05/small-wins-and-feelinggood

4. Triggers, Marshall Goldsmith

5. Fogg Behavior Model; https://behaviormodel.org/

6. From Feedback To Impact; https://talentworldconsulting.com/wp-content/uploads/2023/08/FromFeedbackTo-Impact.pdf

How should we set goals?

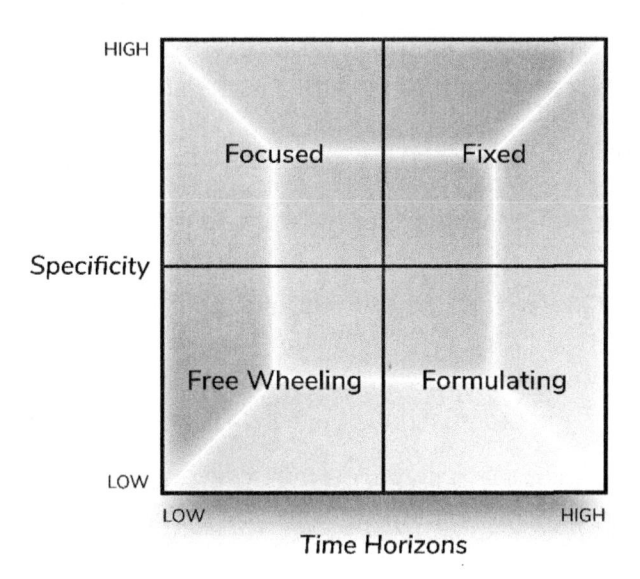

```
HIGH
        |  Focused    |  Fixed       |
Specificity
        |  Free Wheeling | Formulating |
LOW
        LOW          Time Horizons    HIGH
```

I can teach anybody how to get what they want out of life. The problem is that I can't find anybody who can tell me what they want. **Mark Twain**

The positive psychology movement sees goal setting as a key driver of life success. If we are ever troubled by our current life situation, we have failed to translate our dreams of the possible into meaningful, clear and specific objectives. Jim Rohn states: *If you don't design your own life plan, chances are you'll fall into someone else's plan. And guess what they have planned for you? Not much.*

Is this true? This quadrant outlines a more complex pattern to guide the how and when of goal setting. It identifies when goal setting can be a constructive exercise to shape and focus priorities. Alternatively, a counterproductive activity that can backfire.

The two dimensions.

Time Horizons. Which time frame is applied? At one end of the spectrum, the short term focuses attention on objectives for the day, the week or possibly the month. At the other end, goals and plans are set for the next five years and more.

Specificity. How well defined are our goals? Goals can be general, an approximation of the direction of travel. Specific objectives are defined with a clear set of tasks to arrive at the final destination.

Four approaches to goal setting are identified.

Free Wheeling. Here, the short term coincides with the general. This position is an improvisational stance to life. If the future is unknown, and possibly unknowable, this strategy avoids commitments. At best, the life of spontaneity to enjoy the moment and respond to events as they happen. Alternatively, a care free strategy that lacks purpose; a life of hesitation and procrastination which fails to invest in the future.

Slow down and enjoy life. It's not only the scenery you miss by going too fast - you also miss the sense of where you are going and why. **Eddie Cantor**

Focused. Goal setting is short term and specific. This is the life style of organised structure with the reassurance of an established rhythm to each day and week. A planned diary and scheduled calendar provides clarity and meaning to life. No doubt a sensible way to manage time in a busy world around key objectives, this outlook also has the potential to conclude: *where is the life we have lost in living?* A life lived by routine can block opportunities for that energising variety which responds to events as they are encountered.[1]

Goal obsession is the force at play when we get so wrapped up in achieving our goal that we do it at the expense of a larger mission. **Marshall Goldsmith**

Formulating. This stance to goal setting combines a long term time horizon but only in general terms. It provides purpose and meaning around life values and priorities.[2] It creates flexibility to adapt to the slings and arrows of life's contingencies. That is the upside. The downside: a life of hope reluctant to make detailed plans to reach these ambitious goals. This can be the life of *what could have been* which never realises its promise.

I coulda been a contender, I could've been somebody, instead of a bum, which is what I am. **Terry Malloy, On The Waterfront**

Fixed. In this situation, specific goals are set for the long term. This strategy writes down goals for the future. Life does not happen to us. And the more detailed and ambitious our goals the better. An alternative: this life outlook backfires. The Yale study much loved by motivational speakers never took place.[3] The fundamental problem with this approach: we assume our current self knows what will make our future self happy.[4]

When we make music we don't do it in order to reach the end of the composition. If that were the purpose of music, then obviously the fastest players would be best. **Alan Watts**

SO WHAT?

There is a fine line between dreams and reality, it's up to you to draw it. **B Quilliam**

Maybe the solution to this life question is that a sense of direction of travel might be important for some. But that a detour from time to time is no bad idea. For others, *the road is everything ahead of me*.[5]

NOTES

1. Goal Setting Gone Wild;https://www.hbs.edu/ris/Publication%20Files/09-083.pdf?__s=j6rskt1bdsiu832tsvyz

2. Purposive Drift; https://www.porchlightbooks.com/blog/changethis/2007/purposive-drift-making-it-up-as-we-go-along

3. A 1953 graduating class of Harvard MBA students was asked about whether, or not, they had goals. 3% said they had clear, written goals, 13% had goals, just not written down, 84% did not have goals at all. Ten years later, it was discovered that the 3% who had written goals outperformed everyone altogether by earning ten times as much as all of the other 97% combined.
The research was fiction. If Your Goal Is Success, Don't Consult These Gurus; https://www.fastcompany.com/27953/if-your-goal-success-dont-consult-these-gurus

4. *We treat our future selves as though they were our children, spending most of the hours of most of our days constructing tomorrows that we hope will make them happy.* Stumbling Towards Happiness, Daniel Gilbert

5. On The Road, Jack Kerouac. *There was nowhere to go but everywhere.*

How can we best manage the difficulties of life?

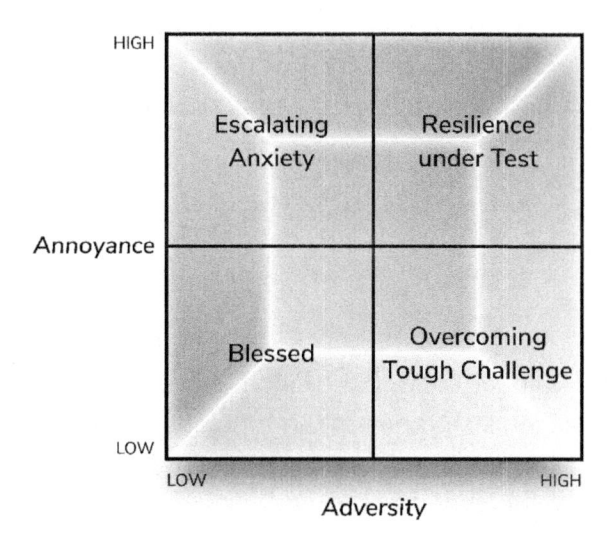

```
HIGH │
     │  Escalating    │  Resilience
     │  Anxiety       │  under Test
     │                │
Annoyance ───────────┼───────────
     │                │
     │                │  Overcoming
     │  Blessed       │  Tough Challenge
     │                │
LOW  │
     └────────────────┴───────────
        LOW                    HIGH
              Adversity
```

Somebody stands in the sunshine; somebody stands in the rain; somebody's shootin' a shotgun; somebody's feelin' the pain; somebody has to spend their life wrapped up in a chain. It's rollin. **Steve Gibbons Band**

Life can be a joyous experience of wonder and delight, fun and laughter and advancement towards fulfilling goals. But it is not always this way. It is sometimes difficult. We are confronted with annoying barriers to progress. Even worse, we encounter harsh adversity. How do we manage the ups and downs of the stuff that life throws at us?

When circumstances are easy it's hard to distinguish ordinary people from extraordinary ones, or to see the extraordinary within ourselves. **Shane Parrish**

This quadrant provides a perspective based on two dimensions.

Adversity. This theme spans the spectrum from the minor hardships we experience during the course of life, through to the major traumas of, for example, a bankrupt business, the breakup of a valued relationship, or worse, the death of a loved one.

Annoyance. If life is just *one thing after another*, annoyances are those episodes of frustrating niggle. From the minor hiccups of an empty toothpaste tube, a garbage bag that bursts in the kitchen or a late train, to the major hassles of the lost house key, a tyre puncture or a missing pet. This is time and energy that could be deployed more productively.

Elephants don't bite. It is the mosquitoes of life that cause the most trouble. **David Lieberman**

Four responses are identified to resilience.

Blessed. In this scenario, both annoyance and adversity are minor. This is a life of peaceful contentment untroubled by disruptive forces. Alternatively, this is the fragile state as outlined by Nassim Taleb.[1] We become vulnerable to the stresses and shocks that will inevitably happen.

Something always goes wrong when things are going right. **Matt Johnson, The The**

Escalating Anxiety. Annoyance is high but adversity is low. A life situation of endless worry to cope with the daily hassles - smartphone alerts, a long and unpleasant commute, noisy neighbours, a difficult teenager. They disrupt our equilibrium and dissipate our energies and time.[2] Over time, this becomes highly stressful and takes its toll. In this circumstance, a rethink is needed to make key changes in life-style before a series of ongoing annoyances become adversity.

Any idiot can face a crisis, but it is day-to-day living that wears you out. **Anton Chekov**

Overcoming Tough Challenge. Annoyance might be relatively low but adversity is high. This is to encounter hurt, pain, suffering and loss. The Nietzschean dictum that what doesn't kill strengthens us provides little consolation during these times. This is the uncomfortable reality that makes us ask: will this too pass?[3]

Resilience under Test. A tough scenario in which both annoyance and adversity combine. Even worse, the interplay between the two multiply for an arduous and aggravating and unrelenting experience. Is there no let up? What have we done to deserve this misfortune?

Antifragility is beyond resilience or robustness. The resilient resists shocks and stays the same; the antifragile gets better. **Nassim Taleb**

SO WHAT?

After all, our worst misfortunes never happen, and most miseries lie in anticipation. **Honore de Balzac**

If a problem has no solution, it may not be a problem, but a fact - not to be solved, but to be coped with over time. The preacher of Ecclesiastes reminds us time and chance happen to us all. Sometimes there is no rhyme or reason for life events. But we can however develop coping strategies to address the minor annoyances that might make it easier to survive the major adversities.[4]

NOTES

1. Antifragile and its Implications; https://fs.blog/antifragile-a-definition/

2. How modern life affects our physical and mental health; https://www.medicalnewstoday.com/articles/318230#The-emergence-of-the-constant-checker

3. This too shall pass; https://simplicable.com/en/this-too-shall-pass

4. Resilience: Build skills to endure hardship; https://www.mayoclinic.org/tests-procedures/resilience-training/in-depth/resilience/art-20046311

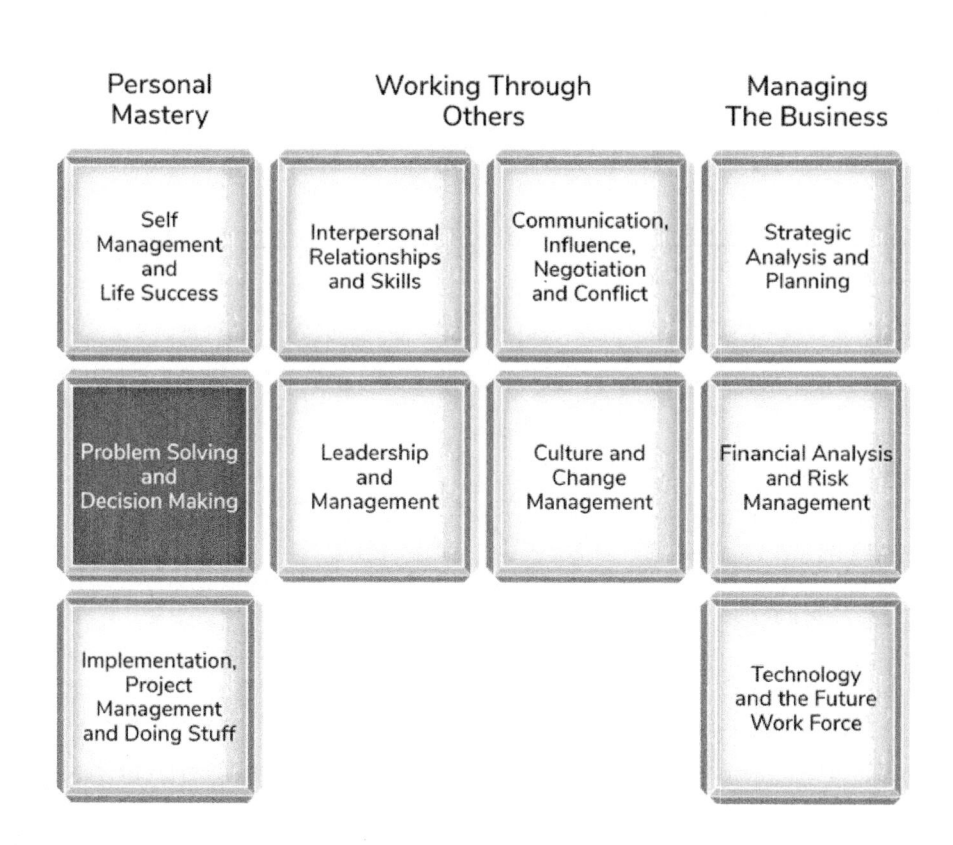

Personal Mastery	Working Through Others		Managing The Business
Self Management and Life Success	Interpersonal Relationships and Skills	Communication, Influence, Negotiation and Conflict	Strategic Analysis and Planning
Problem Solving and Decision Making	Leadership and Management	Culture and Change Management	Financial Analysis and Risk Management
Implementation, Project Management and Doing Stuff			Technology and the Future Work Force

Which problems are best avoided

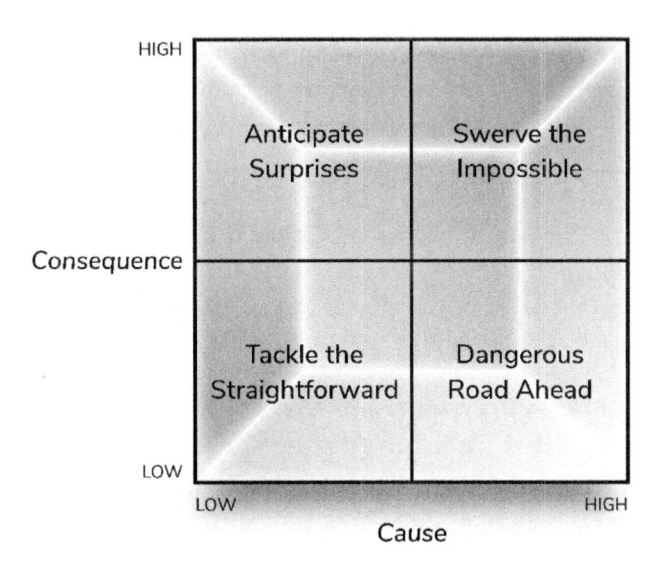

	Low Cause	High Cause
High Consequence	Anticipate Surprises	Swerve the Impossible
Low Consequence	Tackle the Straightforward	Dangerous Road Ahead

If you don't get elementary probability you go through life like a one legged man in an ass kicking contest. **Charlie Munger**

Alexander the Great was challenged to untie a complex knot tied to an ox cart. Whoever could untie the Gordian knot was destined to rule all of Asia. Instead of embarking on the intricacies of untangling the knot, Alexander cut through it with his sword. A seemingly intractable problem was solved through a simple and direct approach.

Some problems seem more difficult than they are. Others, however, are best side stepped. The cliché is that correlation is not causation. Sometimes our associations between cause and consequence are misguided.[1] We see patterns that don't exist[2] and sometimes we fail to recognise the dynamic - simple or complicated - between cause and consequence.

This grid is based on two dimensions to a problem.

Cause. The spectrum in which a single cause provides a simple explanation of effects, through to the phenomena in which many causal variables interact in complex ways.

Consequence. This dimension ranges from few to many consequences. Sometimes the effects are obvious and simple and the results inevitable. Alternatively, the consequences are unpredictable.

Results are what you expect; consequences are what you get. **Ladies Home Journal, 1942**

Against this backdrop, four scenarios emerge.

Tackle the Straightforward. Causes are few and the sequential chain to consequences is direct. This is the principle of: do this and get that. This is the domain of the relatively undemanding problems of life, provided of course our thinking is clear about the connect between what we do and what will subsequently happen. If not, this can be the folly of arrogance.

Anticipate Surprises. When causes are simple but may trigger any number of different possibilities, we should be prepared for the unexpected. We may be delighted that one action sets in motion a variety of positive outcomes. Alternatively, this is the scenario of WTF; we didn't foresee that event.

In the realm of the unexpected, true adventures await those who are willing to take the leap. **Tales of the Unexpected**

Dangerous Road Ahead. Many causal factors are at work and required to be in play to achieve a single consequence. At best, the stars align for an extraordinarily positive result. At worst, this is the principle of the weakest link in a chain. One mis-step undermines the impact of other variables with a negative effect.

A handful of concepts about places, paths, motions, agency, and causation underlie the literal or figurative meanings of tens of thousands of words and constructions. **Steven Pinker**

Swerve the Impossible. Multiple causes interact in a range of permutations for a series of possible outcomes. This complexity, if understood and managed, finds new ways to gain advantage.[3] We identify a pattern that others fail to recognise, a configuration that we can exploit. Conversely, a situation of high unpredictability with unexpected results, and best avoided.

SO WHAT?

You can never do merely one thing. **Garrett Hardin**[4]

Warren Buffett applies the test: do we know our *because*? Can we state the logic behind our thinking to explain clearly to others what we are doing and why, and with what expected outcome?

If we can't, it may be worth tracking back to check our theory of what happens where, when and why.

NOTES

1. Correlation, Causation, and Confusion; https://www.thenewatlantis.com/publications/correlation-causation-and-confusion

2. Spurious correlations. It is amazing to discover for example that the correlation between per capita consumption of cheese and the number of people who died by becoming tangled in their bed sheets was 0.947. http://www.tylervigen.com

3. *Everybody looks for the sweet spot, that situation in which the risks are low and the rewards are high. The trouble is, that when an obvious situation like that arises, everyone rushes to it.* B Zeckhauser and A Sandoski. In the scramble for the sweet spot, rewards are diluted and the risks rise. Look instead at the high risk-high reward opportunities. These might require more time and effort in working through the strategic gains and hazards, but these are the opportunities that others back off from. It is these possibilities, with robust analysis and shrewd decision making, that have the potential to make business breakthroughs.

4. Three Filters Needed to Think Through Problems; https://fs.blog/garrett-hardin-three-filters/

Why do intelligent people do daft stuff?

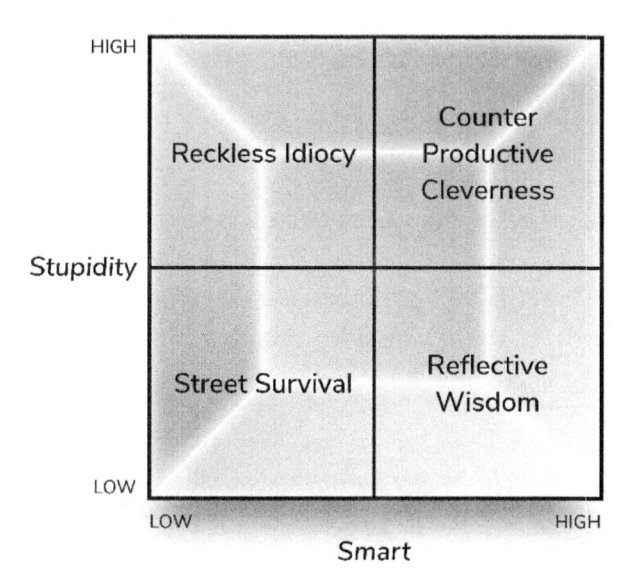

```
         HIGH
          ┌─────────────┬─────────────┐
          │             │   Counter   │
          │  Reckless   │ Productive  │
          │   Idiocy    │  Cleverness │
Stupidity │             │             │
          ├─────────────┼─────────────┤
          │             │             │
          │   Street    │  Reflective │
          │  Survival   │   Wisdom    │
          │             │             │
          └─────────────┴─────────────┘
         LOW
            LOW                    HIGH
                     Smart
```

Other people are trying to be smart. All I'm trying to be is non-idiotic. It's harder than most people think. **Charlie Munger**

It is easy to think that highly intelligent individuals - not least those who report high scores on conventional IQ tests - avoid stupidity. And those who do the stupid stuff of life, lack intelligence. This is not so. Smartness and stupidity are not opposite ends of one continuum. To understand why, this quadrant explores the permutations of smartness and stupidity.

A lot of people start out with 400-horsepower motor and get a hundred horsepower of output. So why do smart people do things that interfere with getting the output they're entitled to? **Warren Buffett**

Smart. The cognitive skills to help us solve problems, a spectrum that runs from limited reasoning power, to the high end of advanced aptitude in analysis and critical thinking.

Stupidity. A dimension to reflect the counter-productive behaviours that get us into difficulty. At the low end, the avoidance of activities that are against our long-term interests. At the other, an almost magnetic attraction to those actions that can only create trouble in life.

Any series of numbers, however positive, evaporate when multiplied by a single zero. **Charlie Munger**

Four permutations emerge.

Street Survival. This combination of low smart and low stupidity describes those who recognise their limitations and avoid situations that might expose these shortcomings. A cautious approach to life. There might not be a big upside, but it is one that avoids the potentially disastrous downside.

I have seen in my time hundreds of plowmen wiser and happier than the rectors of university. **Michel de Montaigne**

Reckless Idiocy. Low smart meets high stupidity. A grouping regularly reported in the Darwin Awards: *the recognition of individuals who have contributed to human evolution by selecting themselves out of the gene pool.*[1] When low intelligence - which fails to recognise its own failings - meets stupidity, it embarks on those actions that are counterproductive, personally and for others.

Last Friday night, I Twitted a photograph of myself that I intended to send as a direct message as part of a joke to a woman in Seattle. Once I realised I posted to Twitter I panicked, I took it down and said that I had been hacked. I then continued with that story, to stick to that story which was a hugely regrettable mistake. **Anthony Weiner, candidate for mayor, New York City**

Reflective Wisdom. A description of high levels of smart and low stupidity, this combination realises the need to stay in the *circle of competence*. This grouping excels at doing what it knows and does best. It side steps those situations that might draw them into activities damaging to their best interests.

Every generation imagines itself to be more intelligent than the one that went before it, and wiser than the one that comes after it. **George Orwell**

Counter Productive Cleverness. High smart is accompanied by high levels of stupidity. This is intelligence deployed against itself. Being right on one set of issues translates into the intellectual arrogance that is right about anything and everything. And the skill to debate logically - to argue for the indefensible - backfires, and reinforces the righteousness of the original position.[2]

Nothing is more hateful to wisdom than excessive cleverness. **Edgar Allan Poe**

SO WHAT?

This quadrant reflects the life wisdom summarised by Charlie Munger: *it's remarkable how much long-term advantage people like us have gotten by trying to be consistently not stupid, instead of trying to be very intelligent.*

Before we attempt the brilliance of our smarts, we should avoid the obvious stupidities.[3]

NOTES

1. Darwin Awards: a site to *commemorate individuals who protect our gene pool by making the ultimate sacrifice of their own lives. Darwin Award winners eliminate themselves in an extraordinarily idiotic manner, thereby improving our species' chances of long-term survival.* https://darwinawards.com/

2. Why do intelligent people do stupid stuff? And are intelligent people more - not less likely - to behave in stupid ways?
https://www.evolveassess.com/blog/psyched-for-business-podcast-episode-07

3. Nincompoopery: How To Find And Kill The Corporate Stupidity That Drives Customers Crazy, John R. Brandt

Why didn't the dog bark?

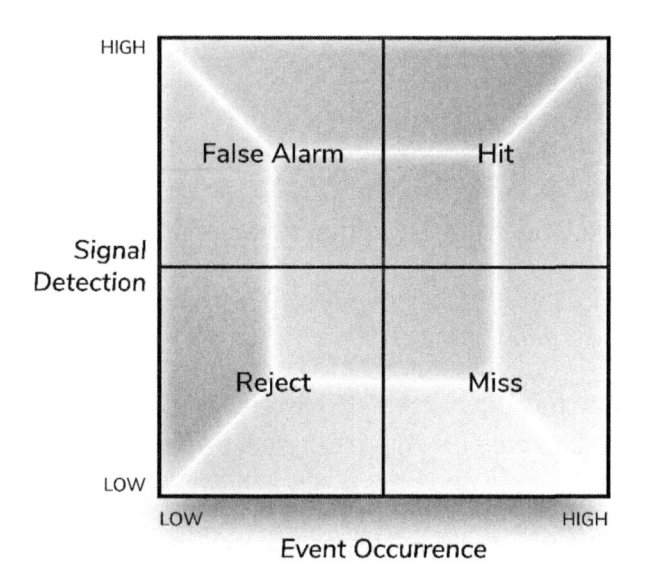

Is there any other point to which you would wish to draw my attention?
To the curious incident of the dog in the night-time.
The dog did nothing in the night-time.
That was the curious incident.
The Adventure of Silver Blaze, Arthur Conan Doyle

The task is to find the needle in the haystack. Science has established a series of protocols - research design, statistical methodologies, peer review, replication - to locate the needle. To apply the jargon, Type 1 errors are the false positives that report something is significant when it isn't.[1] Type 2 errors are the false negatives that say something is not significant when it is.

In life, we find ourselves bombarded with information, noise to make claims on our attention and demand a response. What is true, accurate and meaningful vis a vis what is false, inaccurate and of no consequence? This quadrant helps to find the signal in the noise.[2]

The two dimensions.

Event Occurrence. This asks if something important happened, from a spectrum of *nothing to see here, move on*, to a significant event that requires action.

Signal Detection. This is our radar screen to scan the environment and differentiate the true from the false. At the low end of the spectrum, our detection equipment is faulty. and fails to give accurate readings. At the high end, our mental systems are switched on and sophisticated to spot the signal.

Four responses are highlighted.

Reject. Nothing has happened. No event has occurred and our system has not detected anything. Correctly, we carry on as is.

False Alarm. Nothing has happened, but our mental software locates an event. In this scenario, our systems are activated to respond. The upside of this super sensitivity is caution. That noise *might* after all be a break in to the house, our colleague might be dishonest, and our partner may be cheating on us. The downside: a highly stressful way to live.

There is an important lesson in evaluating human behaviour: never denigrate a behaviour as irrational until you have considered what purpose it really serves. **Rory Sutherland**

Miss. Our signal detection equipment lets us down. Something important has happened, but we have not picked it up. Why? Did we switch off? Were we asleep at the wheel? Did our cognitive biases distort the intake and processing of information? [3] Or did our emotions deny the reality of the situation?

At the end of the day, we're a bunch of apes whose brains were optimised for defending ourselves and our tribes, not for doing unbiased evaluations of scientific evidence. So why get angry at humanity for not being great at something we didn't evolve to be great at? **Julia Galef**

Hit. Our signal detection equipment is at its best to spot with accuracy an instance of importance. It might be an emergency requiring a rapid response. Or it might seem at first sight a relatively trivial incident, but one, if not resolved quickly, has the potential to escalate.[4]

At the heart of science is an essential balance between two seemingly contradictory attitudes - an openness to new ideas, no matter how bizarre or counterintuitive they may be, and the most ruthless sceptical scrutiny of all ideas, old and new. This is how deep truths are winnowed from deep nonsense. **Carl Sagan**

SO WHAT?

When generating information becomes cheap, finding information that matters becomes correspondingly more expensive. **Rory Sutherland**

For our evolutionary survival, our response to potential risk had to be rapid. Our mental software was biased toward the false signal to identify threat. But it makes for an anxious life style.

When fear is in the driving seat we miss the genuine opportunities for gain.

NOTES

1. Why Most Published Research Findings Are False, John Ioannidis; https://www.ncbi.nlm.nih.gov/pmc/articles/PMC1182327/

2. The Noise Bottleneck: When More Information is Harmful; https://fs.blog/noise-and-signal-nassim-taleb/

3. Buster Benson and cognitive biases; https://medium.com/unexpected-leadership/buster-bensons-cognitive-bias-cheat-sheet-453e75eb9fa8

4. Survivorship bias. Abraham Wald and the Missing Bullet Holes; https://medium.com/@penguinpress/an-excerpt-from-how-not-to-be-wrong-by-jordan-ellenberg-664e708cfc3d

Which sources of information can we trust?

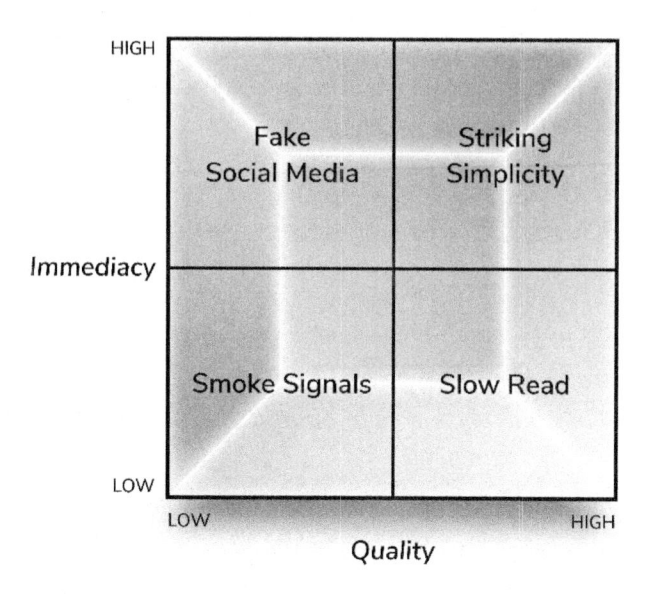

[A 2x2 matrix with Immediacy on the vertical axis (LOW to HIGH) and Quality on the horizontal axis (LOW to HIGH). Quadrants: top-left "Fake Social Media", top-right "Striking Simplicity", bottom-left "Smoke Signals", bottom-right "Slow Read".]

Most problems have either many answers or no answer. Only a few problems have a single answer. **Edmund Berkeley**

Philip Tetlock[1] tracked the accuracy of the forecasts of 284 experts from a range of disciplines including political scientists, economists and journalists, collecting over 27,000 judgements they had made about the future. He looked back to check the accuracy of their predictive powers. The results were awful. *The experts barely outperformed a model based on random guessing.* They were beaten by dart throwing chimps.

Information matters. The information we attend to and ignore shapes our judgements, from the relatively trivial to the significant in life. How do we deal with information overload to locate meaning and wisdom?

Given a thimbleful of facts, we rush to make generalisations as large as a tub. **Gordon Allport**

This quadrant is based on the trade-offs between two dimensions.

Quality. This reflects the accuracy and relevance of our information intake. Low quality is content which is not only incomplete, but often highly misleading to distort our understanding of the world. High, trusted information for insight into the problems we encounter and the potential solutions.

Immediacy. This theme is about timeliness. Low immediacy is slow content, information which takes time to receive and assimilate. High immediacy is the rapid flow of information accessible in the present.

Of the four basic emotions into which they classified tweets, sadness and disgust barely travel. Joy does better. But anger, like a potent virus, spreads the fastest and most widely of all. **Beihang University researchers**

Four informational patterns play out.

Smoke Signals. Here information arrives slowly and is inaccurate. By the time this information reaches us it has been filtered and distorted to the point that any meaningful truth has been lost.[2]

Fake Social Media. This is the speed of low quality information from the feeds of different social media platforms that incorporate the distraction of clickbait advertising. Its immediacy demands our attention. Occasionally it provides insight. But for the most part, *foam and the froth* to be ignored.

A lie is halfway round the world before the truth has got its boots on. **Virgil**[3]

Slow Read. This is information with rich content but requires time to work through and understand fully. In a busy schedule of an overloaded inbox, this source of information is unpopular and largely ignored. But it is content that gives a deeper insight into the issues.

Striking Simplicity. Information presented in a vivid and timely way to gain our attention and capture our interest. Complex issues have been consolidated and summarised to provide meaning. This represents a key priority in the choices we make about our sources of information.

SO WHAT?

In the Information Age, the first step to sanity is FILTERING. Filter the information: extract for knowledge. First for substance. Second for significance. Third for reliability. Fourth for completeness. **Marc Stiegler**

There is no perfect decision, all the time, every time. Speed, based on getting it right 90% of the time, is a better strategy than one that waits to get it right 100% of the time. It helps however if we implement filters to evaluate the quality of information that guides these decisions.[4]

NOTES

1. Philip Tetlock and the dismal track record of expert forecasters; http://www.newyorker.com/archive/2005/12/05/051205crbo_books1

2. Smoke signals were unreliable, not helped by the fact that they could be seen by the enemy. Other systems of transmission evolved including semaphore, used on the cover of the Beatles' Help album. *When we came to do the shot, the arrangement of the arms with those letters didn't look good, so we decided to improvise and ended up with the best graphic positioning other arms.* The shapes that appear on the album actually signify the letters N, U, J and V.

3. Although often attributed to Winston Churchill; https://interestingliterature.com/2021/06/lie-halfway-round-world-before-truth-boots-on-quote-origin-meaning/

4. Ten Commandments for Aspiring SuperForecasters; https://goodjudgment.com/philip-tetlocks-10-commandments-of-superforecasting/

Should we mistrust the experts?

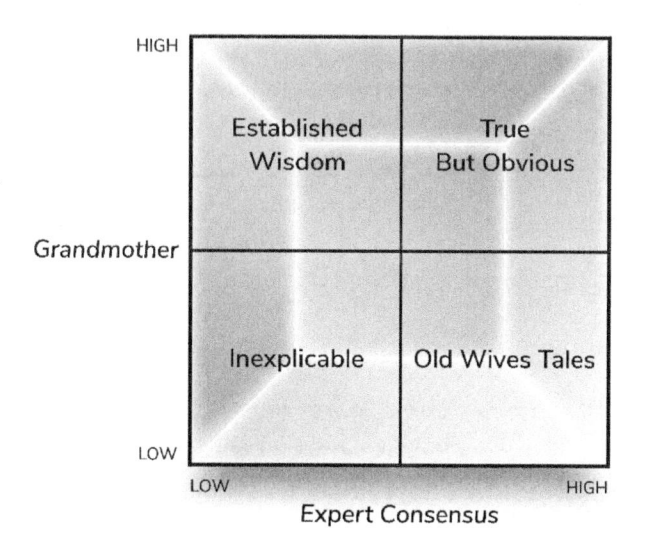

	Low Expert Consensus	High Expert Consensus
High Grandmother	Established Wisdom	True But Obvious
Low Grandmother	Inexplicable	Old Wives Tales

Your grandmother vs. academic researcher: who should you trust? If you hear advice from a grandmother or elders, odds are that it works 90% of the time. On the other hand, if you read anything by psychologists and behavioral scientists, odds are that it works at less than 10%, unless it is has also been covered by the grandmother and the classics, in which case why would you need a psychologist? **Nassim Taleb**[1]

The Nassim Taleb principle does not apply to the complex issues of astrophysics, string theory or nuclear engineering. Here in-depth knowledge and expertise is critical in problem solving. Taleb's critique is targeted at the so-called soft social sciences of economics, anthropology, sociology and psychology - the enterprises that attempt to address the nature of human nature and social interaction.

Order and simplification are the first steps towards the mastery of a subject. **Thomas Mann**

The two dimensions.

Expert Consensus. This identifies the extent to which experts have agreed a body of evidence on which to base their analysis and recommendations. A range from low consensus with major disagreement over a suspect evidence base, through to a high level of consensus that provides a consistent and coherent summary of findings with trust about the implications.

Grandmother. This summarises the level of certainty with which a sensible grandmother makes a statement; a spectrum from the doubtful and largely uncertain, to high, one expressed with full confidence.

Grandmothers are repositories of inherited wisdom. **Nassim Taleb**

Four stances are identified.

Inexplicable. This combines low expert consensus and grandmother uncertainty. These issues, in all likelihood, identify life problems that will never be resolved. Or those that await the genius to cut the Gordian Knot of human psychology.

I think there should be a little bit of uneasiness in everything, because I do think we're all really in a sense living on the edge. So much of life is inexplicable. **Edward Gorey**

Established Wisdom. The experts cannot agree on a body of evidence to provide meaningful conclusions of practical application. In the absence of consensus, it is sensible to fall back on our grandmother's knowledge and place problem solving bets here rather than await the agonising of *more research is needed* from the experts.

If you have perplexing slides you will be admired and respected. You will also be considered an expert. **@AdContrarian**

Old Wives Tales.[2] In this scenario, experts agree on a body of evidence that defies the belief system of our grandmothers. Scientific methodology overturns past assumptions of what does and doesn't work to challenge the mistaken views of our grandmothers. This is extremely rare in the social sciences. Alternatively, an academic consensus that after further replication is later shown to be false.[3]

An expert is one who knows more and more about less and less. **Nicholas Murray Baker**

True But Obvious. This combines a high level of expert consensus with the certainty of our grandmothers. This observation is unlikely to be a breakthrough finding to rethink how we as individuals or as a society operate. It is usually a statement of the blindingly obvious and trivial, adding little to our knowledge base.

What you get from Harvard Business School is a wonderful network of people who were there with you and a set of tools that you can then bamboozle people with for the rest of your life. **Peter Day, Radio 4 business reporter**

SO WHAT?

Human nature hasn't changed for a million years. It won't even change in the next million years. Only the superficial things have changed. It is fashionable to talk about the changing man. A communicator must be concerned with the unchanging man, what compulsions drive him, what instincts dominate his every action, even though his language too often camouflages what really motivates him. **Bill Bernbach**

The position is not that experts in the social sciences can't be trusted, despite recent evidence that much research is flawed.[4] But if their conclusions diverge from folk wisdom, we should be sceptical.[5] And again ask our grandmothers what they think.

NOTES

1. The Intellectual Yet Idiot; https://medium.com/incerto/the-intellectual-yet-idiot-13211e2d0577

2. Old Wives Tales. For example, the carrots improve eyesight misconception. *The association between carrots and vision enhancement originated during World War II, when British pilots claimed improved night vision due to their high carrot consumption. However, this was later revealed as a strategic misinformation campaign to mask advancements in radar technology.*
https://www.silversurfers.com/nostalgia/myths-legends-and-life-lessons-the-fascinating-world-of-old-wives-tales/#:~:text=The%20Origins%20of%20Old%20Wives,when%20scientific%20understanding%20was%20limited

3. For example, the British amateur who debunked the mathematics of happiness; https://www.theguardian.com/science/2014/jan/19/mathematics-of-happiness-debunked-nick-brown

4. Social scientists' predictions were no better than those from a sample of the (non-specialist) general public. Insights into the accuracy of social scientists' forecasts of societal change; https://www.nature.com/articles/s41562-022-01517-1
When a researcher on dishonesty is criticised for dishonest research; https://www.nytimes.com/2023/06/24/business/economy/francesca-gino-harvard-dishonesty.html

5. Experts vs. Imitators; https://fs.blog/experts-vs-imitators/

How to explain mystery

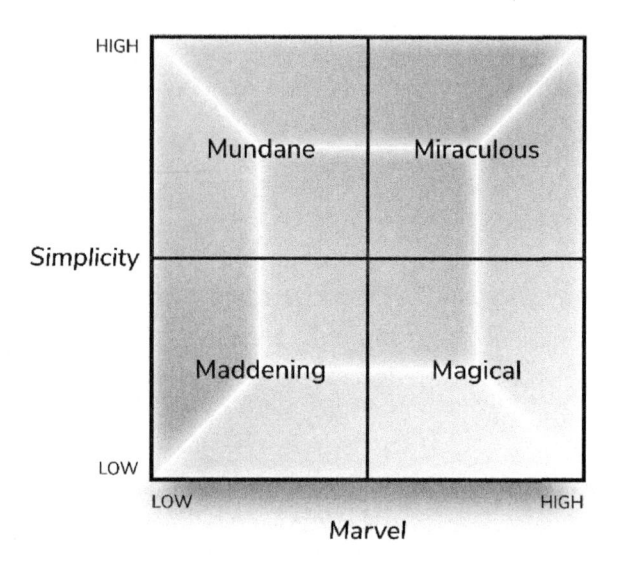

2×2 chart: Y-axis "Simplicity" from LOW to HIGH; X-axis "Marvel" from LOW to HIGH. Quadrants: top-left Mundane, top-right Miraculous, bottom-left Maddening, bottom-right Magical.

The modern mind always mixes up two different ideas: mystery in the sense of what is marvellous, and mystery in the sense of what is complicated. That is half its difficulty about miracles. **GK Chesterton**

There are wicked problems: the genuinely tough issues where we don't even know where to start, never mind where to look for a solution. And there are problems manufactured by any number of vested interests to obfuscate. There are also the extraordinary days of *miracle and wonder*[1] that can be dismissed as one of those things. How do we tell the difference?

There are two methods in software design. One is to make the program so simple, there are obviously no errors. The other is to make it so complicated, there are no obvious errors. **Tony Hoare**

Two dimensions apply.

Marvel. This reflects a sense of wonder at events. At one end of the dimension, the routine of the familiar and expected. At the other, the extraordinary that surprises and amazes.

Simplicity. This spectrum ranges from the highly complicated, events emerging from multiple interacting causes. It is difficult to work out the effects, through to the simple that is startling in its directness.

The ability to simplify eliminates the unnecessary, so that the necessary may speak. **Hans Hofman**

We encounter four types of mystery.

Maddening. This describes those phenomena - low on marvel and low on simplicity. At first, there seems nothing of much wonder to behold. But then, a sense that there is more to this than meets the eye. The reality, typically, is complexity designed and introduced as a smoke screen to state the obvious. And there is, in fact, much less to this than meets the eye.

Everything became sublime, especially the menu of the cafe advertising egg's, sausage's and tomato's. **Michael Foley**[2]

Mundane. High simplicity coincides with low marvel. This is the realm of the ordinary. The stuff of everyday life which is understandable, familiar and comfortable. It easy to say: *nothing to see here. Move on*. But sometimes, what on first impression seems the mundane - through a shift in perspective - becomes the remarkable.

The world is full of obvious things which nobody by any chance ever observes. **Sherlock Holmes**

Magical. This describes the combination of high marvel with low simplicity. When the fakir throws a rope in the air and the assistant climbs it[3], the act requires a complex set of sleight of hand machinations. But the event amazes us, and we suspend our judgement to witness an astonishing event.

People often ask if I perform sleight of hand or if I do real magic. There is a very real difference between the two. Sleight of hand is fast fingers, consummate skill. Real magic is the work of the devil. **Aaron Fisher, The Omen**

Miraculous. Here, we wonder at how such a simple event can explain an extraordinary phenomenon of marvel. This is the miracle of religious faith in which water is turned into wine, and five thousand are fed through two loaves and five fishes. It is also the scientific mystery of how a few mathematical principles and laws can explain much of the complexity of the workings of the natural world. This is the stuff of innovative breakthroughs.

The magic isn't in the trick. It is in the audience's eyes. **David Blaine**

SO WHAT?

James Joyce revealed the richness and strangeness of each day. Marcel Proust revealed the richness and strangeness of each life. **Michael Foley**

It is easy to confuse the mundane and the miraculous. We can get excited by the apparent miraculous when it is the ordinariness of the mundane. As James Randi, the magician and sceptic noted: *if Uri Geller is bending spoons through the paranormal, he's doing it the hard way.* And, sometimes, maybe often, we fail to see the magical in the mundane.

NOTES

1. Paul Simon and The Boy In The Bubble; https://youtu.be/Hk7MCvCHNQA?si=BTQeUaJc6r6dNYak

2. Embracing the Ordinary, Michael Foley; https://www.theguardian.com/books/2012/jul/18/embracing-the-ordinary-michael-foley-review

3. The Indian rope trick; https://www.youtube.com/watch?v=QfDX-a7MQPM

Is it ethical?

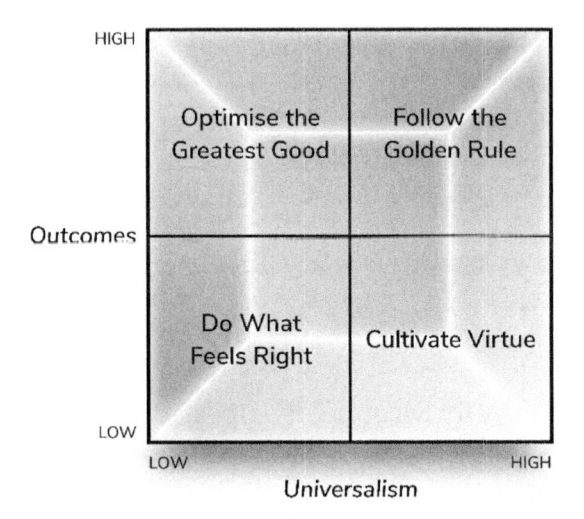

	LOW Universalism	HIGH Universalism
HIGH Outcomes	Optimise the Greatest Good	Follow the Golden Rule
LOW Outcomes	Do What Feels Right	Cultivate Virtue

Was Friedrich Nietzsche - the philosopher with a hammer - correct in proposing that *a moral system valid for all is basically immoral*? What makes something right vs wrong? How do we know the difference? Which ethical beliefs shape our approach to decision making? In business? And in life more generally?

Two themes are important to explain an ethical system.

Universalism. This is the stance that moral conduct and ethical behaviour transcend time and space. At the low end of this range, relativism proposes that principles and values are context dependent and vary across different cultures, societies and for individuals. At the high, objective moral truths apply across all history and geography.

Outcomes.[1] At one end of this dimension, the focus is on inputs - intrinsic virtue and our actions can be right or wrong regardless of the consequences. The other end focuses on ethical outcomes. What matters is not intention, but the end consequences of our actions.

However brilliant an action, it should not be esteemed great unless the result of a great motive. **Duc de la Rochefoucauld**

Four ethical positions can be adopted.

Do What Feels Right. This stance combines relativism and inputs. A situationalist outlook in which we attempt to do what we see as the right thing - appropriate to the specific circumstances we encounter. At best, a well-intentioned approach, adaptable to the issues as we interpret them. At worst, the defence of the sociopath who refuses to accept societal conventions of good and bad to advance their own personal sense of morality.

Sometimes you've gotta put your principles to one side and do the right thing. **St Loius cab driver to Joseph Fletcher**[2]

Optimise the Greatest Good. Relativism intersects with outcomes in this ethical system. What matters is impact not intentions. Moral impact can only be applied in a given context. This draws on a flexible set of rules, contingent on the specific circumstances at the time, for a pragmatic approach to ensure the greatest happiness of the greatest number.

Actions are right in proportion as they tend to promote happiness, wrong as they tend to produce the reverse of happiness. **John Stuart Mill, Utilitarianism**

Cultivate Virtue. This is universalism in combination with attention to moral behaviour. Because we cannot control events in life or take full responsibility for the results of our actions, the only strategy is to follow a moral code based on timeless truths and principles. Alternatively, this is the wringing of hands; the hope that an attempt at virtue will have a positive impact on others.

If you think about what you ought to do for other people, your character will take care of itself. Character is a byproduct, and any man who devotes himself to its cultivation in his own case will become a selfish prig. **Woodrow Wilson**

Follow the Golden Rule. This ethical outlook integrates universalism with a recognition that outcomes matter more than intentions. The Golden Rule[3] - an established moral principle across a range of religious traditions and philosophical systems throughout history - is the guiding principle: *treat others as one would want to be treated by them*. At best, an ethical system concerned not with self but with the impact on others. Conversely, a vague exhortation that lacks guidance across the complexity of a range of moral dilemmas.

Do not do unto others as you would that they should do unto you. Their tastes may not be the same. **George Bernard Shaw**

SO WHAT?

We have in fact, two kinds of morality, side by side: one which we preach but do not practice, and another which we practice, but seldom preach. **Bertrand Russell**

In discussions about morality and ethics, there is the binary logic of right or wrong and good versus bad. This mindset provides clarity and certainty to tackle a range of ethical dilemmas. It can also result in dogmatism, especially when facing the specifics of different cultural expectations and conventions.

Fuzzy logic accepts the world is complex and messy. Trade-offs need to be made in any specific scenario.

NOTES

1. The philosophical jargon is the distinction between a deontological approach - the morality of what should happen, versus teleological - the morality of what in fact happens.
https://www.geeksforgeeks.org/difference-between-teleological-and-deontological/

2. Situational Ethics: Joseph Fletcher;
https://www.allaboutphilosophy.org/situational-ethics.htm

3. The Science of Good and Evil, Michael Shermer

How to decide how to decide

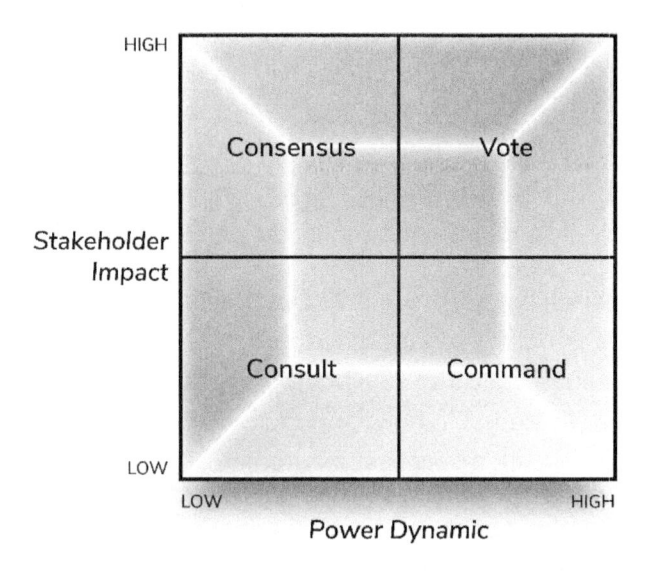

If you like laws and sausages, you should never watch either one being made. Laws are like sausages it is best not to see them being made. Laws are like sausages. **Otto von Bismarck**

The outcomes of a decision - and the success of subsequent implementation - rarely hinge on rational analysis. Process matters. This depends on our positional power as well as the impact on stakeholders affected by the decision.

Two themes shape which decision making process should be applied.

Power Dynamic. This reflects, at one end of the spectrum, the extent to which we are relatively powerless. Here we cannot draw on an array of resources to impose our will. Or, a position in which we are in full command of the situation and can call the shots.

Stakeholder Impact. Seldom is a decision made in isolation. Decisions require others' involvement and backing for a successful outcome. At the low end, there is little need for others' input. At the high end, a range of constituency demands will determine the probability of a successful outcome.

Four decision strategies are identified.

Consult. When a low power dynamic intersects with a low stakeholder impact, this is decision making as a series of conversations about possibilities with no defined agenda. At best, this approach builds awareness of bigger decisions on the horizon. More often, a process of prolonged talk that achieves little.

Consensus. In this scenario, the power dynamic is low but the impact on stakeholders is high. Any attempt to push forward an assertive agenda is misguided, with the likelihood of negative consequences. Time and energy is needed to build and manage coalitions to support the kind of decision with a successful outcome.

Command. When the power dynamic is high and stakeholder impact is low, decision making can be swift. At best, this is the boldness of Napoleon: *to make an omelette, eggs need to be broken*. Misjudged, a decision making process that neglects realpolitik and is exposed when stakeholder influence is higher than anticipated.

The absence of alternatives clears the mind marvellously. **Henry Kissinger**

Vote. The power dynamic is high, as is stakeholder impact. In this scenario, decision making must appeal to a wide audience to gain support. Time consuming it may be. But it establishes legitimacy for a credible outcome to advance decision outcomes.

Democracy is the worst form of government except for all the others that have been tried. **Winston Churchill**

SO WHAT?

Power and influence are not the organisation's last dirty secret but the secret of success for both individuals and their organisations. **Jeffrey Pfeffer**

A decision is only as good as the outcome it achieves to progress our aims in life. But it helps to know which process should be deployed to ensure that this outcome is more likely, and to understand our positional power vis a vis those of others.

NOTES

1. An outlook that was justified after the British people voted him out of office as Prime Minister within months of the end of the Second World War.

How to optimise our decisions

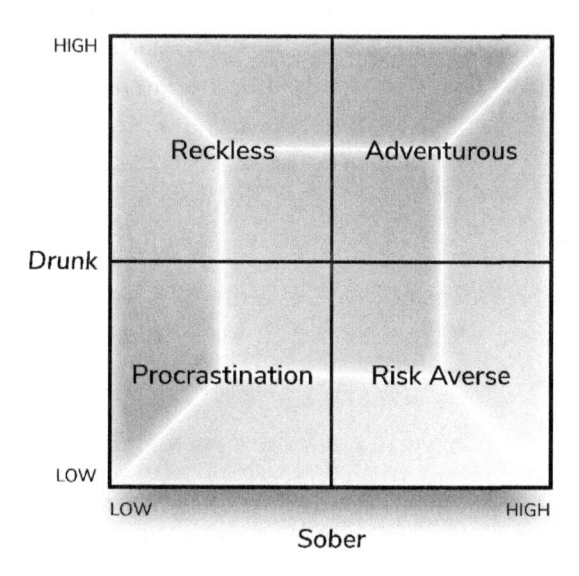

	Low Sober	High Sober
High Drunk	Reckless	Adventurous
Low Drunk	Procrastination	Risk Averse

Herodotus, the Greek historian, reported that the ancient Persians always made important decisions twice. First when they were drunk, and then again when they were sober. Only if the Persians reached the same decision, drunk and sober, would they act on that decision. The approach apparently worked. The Persians dominated much of the Middle East and Central Asia for three centuries.[1]

This quadrant explores two dimensions for effective decision making.

Sober. This is cool headed thinking that approaches problems in a dispassionate and objective way. Low is irrational and illogical. High, a considered and deliberative process.

Drunk. The hot headed impulsiveness in which the emotions are in the driving seat of decision making. At the low end of the spectrum, a detached approach to see the issues clearly. At the other extreme, an exuberant befuddlement.

The piano has been drinking, not me. **Tom Waits**

Four decision stances are identified.

Procrastination. Decision making is stuck. Neither logic or emotion are applied to problems. Decisions remain unresolved. It may be this avoids a decision that does not need to be made. Procrastination after all has its benefits.[2] Or, an important decision to raise complex issues and arouses difficult feelings - and it goes unmade.

I don't catch your drift and I don't catch your plan. **Amy Winehouse**

Reckless. This is the hot headedness of drunkenness without the cool logic of sobriety. Occasionally, this outlook has the advantage of intuitive boldness. Mostly, an impetuosity to be regretted as the consequences of the decision are realised.

You know you've had enough cocktails when you feel exquisitely sophisticated but can't quite say it. **Guy Browning**

Risk Averse. Cool headed sobriety wins over hot headed drunkenness. A logical approach to problems which is alert to risk and anxious about the possibilities of making the wrong decision. This is sensible. It minimises the downside of life's contingencies to avoid failure. Playing it safe however is not a formula for decisions with exceptional positive outcomes.[3]

But then they sent me away to teach me how to be sensible. Logical, oh, responsible, practical. **The Logical Song, Supertramp**

Adventurous. Sober and drunk combines cool and hot headed thinking in which reason and emotion work together in harmony.[4] Problems are analysed and decisions considered with logic and feeling. Rationality is not the sole criterion. It is balanced with intuition and a sense of does this feel right. These are the decisions with the potential to enthuse and energise.

Consider the possibility that the right answer might be any of them. The only wrong answer is to choose none of them. **Oliver Burkeman**

SO WHAT?

The right context is worth 80 IQ points. **Alan Kay**

Different problems require different decision making tactics. But if the outcome of a structured and logical process does not engage, it may be the wrong choice. And, if in the morning after the decision making party and once the hangover clears, the analysis looks misguided, it is probably the wrong option.

NOTES

1. Let's Get Persian;
https://cdn.porchlightbooks.com/legacyassets/system/manifestos/pdfs/000/000/268/original/51.02.GetPersian.pdf

2. The benefits of procrastination;
https://www.medicalnewstoday.com/articles/325108#Why-do-we-procrastinate?

3. Why we need emotions to make decisions;
https://www.thedrum.com/news/2019/01/30/why-emotion-plays-critical-role-decision-making

4. The Master and the His Emissary, Iain McGilchrist;
https://www.theguardian.com/books/2010/jan/02/1

What is the focus of innovation?

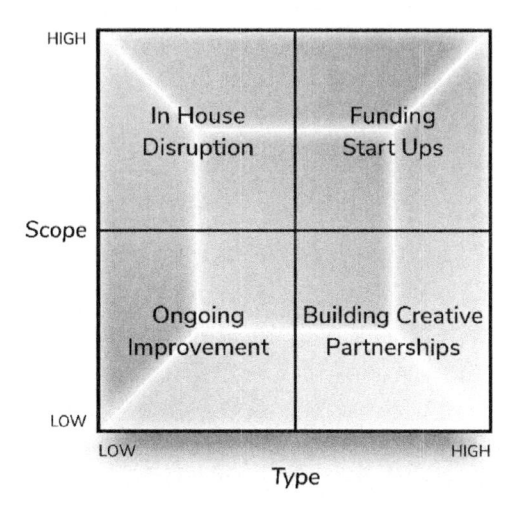

	Type LOW	Type HIGH
Scope HIGH	In House Disruption	Funding Start Ups
Scope LOW	Ongoing Improvement	Building Creative Partnerships

To design a desk which may cost $1,000 is easy for a furniture designer, but to design a functional and good desk which shall cost $50 can only be done by the very best. **Ingvar Kamprad, IKEA**

Innovation comes in all sorts, shapes and sizes. We can fall back on stereotypes to recall the businesses which have been innovative and adopt the so-called best practices of these exemplars. This attempts to replicate a formula to capture past successes. This is not how genuine innovation works.

Enron was named America's most innovative company by Fortune for six consecutive years, from 1996 to 2001.

Two dimensions underpin this innovation matrix.

Type. This reflects the extent of the innovation. Incremental is the search for the day to day, week to week improvements for organisational gain. Radical, the aspiration to find the game changer for transformation.

Scope. This identifies the balance between internal and external innovation. Internal innovation looks for creativity within the organisation for ideas to raise the game. External innovation scans and locates ideas from the wider business environment.

Creativity isn't thinking in limbo and having an idea out-of-the-blue. Creativity is putting things together in a way no one else would think of. **Dave Trott**

Four innovation outlooks emerge.

Ongoing Improvement. This represents a business fundamental, a constant internal focus on incremental innovation. *In every day in every way we are getting better and better.* Criticised by the gurus as a lame attempt at innovation, this follows the Tom Peters' recommendation that 1% gains over 100 activities make a significant impact.

We start from the presumption that our people are talented and want to contribute. We accept that, without meaning to, our company is stifling that talent in a myriad of unseen ways. Finally we try to identify those impediments and fix them. **Ed Catmull, Pixar**

In House Disruption. Innovation is internally focused but the agenda is radical. This is the ambitious programme to encourage employee creativity that develops transformational products and services. At best, the model of an innovation factory to maintain a flow of original outcomes with drum beat rapidity. Alternatively, a flawed enterprise in which individual creativity encounters the barriers of the vested interests of the status quo.[1]

That's cute But don't tell anyone about it. **Senior manager at Kodak to Steve Sasson, the engineer who invented the first digital camera in 1975**[2]

Building Creative Partnerships. Incremental improvement is achieved through access to an array of external agencies. This provides a diversity of fresh thinking through the introduction of contractors, consultants and open source platforms[3] to help rethink long-standing problems. At best, the firm ratchets up its creative power. At worst, a recycle of the conventional ideas of the firms the contractors and consultants last worked with.

Funding Start Ups. This profile accepts that radical innovation is best achieved through diversification to invest in emerging ideas from a range of sources, from universities, think tanks, and the *guy in a garage*.[4] This is the organisation with an innovation portfolio backing ideas from an array of partners. Alternatively, coordination of this innovative flow becomes the challenge. Here, firms lack coherence to prioritise and commercialise the ideas aligned to its overall strategic purpose.

If you want to understand how animals live, you don't go to the zoo, you go to the jungle. **Jorgen Vig Knudstorp, Lego**

SO WHAT?

Learning to collaborate is part of equipping yourself for effectiveness, problem solving, innovation and life-long learning in an ever-changing networked economy. **Don Tapscott**

If there is a formula, it is unlikely to generate genuine innovation. Most progressive organisations play in all four boxes to juggle incremental and radical innovation as well as how best to locate the sources of future innovation. How much they play in each of the four boxes depends on the scale of the long-term business aspiration and a willingness to challenge the current organisational order.[5]

Most big R&D spenders are not really seeking innovations. They are spending money on historical programs, following historical patterns and trying to defend and extend the historical business. **Adam Hartung**

NOTES

1. Skunk Works and the attempt to side-step the institutional barriers to innovation; https://qualitance.com/blog/skunk-works-story-how-to-create-high-speed-projects/

2. This man invented the digital camera in 1975 and his bosses at Kodak never let it see the light of day; https://www.businessinsider.com/this-man-invented-the-

digital-camera-in-1975-and-his-bosses-at-kodak-never-let-it-see-the-light-of-day-2015-8?r=US&IR=T

3. Nikola Tosic and open innovation; https://openinnovation.me/nikolatosic/innovations

4. Steve Wozniak: Apple starting in a garage is a myth; https://www.theguardian.com/technology/2014/dec/05/steve-wozniak-apple-starting-in-a-garage-is-a-myth#

5. The alternative is innovation by theft. We both had a rich neighbour Xerox. I broke into his house to steal the TV and found you had already stolen it. Bill Gates about Steve Jobs; https://folklore.org/A_Rich_Neighbor_Named_Xerox.html

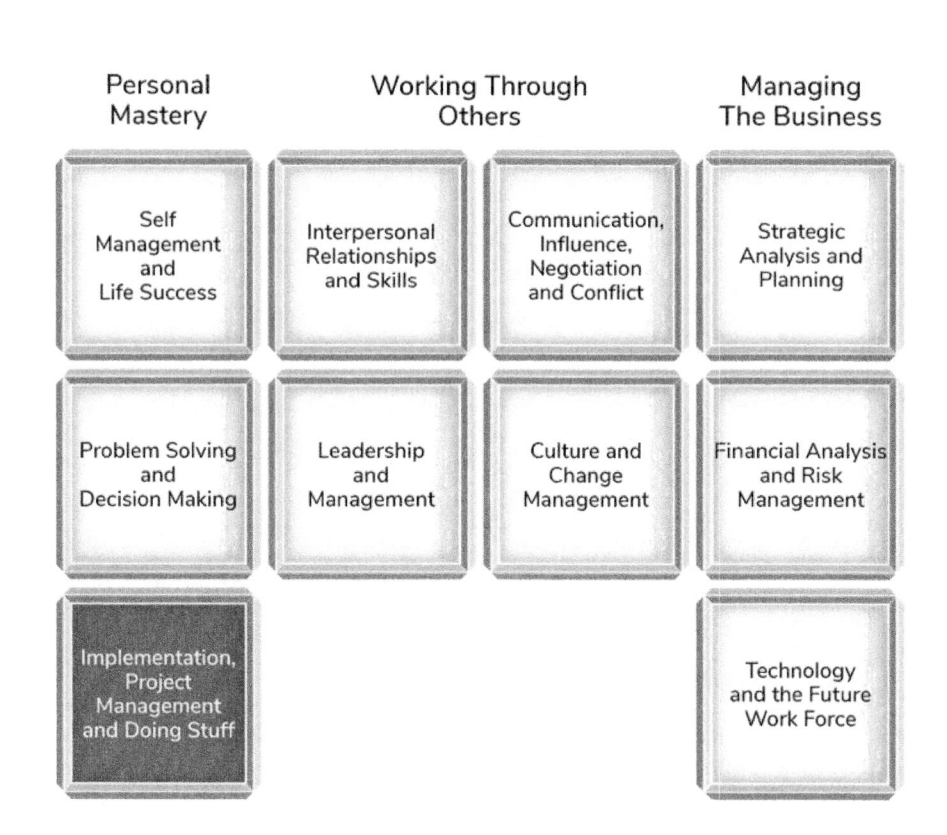

Personal Mastery	Working Through Others		Managing The Business
Self Management and Life Success	Interpersonal Relationships and Skills	Communication, Influence, Negotiation and Conflict	Strategic Analysis and Planning
Problem Solving and Decision Making	Leadership and Management	Culture and Change Management	Financial Analysis and Risk Management
Implementation, Project Management and Doing Stuff			Technology and the Future Work Force

Have we got our priorities right?

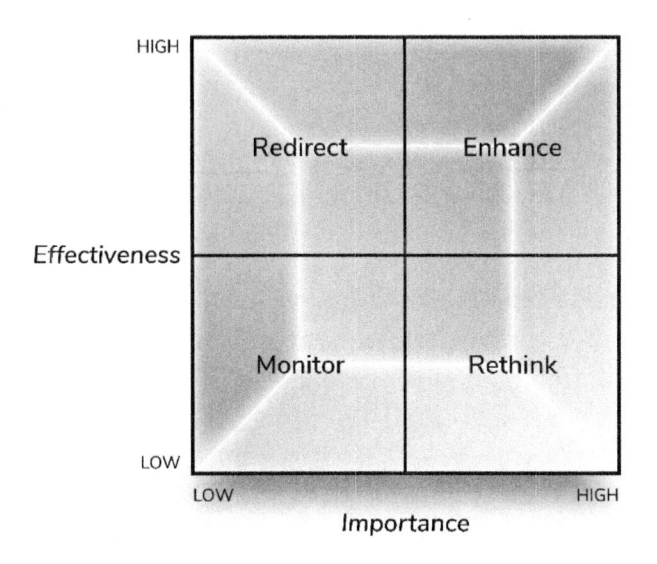

(A 2x2 matrix with Effectiveness on the vertical axis (Low to High) and Importance on the horizontal axis (Low to High). Quadrants: top-left "Redirect", top-right "Enhance", bottom-left "Monitor", bottom-right "Rethink".)

Actions fit into three separate boxes. Box 1 is all about managing the present and improving the current business. Box 2 involves selectively abandoning the past. Box 3 contains the keys to creating the future. **Vijay Govindarajan and Chris Trimble**[1]

The strategic humbug Michael Porter[2] says: *Strategy is choice. Strategy means saying no to certain kinds of things.* In this instance, Michael is correct. Choice also applies to execution. Not every activity can or should be implemented with brilliance. Tough decisions need to be made to determine the focus of effort.

If everything is important, then nothing is. **Patrick Lencioni**

Two dimensions apply.

Importance. The spectrum of relatively low significance to the future, to high, activities becoming increasingly critical to the business.

Effectiveness. This evaluates current organisational activities against the criteria of efficiency, quality and business impact. Low, troublesome processes and practices that are failing. High, activities that are working well for the business.

Four implementation choices are highlighted.

Monitor. These activities are not executed particularly well, but the organisational implications are modest. These are relatively unimportant to the business. They do however need constant review as the operating model changes over time. But for the most part, low priorities requiring little investment.

Redirect. Activities where past activity may have built effectiveness, but are now less relevant to the organisation. This is current practice going through the motions and disconnected from the business's operating model and now wasting resource. Typically functional power dynamics block change. These are the vested interests to challenge and overcome.

Every established order tends to make its own entirely arbitrary system seem entirely natural. **Pierre Bourdieu**

Rethink. High importance activities where effectiveness is low. There is no past legacy to build on and no one is attending to the issues. Or, perhaps, previous practices have lost organisational momentum. The focus now: analyse the specific issues to design and implement imaginative and workable solutions to deploy resource to more critical activities.

At first, we found it hard to believe we could be that bad - but we were. **Vaughn Beals, CEO, Harley Davidson**

Enhance. For high importance activities that are also working well, the challenge is one of continual improvement to identify better and quicker processes to optimise efficiency and quality. This is the game of the 1% improvement which produce compound returns as they accumulate over time.[3]

I like to tell people that all of our products and business will go through three phases. There's vision, patience, and execution. **Steve Ballmer, Microsoft**

SO WHAT?

The first rule of any technology used in a business is that automation applied to an efficient operation will magnify the efficiency. The second is that automation applied to an inefficient operation will magnify the inefficiency. **Bill Gates**

There are three questions facing an organisation. What should we **stop**? Which activities have served the business well in the past but now lack relevance? What should we **continue**? Activities of importance that can be improved. And what should we **start**? Which processes and practices need to be introduced to provide the infrastructure for future gains?

NOTES

1. The Three-Box Approach to Business Model Reinvention: Putting the Idea into Practice; https://hbr.org/2011/09/the-three-box-approach-to-busi-1

2. Michael Porter did not follow his own advice and vanished from strategy conversations when he had to file for bankruptcy as his firm Monitor found itself unable to pay its bills.
https://www.forbes.com/sites/stevedenning/2012/11/20/what-killed-michael-porters-monitor-group-the-one-force-that-really-matters/?sh=6018ba84747b

3. One percent gains; https://jamesclear.com/marginal-gains

How far are we prepared to go?

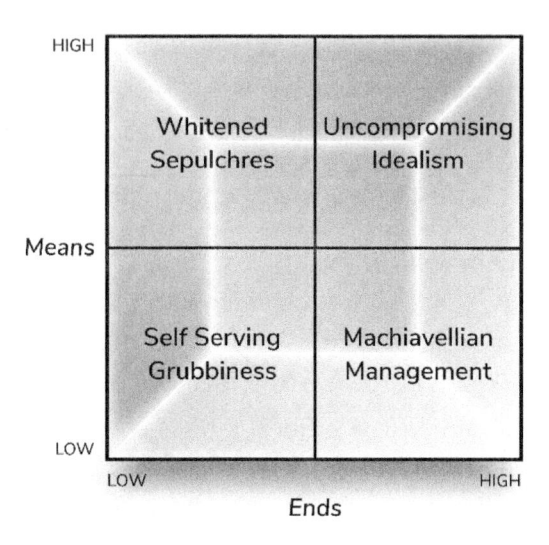

	Ends LOW	Ends HIGH
Means HIGH	Whitened Sepulchres	Uncompromising Idealism
Means LOW	Self Serving Grubbiness	Machiavellian Management

The problem with the rat race is even if you win you're still a rat. **Lily Tomlin**

In any sphere of life - politics, business, family and friendships - there is an ideal of what might be. These provide the noble goals of - if not perfection - at least something worthwhile. But there is also life experienced *as is* and what is possible given the circumstances of the vagaries and contingencies of human nature, interpersonal dynamics and political realities.

This quadrant is based on the two dimensions of Ends and Means. Each is caricatured on a spectrum from Dirty to Clean.

Ends. This represents the overall goal to be achieved. At the low - the dirty end - objectives describe the short-term interests of the self-serving of no benefit to anyone other than the individual. Clean ends describe a more aspirational aim to attain something of lasting impact to the business, wider community and society.

Means. If ends outline the strategic goal, means are the tactics deployed to realise this aim. Low is the dirty; the willingness to draw on expedient methods, however unpleasant or unpopular. At the other end, clean is an uncompromising stance to maintain high standards of moral values and ethical principles in pursuit of our goals.

Put your calling in a lockbox, go out and make a ton of money, and then come back to the lockbox to pick up your calling where you left it. **Po Bronson**

Four strategies explain the process of getting things done.

Self Serving Grubbiness. In this box, ends and the means are both dirty. It may be - faced with difficult life circumstances - this is the only realistic approach for survival. Focus on the here and now and do whatever is required to stay alive.[1] It can also be the stance of the sociopath without a moral compass, whose lack of conscience and empathy operates only to preserve and protect personal interests.

The distance between insanity and genius is measured only by success. **Elliot Carver, Tomorrow Never Dies**

Whitened Sepulchres.[2] This is the puzzle of a box that combines dirty ends with clean means. And much more common than expected. It describes the individual who advances their aims to the detriment of others, but becomes caught up in an appeal of holier than thou hypocrisy. This is playing by the rules - but only as part of a game of exploitation.

The only vice that cannot be forgiven is hypocrisy. The repentance of a hypocrite is itself hypocrisy. **William Hazlitt**

Machiavellian Management.[3] Clean ends meet dirty means in this scenario. Noble objectives require expedient short cuts. Unpleasant compromises have to be negotiated. This is real-politick. Alternatively - and this seems to be the historical pattern - the deployment of dirty means contaminates the noble clean ends.

People are so simple of mind, and so much dominated by their immediate needs, that a deceitful person will always find plenty who are ready to be deceived. **Niccolò Machiavelli**

Uncompromising Idealism. Clean ends meet clean means. The refusal to compromise based on a principled conviction of what is important and how it is best achieved. Its honesty of intention and transparency of tactics can be refreshingly compelling. The hazards of this approach? Many find this candour awkward. It runs the risk of opening up a can of worms that crawl out to much embarrassment.[4] The key danger is the gap between the *ought to be* and the *as is*. A refusal to negotiate trade-offs and agree compromises results in a player on the side-lines distanced from the messiness of real world problems.

If you want to accomplish something in the world, idealism is not enough - you need to choose a method that works to achieve the goal. **Richard Stallman**

SO WHAT?

The end cannot justify the means for the simple and obvious reason that the means employed determine the nature of the ends produced. **Aldous Huxley**

This quadrant asks: how far are we prepared to go for which purpose? It addresses the issue of our own interests vis a vis those of others. Which tactics are we willing to use to advance these aims?

We each make our judgements. Our aspirations of what we see as ideal and the tactics we are prepared to draw on to achieve our aims.

NOTES

1. Screen writers draw on this story line when the lead character is placed in a situation of danger and has to make difficult choices.

2. *Woe unto you, scribes and Pharisees, hypocrites! for ye are like unto whited sepulchres, which indeed appear beautiful outward, but are within full of dead men's bones, and of all uncleanness.* Matthew 23:27

3. Hitler kept a copy of The Prince by his bedside, and Stalin was known to have read and annotated his copy of the book. Business leaders have looked to the work as a cutthroat approach to getting ahead, and the book has been called the Mafia Bible with gangsters, including John Gotti, quoting from its pages. https://www.history.com/topics/renaissance/machiavelli

4. The Untouchables. The Chicago cop Malone to Eliot Ness as they assemble a team to take on police corruption: *If you're afraid of getting a rotten apple, don't go*

to the barrel. Get it off the tree;
https://youtu.be/nl67dSs3dXU?si=PBpxdC_Tmig8_VYa

Is resistance futile?

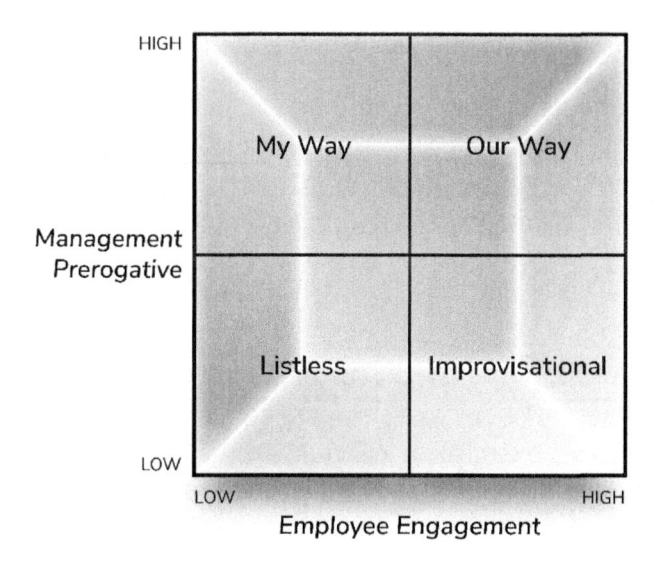

Management Prerogative HIGH	My Way	Our Way
LOW	Listless	Improvisational
	LOW	HIGH
	Employee Engagement	

The result of micromanagement is perhaps tangible in the short run, but more often causes damage for the long term. **Pearl Zhu**

After a spate of suicides in 2016, managers at Foxconn factories - manufacturer of Apple i-phones - ordered new staff to sign pledges that they would not attempt to kill themselves. They had to promise that if they did, their families could only seek the legal minimum in damages.[1]

In developed economies, in the latter part of the 20th century and early 21st century, management for the most part set the agenda. The pluralism of trade unionism and the requirement to negotiate change was in retreat. The only issue for executives was to design a programme of lay-offs - how many and who - when implementing significant organisational change

No doubt the impact of technology, not least AI, will create further workforce disruption. But as the labour market shifts, a strategy of *my way or the highway* is unlikely to sustain for firms hoping for a profitable future.

We do not and cannot accept the principle that incompetence justifies dismissal. That is victimisation. **Peter Sellers, the union leader in I'm Alright Jack**

This quadrant is based on two dimensions.

Employee Engagement. This is the theme of workforce motivation and commitment. At the low end, employees are disengaged, either going through the motions of presenteeism, or worse, proactively dysfunctional. At the high end, employees feel part of an overall purpose and invest personally in the organisation with discretionary effort.

Management Prerogative. At the low end of this spectrum, the organisation integrates employee initiative within the decision making process, an exercise in co-creation. At the high end, the working assumption is that managers have all the answers, know what needs to be done and simply issue instructions with an expectation of compliance.

The way I would measure leadership is this: of the people that are working with me, how many wake up in the morning thinking that the company is theirs? **David Kelley, IDEO**

Four approaches to the workforce are identified.

Listless. Low engagement and low management prerogative combine for organisational drift. This is hands-off management indifference met with employee apathy. Alternatively, a well-meaning managerial cadre talks of employee empowerment, but without the insight or incentives to implement it. In either scenario, there is little expectation of business impact.

We achieved what we achieved in spite of management. **Former BBC Director General, Greg Dyke**

My Way. Low engagement intersects with high management prerogative for a top down approach. A prescriptive and demanding stance towards employees, a workforce that has distanced itself from the organisation's purpose and future. At best, this strategy is a decisive turnaround to restore business performance. *We have got to take the gloves off and have a bare-knuckle fight on some of the things we have to do, because we have to have an effective and prosperous industry.*[2] More typically, the managerial desperation of a rallying cry that goes unheard.

How the hell can I ask people who work for me to travel cheaply if I am traveling in luxury? It's a question of good leadership. **Ingvar Kamprad, IKEA**

Improvisational. In a scenario of high engagement and low management prerogative, decision making places greater emphasis on employee involvement and input. This is strategy as led by the customer based on front line feedback of what is and isn't working. Conversely, the organisational anarchy of competing priorities that lacks consistent purpose and direction.

It is important to keep twirling the pyramid all the time, because it is more important employees listen to the market and not the boss. **Zhang Ruimin, Haier Group**

Our Way. This integrates high employee engagement with a high management prerogative for genuine participation. In situations of major change, co-creation of the solutions is required for new ways of working. The greater the complexity and ambiguity about the best way forward, the higher the need for workforce involvement.

I don't know where we should take this company, but I do know that if I start with the right people, ask them the right questions, and engage them in vigorous debate, we will find a way to make this company great. **Jim Collins, Good To Great**

SO WHAT?

Is there is an optimal way to manage organisational change and integrate the interests of employees and managers? Probably not, especially when the ratio of executive to worker compensation continues to increase.[3] Economic circumstances and shifts in supply and demand in the labour market shape the power balance. However, for most firms, most of the time, resistance will be futile if there is not a shift from management dictat to employee initiative.

NOTES

1. Life and death in Apple's forbidden city; https://www.theguardian.com/technology/2017/jun/18/foxconn-life-death-forbidden-city-longhua-suicide-apple-iphone-brian-merchant-one-device-extract

2. Terence Beckett, DG of the CBI; https://www.newspapers.com/article/the-guardian-g-121180-fp-beckett-bare/113789162/

3. The High Pay Centre estimates that top CEOs had out earned the median annual salary for a full-time worker in the UK by around 1pm on Thursday 4 January, the third working day of 2024.

Do we have - or even need - a plan?

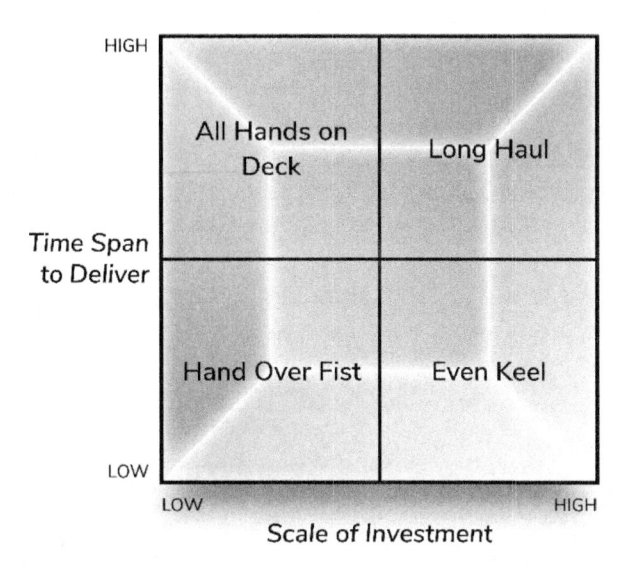

	Scale of Investment	
Time Span to Deliver HIGH	All Hands on Deck	Long Haul
LOW	Hand Over Fist	Even Keel
	LOW	HIGH

It does not do to leave a live dragon out of your calculations, if you live near one. **JRR Tolkien**

By all accounts, London's plan to bid for and run the 2012 Olympics was an outstanding success. In contrast, the plan for a high speed rail line between London and Manchester - HS2 - abandoned in 2023 by the UK government, was a dismal failure. *The 134 miles of track between London and Birmingham would have cost £165m a mile, nearly four times the cost per mile of France's line between Tours and Bordeaux.* Why? What made the difference? And what was the role of planning in explaining the variation in outcomes?

There is no shortage of project management methodologies, from Agile to Scrum to Waterfall. A project manager it seems is now needed to coordinate the range of planning systems in corporate use.

Saying you are doing something that is state of the art means that you are focusing on pursuing excellence rather than cost-effectiveness. **Hamish McRae**

Two themes underpin this quadrant.

Scale of Investment. Low scale means relatively inexpensive. High scale of investment reflects significant resource with the financial discipline and associated time and energy for stakeholder management.

Time Span to Deliver. Time spans can be considered as short, medium, and long term. Short term typically falls into the zone of 3 months to 1 year. Medium is 1 - 3 years. Long term is more than 3 years.

An hour of planning can save you 10 hours of doing. **Dale Carnegie**

Four planning scenarios are played out.

Hand Over Fist. With low investment and short time horizons, this is the zone of rapid impact requiring a minimalist planning infrastructure. This cuts to the chase to do - without the complexity of any detailed methodology. Alternatively, it may be a larger project programme has been chunked into smaller 3 month delivery sub projects. This focuses on quick iterations, feedback, and adaptation based on changing circumstances.

All Hands on Deck. High levels of investment within a short time horizon is the project of urgency. Significant commitments are made for quick delivery. At times, this is the organisational attempt to rectify a fiasco. It is also the planning approach needed when an unexpected opportunity emerges and a narrow window opens up which can be exploited. As an ongoing project management mindset, this runs the risk of employee exhaustion.

Damn the torpedoes. Full speed ahead. **Admiral David Glasgow Farragut**

Even Keel. Low levels of investment intersect with a long time span for delivery. This is project management as a steady incremental process to work through a sequence of phases as part of a sustained activity. At best, a guiding purpose builds momentum to create energy and maintain focus. At worst, this is planning as procrastination to allow budgets to overrun and deadlines slip.

Our goals can only be reached through a vehicle of a plan, in which we must fervently believe, and upon which we must vigorously act. There is no other route to success. **Pablo Picasso**

Long Haul. This is the planning adventure that calls for high levels of investment across a longer time frame. These initiatives require substantial resources with the expectation of a sizeable payoff in future. Systematic planning is critical in large-scale projects to translate an initial strategic concept into profitable reality. The hazard is that circumstances shift, but the oil tanker of the project infrastructure finds itself unable to tack to accommodate new realities.

And the winds and the waves are always on the side of the ablest navigators. **Edward Gibbon**

SO WHAT?

Just because you made a good plan, doesn't mean that's what's gonna happen. **Taylor Swift**

Project planners have an important role in organisational implementation. Problems emerge however when every straightforward task requiring immediate action becomes a thinking exercise than a doing activity. Different challenges - complexity and time scales - demand different approaches to planning, from the fluid and flexible through to the highly detailed and structured. The craft is knowing which tactic is required under which circumstances.[2]

NOTES

1. Lessons from London 2012 Olympics: a crib sheet for major projects; https://www.theguardian.com/public-leaders-network/2013/jan/22/lessons-london-2012-government-projects
HS2 was doomed at the design stage. Its failure is a national embarrassment; https://inews.co.uk/opinion/hs2-doomed-design-state-failure-national-embarrassment-2661861

2. Planning a successful project kick off;
https://www.atlassian.com/blog/productivity/what-is-parkinsons-law

Is there an easy way to project success?

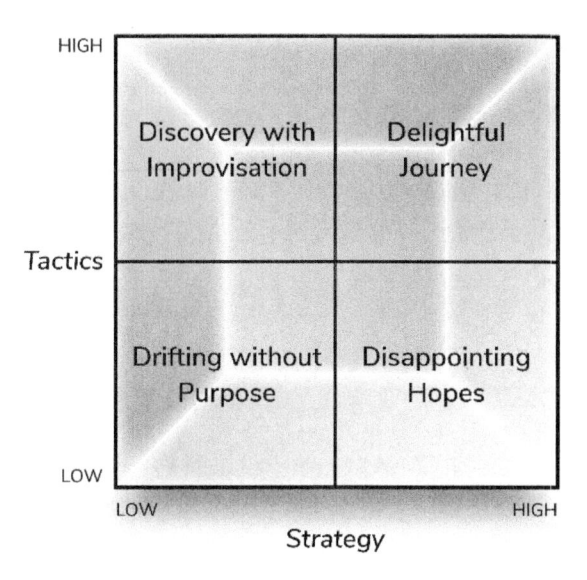

	Low Strategy	High Strategy
High Tactics	Discovery with Improvisation	Delightful Journey
Low Tactics	Drifting without Purpose	Disappointing Hopes

Strategy without tactics is the slowest route to victory. Tactics without strategy is the noise before defeat. **Sun Tzu**

Is there an easy way to manage projects? One that translates an overall game plan into a programme of execution at speed and with quality outcomes? Probably not. But there is a much harder way.

It always take longer than you expect, even when you take into account Hofstadter's Law. **Douglas Hofstadter**

This quadrant maps out two dimensions.

Strategy. This theme runs from low, the lack of a coherent end point, to high, a well formulated game plan with a clear long-term goal is in place.

Tactics. This theme describes the collection of tactics - tools and techniques - that can be deployed for implementation, from a limited range of experience and skill, to an approach that draws on an extensive set of options.

Good tactics can save even the worst strategy. Bad tactics will destroy even the best strategy. **General George Patton**

Four implementation patterns emerge.

Drifting without Purpose. A combination that lacks both a strategy and access to a repertoire of tactics. A project outlook to *go with the flow*. For some organisational activities this approach might work well. There is no fixed agenda of a desired end point. Neither is there much concern with the navigation of means. More often, the currents of business vagaries take these projects out to business sea. Henry Ford famously said: *Failure is simply the opportunity to begin again, this time more intelligently*. This approach to project management does not even begin.

If you don't have a strategy, you're part of someone else's strategy. **Alvin Toffler**

Discovery with Improvisation. For this project, there is no grand master plan. After all, why set long-term goals if it isn't clear what is important to the organisation? What is important today will change tomorrow. This is the flexibility to adapt to circumstances and seize opportunities as they present themselves. Alternatively, this is project management as ad hocery and confusing to team members and stakeholders.

Tactics is knowing what to do when there is something to do; strategy is knowing what to do when there is nothing to do. **Savielly Grigoryevich Tartakower, chess master**

Disappointing Hopes. These projects set long-term aims around a compelling purpose, but run into problems and fail to realise these goals. This grouping lacks access to a compendium of tactics to translate objectives into a sequenced methodology of practical actions and deadlines. Expectations exceed outcomes, and the result is a frustrating experience.

We have developed a collective belief system that persuades us while success is just out there, it is out of reach, locked up in vault, waiting for us to crack the code. One day the tumblers will fall, the safe door will swing open and success will ours. **Les McKeown**

Delightful Journey. Strategy and tactics combine for an effective interplay to realise a long-term purpose based on a flexibility of manoeuvre. This adapts to the ebb and flow of business events. Success is achieved through a sense of purpose with a readiness to work out what is and isn't working. This is the willingness to shift to a different approach as and when circumstances demand.

SO WHAT?

Success is the ability to reach objectives in the shortest time, with the least effort and with the fewest mistakes. **Charles Givens**

Carl Jung said: *the shoe that fits one person pinches another. There is no recipe for living that suits all cases.* True for individuals, it is also true of projects. Different tasks have to be deployed to overcome a range of challenges during the different phases of a business, from start up to growth to turnaround to reinvention.

There is no one blue print for guaranteed project success. But understanding the balance of strategy and tactics - and the fine line between a defined end point and the improvisation of means to get there - is a good starting point.

NOTES

1. The Top 10 Laws of Project Management;
https://stanyanakiev.files.wordpress.com/2011/03/the-top-10-laws-of-project-management.pdf

Are we in control of the project?

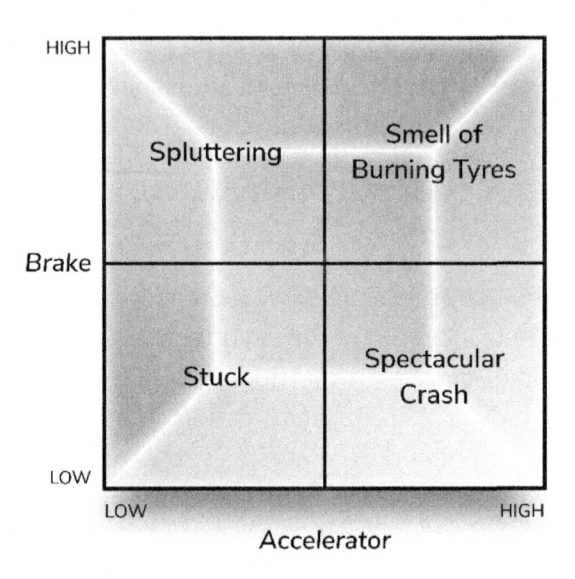

	Low Accelerator	High Accelerator
High Brake	Spluttering	Smell of Burning Tyres
Low Brake	Stuck	Spectacular Crash

How does a project get to be a year late? One day at a time. **FP Brooks Jr**

There are times to speed up. There are also times to slow down. This is project management as reading the road to recognise when to apply the brakes and when to floor the accelerator. Advanced drivers anticipate what is ahead and apply both the accelerator and brake to navigate smoothly through different traffic conditions. Inexperienced drivers misjudge the road ahead. The ride is either very slow or highly risky for themselves, and uncomfortable for the passengers.

In skating over thin ice, our safety is our speed. **Ralph Waldo Emerson**

This quadrant identifies project management scenarios based on two dimensions.

Accelerator. The application of speed to make progress, from the snail like slow to the dangerously fast.

Brake. Utilising the brake in response to any hazards on the road to maintain control at a safe speed.

Four project outcomes are identified.

Stuck. This is project management without either the accelerator or brakes being applied. A project going nowhere. There is no momentum to move it forward. Neither is there a willingness to abandon the project. It stays in organisational limbo, somewhere on the corporate planners to-do list but rarely activated.

Nokia engineers offered about 500 proposals to improve the technology on this project, and none were approved.[1]

Spluttering. Here the brakes are on. But there is no acceleration. This is a project on hold. There may be valid reasons to hold the project back, for example, timings in the budgetary cycle or the need for stakeholder approval. Alternatively, this is the project that lacks corporate commitment and frustrates its sponsors and participants.[2]

The more time you spend in reporting on what you are doing, the less time you have to do anything. Stability is achieved when you spend all your time doing nothing but reporting on the nothing you are doing. **Cohn's Law of project management**

Spectacular Crash. When the accelerator is full on without brakes, this - despite the early thrill of initiating the project - is out of control. Initial enthusiasm gains momentum. The scope of the project becomes increasingly ambitious. Without the brakes of key processes and metrics to evaluate progress and outcomes, this project speeds on before the inevitable pile up.

Insufficient critical reflection meant that clever models built by clever people led to stupid and dangerous decisions. **Anna Lynskey**

Smell of Burning Tyres. Both the accelerator and the brakes are applied. Much energy is deployed in the launch of the project. But there is also resistance and it fails to gain traction. Typically, a project caught between competing political factions of active sponsors and opponents, as well as a few loose cannons. In this situation of organisational tension and political infighting, there is much smoke and smell. No distance is covered.

Killing bad ideas is fine. Killing good ideas isn't all that bad, either. The disaster: keeping an idea barely alive on a life support machine. **Rory Sutherland**

SO WHAT?

I am aware that success is more than a good idea. It is timing too. **Anita Roddick, BodyShop**

Most of business success is the art of timing: when to start, when to pick up the pace, and when to stop. And this applies to project management. Some projects should never be started. Some should be abandoned. For those that do continue, we should read the road ahead and the traffic conditions, and apply both accelerator and brake.

NOTES

1. Nokia's decline. Different business units competed for resources to develop applications for different markets. *Each unit, growing as Nokia expanded, became its own kingdom, each executive a little emperor and people became more concerned about their status and internal promotion than cooperating actively with other departments to produce innovative products.*

2. Power and Pitfalls of Functional Stupidity at Work; https://www.theactuary.com/opinion/2017/03/2017/03/03/stupidity-paradox-power-and-pitfalls-functional-stupidity-work-book

How do we manage project heist?

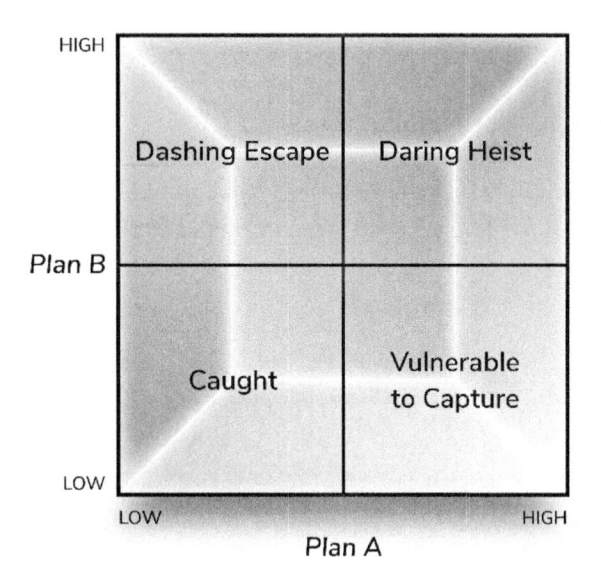

```
         HIGH ┌─────────────────┬─────────────────┐
              │                 │                 │
              │ Dashing Escape  │  Daring Heist   │
              │                 │                 │
       Plan B ├─────────────────┼─────────────────┤
              │                 │                 │
              │    Caught       │   Vulnerable    │
              │                 │   to Capture    │
          LOW └─────────────────┴─────────────────┘
                 LOW                         HIGH
                           Plan A
```

The plan is devised to survive any setbacks, even my death. **Professor, Money Heist**

A gang of robbers plot a raid on a bank. The proceeds - if the job is successful - will be £30 million. Each gang member will receive £5 million. This scenario parallels the typical experience of project team members within an organisation. What plans have been made for implementation? Are contingencies in place to address any setbacks to the original plan?

You're only supposed to blow the bloody doors off. **The Italian Job**[1]

Two dimensions apply.

Plan A. This is the initial plan. At the low end of the spectrum, there is no plan. There is a vague concept relying on ad hoc improvisation to respond to events as they happen. At the high end, a detailed methodology to guide the sequence of activities against defined time-scales and outcomes.

Plan B. The back-up position if Plan A goes wrong. It is possible there is no Plan B. This relies on the assumption that the project brilliance of Plan A will be executed with precision. Failure is not an option. Alternatively, there is a well worked position to fall back on a different strategy.[2]

Four scenarios face the project team.

Caught. When there is no Plan A or Plan B, the members of the Heist are soon captured. The project ends in failure. Improvisation without an alternative course of action may get lucky. More likely, extreme folly ends in project prison.

Get your trousers on. You're nicked. **Inspector Jack Regan, The Sweeney**

Dashing Escape. In the absence of a well-founded Plan A, a back-up position is in place. If Plan A fails as - given the probabilities of previous projects - it will do, there is an exit strategy. The rewards may be modest, but the risks are minimised.

With one bound, Jack was free.[3]

Vulnerable to Capture. Plan A was worked through in meticulous detail. Everything should now proceed in the anticipated sequence of steps and timings. Except that it doesn't. And without a Plan B, options are limited. It may be that the project team is extremely fortunate and escapes. It is also possible that the getaway car doesn't get away, and the team is arrested. This is project management as the arrogance of certainty.

John Bridger: I feel so optimistic. How do you feel?
Charlie Croker: I'm fine.
John Bridger: You see those columns behind you?
Charlie Croker: What about them?
John Bridger: That's where they used to string up thieves who felt fine.

Daring Heist. Plan A has a Plan B. If Plan A works to follow the predicted sequence, the rewards are maximised. And if it doesn't,

Plan B provides the contingency to ensure that there is another escape route, and the risks mitigated.

In this world, everything is governed by balance. There's what you stand to gain and what you stand to lose. And when you think you've got nothing to lose, you become overconfident. **Professor, Money Heist**[4]

SO WHAT?

To achieve great things, two things are needed; a plan, and not quite enough time. **Leonard Bernstein**

Not every organisational task needs a detailed project management methodology. And sometimes the simple becomes unnecessarily complicated through the arrival of an over enthusiastic project manager who wants to impress. But any significant organisational undertaking does require project rigour about contingencies.

And without a back-up plan[5] to accommodate the eventualities of budget over run, delays and sometimes bad luck, the business faces risk.

NOTES

1. The Italian Job; https://youtu.be/Z8WCNOhX4FA

2. Plan C is outside the space of this quadrant. A three by three grid is beyond the scope of this scenario.

3. *There is a delightful story, attributed to more than one publishing house, of the serial writer who disappears in the middle of a story. As he shows no sign of turning up, it is decided to carry on without him. Unfortunately he has left his hero bound to a stake, with lions circling him, and an avalanche about to fall for good measure (or some such situation). Relays of writers try to think of a way out, and give it up. Then at the eleventh hour the missing author returns. He takes the briefest look at the previous instalment and then, without a moment's hesitation, writes: With one bound Jack was free.* Cliffhanger Copout; https://tvtropes.org/pmwiki/pmwiki.php/Quotes/CliffhangerCopout

4. La Casa De Papel (Money Heist); https://youtu.be/hMANIarjT50

5. HS2 high-speed rail plans a recipe for disaster; https://www.theguardian.com/uk/2011/jul/19/hs2-rail-plans-recipe-disaster

Are we playing project chicken?

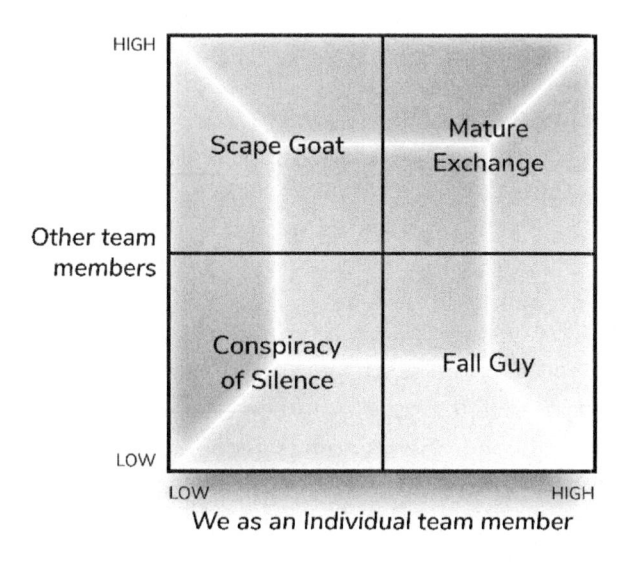

```
HIGH
          |  Scape Goat  | Mature Exchange |
Other team|              |                 |
members   |--------------|-----------------|
          | Conspiracy   |    Fall Guy     |
          | of Silence   |                 |
LOW
          LOW                          HIGH
          We as an Individual team member
```

The six phases of project management: enthusiasm, disillusionment, panic, search for the guilty, the punishment of the innocent, reward for the uninvolved. **Ben Dattner**

Projects follow a predictable script. The first kick-off meeting begins the phase of enthusiasm to generate a feel good factor. Team members express confidence that the project will be delivered to specification and on time within budget. As the project moves onto implementation, the mood shifts.

The 98/2 Rule: people spend 98% of their time talking about flashy things that contribute only 2% to the results overlooking the fact that 98% of the results come from consistently doing the boring basics that few notice. **Shane Parrish**

This quadrant is a variation of the well-known game theory example of Chicken.[1] This is observed in project management reviews when the leader gathers the project team to review progress and take stock of any issues that may affecting time-scales, costs and quality. This is project update time.

The two dimensions.

We as an Individual team member. We face a choice. Keep quiet about any project problems, or speak openly about the difficulties the team is experiencing.

Other team members. Here, colleagues in the project team meeting face a similar quandary. Remain silent about the problems, or express publicly any concerns.

This quadrant explores the interpersonal dynamics and options within a project team meeting.

Conspiracy of Silence. All keep silent. It may not be an explicit strategy agreed in advance by the participants within the meeting. Often it is the unspoken understanding, decoded only through body language. If no one speaks up to highlight any difficulties, the team has bought itself time until the next project meeting. The session therefore works its way around the table with vague updates, questions intended to muddy the waters which go off at a tangent. More equivocations about delivery helps.

In a room where people unanimously maintain a conspiracy of silence, one word of truth sounds like a pistol shot. **Czesław Miłosz**

Scape Goat. As a project member we maintain silence whilst another team member reports their personal difficulties with the project. This is either courage or folly on their part to announce that they are behind schedule. For us and others in the team this is safety, with the bonus of indicating that the failings of this scape goat has undermined everyone's contribution to the project. At this point, the team leader vilifies the scape goat to explain how their lack of performance is responsible for the need to reschedule.

The search for a scapegoat is the easiest of all hunting expeditions. **Dwight Eisenhower**

Fall Guy. In this meeting, we as a team member express openly the challenges we are experiencing. But we find ourselves isolated within the team as others report it is full steam ahead. The project team leader, noting the overall lack of progress, singles us out for special attention. Our personal position will have to be reviewed.

I need to identify unnecessary and unproductive employees so I can cut costs. Does anybody have spare time to join my task force on productivity? Red shirt puts up his hand. Good, good. Anybody else? **The Boss, Scott Adams**

Mature Exchange. All team members take the initiative to express openly the difficulties the project team faces. This provides an honest appraisal of the reasons for problems in the project. At best, a progressive team leader listens to this candid feedback and explores the implications. They accept it is time for a rethink to shift approach and revise the project plan. Alternatively, a defensive leader responds badly to the perceived criticisms, and goes on to undertake a ruthless series of changes to the composition of the team.[2]

SO WHAT?

A person who smiles in the face of adversity probably has a scapegoat. **Stephen Hawking**

This quadrant highlights the importance of trust in organisational life for effective project management. When we second guess others' intentions and they attempt to out-wit our responses, nothing much happens too quickly.

NOTES

1. The classic example of Chicken in game theory involves two drivers in cars heading towards each other on a collision course. If neither driver swerves, both will crash and suffer serious injury or death. If one driver swerves and the other doesn't, the driver who doesn't swerve wins by avoiding the crash, while the other driver loses by appearing to be chicken or cowardly.

2. Or brings in a consultant to colour code the personality profiles within the team. *My daughter who works for (blank) is really upset and angry. The manager has been profiling staff at staff meetings using (blank). She objected to it but has to comply. Her profile is totally "incorrect".*

Can we become more productive?

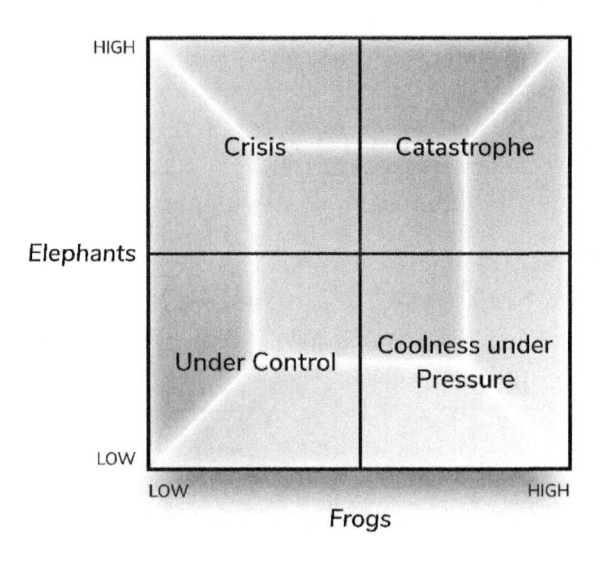

```
                    HIGH
                    ┌─────────────┬─────────────┐
                    │             │             │
                    │   Crisis    │ Catastrophe │
                    │             │             │
        Elephants   ├─────────────┼─────────────┤
                    │             │             │
                    │   Under     │ Coolness under
                    │  Control    │   Pressure  │
                    │             │             │
                    LOW───────────┴─────────────┘
                    LOW                       HIGH
                              Frogs
```

The world is bursting with wonder, and yet it's the rare productivity guru who seems to have considered the possibility that the ultimate point of all our frenetic doing might be to experience more of that wonder. **Oliver Burkeman**

Personal productivity is a billion pound industry. A combination of apps, motivational podcasts, workshops, books and other merchandise promise to optimise our efficiency in personal organisation and time management. And manage the work-life balance. There is the 75% rule, the 85% rule and the 1-3-5 principle, and more.

It is tempting to think that the personal productivity enterprise is part of the problem not a solution.[1]

You have to accept that there will always be too much to do; that you can't avoid tough choices or make the world run at your preferred speed. **Oliver Burkeman**[2]

Two themes identify the challenge.

Frogs. These are the minor tasks that need to be addressed. A small frog is relatively trivial. A large frog is annoying and awkward.[3]

Elephants. The major issues we face in working life. Elephants can appear tiny, sometimes to the point that they are not even visible in the room. Viewed from the distance, elephants appear small. But they become bigger as they approach. Big elephants will rampage through our work plans and priorities to create havoc.

When eating an elephant take one bite at a time. **Creighton Abrams**

Four work patterns emerge.

Under Control. The frog and the elephant are small. There is therefore no immediate problem. Tasks are manageable. Alternatively, the elephant on the horizon is heading in our direction. Here it is easy to become distracted by the small frogs of the day to day stuff as the elephant task moves in closer.

My parents told me I'd never amount to anything because I procrastinated too much. I told them, Just you wait. **Judy Tenuta**

Crisis. Although the frog is small, a large elephant now charges into our lives and commands our urgent attention. This is the disruptive event which - if not addressed rapidly - will have major adverse consequences. Caught up with the tasks of the small frogs, the psychology of denial avoids the presence of these charging big elephants.

I don't like elephants in the room. If there's an elephant in the room, I really want to absolutely examine it. **Frank Skinner**

Coolness under Pressure. The frog is big but the elephant is small, at least at the moment. This scenario represents tasks to tackle and resolve quickly with composure while the elephant remains in the far distance. Alternatively, we avoid swallowing the frog as we fixate on the elephant and the potential danger it represents. This anxiety freezes action.

If it's your job to eat a frog, it's best to do it first thing in the morning. And if it's your job to eat two frogs, it's best to eat the biggest one first. **Mark Twain**

Catastrophe. The frog and the elephant are big. We now face a productivity battle on two fronts. The big frogs are hopping through our diaries and calendar. The big elephant is not only in the room, it is knocking down everything we thought important. This is to move into survival mode to weather the storm and grapple full on with the issues.

Learning to play with a big amplifier is like trying to control an elephant. **Ritchie Blackmore, Deep Purple**

SO WHAT?

Half our life is spent trying to do something to do with the time we have rushed through life trying to save. **Will Rogers**

Small frogs should be swallowed immediately before they become big frogs. And small elephants need close observation to check the speed of approach. The box of Under Control seems the optimal strategy for productivity. It avoids the stresses and strains of hopping frogs and rampaging elephants. But it is worth asking: do we know the difference between frogs and elephants?

NOTES

1. Now It's About Time, Andrew Munro; https://www.amazon.co.uk/Now-about-time-Andrew-Munro/dp/1447607767

2. Four Thousand Weeks: Time Management for Mortals, Oliver Burkeman

3. The CEO who brought down his company recommended the book Five Frogs on a Log: A CEO's Field Guide to Accelerating the Transition in Mergers, Acquisitions And Gut Wrenching Change. A book that can be summarised with the momentous insight: there's a difference between deciding and doing.

Is it possible to idle productively?

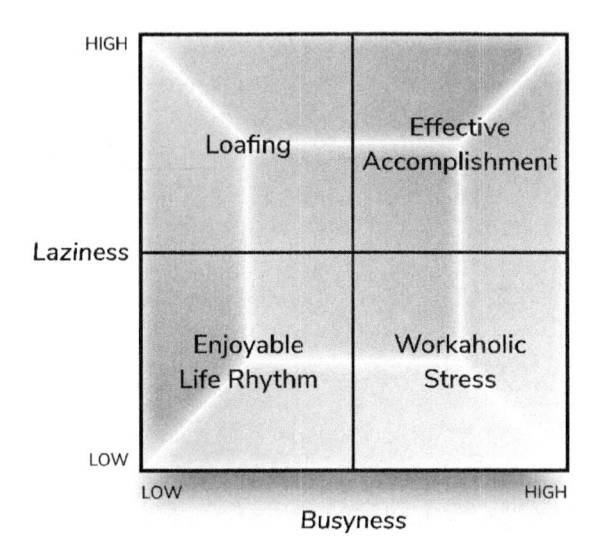

	Low Busyness	High Busyness
High Laziness	Loafing	Effective Accomplishment
Low Laziness	Enjoyable Life Rhythm	Workaholic Stress

No one will believe you solved this problem in one day. We've been working on it for months. Now, go act busy for a few weeks and I'll let you know when it's time to tell them. **Dilbert**

Babe Ruth, one of biggest hitters of home runs in baseball, was apparently motivated to hit the ball out of the stadium because he hated having to run between bases.[1]

In the cult of today's busyness, few are prepared to acknowledge anything other than full on activity within a hectic and demanding schedule. Busyness is now the new conspicuous consumption to keep up the Joneses.[2] It establishes our importance and status.

In an advertising agency, one highly placed complicator can undo the good work of a dozen simplifiers. **Bob Hoffman**

So why - with such busyness - have levels of productivity and innovation stalled?

The secret of the truly successful, I believe, is that they learned very early in life how not to be busy. The truth is many things are worth doing only in the most slovenly, half-hearted fashion possible, and many other things are not worth doing at all. **Barbara Ehrenreich**

It is easy to see busyness and laziness as opposite ends of one spectrum. Busy people deploy energy to get things done. Lazy people withhold energy to avoid doing anything much at all. This is not so. Paradoxical at first sight, the psychology of the two is different.

Our culture's belief that people are secretly lazy deep down and need to be browbeaten into productivity is very old and has far-reaching roots. It dates back to the Puritans and the beliefs they had about hard work, being a signal that a person was morally upstanding. **Devon Price**

The two dimensions for idle productivity.

Busyness. The extent to which we are engaged in the range of life's tasks, work, social and other commitments that take up time and energy. At one end of the spectrum, there is relatively little to do. Life follows a leisurely pace. At the other end, we are preoccupied with an array of activities requiring full attention.

Laziness. The theme that finds it difficult to get going. At the low end, there is no ease or relaxation; it is all go. At the high end of the range, a willingness to idle without pressure to do anything much.

You have to be efficient if you're going to be lazy. **Shirley Conran**

Four work patterns play out.

Enjoyable Life Rhythm. When low busyness coincides with low laziness, the outcome is the productive use of leisure time. A lack of commitments frees up time and energy for a life to be savoured. This is to take time and care in the enjoyment of the little things in life.

What is this life, if full of care, We have no time to stand and stare. **WH Davies**

Loafing. The lack of busyness in combination with high laziness has the potential for a sluggish life style. Everything requires extraordinary levels of energy. It seems better not to do very much at all. Hours become days which become weeks and months, and the years roll by in a state of torpor.

Never do today what you can do as well tomorrow. Delay may give clearer light as to what is best to be done. **Aaron Burr**

Workaholic Stress. High busyness and low laziness is the stance to keep on top of each and every task. At best, this is the intense productivity to sustain motivation to achieve much. At worst, the lack of rest and relaxation creates a restlessness which cannot stop moving and in turn undermines productivity. Time spent becomes more important than tasks achieved.[3]

One of the symptoms of an approaching nervous breakdown is the belief that one's work is terribly important. **Bertrand Russell**

Effective Accomplishment. This combines high busyness and high laziness. Work efficiency is deployed for overall life effectiveness. An outlook to see beyond the immediacy of task demands and a willingness to say no.[4] This provides focus for the important issues with impact.

The difference between successful people and really successful people is that really successful people say no to almost everything. **Warren Buffett**

SO WHAT?

Choose a lazy person to do a hard job because that person will find an easy way to do it. **Frank Gilbreth**[5]

The era of lockdown during the pandemic crisis forced an awkward question for many organisations. It questioned its assumptions about employee productivity. Can we achieve more with less? More results when employees work from home? Different operating models require different working practices. This is true. But some firms discovered that lazy employees - without for example, stressful commutes - became more productive.

You have to keep busy. After all, no dog's ever pissed on a moving car. **Tom Waits**

NOTES

1. From Thinking Better, Marcus du Sautoy

2. Arthur Pop Momand got the last laugh. While he may not have been rich in money, he was rich in time. He lived to be 101 years old, longer than all the Joneses. Five Origin Stories of Keeping up with the Joneses; https://www.sloww.co/keeping-up-with-the-joneses/

3. JP Morgan boss Jamie Dimon recently spoke about his morning routine. He says he gets up at 5am, reads about eight newspapers, and has one cup of coffee (no breakfast). Early rising does not equate to real greatness. Dr Johnson was a far greater man than Jamie Dimon and he famously lay in bed till noon most days. 2. The Idler; https://www.idler.co.uk/article/brits-named-worlds-best-idlers/

4. *That doesn't work for me*. And more on the etiquette of saying no. Are you an Asker or a Guesser? https://www.theguardian.com/lifeandstyle/2010/may/08/change-life-asker-guesser

5. Frank Gilbreth evaluated the motions of workmen to determine the most efficient techniques to perform tasks. He stumbled upon an astonishing fact. He found that he could learn most from the lazy man.
https://quoteinvestigator.com/2014/02/26/lazy-job/

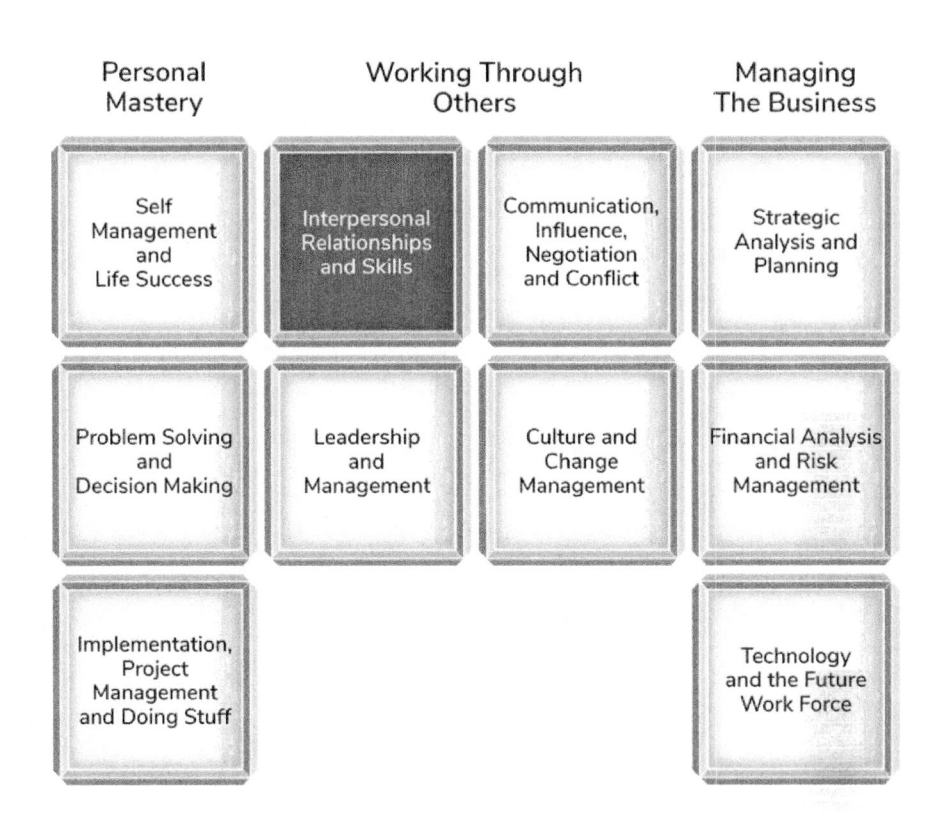

Personal Mastery	Working Through Others	Managing The Business
Self Management and Life Success	**Interpersonal Relationships and Skills**	Communication, Influence, Negotiation and Conflict	Strategic Analysis and Planning
Problem Solving and Decision Making	Leadership and Management	Culture and Change Management	Financial Analysis and Risk Management
Implementation, Project Management and Doing Stuff			Technology and the Future Work Force

Why connections matter

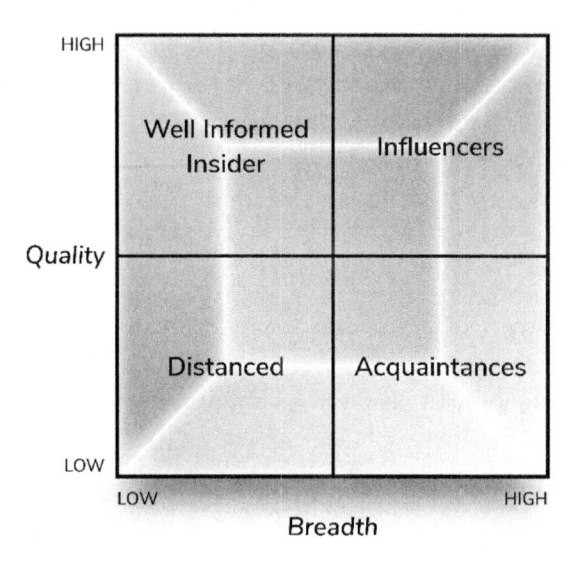

```
         HIGH  ┌─────────────────┬─────────────────┐
               │                 │                 │
               │  Well Informed  │                 │
               │     Insider     │   Influencers   │
               │                 │                 │
    Quality    ├─────────────────┼─────────────────┤
               │                 │                 │
               │                 │                 │
               │    Distanced    │   Acquaintances │
               │                 │                 │
         LOW   └─────────────────┴─────────────────┘
                    LOW                        HIGH
                            Breadth
```

Connectors, people with a special gift for bringing the world together. **Malcolm Gladwell**[1]

No individual is an island. We are social animals. We connect to others in many different ways, through our families, neighbours, friendships, work colleagues, and increasingly through social media. Through these connections we access additional experience, expertise and wisdom. Without connections we limit our options in life. Self-reliance is important. But if we are dependent only on ourselves, we are at a disadvantage vis a vis those with a range of well-developed networks.

A good friend is a connection to life - a tie to the past, a road to the future, the key to sanity in a totally insane world. **Lois Wyse**

Two themes are important.

Breadth. The extent to which we are connected to a range of people. Professionally across different functional disciplines, industries and sectors. Personally, from different generations, social groups and generally those from diverse walks of life. The low end of the spectrum is narrow; the high end, a wide ranging set of connections.

Quality. We may be networked to many different people, but the quality of these connections may be low. Or, we can call on advanced levels of experience, knowledge and expertise from informed and innovative contacts who in turn are also highly connected to more networks of insightful and intelligent contacts.

It is inevitable if you enter into relations with people on a regular basis that you will grow to be like them. **Epictetus**

Four network patterns are identified.

Distanced. These individuals have a limited network and in danger of talking only to themselves. Connections are narrow and of low quality. There is a lack of diversity to provide a range of interactions and multiple perspectives. The risk is of isolation - both socially and intellectually.

If you're a hermit, nothing ever happens in your life. If you're the opposite of a hermit, things happen. **Max Gunther**

Well Informed Insider. This describes those who access experience, expertise and insight but only from a relatively limited domain in life. At best, these connections allow the exchange of knowledge and wisdom based on relationships of trust. At worst, an inner circle that is preoccupied with a narrow set of interests to reinforce each other's convictions to lack engagement with the wider world.

Perhaps the secret of living well is not in having all the answers but in pursuing unanswerable questions in good company. **Rachel Naomi Remen**

Acquaintances. This grouping has extended but shallow contacts across a wide span of different types of people. These relationships are not however well founded. The upside; the opportunity to know someone who knows. Or, this is the social world of superficial interactions. It make it difficult to have conversations of trust to allow the open exchange for a free flow ideas.

I get by with a little help from my friends. **John Lennon**

Influencers. Those individuals who access in-depth experience and expertise across a range of spheres in life. Based on well established relationships of trust from a wide circle of contacts from different fields, these individuals are the boundary spanners, alert to new developments. This is the Medici Effect[2] for creativity, change and innovation.

If you look around the room and you're the smartest person in the room, you're in the wrong room. **Lorne Michaels**

SO WHAT?

It's better to hang out with people better than you. Pick out associates whose behaviour is better than yours and you'll drift in that direction. **Warren Buffett**

Building powerful connections - deep and wide - is not the superficiality of networking[3] to exchange business cards. Connections that make a personal and professional difference take time and energy to build and nurture. These connections provide the multiplier[4] effect to optimise effectiveness.

NOTES

1. Six Degrees of Separation Theory: How We're All Connected; https://www.shortform.com/blog/six-degrees-of-separation-theory/#:~:text=The%20six%20degrees%20of%20separation,Six%20Degrees%20of%20Kevin%20Bacon.%E2%80%9D

2. How the Medici Effect can spark a renaissance in your business; https://bigthink.com/business/medici-effect-business/

3. Five Good Ways Not to Network; https://theundercoverrecruiter.com/5-good-ways-not-network/

4. The Lollapalooza Effect; https://talentworldconsulting.com/wp-content/uploads/2023/08/The-Lollapalooza-Effect-Charlie-Munger-Talent-Assessment.pdf

Are we pleasing or pushing?

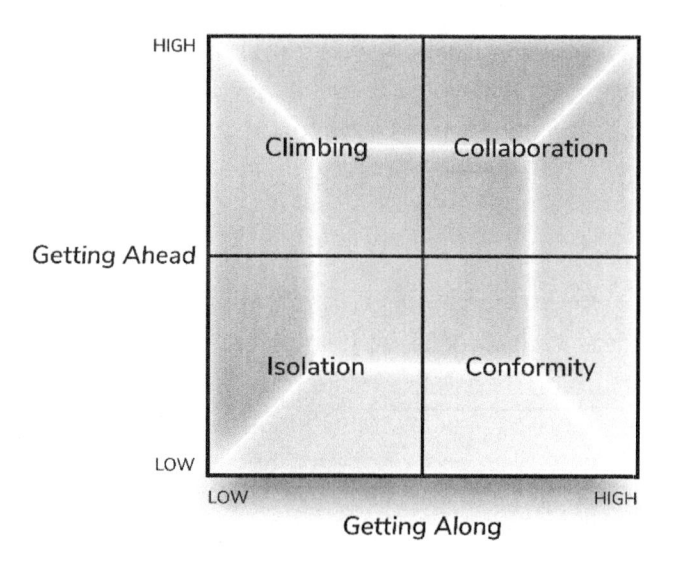

	Getting Along LOW	Getting Along HIGH
Getting Ahead HIGH	Climbing	Collaboration
Getting Ahead LOW	Isolation	Conformity

Because everyone we meet is attempting to get along and get ahead, we're subject to near constant attempts at manipulation. Ours is an environment of soft lies and half smiles that seek to make us feel pleasant and render us pliable. **Will Storr**

After losing his political way, former MP Robert Kilroy-Silk went on to further humiliation to present an absurd TV game show: Shafted. Here Kilroy-Silk posed the big question in life: Share or Shaft?[1]

Human nature and its impact on interpersonal behaviour is underpinned by two driving forces: cooperation and competition. Our own personality and the dynamic with others we encounter is key to interpersonal relationships. It explains why some relationships work and others don't. And how we can optimise our impact in different life situations.

The two dimensions of social interaction.

Getting Along. This is the recognition that - as social beings - our activities and achievements are highly dependent on others, our family, friends and work colleagues. At the low end, there is a reluctance to engage with this connected reality. At the other extreme, we play nice for the happy harmony of cooperation.

Getting Ahead. We have ambitions for greater status and influence in life.[2] At the low end, aspirations for further progression are modest. At the high end, this is intense ambition to seek greater success, typically to achieve career promotion and financial status.

Four interpersonal permutations emerge.

Isolation. Low getting along and low getting ahead describes the independent minded individual who follows their own path in life. It is an uncompromising resistance to others' expectations, and a reluctance to adapt to social conventions. Alternatively, this highlights the lonely person who has become detached from interpersonal interactions, missing the opportunity for an enriching life experience.

Isolation doesn't bother me at all. It gives me a sense of security. **Jimmy Page, Led Zeppelin**

Climbing. When getting ahead is much more prominent than getting along, this is competitive advancement. At best, this individual is single minded in pursuit of an important cause. A life stance that refuses to be deflected by others' expectations of what they should or shouldn't do. At worst, the self-serving individual who wants to win at all costs, prepared to undermine others' efforts and goals to achieve their own objectives.

I'm in competition with myself and I'm losing. **Roger Waters, Pink Floyd**

Conformity. High getting along intersects with low getting ahead. The desire to cooperate makes for an agreeable and easy going interpersonal style. Others find this individual highly approachable, mainly because they represent little threat to their own ambitions. Alternatively, a scenario in which a lack of push to advance personal aspirations is exploited by self-seeking others.

If you can't do something, saying so right away usually makes it much easier for everyone. **Oliver Burkeman**

Collaboration. Getting ahead and getting along combine for a cooperative win-win scenario in social interactions. At best, these individuals are part of a highly motivated group, of ambitious individuals. This helps everyone raise their game for personal and collective benefit. Interpersonal dynamics can also be bracing in this situation. Well managed, against a backdrop of mutual trust, this represents a genuine win-win for all participants. Alternatively, game theory[3] indicates that one defecting player who wants to get ahead can shift the overall mood to trigger conflict.

Winning isn't getting ahead of others; it is getting ahead of yourself. **Roger Staubach**

SO WHAT?

You'll never get ahead of anyone as long as you try to get even with them. **Lou Holtz**

Wires often get crossed in interpersonal encounters. Our competitive instinct can be viewed with suspicion by others. Or, our good nature to cooperate is exploited.

Knowing the dynamics at play with others helps establish how much to please and how far to push.

NOTES

1. In one of TV's most embarrassing moments, Robert Kilroy-Silk explains the dilemma; https://youtu.be/vyBhEyVFFW0?si=RVP_wpkt4LZ433bW The game show format was based on the Prisoner's Dilemma. But a combination of a clunky format, dismal production values and Kilroy-Silk's leaden delivery resulted in disastrous viewing figures. The programme was canned.

2. In evolutionary psychology, this brain feature of competition to advance opened up opportunities to access greater resource, not least in better mating options and plentiful food supplies.

3. Game theory and competitive versus cooperation. The best strategy in iterations of plays seems one of Tit For Tat. First cooperate, then in subsequent rounds do

whatever the opponent did last time. So if initial cooperation is punished with defection, reciprocate in kind.

Who is OK?

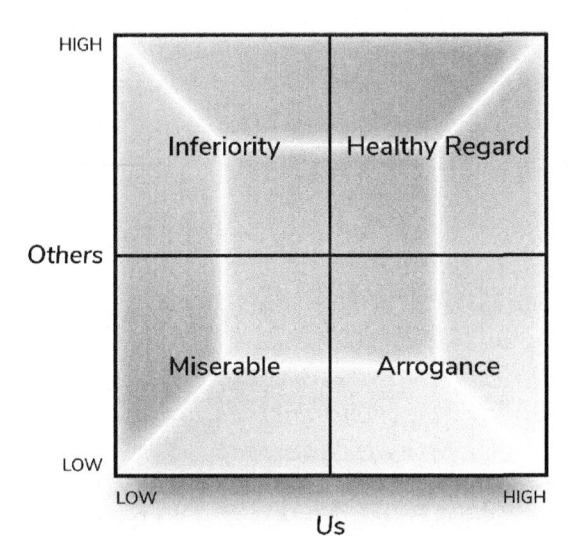

```
        HIGH
          │
          │   Inferiority    │  Healthy Regard
          │                  │
  Others  ├──────────────────┼──────────────────
          │                  │
          │    Miserable     │     Arrogance
          │                  │
        LOW
          └──────────────────┴──────────────────
              LOW                      HIGH
                           Us
```

Intimacy is a game-free relationship, since goals are not ulterior. Intimacy is made possible in a situation in the absence of fear. **Thomas Harris**

The self-help book by Thomas Harris I'm OK You're OK, based on Transactional Analysis, was a best seller. It shipped 15 million copies. Despite the criticisms[1] it tapped into an important observation: the dynamic of our interpersonal encounters and relationships is based not only on others but on how we feel about ourselves.

If there's anything more important than my ego around, I want it caught and shot now. **Zaphod in Douglas Adams' Hitchhikers' Guide to the Galaxy**

The two dimensions that underpin this interplay.

Us. We feel OK. We don't feel OK

Others. They feel OK. They don't feel OK.

Four patterns emerge in this adaptation of the Harris model.

Miserable. We are not OK and the other is not OK. This makes for an unhappy interpersonal scenario. It runs the risk of passive aggressive behaviour spanning a sense of hopelessness to inappropriate over reactions towards others' conduct.

In my life, oh, why do I give valuable time to people who don't care if I live or die? Why do I smile at people who I'd much rather kick in the eye? But heaven knows I'm miserable now. **Morrissey, The Smiths**

Inferiority. We are not OK but others are. This is helplessness to blame ourselves for any misunderstandings and mistakes within a relationship. A vulnerable position that can be exploited by others.

The moment of crisis had come, and I must face it. My old fears, my diffidence, my shyness, my hopeless sense of inferiority, must be conquered now and thrust aside. **Rebecca, Daphne du Maurier**

Arrogance. We are OK but others are not. There may be any number of life circumstances underpinning the situation, not least differences in status and power. The risk: a dismissive attitude towards others that operates in a high handed manner.[2]

Be careful not to mistake insecurity and inadequacy for humility! Humility has nothing to do with the insecure and inadequate! Just like arrogance has nothing to do with greatness. **C Joybell C**

Healthy Regard. We are both OK. This is interpersonal life based on self-confidence and mutual respect in which we and others both feel acknowledged and valued. It may be there is a risk of an interpersonal conspiracy to shore up self-esteem. But for the most part, this is the foundation for openness and trust to develop over time for rewarding relationships.

There are two types of people. Those who come into a room and say, Well, here I am, and those who come in and say, Ah, there you are. **Frederick Collins**

SO WHAT?

Every person's map of the world is as unique as their thumbprint. There are no two people alike. No two people who understand the same sentence the same way. In dealing with people, you try not to fit them to your concept of what they should be. **Milton Erickson**

Relationships can be difficult. Rarely are any difficulties simply about us. It's not all about me. Sometimes, maybe often, the issue is the complex dynamic with our partners, family, friends and colleagues - and their views of who is and isn't OK.

A good check in. Is me or the other? Or both?

NOTES

1. Wendy Kaminer used a variation of the title for her spoof of the self-help craze, I'm Dysfunctional, You're Dysfunctional, with the advice: *First, promote the prevailing preoccupation of the time - either health or wealth, and then package platitudes about positive thinking, prayer or affirmation therapy as sure-fire, scientific techniques.*

2. Exemplified by Fritz Perls of the est movement who is known for: *I do my thing and you do your thing. I am not in this world to live up to your expectations. And you are not in this world to live up to mine. You are you, and I am I, and if by chance we find each other, it's beautiful. If not, it can't be helped.* Despite the rhetoric, the reality was different. Perls was a deeply unpleasant individual. *I've beaten up more than one bitch in my life. And there are thousands of women like her in the States. Provoking and tantalizing, bitching, irritating their husbands and never getting their spanking.*
More on the feet of clay of well-known psychotherapists. The Shadow Side of the Great Psychotherapists, Timothy Thomason;
https://openknowledge.nau.edu/id/eprint/2346/7/Thomason_T_2016_The_Shadow_Side_of_the_Great_Psychotherapists(1).pdf

How do we build trust?

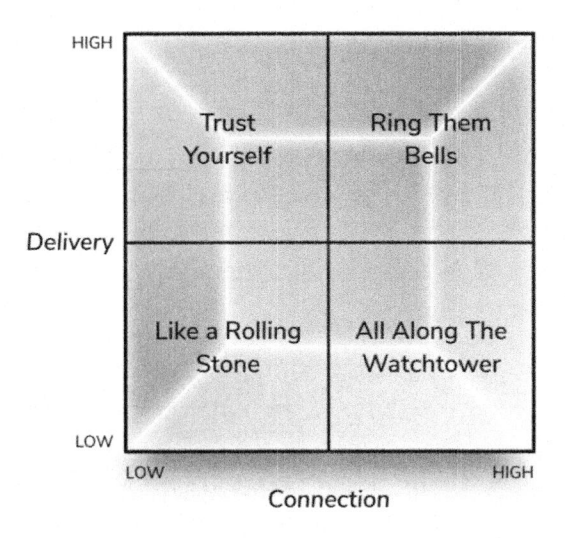

[Figure: 2x2 matrix with axes "Delivery" (Low to High) and "Connection" (Low to High). Quadrants: Low Connection / High Delivery = "Trust Yourself"; High Connection / High Delivery = "Ring Them Bells"; Low Connection / Low Delivery = "Like a Rolling Stone"; High Connection / Low Delivery = "All Along The Watchtower".]

Never trust anyone over 30[1] Bob Dylan famously said in the 1960s during the US civil rights movement of the 1960s. Since then the back catalogue of Dylan has been used in adverts for Airbnb, Bank of Montreal, Brother Printers, Chrysler, Google, Pepsi, Victoria's Secret, and more.

Who do we trust now?

But I did not trust my brother. I carried him to blame. Which led me to my fatal doom. To wander off in shame. **Bob Dylan**

Two themes interact for a relationship of trust.

Connection. This theme taps into empathic understanding. This builds emotional bonds and mutual understanding. At the low end, a closed and guarded stance that puts up barriers to intimacy. At the high end, a sense of genuine care for others and openness about our own feelings. Reciprocity builds further trust.

Delivery. This dimension reflects competence to operate with consistency, over time, for positive outcomes. At the low end, a haphazard approach. Others begin to doubt our willingness to honour our commitments. At the high end of this range, others are confident that we will do what we say we will.

Four stances to trust can be identified.

Like a Rolling Stone. This combines a lack of emotional connection and a reluctance to commit to action. Perhaps life has left us betrayed, disillusioned or damaged. Personally, this is troublesome. At the corporate level this is a world of hypocrisy and humbug. The business who says *your call is important to us* and leaves us waiting 50 minutes for a curt response.

How does it feel to be on your own with no direction home. Like a complete unknown. Like a rolling stone? **Bob Dylan**

Trust Yourself. This is the self-reliance to avoid relationships that might be exploited. At best, an independence of mind and decision making to get things done our way. *Down to Gehenna or up to the throne, he travels the fastest who travels alone*. Alternatively, this is a life of suspicion, if not hostility towards others that makes life much harder than it needs to be.

Trust yourself to do the things that only you know best. **Bob Dylan**

All Along the Watchtower. An emotional connection is made. There is little anticipation however of a positive outcome from this relationship. This can be the relaxed relationship of low expectations. Trust is built and maintained, but only because there is a hesitation to put trust to the test. This becomes the fear of hope that will disappoint. And an outlook that constrains long term mutually beneficial relationships.

No reason to get excited. The thief, he kindly spoke. There are many here among us. Who feel that life is but a joke. **Bob Dylan**

Ring Them Bells. Emotional connection intersects with outcomes.[1] At best, this is the virtuous cycle in which mutual understanding and empathy build a relationship to achieve and sustain results that draws on our and others' relative talents. But trust can be fragile. Misunderstandings become problems that escalate to conflict. Our initial trust in others breaks, and we begin to doubt our judgement.

Ring them bells for the time that flies. **Bob Dylan**

SO WHAT?

Cause something is happening and you don't know what it is. Do you, Mr. Jones? **Bob Dylan**

Who can we trust? And how much are we prepared to disclose our vulnerabilities and shortcomings? Too little trust and we run the risk of putting up the kind of barriers that block emotional connection. Too much, and the hazard of exploitation by those who gain, to our disadvantage.

NOTES

1. Misattributed to Bob Dylan, it was the phrase of student activist Jack Weinberger in the 1960s.

Are we gaining or losing?

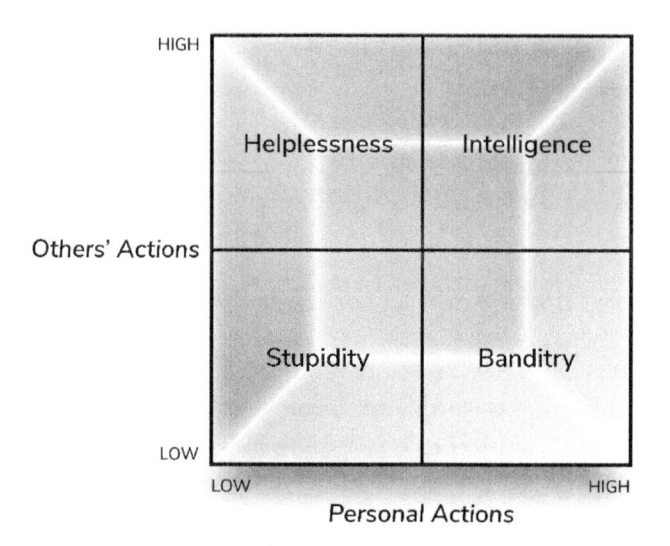

	Personal Actions LOW	Personal Actions HIGH
Others' Actions HIGH	Helplessness	Intelligence
Others' Actions LOW	Stupidity	Banditry

Always and inevitably everyone underestimates the number of stupid individuals in circulation. **First Basic Law of Human Stupidity, Carlo Cipolla**[1]

One of the extraordinary features of human nature is the length to which it will go to do the stupid. This is not only the stuff that is damaging to others, but also personally to ourselves. This behaviour undertakes activities damaging to our physical and mental well-being.[2] Add to the mix our foolish interactions with others, and the opportunity for stupidity is limitless.[3]

In the spirit of Charles Darwin, the awards commemorate individuals who protect our gene pool by making the ultimate sacrifice of their own lives. Darwin Award winners eliminate themselves in an extraordinarily idiotic manner, thereby improving our species' chances of long-term survival. **Darwin Awards**

This quadrant provides an insight into the transactions of interpersonal life to identify the winners and losers as part of our exchanges with others.

I've often said, the only thing standing between me and greatness is me. **Woody Allen**

Personal Actions. At the low end of the range, we experience a loss that puts us in a worse position. At the high end, a gain that results in a positive personal outcome.

Others' Actions. Within the dynamics of interpersonal encounters, do others gain or lose from their transactions with us? At one end, they lose. At the other, we win.

This highlights four patterns of win and loss.

Stupidity. The outcome when another's loss is associated with a personal loss to us. It is not simply that no one wins. Everyone loses. This may be unintentional, a consequence of a mindlessness that fails to recognise the rules of the game. But sometimes, maybe surprisingly often, this is the folly of the ego stance that persists in an interpersonal transaction with an unsustainable position that is damaging to everyone's interests.

Never attribute to malice that which can be adequately explained by neglect, ignorance or incompetence. **Hanlon's Razor**

Helplessness. We are part of an interpersonal game in which others' gains mean a loss for us. A plus for others from the transaction is a minus for us. This might be a conscious acceptance of a dynamic of dependency to acknowledge - for any number of reasons - a weak position. At worst, an exchange of exploitation in which others take advantage of our vulnerabilities.[4]

When a true genius appears in the world, you may know him by this sign, that the dunces are all in confederacy against him. **Jonathan Swift**

Banditry. Our personal gains in this transaction represent a loss for others. At its most extreme, this is theft to take from the other. We exploit the naivete of the helpless. A possibility as a one off exchange if we are cynical. But typically over time, we gain a reputation for bad behaviour and others are reluctant to deal with us.

The bandit's actions follow a pattern of rationality: nasty rationality, if you like, but still rationality. The bandit wants a plus on his account. **Carlo Cipolla**

Intelligence. In contrast to stupidity, our personal gains correlate with others' gains. This is the exchange of mutual benefit and the basis of a long-term relationship. A virtuous cycle begins: high levels of trust and benefit escalate gains for everyone.

When you play games where other people have the aptitude and you don't, you're going to lose. You have to figure out where you have an edge and stick to it. **Charlie Munger**

SO WHAT?

You yourself will always be the worst enemy you can encounter. You yourself lie in wait for yourself in caves and forests. **Friedrich Nietzsche**

Sometimes we are our own worst enemy. In our innocence, we fail to recognise the impact of others' counter-productive behaviour. However damaging to themselves, it also has a negative consequences for us.

This quadrant highlights the need to think reward and risk, and long-term and short-term: who is winning and losing, and to which end?

NOTES

1. The Basic Laws of Human Stupidity, Carlo Cipolla; https://bonpote.com/en/the-5-basic-laws-of-human-stupidity/
The Second Basic Law states that the probability that a certain person is stupid is independent of any other characteristic of that person.

2. The Darwin Awards are typically won by men. 282 Darwin Awards were awarded to males and just 36 awards given to females. Examples include the man who slipped when using a belt sander as an auto-erotic device and lost a testicle. Repairing his scrotum with a staple gun, he was able to salvage his remaining testicle thus failing to eliminate himself completely from the gene pool.
https://www.bmj.com/content/349/bmj.g7094

3. A Stupidity-Based Theory of Organizations, Mats Alvesson and André Spicer

4. A skilled exploiter is effective in explaining why our apparent losses and their gains are just one of these things.

Are we too popular?

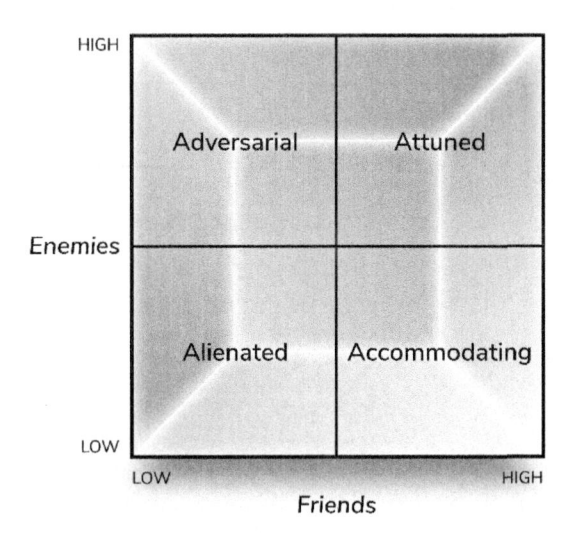

```
HIGH
        |  Adversarial  |   Attuned
Enemies |---------------|-------------
        |   Alienated   | Accommodating
LOW
          LOW                    HIGH
                  Friends
```

What matters isn't being applauded when you arrive - for that is common - but being missed when you leave. **Baltasar Gracián**

In life we encounter different kinds of people. Some we respect and admire, and these feelings are reciprocated. These are trusted friendships. Others trigger animosity through any range of emotions from fear to envy to outright hostility. It is not always easy to work out the dynamic of these relationships. Who is a reliable friend? Who is a dangerous enemy?

The Texan turned out to be good-natured, generous and likable. In three days, no one could stand him. **Joseph Heller, Catch 22**

Friends. This reflects the breadth and depth of our positive relationships with others. Low: we lack access to the trust of family members, broader social connections and work colleagues. High, and we call on a set of supportive relationships concerned to advance our interests.

Enemies. This theme identifies the grouping who oppose us, sometimes directly, more typically indirectly. Even worse, these individuals dislike us, and take pleasure from our personal misfortunes.

Keep your friends close, but your enemies closer. **Michael Corleone, The Godfather**

Four groupings emerge from this quadrant.

Alienated. A combination of low friends and low enemies is one of social isolation. This is a stance of interpersonal distance to avoid relationships that might help or hurt us in life. This is the Paul Simon philosophy: I Am A Rock: *I have my books. And my poetry to protect me. I am shielded in my armour. Hiding in my room. Safe within my womb. I touch no one and no one touches me. I am a rock. I am an island. And a rock feels no pain. And an island never cries.*

A wise person gets more use from his enemies than a fool from his friends. **Baltasar Gracian**

Adversarial. This reflects the ratio of high enemies to low friends. At best, an uncompromising stance in life to defend key principles, however unpopular they might be with others. More likely, an outlook of belligerence or even paranoia that others find objectionable to avoid contact with us.

You have enemies? Good. That means you've stood up for something, sometime in your life. **Winston Churchill**

Accommodating. In this scenario, within the circle of our connections, friendship levels exceed those of enemies. This is a pleasing and engaging interpersonal stance to gain affection and admiration.[1] At worst, this is the people pleaser to avoid challenge, controversy and conflict, exploited by others who take advantage of our naivete.

It is easier to forgive an enemy than to forgive a friend. **William Blake**

Attuned. This box reflects the balance of friends and enemies, alert to the social dynamics within the range of our interpersonal connections and encounters. Here the good in others is identified to build momentum for trusted and long-term relationships. This approach is also shrewd to look beneath the surface of social situations to see the potential for any negative and hostile attitudes and behaviour towards us.

There are two things people want more than sex and money. Recognition and praise. **Mary Kay Ash**

SO WHAT?

It is difficult to say who do you the most mischief, enemies with the worst intentions, or friends with the best. **Edward Bulwer-Lytton**

Bob Marley, the wise philosopher, commented: *your worst enemy could be your best friend and your best friend your worst enemy.* Do we know who are our true friends? And who are potential adversaries?

NOTES

1. The liberating truth is: they're probably not thinking about you. Oliver Burkeman on how to quit people pleasing;
https://www.theguardian.com/lifeandstyle/article/2024/aug/24/oliver-burkeman-book-extract-meditations-for-mortals-people-pleasing

Who is kidding who?

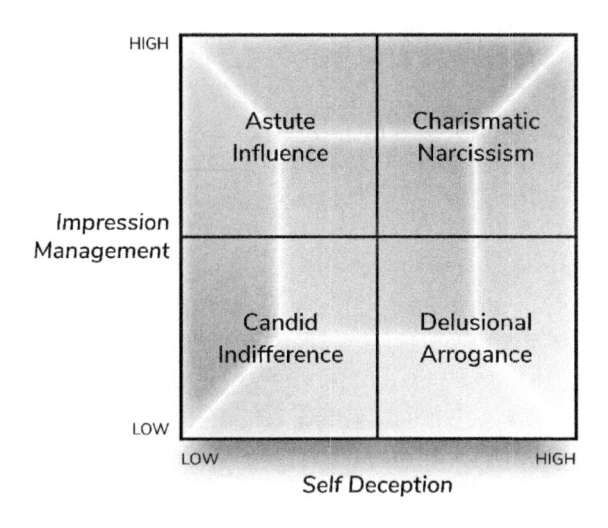

Everyone has the ability to do anything I do and much beyond. Some of you will and some of you won't. For those who won't, it will be because you get in our own way. Not because the world doesn't allow you. **Warren Buffett** In life we aim to make a positive impression on those we encounter. From a meeting with a first date to a job interview through to a dinner party with the new neighbours, the expectation is that we put our best foot forward to convey our best. It also helps if we truly believe that we are the intelligent, hardworking and trustworthy person that we project. This is the evolutionary strategy in which *we deceive ourselves the better to deceive others.*

Liars are not liars if they believe the lie. **Michael Shermer**[1]

Who are we kidding? Ourselves? Others? Both?

Self Deception. This operates at the unconscious level to maintain high levels of self-esteem. At the low end, a critical insight into ourselves and an unflinching view of our failings and frailties. At the high end of the spectrum, our self-deception provides an inflated and distorted image of ourselves.

Impression Management. This reflects the motivation and skill to project a positive image of who we are to others. At the low end of the range, an indifference to others' perceptions and opinions, one that makes little attempt to be anything other than ourselves. At the high end is the need to be viewed positively by others.

Oh, the audacity of authenticity! You're going to confuse, piss off and terrify lots of people - including yourself. **Brené Brown**

This mix of motivations - unconscious and conscious - highlights four interpersonal stances.

Candid Indifference. Levels of self deception and impression management are both low. This combination is one of supreme self-confidence based on a well-founded self-image resistant to any expectations of social gamesmanship. No attempt is made to manufacture and sell the *me product* to others. The risk is that a strategy of *take me as you find me* backfires when others decide not to take what they find.

Nothing in the world is harder than candour, and nothing is easier than flattery. **Fyodor Dostoyevsky**

Astute Influence. Low levels of self deception interact with high impression management. This is insight into our personal strengths to project them effectively for optimal social impact. This approach recognises our shortcomings and limitations. It ensures these potential vulnerabilities are not exploited by others. There is also the hazard in which a cunning canniness is detected by others who find this approach overly scheming.

The first principle is that you must not fool yourself and you are the easiest person to fool. **Richard Feynman**

Delusional Arrogance. High levels of self deception meet low levels of impression management. This interpersonal stance is the ill-founded confidence in our personal brilliance without any need to establish or prove our genius. Here the thinking is: my talents speak for themselves. It is true that we can fool some of the people some of the time. Typically, over time, when these talents speak, no one is listening.

I am being frank about myself in this book. I tell of my first mistake on page 850. **Henry Kissinger**

Charismatic Narcissism. High self deception and high impression management is an intriguing combination. A lack of self-awareness has the upside of a thick skin that is unembarrassable in the effort to influence others. It is an interpersonal approach with the potential to fascinate and captivate others in the short-term. Its extravagant hype and, at times, blatant lies, can be breathtaking. Others can be mesmerised by the sheer audacity of this approach. Longer-term, once they catch their breath, the charlatanism is exposed.[2]

I am a very stable genius. **Former US President Donald Trump**

SO WHAT?

We are so accustomed to disguise ourselves to others that in the end we become disguised to ourselves. **Duc La Rochefoucauld**

The question is not are we kidding ourselves. We always are. The issue is how much are we kidding ourselves. Are we deluded in our interactions with others?

And if our response to feedback triggers defensiveness, we might be fooling ourselves more than we thought.

NOTES

1. A review of deceit and self-deception by Robert Trivers;
https://www.theguardian.com/science/2011/oct/07/deceit-self-deception-robert-trivers
Surprising results that counter the popular idea that knowing yourself is good for you; https://www.scientificamerican.com/article/new-insights-into-self-insight-more-may-not-be-better/

2. How to Be a Charlatan and Make Millions: A Ten Step Programme to Change Your Life, Jim Williams

What is the destructive dynamic of relationships?

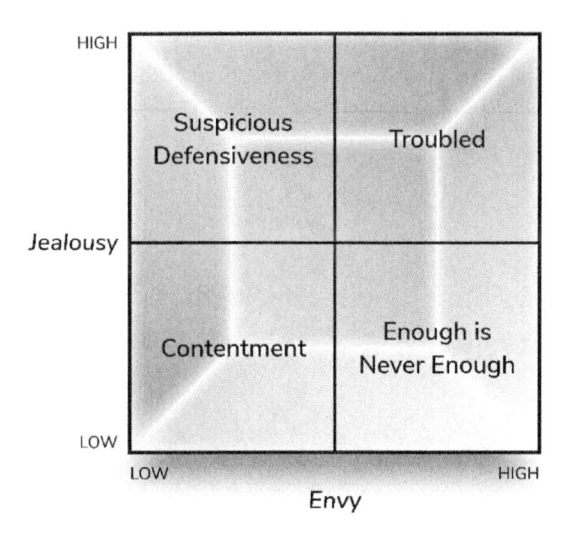

	Low Envy	High Envy
High Jealousy	Suspicious Defensiveness	Troubled
Low Jealousy	Contentment	Enough is Never Enough

Israel loved Joseph more than all his children, because he was the son of his old age: and he made him a coat of many colours. And his brethren envied him. **Genesis 37**

The medievalists identified seven deadly sins, the vices that hold us back from a life of virtue. Envy was the deadliest. Or, as Charlie Munger expressed it: *envy is a really stupid sin because it's the only one you could never possibly have any fun at. There's a lot of pain and no fun.*[1]

Often confused with jealousy, psychologically, envy is different. Nonetheless, both have destructive power to harm not only our relationships with our partner, our friends and work colleagues, but to damage ourselves.

And I saw that all labour and all achievement spring from man's envy of his neighbour. This too is meaningless, a chasing after the wind. **Ecclesiastes**

This quadrant of counterproductive behaviours is based on two dynamics.

Envy. The emotion we experience when we long for something of others: their qualities, achievements or possessions. We compare ourselves unfavourably to others, and resent their status vis a vis our own position. Low envy, and we are untroubled by others' success. High envy becomes a nagging discontent with a feeling of injustice at what we see as the imbalance in relative fortunes.[2]

Jealousy. In contrast to envy, jealousy is the fear of what others might take from us. This is the concern about the loss of a valued relationship. Low jealousy detects little threat to what we have. High jealousy is that fearful insecurity alert to potential loss that becomes possessive.[3]

Jealousy contains more of self-love than of love. **Duc de la Rochefoucauld**

Four emotional responses emerge.

Contentment. Low envy and low jealousy intersect for a confident position, comfortable in interpersonal situations. There is no sense of the inferiority complex of envy or of the suspicion of jealousy. A more cynical interpretation would propose that is a life stance of naivete based on a complacency, failing to recognise interpersonal rivalries and sensitivities.[4]

The more humble a man is before God the more he will be exalted. The more humble he is before man, the more he will get rode roughshod. **Josh Billings**

Suspicious Defensiveness. The combination of low envy and high jealousy is life lived on the back foot. This is less of a comparison of our position relative to others' achievements. It is a stance of heightened sensitivity to the threat from those who want to take what we already have. This interpersonal style can be demanding and exhausting, both for the individual and others whose commitment and loyalty are questioned.

Our envy always lasts longer than the happiness of those we envy. **Duc de la Rochefoucauld**

Enough is Never Enough. Levels of jealousy are low but envy is high. Interpersonal judgements are made less about who can take from us and more directed towards those who trigger dissatisfaction with our own situation. At best, with emotional maturity, this position translates into aspirations for personal advancement. It can also be an outlook of resentful bitterness to view the achievements of others as a criticism of ourselves.

It is not enough to succeed. Others must fail. **Gore Vidal**

Troubled. When high envy and high jealousy interact, the outcome is one of personal and interpersonal difficulties. Life becomes turbulent. A range of malicious tactics are deployed to undermine others, for example, to trigger mean spirited gossip, harsh sarcasm and aggressive mockery. Relationships of trust and respect are undermined. This stance is also damaging us as individuals. There is a frustration that life is not fair which becomes a generalised sense of the injustice of the world.[5]

Nothing arouses ambition so much in the heart as the trumpet-clang of another's fame. **Baltasar Gracian**

SO WHAT?

They will envy you for your success, your wealth, for your intelligence, for your looks, for your status, but rarely for your wisdom. **Nassim Taleb**

Both emotions are part of who we are and can be motivating - if understood and well managed. Both can also be extremely damaging. Together envy and jealousy are highly destructive, personally for ourselves and in the disruption to our interpersonal relationships.

Aristotle suggested a solution: worry less about others and more about ourselves and our own achievements.

NOTES

1. There seems to be a general taboo against a discussion of envy. If so, what accounts for the taboo? Charlie Munger and human misjudgement; https://fs.blog/great-talks/psychology-human-misjudgment/

2. Envy arises only in the context of which social comparisons we choose to make or not make based on what is important to us and our sense of self-worth. Envy, for example, rarely extends to outstanding artists, musicians or Olympic athletes. It is more commonly triggered by the successes of other family members, friends and immediate work colleagues.

3. Jealousy is nuanced. We suffer when a partner dies. This is grief not jealousy. But if we identify a threat of losing that partner to someone else - a rival - jealousy is aroused.

4. In evolutionary terms, both envy and jealousy have adaptive value. Envy can be the driver of the competitive spirit that seeks advancement. And jealousy is a protective strategy to avoid threats to our standing from rivals. Both are important mechanisms for survival and reproductive success.

5. This may be true. But as Max Gunther points out in How To Get Lucky, bad luck is just bad luck. The universe knows nothing of fairness.

How to find a partner in life

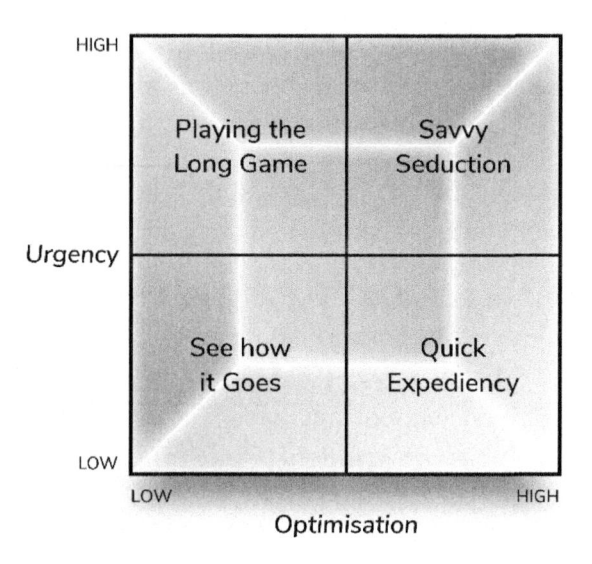

	LOW Optimisation	HIGH
HIGH Urgency	Playing the Long Game	Savvy Seduction
LOW	See how it Goes	Quick Expediency

It is the wicked deception of love that it begins by making us dwell not upon a woman in the outside world but upon a doll inside our head, the only woman who is always available in fact, the only one we shall ever possess. **Marcel Proust**

There are different tactics to find a partner in life: traditional dating to meet others through friends, social events, or in the work place. Blind dating to go on a date, typically set up by a friend or family member, with someone that we have not met. On line dating to locate the individual who provides the perfect fit with our personal profile. Or, the use of a professional matchmaker.

Which strategy underpins our quest for this life partner? Is there an algorithm[1] to guide our tactics?

Two dimensions shape our approach.

Optimisation. This criterion represents our level of aspiration to locate a life mate. At the low end of the spectrum, realism requires that compromises have to be made. There are lots of fish in the sea. At the other end, the ideal of the one and only who can make us happy in life.

Urgency. This theme highlights the speed with which a life partner must be found. Many complex factors influence the need for urgency, age, perhaps being the most obvious. The mix also includes financial demands, family expectations and social pressures.

Against the trade-offs between optimisation and urgency four search strategies are highlighted.

See how it Goes. This combines low urgency with low optimisation. This is the outlook of take life as it comes with no expectations of a potential mate. If it happens, it happens. This has the virtue of keeping options open without any prospect of finding the perfect partner quickly. The downside: personal circumstances and motivations change. This strategy then becomes take what is left on the shelf.

Well, I'm sure you'll find someone somewhere who'll have you. **JK Rowling, Harry Potter and the Goblet of Fire**

Playing the Long Game. This approach takes time to improve the probability of finding the perfect partner. Standards are high, and there is no imperative for speed. This is a reflective and deliberative approach under no pressure to make commitments quickly. Alternatively, the stance of the fantasist who finds themselves running out of options and is out-manoeuvred by less cautious rivals.

Quick Expediency. A dating strategy in a hurry to find a partner, pretty much any partner who passes the minimum threshold of acceptability. Within some highly specific conditions, this is understandable. Under pressure to find someone, anyone, it is a high risk approach for a future dysfunctional relationship.

What makes a date so dreadful is the weight of expectation attached to it. There is every chance that you may meet your soulmate, get married, have children and be buried side by side. There is an equal chance that the person you meet will look as if they've already been buried for some time. **Guy Browning**

Savvy Seduction. The most ambitious of all strategies: a game-plan to optimise speed and quality. There is a motivation to get on with it but without any compromise in the ideal of that partner. It may be a strategy of romantic brilliance. Or one that has to come to terms with frequent rejection. A thick skin prepared to accept set-backs in combination with astute interpersonal skills can achieve its objectives.

My ex, may he rot in hell forever. **Things You Shouldn't Say on a Date, Gena Showalter**

SO WHAT?

Life is a series of trade-offs. This quadrant asks us to balance the ideal versus the possible within the constraints of time in the choice of a life partner. There may be an algorithm for most. But on average, most of us are not average.

Which strategy will accommodate the ideal versus speed?

NOTES

1. Building, Searching and the Algorithm for Finding the Best Spouse; https://www.scotthyoung.com/blog/2015/07/07/building-searching/

Will this relationship survive?

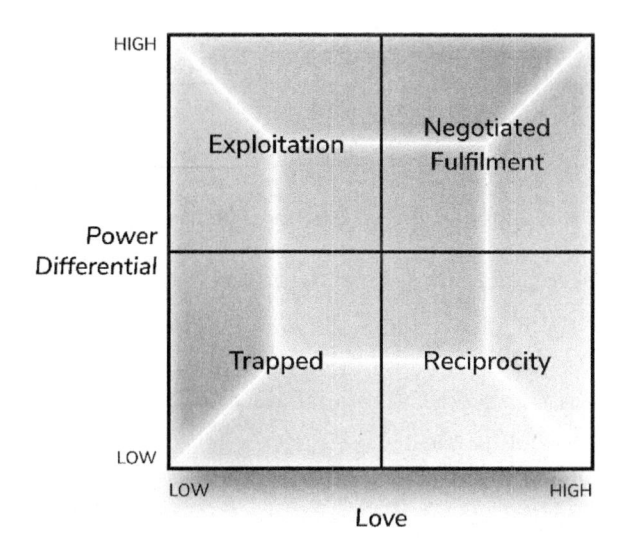

[Figure: 2×2 matrix with Power Differential (LOW to HIGH) on vertical axis and Love (LOW to HIGH) on horizontal axis. Quadrants: High Power Differential / Low Love = Exploitation; High Power Differential / High Love = Negotiated Fulfilment; Low Power Differential / Low Love = Trapped; Low Power Differential / High Love = Reciprocity.]

When you fall in love, it is a temporary madness. It erupts like an earthquake, and then it subsides. And when it subsides, you have to make a decision.
Louis de Bernières, Captain Corelli's Mandolin

Relationships work and don't work for many complex reasons. Some relationships which at first sight seem like a marriage made in heaven turn out to be highly dysfunctional and more like the inner circle of Dante's Hell. Others, which in theory shouldn't work, are in fact happy and rewarding experiences for both parties. But some patterns are highly predictive of partnership breakdown.[1]

Happy families are all alike; every unhappy family is unhappy in its own way.
Leo Tolstoy

Two variables are critical in relationship dynamics.

Love. The theme that runs the spectrum from a lack of feeling which is distanced and cold, to those emotions of warm intimacy and care.

Power Differential.[2] This indicates the balance of power within a relationship. A low differential reflects relative equality in the mix of assets, resources and overall contribution brought to the relationship. A high differential: one partner has a much greater power advantage to the other.

The power in all relationships lies with whoever cares less. **Connor Mead**

Four relationship scenarios are played out.

Being single is better than being in a toxic relationship. Being in a great relationship is better than being single. **Shane Parrish**

Trapped. A combination of low love and a low power differential. It may be a relationship of relative equals, but equals who don't love each other. The relationship continues as an expedient response, sometimes through strickened financial circumstances and limited life options. It lacks a healthy future.

I wish I knew how to quit you. **Annie Proulx, Broke Back Mountain**

Exploitation. Levels of love are low, and there is a significant power difference between the parties. This may be a well calculated relationship; an explicit understanding of the rules of this specific interpersonal game. Alternatively, this scenario allows the partner with most power to take control of the situation and advance their own interests to the neglect of the other.

Tell me what to do. Show me how to behave. I'll do anything you say. **Choderlos de Laclos, Dangerous Liaisons**

Reciprocity. This is a loving relationship in which no one partner has a clear power advantage. In this scenario, at best, each player operates within an environment of respect and trust based on equal contributions to the partnership.

Negotiated Fulfilment. High levels of love coincide with a large power differential. This may be the acceptance that one partner draws on greater assets and resources to make the relationship work in a productive way. And it is a meaningful and rewarding experience for both. Alternatively, this dynamic has the potential to shift, sometimes very quickly, to the exploitation of the dependent partner.

Some people ask the secret of our long marriage. We take time to go to a restaurant two times a week. A little candlelight, dinner, soft music and dancing. She goes Tuesdays, I go Fridays. **Henry Youngman**

SO WHAT?

Adversarial power relationships only work if you never have to see the bastards again. **Peter Drucker**

Relationships are not static. The dynamics ebb and flow over time as each individual changes and expectations shift. Give and take is always being negotiated however implicitly. An insight into love and power helps understand the likelihood of immediate survival and the long-term possibility to thrive.

NOTES

1. The Four Horsemen Of The Apocalypse: 4 Relationship Habits That Predict Divorce; https://www.mindbodygreen.com/articles/four-horsemen-gottman-research

2. Power in a relationship is a complex area. It reflects the balance of supply and demand of resources and the associated expectations. A billionaire, for example, may be relatively powerless, if they are in need of sex which is withheld by the other partner.

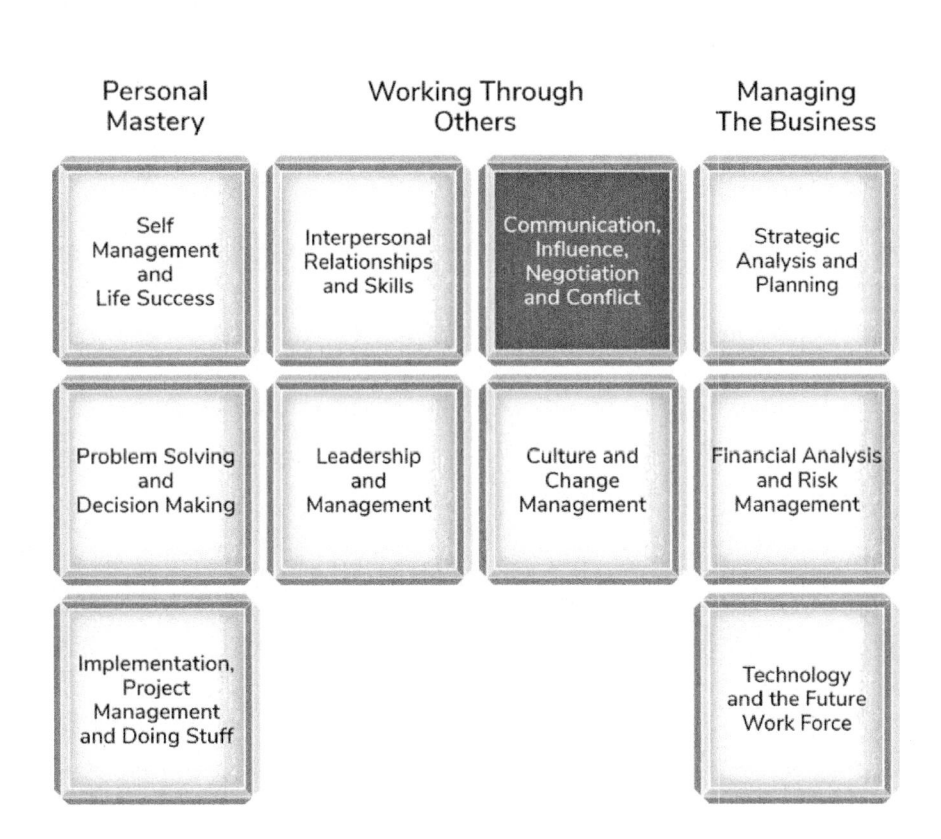

Personal Mastery	Working Through Others		Managing The Business
Self Management and Life Success	Interpersonal Relationships and Skills	Communication, Influence, Negotiation and Conflict	Strategic Analysis and Planning
Problem Solving and Decision Making	Leadership and Management	Culture and Change Management	Financial Analysis and Risk Management
Implementation, Project Management and Doing Stuff			Technology and the Future Work Force

Is our firm communicating with impact?

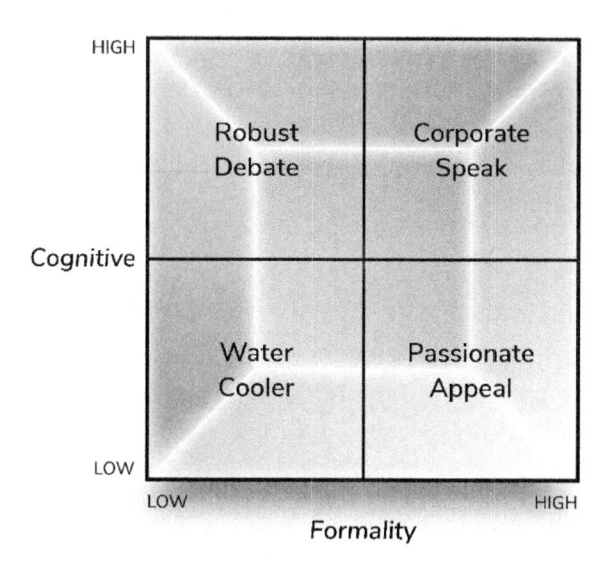

	Formality LOW	Formality HIGH
Cognitive HIGH	Robust Debate	Corporate Speak
Cognitive LOW	Water Cooler	Passionate Appeal

Given the double whammy that people don't think before they speak and that people aren't listening anyway, it's not surprising that communication is our number one problem. **Guy Browning**

Employee surveys deliver the same result, time after time. Communication is a problem. Why is this still an ongoing issue for companies? Firms spend significant time and effort to improve the flow the information down, up, across and outside the organisation. Sometimes these firms even set up a corporate communications department or hire a public relations firm to overcome the problem.[1]

This quadrant[2] suggests that communication is complex and nuanced. Without insight into the dynamics and barriers of effective communication processes, companies will continue to be in an uncomfortable place: talking without much employee listening.

To put it briefly, the secret is to put it briefly. But you always think that's what you're doing, until experience teaches you that you aren't being brief enough. **Clive James**

Two dimensions are highlighted.

Formality. This spans the spectrum from low, the informality of day to day interactions to share information and views within and across work groups, through to the formal: structured and officially approved communication content and media. An array of approaches typically are typically deployed: company-wide announcements, video and conference call presentations, senior executive briefings and newsletters.

Cognitive. Communication can be directed principally at our hearts or our minds. At the low end of this scale, emotionality appeals to the heart to evoke sentiments and feelings to shift behaviour. At the other end, cognitive is aimed at our minds, the use of facts and figures and rational argument to change attitudes.

Four communication patterns emerge.

Water Cooler. Communication is largely informal and based on emotion. This is how information is primarily shared within most organisations. Communication emerges from a series of interactions as colleagues discuss events, share opinions and arrive at judgements about what is and isn't working for them personally. At best, bottom up communication that reflects the employee experience of business reality. Alternatively, the firm is at the mercy of whispering gossip. Unfounded hearsay and speculation become damaging rumour.

Did you hear that Mark is planning to propose to Sarah soon? Yes, a little birdie told me.

Robust Debate. This combines the informal and cognitive. There is less social activity to exchange feelings; more the encouragement of frank discussions - at every level - about the challenges facing the firm. This is played out in ongoing briefings and meetings, corridor conversations, away days and weekend retreats. Communication tackles the issues in a candid way to provide informed feedback. This is the bracing debate admired by Ray Dalio in his principles of radical transparency.[3] However, without a formalised structure and a disciplined process for agreement and decision making, the *last person arguing wins*.

If you haven't got anything nice to say about anybody, come sit next to me. **Alice Roosevelt Longworth**

Passionate Appeal. Communication is formalised to engage the hearts of employees. This is the introduction of corporate events with the hoopla of the motivational speaker, the excitement of an awards ceremony and organisation of fun activities to involve everyone in a spirit of cooperation. And the CEO rounds things up to ask the workforce to *fight with every inch*.[4] At best, this tactic provides an inspirational experience for employees who feel part of a business that cares. It is also a cynical smoke screen to avoid addressing the deep seated issues facing the company.

Corporate Speak. High formality and high cognitive is the fallback position of organisational communication. Largely top down, formalised in official statements that require layers of approval to finalise, this is the strategy of persuasion through facts and figures, accompanied with visuals of projected growth. At one level this is sensible. Organisations need to establish goals and priorities and explain the strategic logic behind decisions. This requires repetition and reinforcement. Conversely, a failing approach, and a mismatch with social exchanges. Rhetoric is very different to experienced reality.

He didn't know the names of the trees and the flowers but he knew rhubarb crumble sales. **Reginald Perrin**

SO WHAT?

The single biggest problem in communication is the illusion that it has taken place. **George Bernard Shaw**

If there was an easy answer to the challenge of communication, it would have been solved by now. Instead there is a mix of the four boxes. Each has an upside but also a downside. However, any firm that relies on the formality of corporate speak will fail to connect with the emotional realities of the workforce.[5]

NOTES

1. Corporate communications and public relations. Surprisingly, the Edelman Trust Barometer found that Mexico and Colombia had the highest levels of employee trust. Edelman itself had its own issues with trust; https://www.theguardian.com/sustainable-business/2015/jul/07/pr-edelman-climate-change-lost-executives-clients

2. This quadrant is based on a framework developed by the consulting firm, The Oxford Group

3. Trust in Radical Truth and Radical Transparency; https://www.principles.com/principles/f6412dca-b3f9-4dd0-bb65-274869dd21ed/

4. This was the approach adopted by Fred Goodwin, former of CEO of Royal Bank of Scotland. The tax payer had to bail out the business to the tune of £45 billion. In a variation of this, the CEO appeals to fear. Nokia CEO Stephen Elop rallies troops in brutally honest memo? Nokia and the burning platform; https://www.engadget.com/2011-02-08-nokia-ceo-stephen-elop-rallies-troops-in-brutally-honest-burnin.html?

5. Communicating with Ros Atkins. Martin Lewis, personal finance journalist and campaigner; https://www.bbc.co.uk/sounds/play/m0020z5l

Are our meetings productive?

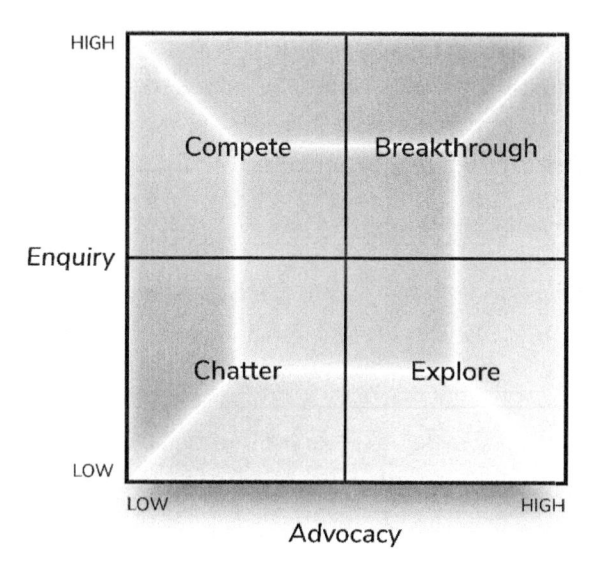

	Low Advocacy	High Advocacy
High Enquiry	Compete	Breakthrough
Low Enquiry	Chatter	Explore

Half of every working day is spent in meetings, half of which are not worth having, and of those that are, half the time is wasted. Which means that nearly one third of office life is spent in small rooms with people you don't like, doing things that don't matter. **Guy Browning**[1]

The average white collar employee spends upwards of 35% of their working time in meetings. This is unproductive and unsustainable. Management teams are looking for creative ways to bring that figure down. Facebook and the Canadian e-commerce firm Shopify, for instance, have introduced no-meeting Wednesdays. Amazon launched the two-pizza rule, where all meetings should be small enough that participants can be fed with two pizzas.[2]

The prevalence of unproductive meetings may be a by-product of the 2020 pandemic when meetings were scheduled to stay connected with colleagues. Many businesses haven't managed to find an equilibrium post lockdown. Some have resorted to cancelling meetings altogether.

Purpose and structure are key to the productive use of employee time. Also critical, the balance in meetings between advocacy and enquiry.[3]

People say that the secret of a good meeting is preparation. But if people really prepared for meetings, the first thing they would realise is that most are unnecessary. In fact, a tightly run meeting is one of the most frightening things in office life. **Guy Browning**

The two key themes for this quadrant.

Advocacy. Low advocacy is more about listening than making a point of view. High advocacy is more assertive to state one's view with clarity and cogency.

Enquiry. Low enquiry lacks an interest in others' views. High enquiry wants to find out other peoples' perspectives, and ask why they hold the view that they do.

Four types of meetings can be described.

Chatter. Low advocacy and low enquiry is the meeting which has too many observers. Or participants have withdrawn emotionally from the organisation. Chatter does allow the opportunity for people to get to know each other. Chatter however quickly becomes aimless conversation without purpose for team members and of no organisational gain.

For me, true luxury can be caviar or a day with no meetings, no appointments and no schedule. **Michael Kors**

Compete. In high advocacy and low enquiry meetings, there is a sense of competition. Who can advance their point of view to the exclusion of others to win the argument? At best, a robust and bracing exercise to put an end to chatter. More typically, this is a meeting of *I win you lose*. Ego - not informed argument - drives the agenda and outcomes.

Watch out for fast talkers, people who articulately and assertively say things faster than they can be assessed as a way of pushing their agenda past other people's examination or objections. **Ray Dalio**

Explore. Low advocacy and high enquiry turns quickly into a talking shop with no motivation to reconcile different perspectives and achieve an agreed outcome. Well facilitated, however, exploration meetings ensure all views are given airtime without the pressure of defending a particular position.

Breakthrough. High advocacy and high enquiry fosters two-way communication and learning. I state my views and I inquire into yours. I invite you to state your views and you inquire into mine. It is built on active and generous listening based on an open mind to see things from others' perspectives. Run with authenticity and sincerity, an engaging encounter for all participants with the potential for breakthrough outcomes for organisational productivity and innovation.

SO WHAT?

You have a meeting to make a decision, not to decide on the question. **Bill Gates**

Bob Weir observed: *meetings can be a lot of fun or they can be frustrating*. Fun is the enjoyable experience in which a lively debate with colleagues results in conclusions that have impact. Frustrating is the scenario of a lopsided discussion. The key issues are not addressed and decisions go unmade.

Whether a meeting is fun or frustrating hinges on the balance between advocacy and enquiry.

NOTES

1. Are meetings a waste of time or necessary for growth?
https://www.businessleader.co.uk/are-meetings-a-waste-of-time-or-necessary-for-growth/

2. Given the frugality of Jeff Bezos, probably very small pizzas; https://www.independent.co.uk/life-style/billionaires-frugal-habits-jeff-bezos-warren-buffett-carlos-slim-a8174081.html

3. This was introduced in the work of Rick Ross and Charlotte Roberts in The Fifth Discipline Field Book.

Are we boring?

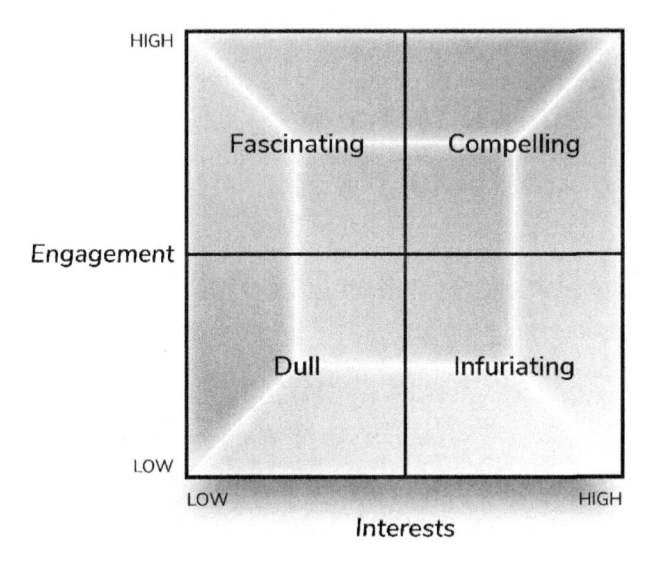

```
              HIGH
                   ┌─────────────┬─────────────┐
                   │             │             │
                   │ Fascinating │  Compelling │
                   │             │             │
 Engagement        ├─────────────┼─────────────┤
                   │             │             │
                   │    Dull     │ Infuriating │
                   │             │             │
               LOW └─────────────┴─────────────┘
                   LOW                       HIGH
                            Interests
```

When I left the dining room after sitting next to Mr. Gladstone, I thought he was the cleverest man in England. But after sitting next to Mr. Disraeli, I thought I was the cleverest woman in England. **Winston Churchill's mother**

Robert Greene points out: *bores provoke a level of rage that seems disproportionate to their offence.* Why?[1] This asks the question no one wants to answer: am I boring? It is a difficult area to confront. We accept any number of personal shortcomings in, for example, our memory or time management. The criticism of boring however stings. Why?

There are multiple factors underpinning the Boring Quotient.[2] Consistently two themes emerge from the research.

Interests. This reflects a life outlook of activities and passions to capture our attention and imagination. From the narrow and one dimensional to the broad that incorporates variety and complexity across a range of different life pursuits.

Engagement. This dimension pulls together a mix of traits, qualities and skills - our social awareness, active listening, enthusiasm and interpersonal flexibility - to gain attention. Low disengages others; they switch off rapidly. High, a connection to draw people into a conversation and the basis for a stimulating conversation.

A yawn is a silent shout. **GK Chesterton**

Four conversational patterns are identified.

Dull. A narrow set of interests in combination with low engagement is the repetition of the one thing without the self awareness to evaluate conversational impact. A monologue preoccupied with a single topic lacking humour and charm.

They're the people whose idea of human interaction seems to be turning up the volume on the monologue that's always going on in their heads. **Mark Edmundson**

Fascinating. The intersect of narrow interests and high levels of engagement. Despite, or maybe because of, the focus on a specific issue and in-depth knowledge, there is a passion to enthuse and energise others. It can be appealing. But too often the effect wears off quickly. Others lose interest in what they come to see as an obsession.

What did men get excited about before railways? **Guy Browning**

Infuriating. A broad set of interests and low levels of engagement. At best, an attempt to connect with others by exploring areas of mutual interest. It can also be a bewildering experience for others. At worst, the stereotype of the Bateman[3] golf club bore who talks with conviction about everything but knows nothing.

Perhaps the world's second worst crime is boredom. The first is being a bore. **Cecil Beaton**

Compelling. A broad span of life interests combine with a flexible interpersonal style to stimulate an interactive conversation. Here, knowledge is worn lightly to draw others into wide ranging discussions that attract and captivate. The downside: too much of a good thing can be a bad thing. Others begin to find this repertoire of interpersonal showmanship exhausting.

The nice thing about being a celebrity is that if you bore people they think it's their fault. **Henry Kissinger**

SO WHAT?

One of the chilling things in life is the realisation that you are a bore. **Guy Browning**

The tough reality is that we are all boring to some people in some encounters. But if a consistent pattern emerges over time across different situations and groups of people that we are boring, we can either dismiss the issue, or do something about it.

Perhaps the worst strategy to avoid being a bore is the attempt to be interesting. Oliver Burkeman points out: this self-centred approach makes us even more boring. Maybe the solution starts by asking others about themselves rather than talking about what is important to us. As long as they are not a bore.

NOTES

1. Mark Edmundson offers some wisdom on bores;
https://peripateticpraxis.wordpress.com/2009/09/18/mark-edmundson-offers-some-wisdomon-bores/

2. The most boring person in the world has been revealed by University of Essex research. People expect to be paid a minimum of £35 a day to spend time with them as recompense.
https://www.essex.ac.uk/news/2022/03/18/the-most-boring-person-in-the-world-discovered-by-researchers

3. The Man Who; http://www.hmbateman.com/about.htm

Why arguments rarely end well

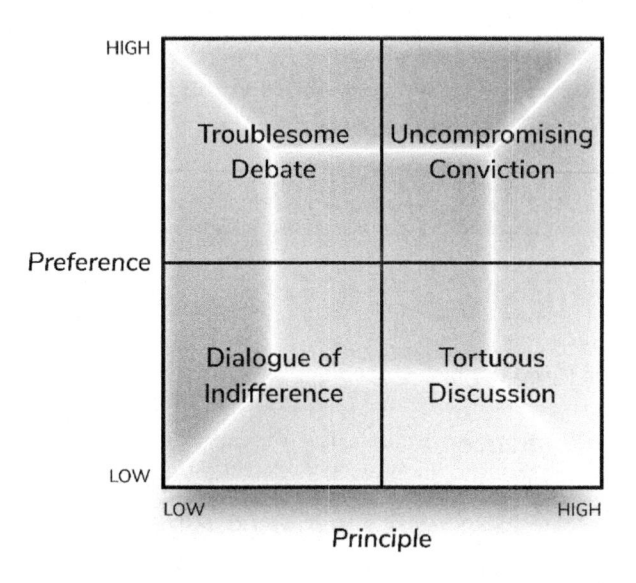

	Low Principle	High Principle
High Preference	Troublesome Debate	Uncompromising Conviction
Low Preference	Dialogue of Indifference	Tortuous Discussion

I argue very well. Ask any of my remaining friends. I can win an argument on any topic, against any opponent. People know this and steer clear of me at parties. Often, as a sign of their great respect, they don't even invite me. **Dave Barry**

We assume that arguing is a cognitive activity in which logic and reason will change minds. It misses a fundamental point. An argument is an interpersonal exchange. At one level, an argument is about rational persuasion to marshal facts and convince others that we are right and others are wrong. If we shift perspective to see an argument as a struggle for power and status, we gain a better insight into the dynamics of the process, and why there is rarely a satisfactory conclusion.

Suckers try to win arguments; non-suckers try to win. **Nassim Taleb**

This quadrant hinges on two dimensions.

Principle. The stance of rigour about an important truth.[1] At one end of the spectrum, people have no overwhelming evidence or reasoned conclusions to justify a position. At the other, convinced of the correctness of their beliefs, marshal an array of rhetorical ploys.

Preference. This dimension spans a range of feelings. At the low end, there is no emotional investment. If the argument goes badly, ego does not suffer. At the high end, a combination of personal sensibilities and feelings drive strong emotions to ensure intensity of debate.

We oftener appear to have a decided character from persistently following our temperament than from persistently following our principles. **Friedrich Nietzsche**

Four types of argument play out.

Dialogue of Indifference. Here, there is not much principle or preference to shape the conversational agenda. This is not an argument with any conviction. It is a friendly freewheeling debate. These conversations can span the trivial to the profound. But there is no *dog in the fight* - morally, intellectually or emotionally - to trigger passions. Paradoxically, these discussions are often the most interesting and illuminating encounters we experience with others.

Don't for heaven's sake, be afraid of talking nonsense! But you must pay attention to your nonsense. **Ludwig Wittgenstein**

Troublesome Debate. When principle is confused with preference there is potential to talk at cross purposes. There is more heat than light. There is in fact not much at stake. There are no fundamental differences based on coherent ethical or moral judgements. But preference overwhelms principle. The *as is* of preference becomes - in the intensity of the struggle for domination in the social encounter - the *ought to be* of principle.

Reverend Sydney Smith, while walking down the street in a residential neighbourhood, came upon two women who stood in their respective yards and howled insults at each other. They will never agree, said Smith, because they are arguing from different premises.

Tortuous Discussion. The dynamics of high principle and low preference are rare. This is the individual in a state of objective detachment who follows the rigour of their logical reasoning to maintain a distance from their personal emotions.[2] In arguments, others can find this disturbing. It is an unusual experience. As a consequence, others are bewildered and conversations can be awkward.

Uncompromising Conviction. This is a dangerous box. It moves into the territory of high principle and high preference. At best, arguments are presented to combine intellectual rigour with emotional passion. This is the rhetoric of civil rights campaigner Martin Luther King in his *I have a dream* or *I have been to mountain* speeches of the 1960s.[3] Logic is accompanied with passion for persuasive force. Alternatively, a rhetorical farce in which preference is stated as an uncompromising principle. Arguments are summoned to defend an emotional commitment. Any number of linguistic tricks can be called on to indicate the righteousness of the opinion. Rarely an argument that can be won in this interpersonal encounter.

It is easier to fight for one's principles than to live up to them. **Alfred Adler**

SO WHAT?

Never let your ego get so close to your position that when your position goes, your ego goes with it. **Colin Powell**

Most arguments cannot be won to the satisfaction of either player, in face to face encounters or in social media exchanges. Avoid them. But if an argument is unavoidable, check if the issue in dispute is principle or preference, or both.

NOTES

1. The Book of the Grotesque, Sherwood Anderson;
https://faculty.weber.edu/jyoung/English%202500/Readings%20for%20English%202500/Book%20of%20the%20Grotesque%20by%20S.pdf

2. This tactic is often sneaky and well disguised. Jordan Peterson is the maestro of this game in his pretentions to display scientific objectivity. The wagging fingers of

hyphenated commas, and his one trick pony trick to be specific, represent a failing attempt to conceal his own ideological convictions.

3. Martin Luther King and rhetoric;
https://youtu.be/Oehry1JC9Rk?si=hGaQqCMQymoucOP6

Can we improve the chances of winning an argument?

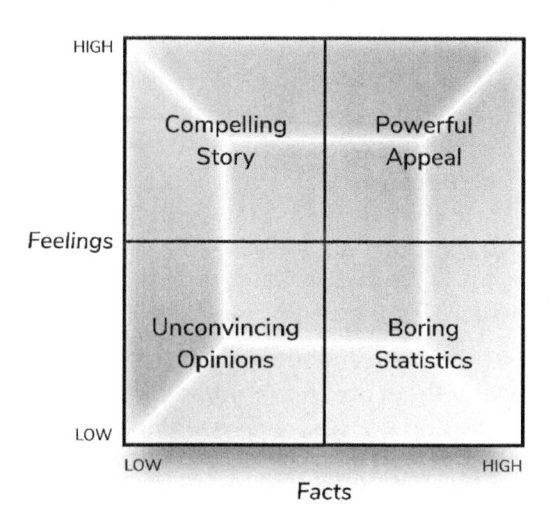

```
         HIGH
              ┌──────────────┬──────────────┐
              │              │              │
              │  Compelling  │   Powerful   │
              │    Story     │    Appeal    │
              │              │              │
   Feelings   ├──────────────┼──────────────┤
              │              │              │
              │ Unconvincing │    Boring    │
              │   Opinions   │  Statistics  │
              │              │              │
         LOW  └──────────────┴──────────────┘
               LOW                      HIGH
                         Facts
```

Here's a foolproof method for triggering a futile, frustrating argument with your partner, best friend, parent, child - anyone, really. First, make an observation that's factually correct, but implies a critical judgment. **Oliver Burkeman**[1]

Arguments rarely end well. Should we therefore abandon any attempt at persuasion? After all, in the billions of social media posts, there is no recorded instance of anyone saying: *you are completely right. I was completely wrong*. Or, should we continue to engage with others to influence discourse across a range of social, business, scientific and political affairs? Should we argue with our partner, family and friends? Is this a productive use of our time?

To understand the dynamics of an argument, two themes are relevant.

Facts. This dimension is the deployment of data to support or oppose a given opinion. Some positions lack grounding in research or objective analysis. These are expressed opinions without a coherent evidence base. At the high end, relevant data is summarised in a cogent way to work logically from premise to conclusion.

Feelings. This represents the rhetoric with emotional appeal. At one end of this range, it is the belief that facts speak for themselves, full stop. At the other, feelings provide the motivational narrative to explain and justify the righteousness of an argument.

Never call a behaviour irrational until you really know what the person is trying to do. **Rory Sutherland**

Four argumentative positions are identified.

Unconvincing Opinions. When facts and feelings are absent in a debate, this is an argument going nowhere fast. This is a series of half-baked opinions without emotional investment and a sequence of interactions to go through the motions. Players in this discussion are bored and now boring each other.

There are no uninteresting things, only uninterested people. **GK Chesterton**

Compelling Story. Facts are low but feelings are high. Emotions are deployed to advance the argument. There are any number of rhetorical tricks and tactics to dismiss the facts. After all most published research is wrong. Isn't it?[2] Emotions replace the facts to appeal to truthiness.[3] Dull statistics that can be questioned fail to engage the emotions that anecdotes evoke.

Boring Statistics. In this debating scenario, the facts are presented to explain a logical sequence. Data is intended to form robust conclusions. This is an objective and dispassionate presentation of the issues. Rarely does it work. Few people are convinced by a display of facts and figures, or even the data visualisation of a pie chart or histogram. Persuasion needs the context of a story.

Powerful Appeal. This is the argument that is convincing. When facts and feelings combine, facts provide the reassurance that the argument is solid and founded on robust evidence. Feelings resonate with the listener to connect with their own life experience. This argument makes sense at a personal level. We believe this truth.[4] At best, this is rhetoric to appeal to overcome opposition and gain support. Exercised with cynicism, it is the manipulation of both our thoughts and feelings to prop up an unsustainable position.

People are so different, so fascinating, each in his or her own specific world, waiting to crash into and effect another. Waiting to discover things about themselves, little details and preferences to build an identity out of. **Vee Hoffman**

SO WHAT?

Discussion is an exchange of knowledge; an argument an exchange of ignorance. **Robert Quillen**

Arguments are played out in a context of power dynamics and expectations of the rules of the communication game. Different rhetorical tactics are required for different occasions. But if we can't integrate both facts and feelings, we have a high chance of losing the argument.

Sean Spicer, our press secretary, gave alternative facts. **Kellyanne Conway**

NOTES

1. How to pick (and stop) an argument;
https://www.theguardian.com/lifeandstyle/2016/feb/19/how-to-pick-and-stop-an-argument-oliver-burkeman

2. Why Most Published Research Findings Are False, John Ioannidis;
https://journals.plos.org/plosmedicine/article?id=10.1371/journal.pmed.0020124
The figure of 70% is probably an overstatement, but still uncomfortably high.

3. Truthiness: a seemingly truthful quality that is claimed for something not because of supporting facts or evidence but because of a feeling that it is true or a desire for it to be true.

4. When Jon Stegner saw that his company, a manufacturer, was wasting vast sums of money, he knew he'd have to persuade his bosses to do something. Stegner asked a summer student to investigate a single item - work gloves. The eager student reported that the factories were purchasing 424 different kinds of gloves, from different suppliers and at different prices. Gloves that cost $5 at one factory were being billed at $17 in another. Stegner could have summarised the evidence in a single spreadsheet and presented his findings in a pie chart, arguing

for better purchasing cost control. Instead he collected a specimen of all 424 gloves with their price tags and piled them on the boardroom table, and invited his bosses to see them.

Can we resolve conflict?

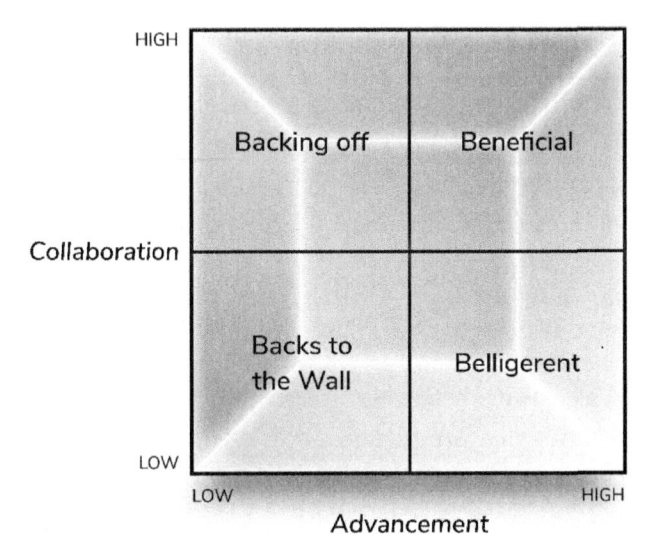

HIGH	Backing off	Beneficial
Collaboration		
LOW	Backs to the Wall	Belligerent
	LOW	HIGH
	Advancement	

In The Hunt for Red October, Ramius, the Soviet submarine captain, sees that an enemy torpedo has been fired and is heading quickly towards his sub. He orders that the sub, Red October, races directly towards the torpedo. By moving rapidly, Captain Ramius changes the target distance to disrupt the torpedo's programming. Instead of running away from the problem, Ramius' strategy of moving towards danger disarms the threat.

When we interact with people from different backgrounds with varying aspirations, experiences and aptitudes to work together, conflict is inevitable. Conflict can be constructive. It creates a dialogue in which both parties benefit. Conflict can also be a destructive force with negative consequences to create lingering resentment damaging to future relationships.

Take anything that you want but remember the bill must be paid. **Steve Gibbons Band**

Two dimensions underpin the resolution of conflict.

Advancement. Do we see conflict as a positive? At the low end of the spectrum, conflict is a hazard to be avoided at all costs. At the high end, conflict is viewed as an opportunity for future gain.

Collaboration. This identifies the level of cooperativeness deployed to overcome conflict. In low collaboration, our individual agenda furthers our ambitions or addresses our personal concerns. In high collaboration, a willingness to involve others and work towards positive outcomes for everyone.

Four modes[1] emerge from the interplay of these two themes.

Backs to the Wall. In a permutation of low advancement and low collaboration, a defensive attitude is adopted. This may be a valid response to protect our current position from others' unreasonable demands. We focus on the preservation of our present interests. At worst, the tactics of emotional immediacy to dismiss the legitimate concerns of other parties that blocks future cooperation.

A defence mechanism is a method of response intended to spare us pain; the problem is that in the act of defending ourselves in the immediate term, we harm our longer-term chances of dealing with reality.[2]

Backing Off. In low advancement and high collaboration, conflict is an intolerable experience, one in which disagreement or opposition trigger unpleasant emotions. The upside of this stance: empathy towards others' needs and a desire to accommodate their interests. The downside: in seeking happy harmony with others, we duck the difficult issues. Others' gains become our personal losses.

Try for just a single day, a whole day when you refuse to acknowledge fear of failure, fear of making yourself look like an idiot, fear of losing your lover, fear of losing your job, fear of your boss, fear of anything and of any kind. Fear will creep back, usually at three in the morning. Laugh at it and tell it to take a hike. **Felix Dennis**

Belligerent. In high advancement and low collaboration, conflict is relished. In situations of obvious inequity and injustice, this forceful and direct operating style challenges unacceptable compromises. Alternatively, this approach looks to get our retaliation in first when our personal position is threatened. An aggressive manner alienates others and undermines the possibility of a satisfactory conclusion.

Aggression is what I do. I go to war. You don't contest football matches in a reasonable state of mind. **Roy Keane, Manchester United**

Beneficial. The combination of high advancement and high collaboration is a measured response to conflict. This operating approach determines which battles are important and can be won. It avoids those which either don't matter that much or will result in defeat. The potential risk: an ambivalent stance that shifts between assertive and accommodating styles and confuses others.

The person who looks for a fight gets attention. But the one who looks for a compromise gets ahead. **Sam Rayburn**

SO WHAT?

Know when to hide, know when to run; know when to fight. **Multiplayer strategies for the Red Faction computer game**

If we aren't experiencing conflict, ask why? Maybe we are not pushing hard enough. And saying yes rather than no. Or, are we in denial to ignore the difficult issues that will escalate into a bigger set of problems?

Most people dislike conflict and will go to any lengths to avoid dealing with it. This can this work in our favour when we recognise the power dynamic is on our side. It also helps if we also know when we need to back off to wait for a more favourable time.

NOTES

1. Conflict management styles;
http://webhome.idirect.com/~kehamilt/ipsyconstyle.html

2. Anna Freud and defence mechanisms; https://www.theschooloflife.com/article/the-great-psychoanalysts-anna-freud/

What is our negotiational style?

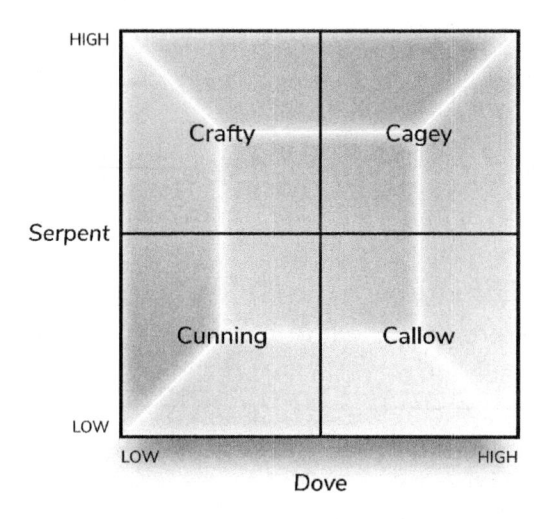

	Dove LOW	Dove HIGH
Serpent HIGH	Crafty	Cagey
Serpent LOW	Cunning	Callow

Be ye therefore wise as serpents, and harmless as doves. **Matthew 10:16**

In principle, each negotiational encounter is approached with objectivity to clarify the issues, explore the range of options and work out a solution to optimise outcomes for everyone. In practice, this is not how it works in the rough and tumble of bargaining. Instead, we and others bring a preferred style into discussions which shape the dynamic and either limit or expand our options and outcomes.

You may be deceived if you trust too much, but you will live in torment if you do not trust enough. **Frank Crane**

This quadrant is based on two dimensions of negotiation.

Dove. A starting point of harmony to establish trust. At one end of the spectrum, the naïveté to assume the best intentions of all parties to achieve a positive outcome. The other end, one of scepticism, and a default position of suspicion of others' intentions.

Serpent. This applies shrewdness to negotiation. At the low end of the range, the foolish which is badly prepared, misreads the complexities of the issues and blunders through the phases of the process. At the other, the astute who is well organised and savvy to judge the optimal tactics and juggle the art of the possible.

Now the serpent was more crafty than any of the wild animals the LORD God had made. He said to the woman, "Did God really say, 'You must not eat from any tree in the garden? **Genesis 3:1**

Four negotiational styles are identified

Cunning. The combination of low dove innocence and low serpent wisdom has the potential to duck and dive in negotiations. This is the street survival strategy to wing it to identify an edge. This expediency becomes counterproductive when confronted with an experienced negotiator in possession of the facts who applies analytical logic and flexible problem solving to the discussions.

I have a plan, sir. **Baldrick**
A cunning and subtle one? As cunning as a fox who's just been appointed Professor of Cunning at Oxford University? **Blackadder**

Crafty. Low dove innocence intersects with high serpent wisdom. This strategy takes advantage to exploit any vulnerabilities in the position of others. Crafty is well organised to put forward proposals that expose any weaknesses. It is ruthless to keep pushing to make additional demands. A crafty strategy also backfires when it presses too hard and alienates the other party.

The crafty person is always in danger; and when they think they walk in the dark, all their pretences are transparent. **John Tillotson, former Archbishop of Canterbury**

Callow. High dove innocence lacks serpent wisdom. This approach assumes positive intentions and that negotiations will be conducted in good faith. At best, discussions get off to a good start to build momentum for more extensive negotiation. This tactic fails when opposed by unsympathetic others who are uncompromising and refuse to shift from their initial demands.

Look around the table. If you don't see a sucker, get up because you're the sucker. **Amarillo Slim, poker champion**

Cagey. High dove innocence combines with high serpent wisdom. This operating style assumes positive outcomes are achievable and looks to build trust within the process. It holds back from premature commitments, and is circumspect in allowing discussions to evolve. It reframes the issues to keep the negotiation on track with the other party. Serpent wisdom has a backup position to withdraw from the discussions if good faith is not reciprocated.

Just one more thing. **Lieutenant Columbo**[1]

SO WHAT?

The single most powerful tool for winning a negotiation is the ability to get up and walk away from the table without a deal. **Paul Gauguin**

What is our fundamental approach to negotiation? The bottom line: are we innocent as doves? And as wise as serpents?

Do we have the flexibility to shift our approach contingent on the specifics of each negotiational situation we encounter?

NOTES

1. Use the Columbo Question; https://leadingstrategicinitiatives.com/2011/07/19/use-the-columbo-question-to-get-strategic-information/

Are our negotiational tactics working for us?

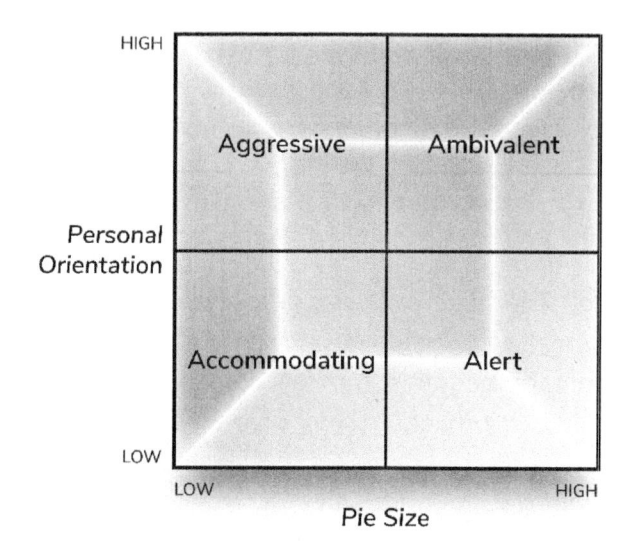

```
                    HIGH ┌─────────────┬─────────────┐
                         │             │             │
                         │  Aggressive │  Ambivalent │
                         │             │             │
              Personal   ├─────────────┼─────────────┤
            Orientation  │             │             │
                         │Accommodating│    Alert    │
                         │             │             │
                    LOW  └─────────────┴─────────────┘
                         LOW                       HIGH
                                  Pie Size
```

Nikita Khrushchev, President of the Soviet Union, attends a United Nations conference in the mid-1960s. In an apparent display of anger at U.S. policy, Khrushchev pounds the lectern with his shoe. Photographic evidence indicates that he was wearing both shoes at the time. So where did the third shoe come from?

To negotiate, you have to work on making the pie as big as possible.
Anthony Iannarino

Negotiation is a key skill that spans a spectrum of activities. From buying a car, asking the boss for a salary raise, resolving a messy divorce, through to the complexities of political diplomacy. Effectiveness and impact in this area has important life consequences.

When you are in a pie eating contest, the prize is more pie.[1]

Two dimensions apply.

Pie Size. This summarises what is at stake in the negotiation. At the low end of the spectrum, pie size is fixed. Each party must compete for the biggest slice. At the high end, the size of the pie is part of the negotiation and how it might either shrink - for example, extended discussions that are costly or expanded for greater value for all.

Personal Orientation. This highlights preferences in operating style. Cooperative is the outlook to look for mutually beneficial outcomes. Competitive, a stance motivated to win to advance personal interests.

Four negotiational patterns are highlighted.

Accommodating. The pie is fixed, and there is a cooperative willingness to agree who gets how much of this pie. At best, an acknowledgement of negotiational realities to build a long-term relationship for discussion about future pies. Alternatively, this is the acceptance of the current parameters of the situation, concedes too readily, and overlooks opportunities to rethink what is being negotiated.

Anybody who gets away with something will come back to get away with a little more. **Harold Schonberg**

Aggressive. A fixed pie and a competitive approach to push for the biggest slice. This advances an array of arguments to demand a winning personal outcome. The upside: this tactic does sometimes walk away with more pie. Probably best as a one-off negotiation. The hazard: an approach that finds itself competing for a slice of a pie that will become smaller in future.

We cannot negotiate with people who say what's mine is mine and what's yours is negotiable. **JF Kennedy**

Alert. This combines cooperation with a motivation to explore options for a larger pie. This reframes the issues to shift the stakes and optimise the size of the pie. This is negotiational versatility, responsive to others' proposals and manage the trade-offs to achieve longer-term objectives. A collaborative approach, it can also be vulnerable to an antagonistic position that focuses on immediate gains.

Grow the pie and shrink the ego. **Lex Benjamin**

Ambivalent. A competitive outlook that adopts flexible tactics to open up ways that will optimise the gains for all parties. At best, a relentless strategy to leave no stone unturned in searching for options that shift what is at stake: how to increase the size of the pie. Conversely, a demanding but confusing strategy that is viewed as equivocation and alienates the other party.

SO WHAT?

You must never try to make all the money that's in a deal. Let the other fellow make some money too because if you have a reputation for always making all the money, you won't have many deals. **John Paul Getty**

Each negotiational scenario throws up its own distinctive challenges. Any predetermined stance is high risk. A combination of preparation and flexibility optimises our negotiating position. It helps however to acknowledge our own operating preferences - our strengths and potential shortcomings - and when the size of the pie can be negotiated for greater value.[2]

NOTES

[1] Contestants must place their hands behind their backs while eating the pie. Contestants must not touch/eat any pie until the start signal is given. The first person to finish their pie will throw their hands in the air to end the contest and be declared the winner.
There is another interpretation: success at work means more work demands which in turn continues a cycle of additional work commitments.
https://douglastsoi.substack.com/p/work-is-a-pie-eating-contest

[2] Insights from Scotwork; https://www.scotwork.com/resources/

Do we present with impact?

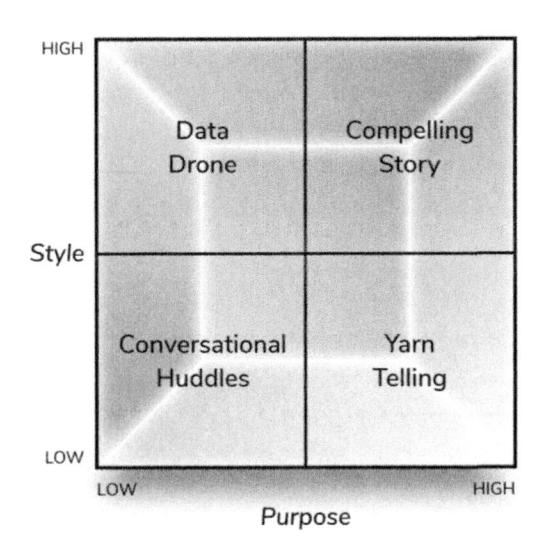

```
         HIGH
              |
              |  Data          Compelling
              |  Drone         Story
              |
    Style  ---+---------------------------
              |
              |  Conversational   Yarn
              |  Huddles          Telling
              |
         LOW  |_____
              LOW                    HIGH
                      Purpose
```

Show up early. Never apologise in the introduction. Finish early. **Edward Tufte**[1]

The anticipation of making a presentation is the stuff of a cold sweat for many. For 75% of us, it is a stressful experience. But organisational life requires us to speak to others. Even worse it requires us to attend presentations when we would prefer to be somewhere else. But speak and listen we must; a range from the cheese of David Brent type motivational speakers[2] to the dull deck of the Finance Director explaining a change in budget policy.

Your audience has got a long list of things that they'd rather be doing than listening to you. **Alex Merry**

Presentations are shaped by two dimensions.

Purpose. Is our communication now or there? At the low end, we convey key facts and figures about the current situation. High is persuasion to a point of view for the longer-term. The agenda is to appeal to hearts and minds to elicit change.

Style. This theme reflects presentational context and the expectations of the audience. Low formality is the casual approach, usually highly interactive to encourage questions and a free flow of discussion. High formality is the structured presentation to follow a corporate script and discourage questions or debate.

My best advice is to not start in PowerPoint. Presentation tools force you to think through information linearly, and you really need to start by thinking of the whole instead of the individual lines. **Nancy Duarte**

Four presentational stances emerge.

Conversational Huddles. High information and low formality. This is the team briefing to give colleagues the facts and figures to help prioritise the day, week and month based on key statistics for review and action planning. This typically combines an opportunity for questions and discissions.

Data Drone. High on information and formality, the wonk armed with a deck of numbers and histograms speeds through the session to overwhelm the audience. Few in the audience get it. And there is no opportunity for debate. Nonetheless, the objective has been achieved. A baffling array of statistics in a display of expert showmanship.

Yarn Telling. This presentational tactic is informal but motivated to persuade the audience. This is the stuff of cosy anecdotes and heart-warming case studies, but with no defined outcome. A few chuckles keep listeners engaged. This is entertainment not enlightenment. A positive experience at the time, it lacks a sustainable impact.

There's always room for a story that can transport people to another place. **JK Rowling**

Compelling Story. A presentation to combine formality with persuasion. This stance marshals the facts in a compelling way to connect to the concerns of the audience. It provides a convincing summary of the issues for action. This is rhetoric at its best.

Alternatively, an uncomfortable message that listeners are not prepared to acknowledge

Listen with your ears. Listen with your eyes. Listen with your heart. **Guy Browning**

SO WHAT?

When deciding between giving a longer or shorter presentation, pick shorter. I wish you had talked longer are six words you'll seldom hear from audiences. **Sam Harrison**

Different audiences have different expectations. Do we go with the fun of the light hearted chortle? Or face embarrassment?[3] Or are we prepared to challenge listener expectations and be challenged by the audience?

Which presentational tactics will achieve our goal?

NOTES

1. PowerPoint is the work of the devil; http://mingus.as.arizona.edu/~bjw/software/fightppt.html

2. David Brent: Motivational Speaker; https://youtu.be/mXytRC0k-K8?si=k96zddpZJgQIRR3d

3. Boris Johnson praises Peppa Pig in bizarre CBI speech; https://youtu.be/8zHURhs0DbM?si=Ly6sY3WLv4GBuXGl

Are we having a big conversation?

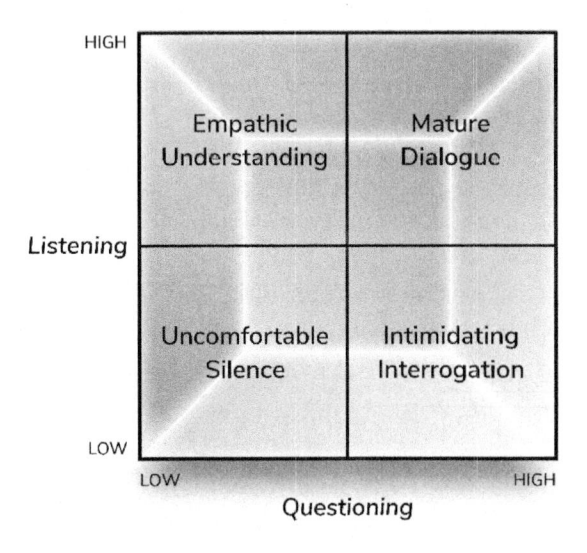

	Low Questioning	High Questioning
High Listening	Empathic Understanding	Mature Dialogue
Low Listening	Uncomfortable Silence	Intimidating Interrogation

Jazz never seems to begin or end. Jazz isn't methodical, but jazz isn't messy either. Jazz is a conversation, a give and take. Jazz is the connection and communication between musicians. **Nat Wolff**

Conversations matter. From the Board room and a discussion about strategic options to the line manager confronting the bad behaviour of a team member, through to the first night of a date. The exchange of information and opinions - and its balance - is critical to establishing a meaningful dialogue.

The question am I the best lover you have ever had is a bad question. There is only response that can make us happy. What do you like most about my love making is a good question. There is only one response that make us unhappy. **Daniel Gilbert**

In this quadrant, a big conversation hinges on two themes.

Questioning. This dimension reflects not only the quantity of questions, but the tone and style in which questioning[1] is framed. Low reflects a conversational stance that talks. High, an approach that asks.

Listening. This spans the spectrum from the rude that fails to recognise others' responses, through to that proactive approach in which others feel acknowledged and affirmed. At the low end, little is heard. At high, active and attentive listening in the moment.

If A equal success, then the formula is A equals X plus Y and Z, with X being work, Y play, and Z keeping your mouth shut. **Albert Einstein**

This maps out four conversational patterns.

Uncomfortable Silence. This interpersonal event is not a conversation. It may be the wrong people at the wrong time and in the wrong space. It is an awkward encounter between two people who fail to connect. Neither is interested in the others' views or willing to make the first move to initiate a dialogue.

I know how it is. Saying too much. Saying too little. Who says enough? Just enough? That's not what I meant - not what I meant at all. **Jeanette Winterson**

Empathic Understanding. Low questioning in combination with high listening is the conversational rhythm to allow others to express themselves fully. There is no anticipation of immediacy of response to put the other on the spot or make rapid judgements. At best, this gives others the opportunity to breathe, open up and talk freely about the issues they face and share any concerns they have. Alternatively, the caricature of the counselling style which leaves others with a sense of talking into space.[2]

I learned that you actually have more power when you shut up. **Andy Warhol**

Intimidating Interrogation. Conversation is out of kilter. One party seizes the initiative to bombard the other with a series of questions. In some interpersonal encounters, where there is an urgent need to get to the facts, a valid tactic. But in most contexts, this is a conversation moving quickly into shut down mode. Others feel on the back foot and under pressure, and trust is not established.

If you don't like what's being said, change the conversation. **Don Draper, Mad Men**

Mature Dialogue. This is conversational tennis between two equal players. One question triggers a thoughtful response which is heard and understood, which in turn leads to another question. The conversational ball goes back and forward over the net. The upside: a mutual respect between the players to build a constructive exchange to open up an informed debate. Occasionally, this balance of questioning and listening becomes a battle of competing egos. Less a game of baseline play, and more one of rhetorical serve and volley.

Knowledge speaks, but wisdom listens. **Jimi Hendrix**

SO WHAT?

Great questions are a much better indicator of future success than great answers. **Ray Dalio**

The balance of a conversation and the dynamics of questioning and listening hinge on context. The specifics of the situation - power differentials, the implicit and explicit objectives of participants, personal chemistry - shape the rules of engagement. But over repeated interactions across different situations, it is useful to check if we are listening or lecturing.

NOTES

1. 16 types of questions you need to know; https://nulab.com/learn/collaboration/the-8-essential-questioning-techniques-you-need-to-know/

2. Two psychoanalysts are walking towards each other down a street. As they approach each other, one says *Well hello.* The other replies, *Good day to you.* Both continue past each other and think to themselves: I *wonder what he meant by that?*

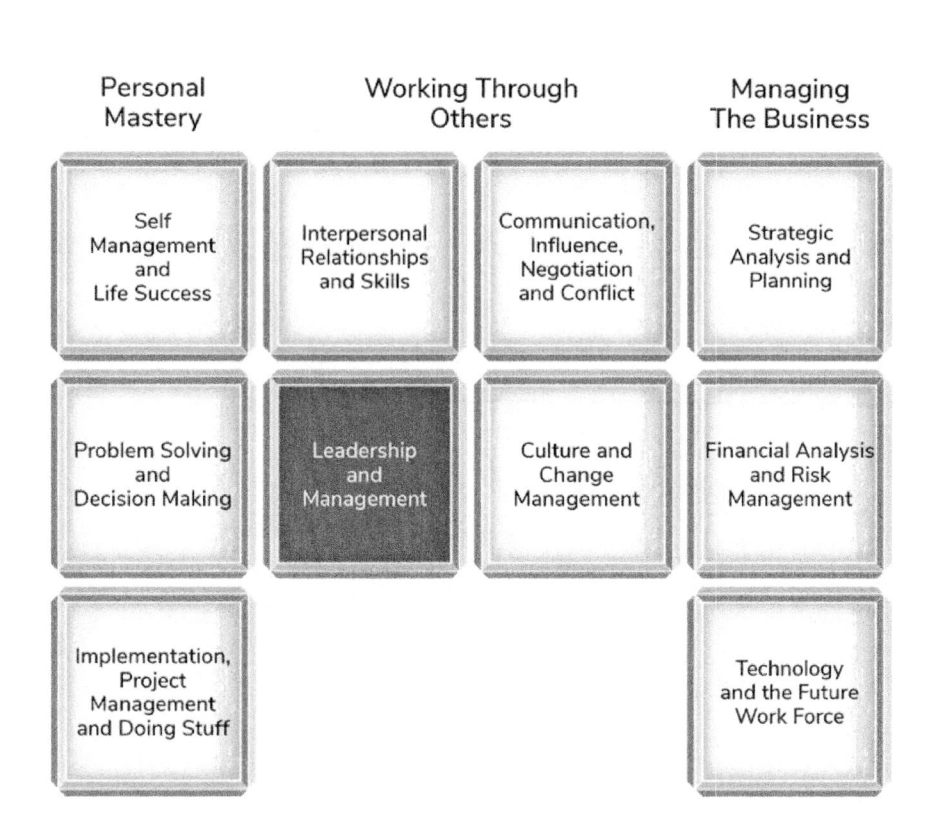

Personal Mastery	Working Through Others		Managing The Business
Self Management and Life Success	Interpersonal Relationships and Skills	Communication, Influence, Negotiation and Conflict	Strategic Analysis and Planning
Problem Solving and Decision Making	Leadership and Management	Culture and Change Management	Financial Analysis and Risk Management
Implementation, Project Management and Doing Stuff			Technology and the Future Work Force

Are we for real?

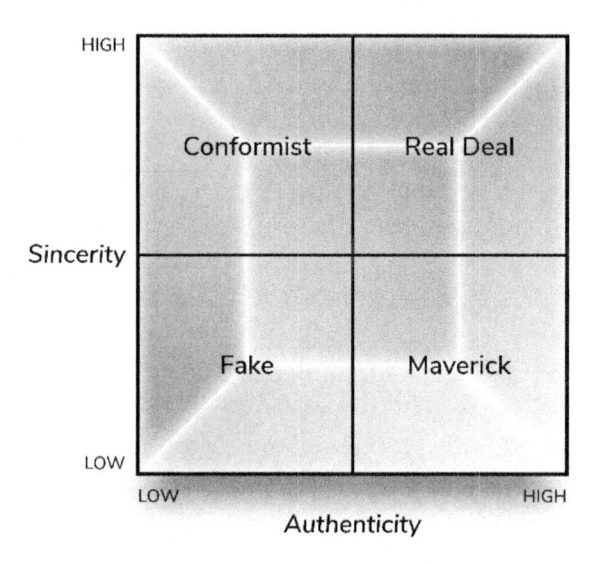

(2x2 matrix: x-axis Authenticity Low→High, y-axis Sincerity Low→High. Quadrants: Conformist (low authenticity, high sincerity), Real Deal (high authenticity, high sincerity), Fake (low authenticity, low sincerity), Maverick (high authenticity, low sincerity).)

Authenticity generally means acting in accordance with our inner selves. We're authentic when we express what we truly feel. Sincerity is about behaving in accordance with the demands of our role. We're sincere when we meet our obligations and fulfil our responsibilities. **Phil Rosenzweig**

Authenticity has become a buzz word in recent times. Brands are encouraged to be authentic. Or to rediscover something that is real if they have lost it. Or at least pretend they have it. Organisations should be authentic work places to encourage employees to bring their true selves into work. And leaders need to dig deep to find their true selves if they are to optimise their effectiveness. The problem with this emphasis: it forgets Lionel Trilling's distinction between authenticity and sincerity.[1]

Always be a first-rate version of yourself and not a second-rate version of someone else. **Judy Garland**

For Trilling, authenticity is more inward focused, a private virtue based upon staying true to oneself. In contrast, sincerity is outward focused, more public facing to reflect our behaviour towards others.

It is the balance between the inner and outer life that often creates tension in our social interactions.

Authenticity. The inner perspective of consistency of one's own beliefs and values, and a recognition of one's uniqueness as an individual without conforming to others' expectations.

Sincerity. The dimension of honesty and truthfulness in our transactions with others, without deceit or hypocrisy to operate in an open and transparent way.

Four outlooks emerge from the interplay.

Fake. Neither authentic or sincere in their interactions, these leader lack personal principle and professional responsibility. In highly politicised or corrupt environments this grouping might do well, operating on the maxim of fake it till you make it. Over time, losing touch with their own beliefs and neglectful of social obligations, these individuals move into dysfunction.

Sincerity is the key. If you can fake that, you've got it made. **George Burns**

Conformist. This leadership group lacks a clear self-identity. It looks to social conventions to provide a behavioural blueprint. At best, ego is put to one side on behalf of service to others. At worst, this is the individual without principle who follows the crowd. Without well-defined values to provide personal standards, these leaders compromise easily to accommodate others' expectations.

When you're just like everybody else, you've nothing to offer other than your conformity. **Wayne Dyer**

Maverick. High on authenticity but low on sincerity, this is an uncompromising approach. This leader remains true to their principles regardless of the social impact. At best, the organisational dissident who rejects cultural expectations and refuses to play the rules of the game. They become a creative force for disruption. Alternatively, the heretic who - by challenging current conventions -

becomes side-lined. These individuals lose credibility as serious players.

Be yourself; everyone else is already taken. **Oscar Wilde**

Real Deal. There is alignment between the inner and outer worlds. These leaders are who they seem to be. And seem to be who they really are. There is consistency between what they think, say and do. They are viewed as genuine and honest people trusted to deliver on their commitments. There is a risk that in some work environments - where pragmatic expediency takes precedence over principled action - this group becomes unpopular for the challenge it provides.

SO WHAT?

Straight up is a way of serving a drink. It is also a way to climb a mountain and of living a life. **James Ullman**

This quadrant highlights a tension in organisational life. On the one hand, the pursuit of what is personally important to us. On the other hand, a recognition of the need to fulfil several obligations.

There is no easy resolution. But as Anne Morrow Lindbergh[2] reminds us: *the most exhausting thing you can do is to be inauthentic.*

NOTES

1. Sincerity and Authenticity, Lionel Trilling; https://medium.com/adams-notebook/lionel-trilling-sincerity-and-authenticity-1972-e0934fa65aab

2. Truth is truth whoever says it. The extraordinary Anne Lindbergh; https://www.theguardian.com/news/2001/feb/10/guardianobituaries

What kind of leader do we want?

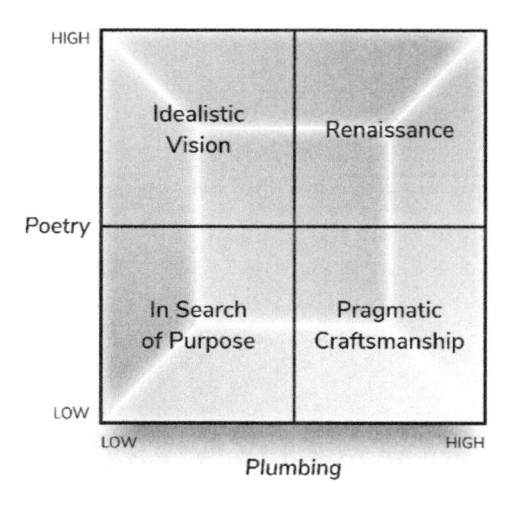

	Low Plumbing	High Plumbing
High Poetry	Idealistic Vision	Renaissance
Low Poetry	In Search of Purpose	Pragmatic Craftsmanship

I first set eyes on him in the autumn of 1983. I imagined him in lederhosen in the Black Forest with an axe over his shoulder, looking for ogres to kill. **A misty eyed Toby Young on disgraced ex UK Prime Minister, Boris Johnson**[1]

Leadership - as Jeffrey Pfeffer points out in Leadership BS - is often over-stated. The heroism of the leader is much more appealing than the routine of the manager. Peter Drucker reminds us that the distinction between leadership and management is arbitrary. Leaders must manage and managers must lead. Nonetheless, the romanticisation of leadership continues.[2]

This quadrant hinges on two dimensions which identify four leadership permutations.

Plumbing. The theme of the organisational fixer, ranging from at the low end, the hapless individual who doesn't know the difference between a business spanner and a wrench, to the skilled professional who tackles the organisational infrastructure to get things done.

Poetry. This is the deployment of language in organisational life. The spectrum runs from the inarticulate who finds it difficult to express themselves, through to the highly eloquent, whose mastery of communication is compelling and convincing.

There is something about a bureaucrat that does not like a poem. **Gore Vidal**

In Search of Purpose. When low plumbing meets low poetry, this group is pointless. It is difficult to know its organisational contribution. With little capacity to fix and a limited aptitude to express, these individuals only survive and progress thanks to the Peter Principle.[3] They are promoted to get them out of the way of those who either can do or talk.

He turned TI's low-cost policy into a fanatical obsession by building in control mechanisms that completely squashed any opportunity for individual initiative, thought, or innovation. **On Fred Bucy, Texas Instruments**

Idealistic Vision. Low plumbing and high poetry is the individual with the art of oratory to outline a future of possibilities, but with little insight into the practicalities of realising that future. The converse of Pragmatic Craftmanship, this group flourishes when the business is running well. But with a bad habit of ignoring the leak that is about to become an organisational torrent, these leaders are exposed when the pipes overflow.

Sell the sizzle and the steak.

Pragmatic Craftsmanship. High plumbing and low poetry is the set of individuals who roll up their sleeves to put in place systems and structures for future business success. They know to tackle the difficult stuff when problems emerge. But do so with a grunt. This group lacks eloquence to explain what they do and why. These individuals simply know a job has to be to be done. Highly valued when the business is flooding, these individuals are often ignored until the next round of tough challenges occur.

Renaissance. A rare combination. Very few leaders combine plumbing with poetry. This is the exceptionalism of versatility. On the one hand, these individuals display the practicality to implement a robust infrastructure of systems and processes to support the business. They know how to trouble shoot the problems which inevitably will occur. On the other hand, they demonstrate outstanding skills to articulate a compelling narrative to engage the workforce through the ups and downs of organisational life.

It can be poetry, but it also needs plumbing. **Kevin D Wilde**

SO WHAT?

The leader has to be practical and a realist, yet must talk the language of the visionary and the idealist. **Eric Hoffer**

Organisations face different challenges in the strategic cycle - from start up to expansion to turnaround to reinvention. And this requires different leadership responses. The issue in promotion and succession is to ensure breath of both leadership stances: poets and plumbers.

To paraphrase Woody Allen, *there might be a poet but trying finding a plumber on a Sunday morning.*

NOTES

1. Toby Young also described Boris Johnson as a cross between Hugh Grant and a silverback gorilla. Given his downfall and disgrace, a better image of Johnson might be a combination of Hugh Hefner and the pest of a silverfish.

2. The romanticisation of leadership; Donald Clark, Leadership and the weasel word;
http://donaldclarkplanb.blogspot.co.uk/search?q=Leadership:+the+weasel+word+that+led+to+bad+management

3. The Peter Principle; https://www.mindtools.com/as1yww0/how-to-avoid-the-pitfalls-of-the-peter-principle. A variation of this principle; Imhoff's Law: t*he organisation of any bureaucracy is very much like a septic tank. The really big chunks rise to the top.*

Why is strategic leadership so difficult?

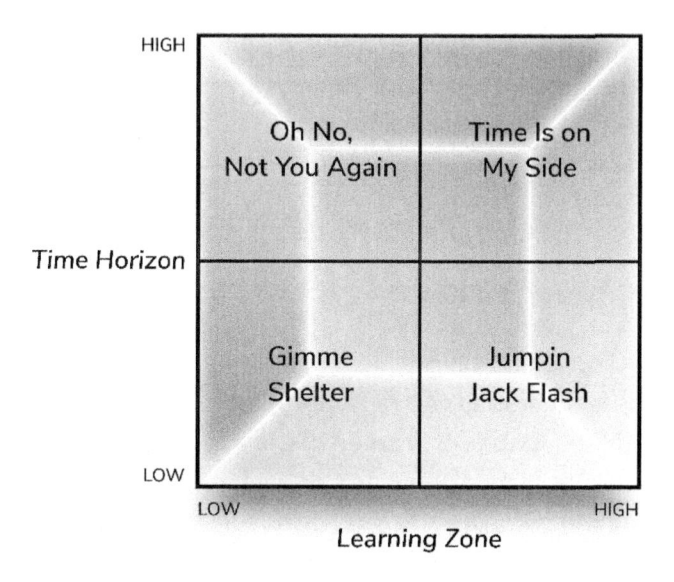

```
         HIGH
              ┌─────────────┬─────────────┐
              │             │             │
              │   Oh No,    │  Time Is on │
              │ Not You Again│   My Side   │
              │             │             │
Time Horizon  ├─────────────┼─────────────┤
              │             │             │
              │   Gimme     │   Jumpin    │
              │   Shelter   │  Jack Flash │
              │             │             │
              └─────────────┴─────────────┘
         LOW
              LOW                       HIGH
                    Learning Zone
```

Everything in strategy is very simple, but that does not mean that everything in strategy is very easy. **Karl von Clausewitz**

When Steve Jobs returned to Apple in 1997, it was on the brink of bankruptcy. He implemented a series of initiatives to revive the struggling tech giant. Through these decisions, he transformed Apple from a company on the verge of collapse[1] into one of the most valuable and influential companies in the world. His ability to operate on a multi-year time horizon to foresee and shape market trends, a commitment to innovation and quality, and a focus on customer experience, illustrate strategic leadership.

Why do many executives find strategy so difficult? This quadrant is based on two dimensions.

If the only tool you have is a hammer, you tend to see every problem as a nail. **Abraham Maslow**

Learning Zone. A willingness to face into change and challenge. At the low end of this range, it is tempting to operate within the familiarity of our comfort zone. At the other, a readiness to grapple with the different to stretch and take on novel problems and find alternative solutions.

Time Horizon. What is the time-span of the challenges we face? A short time horizon, and success or failure is determined relatively quickly. A longer time horizon creates a different set of challenges and a more complex set of problems.[2]

No two people living at the same time live in the same time. **Elliott Jaques**

Four leadership stances are identified.

Gimme Shelter. These are the business problems within our comfort zone with a short time span. At best, this optimises our impact to achieve immediate results. With experience, we establish a reputation for delivery. Alternatively, this is firefighting to reframe issues to simplify the complex and ambiguous as a set of operational problems, problems which have a bad habit of recurring.

What you find is there's never just one cockroach in the kitchen when you start looking around. **Warren Buffett**

Oh No, Not You Again. The combination of a low learning zone and long time horizon reflects the leader who excels in an unchanging business landscape. A far-sighted perspective draws on significant experience and expertise to articulate a stable and sustainable strategic outlook. At worst, a stance that assumes *what takes the hill will keep the hill* and lacks the flexibility to accommodate a different set of futures.

It is the business of the future to be dangerous. **Alfred North Whitehead**

Jumpin Jack Flash. A high learning zone intersects with a short time horizon. This is strategy motivated by personal restlessness to keep exploring new possibilities for improvement today. The upside: a questioning and challenging mind set to encourage experimentation and innovation. The downside: a haphazard approach lacking consistency around a guiding strategic purpose.

Sometimes I've believed as many as six impossible things before breakfast.
Red Queen, Through The Looking Glass

Time Is on My Side. High learning zone and high time horizon combine for the exploratory outlook motivated to take on new challenges as part of a long-term game plan. This is leadership without the burden of a dominant mind set of fixed beliefs; it questions assumptions about the future. The downside: this executive is dismissed as the dreamer of what might be, and becomes sidelined in the expediency of today's debates.

The power of replacing conventional thinking with radical rationality - and both history and happy shareholders can attest to the massive returns this approach can generate. **Brendan Mathews**

SO WHAT?

Warren Buffett observed: *someone's sitting in the shade today because someone planted a tree a long time ago.*[3]

When the dynamics of human nature and organisational incentives coincide, it is not surprising that strategic leadership is difficult. It requires a willingness to rethink current assumptions of business success and accept the uncertainty of a different future. It is often much easier to stick with what we know now rather than intentionally drive to a new future. Strategic leadership, over a longer time horizon, crafts the new, especially in times of turbulence. This requires abandoning the *tried and tested*.

NOTES

1. In an irony of business life, Bill Gates' Microsoft gave Steve Jobs a life line. Why Microsoft Saved Apple From Bankruptcy; https://medium.com/cornertechandmarketing/why-microsoft-saved-apple-from-bankruptcy-930f530c18e6#

2. Timespan of discretion is the key theme in the work of Stratified Systems Theory by Elliott Jaques; https://www.talkingaboutorganizations.com/e48/

3. New College Oxford was built in the late 14th century. In the 19th century, it became necessary to replace the giant oak beams in the ceiling of the common room. New College, worried about the lack of new oak beams, contacted the

Oxford forester to discuss the problem. The forester explained that the individual who had built the original ceiling in the 14th century had also planted the trees to replace the beams. They stood on Oxford University land waiting to be felled.

Are we in leadership flow?

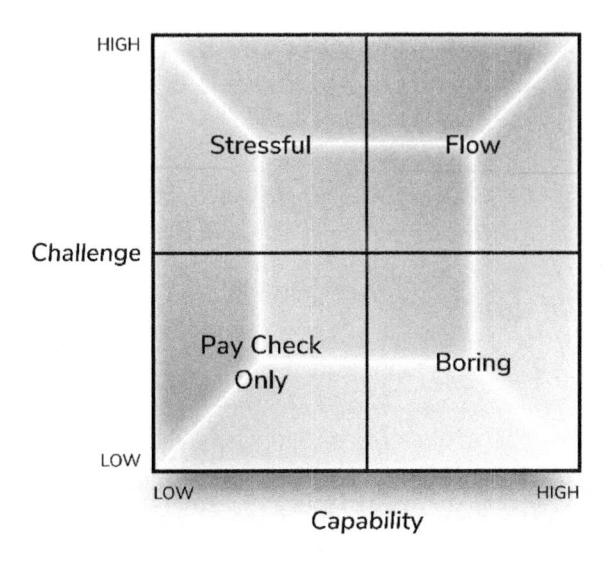

*Flow is the **Fascination** with what we're doing. Becoming **Lost** in what we're doing. At **One** with what we're doing. **Wholly** involved in the task. Flow is the time when your physical and psychological energies are caught up in the task. Flow is the moment of your optimum productivity and creativity. Learn how to find those times of flow.*[1] **Mihaly Csikszentmihalyi**

Mihaly Csikszentmihalyi outlined the concept of flow: a state in which we are fully immersed in the task at hand to experience optimal engagement and focus, often losing track of time in the process. The ego falls away. Time flies. Every thought, action, and movement follows from the previous one - like playing jazz.[2]

It is impossible to enjoy a tennis game, a book, or a conversation unless attention is fully concentrated on the activity. **Mihaly Csikszentmihalyi**

Two dimensions are key to understanding the flow experience.

Capability. This summarises the talents and skills we bring to a situation. Low capability and we feel overwhelmed and out of our depth. High at the other end of the spectrum deploys a range of cognitive and emotional skills, and we feel in control.[3]

Challenge. This reflects the complexity of the task and the time for a successful outcome. Low challenge is simple and straightforward. High challenge, a demanding and difficult set of problems only overcome over an extended period.

Research has shown that capability grows over time. As individuals we all do our best to go with the grain of that growth, to find challenges that stretch but do not over or underwhelm us; that are just right for us at each stage of our growth. **Gillian Stamp**

Four scenarios emerge.

Pay Check Only. Capability and challenge are both low. Tasks are neither difficult or stimulating. They can be completed on autopilot without mindful attention. This is leadership reality; some tasks are effortless and don't engage. Problems emerge when we adopt this default position for more demanding tasks.

Stressful. Challenge is high but capability is low. This is an inevitable part of a transition, from first line leadership to take on increasing responsibilities to progress through organisational levels and face tougher problems. However, when this pattern recurs over time, it becomes a difficult experience, personally and with negative consequences for the organisation.

Boring. Capability is high but challenge is low. This is leadership life that might be efficient in the short term. The lack of challenge however fails to encourage personal development and growth for the long term. This is leadership that coasts. The hazard here is that team members of this leader also begin to disengage.

Is life not a thousand times too short for us to bore ourselves? **Friedrich Nietzsche**

Flow. Both capability and challenge are matched. This is the leader immersed in a task to draw on a range of skills to meet the demands they face. Challenge builds capability for engagement for heightened levels of future performance.

Greatness is in many of us, but only if we rise to the demands of life. Greatness arises only when tested. **Will Durant**

SO WHAT?

Got my mojo working. **Muddy Waters**

Flow is an unrealistic expectation for all leadership tasks. Some stuff simply needs to be done without any anticipation of engaging fulfilment.

But if we find ourselves rarely in flow, we might ask if we are in the wrong role and need to rethink how to recraft our roles for greater engagement.[4]

NOTES

1. How Coaching Creates Creative Flow;
http://www.wishfulthinking.co.uk/blog/2006/04/26/how-coaching-creates-creative-flow/

2. Charlie Parker and Coleman Hawkins 1950;
https://youtu.be/stpH4ywM0R8?si=nzp2YHP6CSNmkC5t

3. Elliott Jaques argues that cognitive complexity is required to match the complexity of the task at hand, and highlights the importance of timespan of discretion. This is the maximum length of time before the results of one's decisions and actions can be evaluated. Time Span of Discretion and Scope of Complexity;
https://www.linkedin.com/pulse/time-span-discretion-scope-complexity-ruth-malan/

4. Recrafting Work: A Model for Workplace Engagement and Meaning;
https://core.ac.uk/download/pdf/214132575.pdf

Who is in our team?

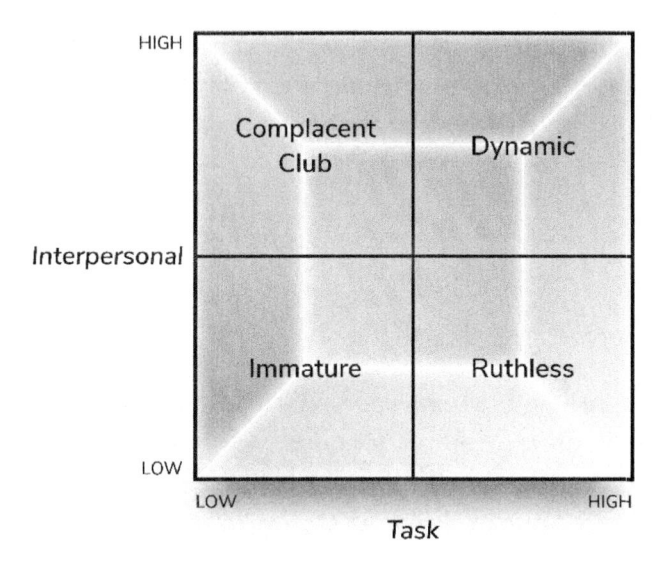

Interpersonal HIGH	Complacent Club	Dynamic
LOW	Immature	Ruthless
	LOW — Task — HIGH	

The leaders who work most effectively, it seems to me, never say I. And that's not because they have trained themselves not to say I. They don't think I. They think we. They think team. This is what creates trust, what enables you to get the task done. **Peter Drucker**

Or, as David Brent of The Office observed: *there may be no I in team, but there's a ME if you look hard enough.*

There has been a shift from personal heroics to recognise the dynamics of a collective effort and the impact of a well-functioning team. Globally, billions are now spent on a range of team assessment and development activities, the gamut of the personality typing of colour profiling systems[1] through to the heartiness of outward bound type adventures. The evidence is mixed about the business impact of these different interventions. Nonetheless, effective teams matter.[2]

This quadrant is based on the two dimensions of task and people.

Task. This reflects the extent to which a team understands its purpose and positioning within the organisation, and is equipped with the resource and skills to undertake its challenges, a spectrum from the clueless through to the focused.

Interpersonal. The dynamic of trust to draw on a shared understanding of individual differences, the contribution of different personalities and the proactive management of diversity within the team. This ranges from the highly toxic team to a set of constructive relationships within the group and with other work areas.

The secret of managing is to keep the guys who hate you away from the guys who are undecided. **Charles Stengel**

Four team archetypes emerge.

Immature. Low task and low interpersonal is the scenario of a team as a work in progress, getting to grips with its role within the organisation and finding its feet to work out the rules of engagement. Alternatively, the vicious cycle in which unpleasant team members cannot get along and whose bad behaviour constrains team impact, which leads to frustration from its stakeholders.

Complacent Club. Team members operate in happy harmony enjoying the interactions within the work group but lack a task focus. It may also be a team detached from business reality. Its lack of consistent delivery comes under increasing criticism from key stakeholders.

When a great team loses through complacency, it will constantly search for new and more intricate explanations to explain away defeat. After a while it becomes more innovative in thinking up how to lose than thinking up how to win. **Pat Riley**

Ruthless. When a team attends to the dimension of task but neglects the interpersonal dynamic, the work group focuses on short-term results. At times, this may be inevitable: a necessary response to turn around a team that is in trouble. Sometimes teams face immediate challenges and social niceties are put to one side to deal with a crisis. However, if a habitual pattern, this is the trajectory of team dysfunction and a decline in future business results.

Bring me the liver of that asshole. I will eat it for breakfast. **Leo Apotheker, former CEO HP[3]**

Dynamic. When the themes of high task and high interpersonal intersect, this is growth to move into the virtuous spiral of an improvement in business outcomes that in turn inspires further team development and group cohesion for greater effectiveness. The hazard here is team retention to ensure an increasingly confident and capable group of team members are rewarded - individually and collectively for its achievements.

It is amazing what you can accomplish if you do not care who gets the credit. **Harry S Truman**

SO WHAT?

There is an ongoing tension within any team that reflects competing forces: team member happiness vs stakeholder demands, support versus challenge, immediate results versus sustainable impact.

As a leader, if we are not managing both the task and interpersonal aspects of the team, we are not leading.

NOTES

1. The 5 phases of personality profiling in team development: 1. 95% of the time the team leader is a Fiery Red who now expects the other colours within the team to accept their flaws. The one Green Earth feels isolated. 2. A trust building game that manages to achieve the opposite when the Sunshine Yellow gets distracted and the Cool Blue lands badly and hurts himself. 3. The cheery exercise involving abseiling in which bonding between members is mandatory. Any criticism of this activity by the Earth Greens to indicate the risks for team members with a disability is viewed as not in the spirit of the event. 4. After dinner, the Cool Blues and Earth Greens head off to bed early, leaving the Fiery Reds and Sunshine Yellows to argue in the bar. 5. Back to work and unresolved conflicts of power, status and rewards continue.

2. High-performing Teams: An Evidence Review; https://www.cipd.org/globalassets/media/knowledge/knowledge-hub/evidence-reviews/2023-pdfs/8388-high-performing-teams-scientific-summary-may23.pdf

3. Like Dick Fuld of Lehman Brothers - *when I find a short-seller, I want to tear his heart out and eat it before his eyes while he's still alive* -this outlook seems predictive of business decline.

Are we at risk of group think?

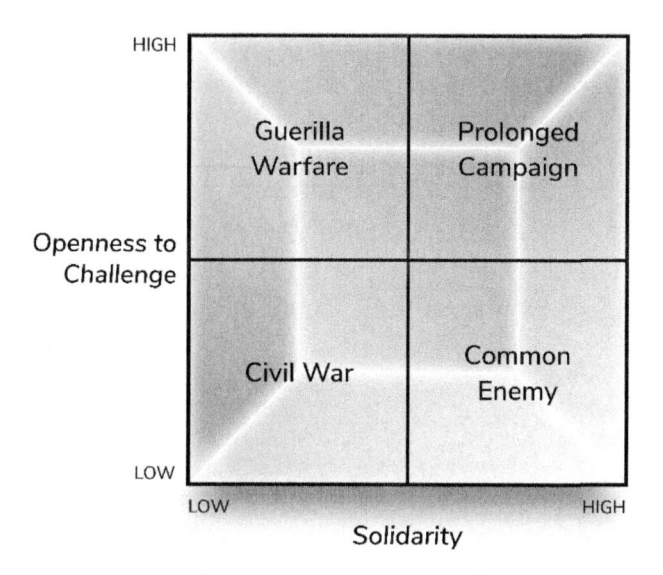

	Low Solidarity	High Solidarity
High Openness to Challenge	Guerilla Warfare	Prolonged Campaign
Low Openness to Challenge	Civil War	Common Enemy

How pleasant is the sound of even bad music and bad motives when we are setting out to march against an enemy. **Friedrich Nietzsche**

In 1961, the U.S. government planned to invade Cuba to overthrow the revolutionary Fidel Castro. Despite concerns, President Kennedy and his team of advisors proceeded. The pressure to maintain unity among the advisors led to an inadequate evaluation of potential problems and alternatives. Critical viewpoints were suppressed. Dissenting opinions were discouraged or were outright ignored. The botched result - the Bay of Pigs fiasco - became a significant embarrassment for the U.S. government. JF Kennedy asked: *how could we have been so stupid?*[1]

The main misfortune was the loss of confidence in the value of one's own opinion. People imagined that it was out of date to follow their own moral sense, that they must all sing in chorus. **Doctor Zhivago, Boris Pasternak**

This quadrant is based on two dimensions of how teams think.

Solidarity. The theme of alignment within a group. In low solidarity, a divergence of views and perspectives lacks consensus amongst participants. In high solidarity, agreement around key assumptions and beliefs, and a motivation to maintain harmony for camaraderie.[2]

Openness to Challenge. To what extent is the work group isolated from business realities, or willing to accept feedback about the problems it needs to address? In low openness, a team becomes detached from organisational imperatives. At the high end, the group encourages honesty to discuss the difficulties it faces.

Beware of group think: the fact that no one seems concerned doesn't mean nothing is wrong. **Ray Dalio**

Four patterns within work groups emerge.

Civil War. In a scenario of low solidarity and low openness, the team is at war with itself. There is a lack of interpersonal trust which cannot even agree on the challenges that need to be addressed, never mind how to resolve contentious issues. Over time, a victor within the work group might finally emerge after much attrition. But it is unclear what has been won.

Guerilla Warfare. A team which combines low solidarity and high openness. This is leadership expediency to address with candour the issues facing the business; a pragmatism to get on top of problems. No social niceties are asked for or expected. The risk: a mercenary attitude to organisational effectiveness in which low levels of interpersonal trust trigger political gamesmanship.

The opposite of groupthink - rancour and dysfunction - is also a danger. Team members must disagree without being disagreeable. **Philip Tetlock, Superforecasting**

Common Enemy. When high solidarity meets low openness, the group comes together to face an agreed threat. At best, this engages energy to direct and coordinate effort to overcome an immediate challenge. Conversely, this is leadership within a delusional team, fighting the wrong battle at the wrong time. Even more risky, the illusion of invulnerability with the confidence to take on future wars.

The war, therefore if we judge it by the standards of previous wars, is merely an imposture. **George Orwell**

Prolonged Campaign. In business there is no final victory. Instead there is a series of battles to be fought. In this permutation of high solidarity and high openness, there is a shared understanding of problems. At best, an executive commitment to work together through *fire and rain* as part of a guiding purpose. At worst, battle fatigue sets in and leaders become exhausted by the need to fight another day.

Coming together is a beginning. Staying together is progress. Working together is success. **Henry Ford**

SO WHAT?

Solidarity is great for a group that needs to work in unison or march into battle. Solidarity engenders trust, teamwork, and mutual aid. But it can also foster group think, orthodoxy, and a paralysing fear of challenging the collective. Solidarity can interfere with a group's efforts to find the truth. **Greg Lukianoff and Jonathan Haidt**

If everyone agrees with our views, we are in leadership trouble. Wise leaders encourage debate and challenge within the team to ensure different views are heard and worked through.

Or adopt the strategy of Samuel Goldwyn: *I don't want any yes-men around me. I want everybody to tell me the truth even if it costs them their jobs.*

NOTES

1. Less group think and more politico think; The group think myth and the real reasons many teams make bad decisions; https://powerofus.substack.com/p/the-groupthink-myth-and-the-real

2. James Montier highlights the eight symptoms of group think: An illusion of invulnerability and an excessive optimism that encourages taking extreme risks. Collective rationalisation. Members of the group discount warnings and do not reconsider their assumptions. Belief in inherent morality. Members believe in the rightness of their cause and ignore the ethical or moral consequences of their decisions. Stereotyped views of out-groups. Direct pressure on dissenters. Members are under pressure not to express arguments against any of the group's views. Self-censorship. Doubts and deviations from the perceived group consensus are not expressed. Illusion of unanimity. The majority view and judgments are assumed to be unanimous. Mind guards are appointed. Members protect the group and the leader from information that is problematic or contradictory to the group's cohesiveness, view, and/or decisions.

How do we gain promotion?

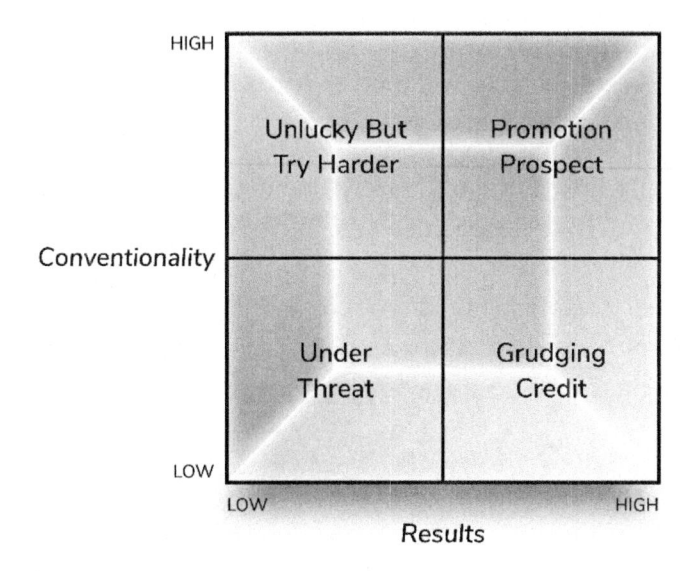

	Low Results	High Results
High Conventionality	Unlucky But Try Harder	Promotion Prospect
Low Conventionality	Under Threat	Grudging Credit

Although you may think that people instinctively want to make the best possible decision, there is a stronger force that animates business decision-making: the desire not to get blamed or fired. **Rory Sutherland**[1]

It is appraisal time. Our line manager has been mandated to conduct a formal review of our performance over the last twelve months. We anticipate this will be an uncomfortable conversation, for us personally as well as for the manager.[2] We also plan to raise the issue of a salary raise and discuss our prospects for promotion.

This quadrant adapts Rory Sutherland's framework to outline the two themes that underpin a performance and/or talent conversation.

Results. Has the individual delivered against their objectives? An extremely fuzzy area that in part explains the awkwardness of the discussion. The causes and consequences of performance are vague. At one end of the range, a perception of failure. At the other, of success.

Conventionality. This describes the extent to which an employee complies with cultural expectations. At the low end of the spectrum, the independent maverick. At the conventional end, the highly socialised employee who fits in extremely well to conform to organisational norms.

Four conversational outcomes are played out.

Under Threat. This performance review combines low results with unconventionality. The employee has not delivered and their operating style is viewed as unhelpful, if not extremely disruptive. Attention is given to an action plan to turn around the situation with the prospect of dismissal. Conversely, this is the challenging employee who has failed because of a lack of management support.

It is much easier to be fired for being illogical than it is for being unimaginative. **Rory Sutherland**

Unlucky But Try Harder. Low results and high conventionality coincide for an expression of management regret and sympathy. This is the loyal employee who has done their best in the face of difficult circumstances, but been unable to deliver on agreed commitments. Or, often the ally of the manager who has avoided any confrontation over misguided plans for the business area.

Big companies have procedures that make it nearly impossible to fire anybody. If you have no career ambition and no pride you can take great advantage of this situation. **Dilbert, Scott Adams**

Grudging Credit. In this performance review, we encounter the employee of low conventionality who succeeds. This places the appraising manager in a difficult position. An awkward and disliked team member has delivered on their objectives. The response: modest praise through gritted teeth.

It is safer to be criticised for not doing anything, than it is to blamed for doing something badly. **Philander Chase Johnson**

Promotion Prospect. In this scenario, results have been achieved through the conventionality of an acceptance of the corporate norms. For the line manager, a refreshing break from the conversations in the other three boxes. The individual is given the nod and the wink that their job will be safe in the event of another restructure. There is every possibility of future advancement. Alternatively, longer-term - this conversation repeated throughout an organisation - results in a talent pipeline that lacks diversity.

SO WHAT?

I didn't get where I am today without knowing God moves in mysterious ways.
CJ, The Fall and Rise of Reginald Perrin[3]

When the outcomes of organisational success are difficult to evaluate objectively, managers are forced to rely on inputs.[4] And a key input is the extent to which the *face fits*. This is an obvious business hazard. When any challenge to the prevailing norms is fired or sidelined from future advancement, complacency to protect the status quo becomes the dynamic of decline.

NOTES

1. Alchemy, Rory Sutherland

2. Big Keith's Appraisal; https://youtu.be/IkYUDQCYGHA?si=0dI3UEJPqKnC7rat

3. I didn't get where I am. The Fall and Rise of Reggie Perrin; https://www.youtube.com/watch?v=drlPblWAz-E

4. An alternative. Randomness. *Kelvin MacKenzie, ex editor of The Sun and of LiveTV hit on a ruse for cutting costs and amusing himself at the same time. He would walk in to the studio or production gallery and fire someone at random. If this summary loss of personnel did not appear to affect the live broadcast happening at the time, he'd regard the financial saving as well made.*

Who should we promote?

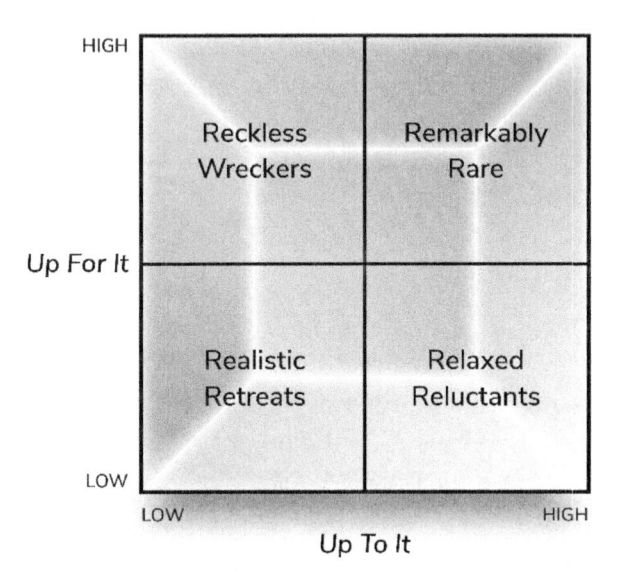

	LOW (Up To It)	HIGH (Up To It)
HIGH (Up For It)	Reckless Wreckers	Remarkably Rare
LOW (Up For It)	Realistic Retreats	Relaxed Reluctants

One reason so many employees are incompetent is that the skills required to get a job often have nothing to do with what is required to do the job itself.
Laurence J. Peter[1]

Professor Adrian Furnham at University College London observes that when an organisation addresses the issue of succession to review the choice of candidates and who might be in the running for progression to more senior roles, it faces two questions: a*re they up to it and are they are up **for** it?*[2]

Sociopaths, in their own best interests, knowingly promote over-performing losers into middle-management, groom under-performing losers into sociopaths, and leave the average bare-minimum effort losers to fend for themselves.
Venkatesh Rao[3]

This quadrant identifies the interplay of these two questions.

Up To It. This summarises a mix of capability and character indicative of an individual well equipped for greater responsibility in future. Low, and the absence of the qualities for advancement. High, the experience and skill set to progress further.

Up For It. The theme of ambition to aspire to greater status and power. Low represents a lack of career motivation to take on greater responsibility. High, the desire to move through the levels of the organisational hierarchy.

Some are born mediocre, some may achieve mediocrity, and some have mediocrity thrust upon them. With Major Major it had been all three. **Joseph Heller, Catch 22**

Four promotion prospects are identified.

Realistic Retreats. This grouping recognises its limitations and accepts it has reached its level in the organisational hierarchy. These individuals understand the Peter Principle and have no aspirations to progress. Instead, the focus: to deliver on commitments at the current level. Often neglected, these individuals put in an organisational shift without making too much fuss about it.

The very substance of the ambitious is merely the shadow of a dream. **William Shakespeare**

Reckless Wreckers. High ambition but low capability to progress is a damaging combination. It is the candidate whose enthusiasm and energy helps make them look and sound the part. It is also the lack of talent to deliver on the promise of the career sales pitch. For organisations lacking an objective and systematic system for performance and talent reviews, these individuals progress quickly. And are eventually exposed as over-promoted and damaging to the business.

Wrecker: I'm fine. It'll take more than a blaster shot to take me down.
Echo: You were down.
Wrecker: Yeah, well, not for long. **Star Wars**

Relaxed Reluctants. For those who are up to it but not up for it, the focus is on performance and contribution right now. This group is not distracted by the dreams of what might be in the next promotion. Often neglected in succession reviews, these individuals refuse to participate in the corporate games of impression management and political manoeuvres.

Bill Tindall had had years of management experience. One engineer who worked for him said that Tindall liked remaining the deputy in the divisions where he worked because it gave him more actual ability to get things done, more manoeuvring room, and considerably less bureaucratic hassle. **The Man Who Saved Apollo**[4]

Remarkably Rare. When up to it and up for it coincide, this is the succession candidate whose talents have made a significant business impact with indicators of a further contribution to be made in future. These individuals are motivated to progress to take on larger responsibilities and have greater organisational influence. Highly valuable, but not always valued, these exceptional individuals often become the focus of peer rivalry which looks to undermine their position and future advancement.

SO WHAT?

Keep your shoulder to the wheel, your nose to the grindstone, your ear to the ground, and your hands to yourself. And if you can get a damn thing done in that position, please let me know how you did it. **Marcel Rocca**

Succession planning and career development should be two sides of a coin. Those up **to** it and those up **for** it could be expected to represent the emerging generation of professionals and leaders for key appointments. Instead, the up for it factor often runs ahead of the evaluation of up to it. When organisations reward self-serving advancement rather than those who could make a bigger business contribution, the outcome is predictable.

There is an alternative; we rely on random promotion. And even better, we randomly choose the people who will make the promotion decisions.[5]

NOTES

1. The Peter Principle. In a hierarchy, every employee tends to rise to his level of incompetence. Peter goes on to ask: *Sometimes I wonder whether the world is being run by smart people who are putting us on or by imbeciles who really mean it.* The Lateral Arabesque is a variation of the Peter Principle: the pseudo promotion in which the incompetent person is not raised in rank but given a longer job title and a new office in a remote part of the building.

2. Talent review: the mysterious meeting where all the managers lock themselves in a room and talk about you; A Little Less Plotting And A Lot More Conversation Please: 9 Tactics for Talent Reviews with Business Impact; https://talentworldconsulting.com/wp-content/uploads/2023/08/A-Little-Less-Plotting-Talent-Reviews.pdf

3. The Gervais Principle, Or The Office According to The Office; https://www.ribbonfarm.com/2009/10/07/the-gervais-principle-or-the-office-according-to-the-office/

4. The opposite of the Peter Principle; https://www.johndcook.com/blog/2020/06/07/opposite-peter-principle/

5. Random promotion may be best, research suggests; https://www.theguardian.com/education/2010/nov/01/random-promotion-research

Who should we demote?

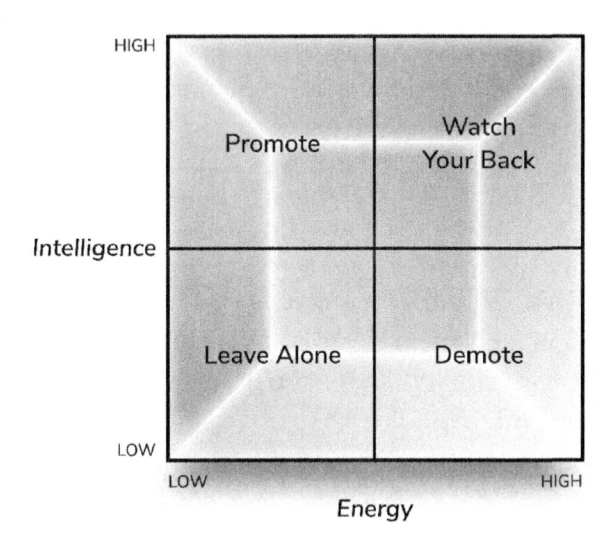

```
         HIGH
              ┌──────────────┬──────────────┐
              │              │    Watch     │
              │   Promote    │   Your Back  │
              │              │              │
Intelligence  ├──────────────┼──────────────┤
              │              │              │
              │  Leave Alone │    Demote    │
              │              │              │
         LOW  └──────────────┴──────────────┘
              LOW                        HIGH
                         Energy
```

Whoever is stupid and industrious must be got rid of, for they are too dangerous. **General Kurt von Hammerstein-Equord**[1]

Career development and succession management largely operate on the assumption of onwards and upwards. In a distant corporate past, dead man's shoes[2] was the trigger for promotion. Now succession - who gets which next big job - is largely driven by organisational restructure or the domino effect of external hires.

The process finds it difficult to deal with the *mad, bad and sad* of business life, those individuals in key positions blocking the pipeline of emerging professional and management talent.

Talent is indispensable, although it is always replaceable. Just remember the simple rules concerning talent. Identify it, hire it, nurture it, reward it, protect it. And when the time comes, fire it. **Felix Dennis**[3]

Two dimensions are key to identifying problematic career patterns.

Energy. At one end of the spectrum, the grouping of the idle who in all likelihood, will never be engaged, having adopted the habit of resting before they get tired. At the other end, the eager beavers who apply themselves to each and every task with extraordinary levels of enthusiasm

Intelligence. This reflects the range of those who struggle to make sense of the world and work out what is happening, through to the informed and thoughtful who identify the issues, clarify problems and generate solutions.

This interplay highlights four kind of prospective employees.

Leave Alone. This grouping combines both low energy and intelligence. No doubt colleagues will complain about their indolence and lack of proactivity. But for the most part, these individuals do not represent a management priority. They do relatively little harm.

It will soon be difficult to put up a shelf without a degree in shelf putting up. **Tom Hodgkinson, The Idler**

Promote. These employees combine low energy and high intelligence. This is the individual without the arrogance to assume they can do everything. They delegate effectively to give team members time and space to think. A neglected grouping in classic performance potential mapping, their progression should be accelerated.[4]

You must be a lazy person if it takes you ten hours to do a day's work. What I do is get good people, and I never give them orders. **Andrew Carnegie**

Demote. High energy and low intelligence. This employee is *a menace, and must be fired at once. They create irrelevant work for everybody.* This grouping is a hazard for managers. When given scope, they are highly damaging to organisations. Unfortunately, these individuals often appear in the top right box of the typical performance potential map.

Watch Your Back. Employees of high energy and intelligence are a risk for any self-serving and ambitious line manager. At best, these employees drive performance to improve overall work effectiveness and business outcomes. Nonetheless, the hazard is that these high performers outshine the manager to become a threat to their own position.

Talent reviews. That's where you look after old friends and settle old scores. **Workshop delegate[5]**

SO WHAT?

Somebody once said that in looking for people to hire, you look for integrity, intelligence, and energy. And if you don't have the first, the other two will kill you. If you hire somebody without integrity, you really want them to be dumb and lazy. **Warren Buffett**

The Charlie Munger rule of: *avoid the stupid before starting the brilliant* applies. When an organisation fails to address the hapless and hopeless, not only is team effectiveness damaged in the short-term, longer-term, those of intelligence and energy leave.

NOTES

1. *I divide my officers into four classes as follows: the clever, the industrious, the lazy, and the stupid. Each officer always possesses two of these qualities. Those who are clever and industrious I appoint to the General Staff. Use can, under certain circumstances, be made of those who are stupid and lazy. Those who are clever and lazy qualify for the highest leadership posts. They have the requisite and the mental clarity for difficult decisions. But whoever is stupid and industrious must be got rid of, for they are too dangerous.* General Kurt von Hammerstein-Equord, 1933
The Person Who is Clever and Lazy Qualifies for the Highest Leadership Posts; https://quoteinvestigator.com/2014/02/28/clever-lazy/

2. While waiting for a dead man's shoes you could probably earn a better pair.

3. Getting fired and why an employee desk was set on fire; https://www.rightattitudes.com/2010/02/03/folklore-origin-expression-you-are-fired/

4. Acceleration: Seven principles to speed up leadership development in a tough world; https://talentworldconsulting.com/wp-content/uploads/2023/08/Acceleration-LeadershipDevelopment.pdf

5. A Little Less Plotting: 9 Tactics for Talent Reviews with Business Impact; https://talentworldconsulting.com/project/a-little-less-plotting-talent-reviews

What leadership legacy will we leave?

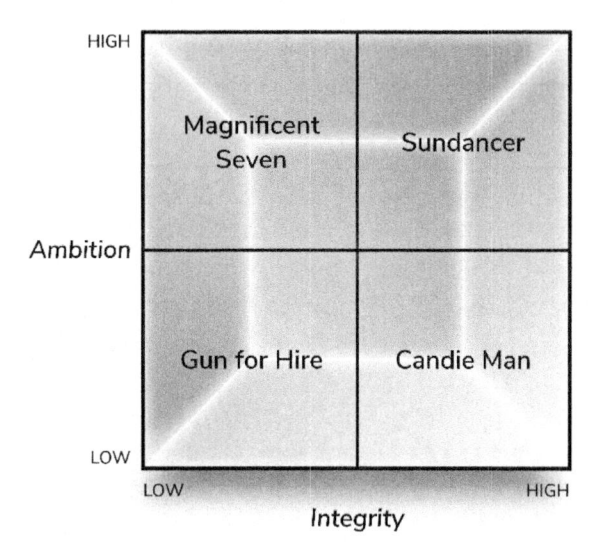

```
HIGH
        |  Magnificent  |  Sundancer   |
        |    Seven      |              |
Ambition|---------------|--------------|
        |  Gun for Hire |  Candie Man  |
        |               |              |
LOW
         LOW                      HIGH
               Integrity
```

The greatness of a person is not in how much wealth they acquire, but in their integrity and ability to affect those around them positively. **Bob Marley**

In April 2010, a blowout occurred at Deepwater Horizon, an offshore rig drilling in the Mexican Gulf. It caused an explosion that killed 11 crewmen. Horizon sank, but the well gushed at the seabed causing the largest marine oil spill in history.

The Gulf of Mexico is a very big ocean. The amount of volume of oil and dispersant we are putting into it is tiny in relation to the total water volume. **Tony Hayward, CEO, BP**[1]

A week after the explosion, Hayward asked his executive team: *what the hell did we do to deserve this?* BP ended up paying $65 billion in criminal and civil penalties, damages and cleanup costs for the largest environmental disaster in U.S. history.

The word character - kharakter - means the mark that is left on a coin during its manufacture. Character is also the mark left on you by life, and the mark we leave on life. **James Kerr, Legacy**

This quadrant is based on two dimensions of a leadership legacy.

Integrity. At the low end, the expedient willingness to say and do whatever advances our own position, regardless of truth. At the high end, consistency around key values to align our conduct with our words. This is the moral compass that results in honesty and sincerity.

Ambition. At the low end, a contentment with our current business circumstance. There is no need to push on for greater power, status, wealth or fame. At the high end, a concern that life should and can get better. There is a nagging suspicion that this is not as good as it gets, and we should be more successful.

You must own everything in your world. There is no one else to blame. **Jocko Willink, US Navy SEAL**

Four stances are identified.

Gun for Hire. When low integrity and low ambition combine, this is the drifter as the grifter. At best, this is leadership life to tackle the unpleasantness of short term business troubles, unencumbered with any sense of organisational loyalty. At worst, a cynical outlook to get by without purpose and principle.

I'll keep the money and you can have the rope. **Blondie, The Good, The Bad and the Ugly**

Magnificent Seven. Low ambition and high integrity intersect for a principled leadership outlook without interest in financial security or career progression. At best, the grouping in business life that refuses to play the conventional game and provides a refreshingly candid perspective. Alternatively, this leader may lose out in the corporate shoot out of politics.

He doesn't give a hoot about money. A man in this line of work who doesn't care about money? Men in this line of work are not all alike. Some care about nothing but money. Others, for reasons of their own, enjoy only the danger. **The Magnificent Seven**

Candie Man.[2] High ambition and low integrity combine for the leader who does whatever is needed to advance personal goals. Here there is no principle, only a competitive drive to do whatever is required to further their objectives. Much loved by firms who need a lack of scruple to take on the highly unethical, these Machiavellian leaders are unloved by their colleagues.[3]

I don't give a shit. When I'm gone they can grill me and throw the ashes where they please, say what they like. **Harold Robbins**[4]

Sundancer.[5] A combination of high ambition and high integrity: the leader who does the right thing today against a longer-term purpose for tomorrow. This is the driven individual who wants to advance, but only within their own professional and ethical imperatives. At best, highly inspirational individuals whose impact is respected and remembered. The downside: an uncomfortable grouping who face the confederacy of dunces.[6]

You know, when I was a kid, I always thought I'd grow up to be a hero. **Butch Cassidy**

SO WHAT?

When people say to me: Oh, would you rather be thought of as a funny man or a great boss? My answer is always the same: to me, they're not mutually exclusive. **David Brent, The Office**[7]

How will the world remember us as leaders? As someone who made a positive impact on others, viewed with fondness and gratitude? Or a nasty stain that was a damaging and destructive force?

NOTES

1. Tony Hayward at first insisted that BP was not at fault for the explosion on the Deepwater Horizon on 20 April and the subsequent oil spill. *Well, it wasn't our accident, but we are absolutely responsible for the oil, for cleaning it up, and that's what we intend to do.* The SODDI defence ("some other dude did it") doesn't get CEOs of major companies off the hook.

2. Candie Man in Quentin Tarantino's Django Unchained; https://youtu.be/t-Cqmgg9Dsk?si=UGDd0Jaef4cC9yEX

3. It is rumoured that when disgraced CEO Fred Goodwin left Clydesdale Bank to join the ill-fated RBS, his colleagues held a party to celebrate his departure.

4. *Harold destroyed himself, not with booze, drugs or women. He destroyed himself with success.* Harold Robbins: The Man Who Invented Sex, Andrew Wilson

5. Butch Cassidy and the Sundance Kid

6. A Confederacy of Dunces, John Kennedy Toole - taken from the quote by Jonathan Swift: When a true genius appears in the world, you may know him by this sign, that the dunces are all in confederacy against him.

7. More insights from David Brent, The Office;
https://www.radiox.co.uk/features/david-brents-funniest-quotes-from-the-office/

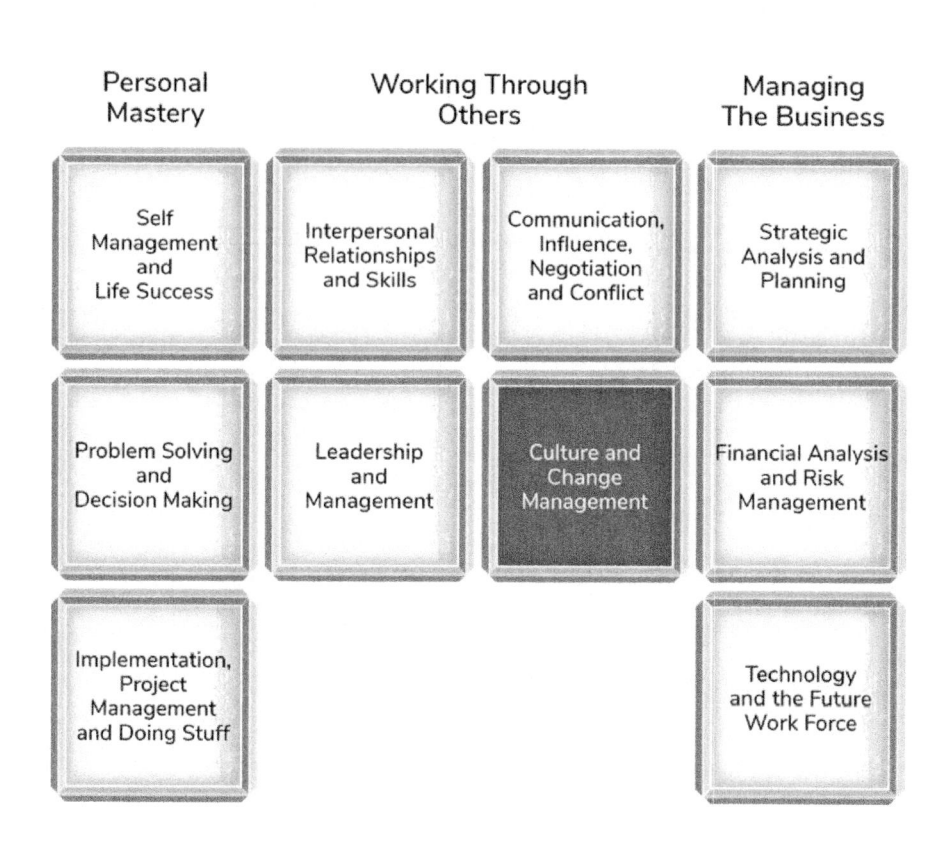

Personal Mastery	Working Through Others		Managing The Business
Self Management and Life Success	Interpersonal Relationships and Skills	Communication, Influence, Negotiation and Conflict	Strategic Analysis and Planning
Problem Solving and Decision Making	Leadership and Management	Culture and Change Management	Financial Analysis and Risk Management
Implementation, Project Management and Doing Stuff			Technology and the Future Work Force

Are the firm's values of much value?

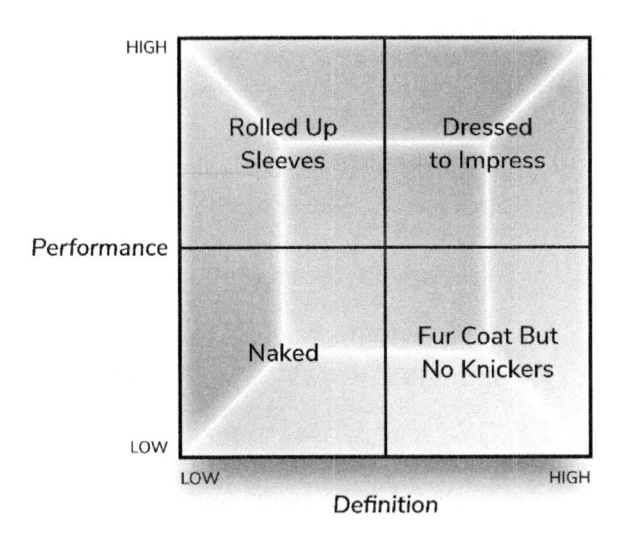

```
                HIGH
                 |
                 | Rolled Up  | Dressed
                 | Sleeves    | to Impress
                 |            |
  Performance    |------------|------------|
                 |            |
                 | Naked      | Fur Coat But
                 |            | No Knickers
                 |            |
                LOW
                   LOW              HIGH
                       Definition
```

For me the ideal number is zero. Values may be important, but they are also slippery. The minute anyone tries to write them down they become trite and unhelpful. **Lucy Kellaway, former Financial Times columnist**

How important is a corporate mission statement and defined set of values to business success? It is now a corporate mantra that an organisation must articulate its beliefs about what matters and how it intends to operate. These values are the guiding principles for strategic decisions, to shape structure and organisational design, and reinforce culture and working practices. But what if this approach adds little value?

Lucy Kellaway reviewed the values of the FTSE 100 companies. 83 had an explicit statement of values; 17 had none. Over the past 10 years she found that the 17 value-less companies had outperformed the others in the FTSE 100 Index by about 70%.[1] Why?

This quadrant is based on two dimensions.

Definition. Every organisation does have values of some sort but not all are explicit. This dimension runs from loose to tight. Loose, the company without posters and the paraphernalia of mouse mats, coffee cups, baseball caps etc. Tight, that set of values articulated in detail which become embedded within recruitment, induction and performance management processes.

Performance. This spans the spectrum from the organisations with dismal financial outcomes vis a vis those who delight their stakeholders, reflected in a permutation of share price, profitability, and positive customer and employee perceptions.

Four permutations of corporate values emerge.

Naked. The combination of loosely defined values and low performance is exposed. Some of these firms do survive and just about maintain a presence in the market place. But, as Warren Buffett pointed out: *only when the tide goes out do you discover who's been swimming naked.* These firms are highly vulnerable to adverse market conditions.

You're a mess. You've gone wrong somewhere pal. **Irvine Welsh**

Rolled Up Sleeves. Loosely defined values intersect with high levels of business performance. These firms cut to the chase to block any attempts by external public relations firm or internal corporate communications team to take control of the values with the hoopla of brand guidelines, corporate videos[2] and cheesy merchandise. It is probably this category of firms which Lucy Kellaway highlights; the minimalists who let results do the talking. When genuine values are embedded within a firm's culture, this works well. The risk is that, over time, the **what** of results and the exhortation to *just do it* takes priority over the **how** these results are achieved.

If someone goes out of their way to tell me they are honest or creative, I immediately conclude the reverse. **Lucy Kellaway**

Fur Coat But No Knickers.[3] Tightly defined values are not associated with business performance. This is a business preoccupied with impression management to look and sound the part. Or, a business that doesn't feel comfortable in its own skin. It struggles to make sense of its sense of purpose and work out the rules of engagement. Some do find this purpose. Others continue the futile exercise in search of greater precision and more effective communication tactics. Just as a frequently changing strategy is no strategy, constant revisions to values indicate an organisation without purpose.

Out of 24, only five correctly identified their company's values, and in three cases it was because they had been on the committees that drafted them. The remaining 19 each raised a hand confidently - only to pick out the wrong values. **Lucy Kellaway**

Dressed to Impress. Tightly defined values are matched with high levels of performance. For these firms, there is clarity about the what and how of business results. In a virtuous cycle, organisational success reinforces a commitment to the existing values which in turn drives further performance. Conversely, in a vicious cycle, success is largely an outcome of luck[4] that perpetuates the myth that positive outcomes are achieved - because of - rather than despite these values.

SO WHAT?

When you don't dress like everybody else, you don't have to think like everybody else. **Iris Apfel, fashion designer**

This quadrant addresses the challenge of how to communicate the rules of engagement within a company. Do we set up an internal committee or hire a consulting firm to define and articulate our values?

Maybe we simply ask our senior leaders to behave the way they do. And then after a few months: ask employees which values do they see in action?

NOTES

1. There are different interpretations of this finding. One is obvious; values don't matter. We doubt that. Our guess is that the 17 value-less companies did in fact have values. They just didn't see a need to write them down and make them part of an internal communications campaign. They just got on with the business of

business without needing to defend and promote these values. Alternatively, the firms that didn't really know their purpose felt under pressure to come up with something.

2. Oh happy day when Ernest & Young showed me the better way; https://youtu.be/Malq9o1H1yo Check out 4.09. Unfortunately, Ernest & Young forgot the first rule of hole digging. https://youtu.be/s9EyK02X2nc

3. Ilford folk call Dagenham a corned-beef city. The Dagenham East End Cockney reply: In Ilford, they're all fur coats and no drawers.

4.The Success Equation: Untangling Skill and Luck in Business, Sports, and Investing, Michael Mauboussin

How much change is possible?

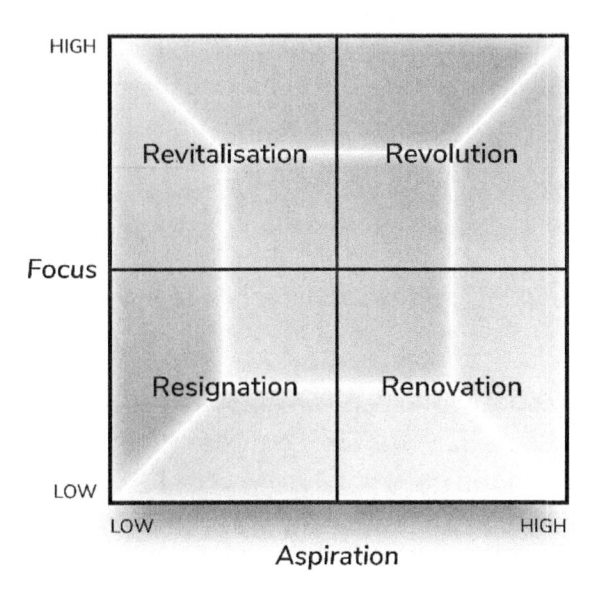

	Low Aspiration	High Aspiration
High Focus	Revitalisation	Revolution
Low Focus	Resignation	Renovation

The optimist thinks this is the best of all possible worlds. The pessimist fears it is true. **Robert Oppenheimer**

Change we are told is the only constant in VUCA world. Like the Red Queen in Alice in Wonderland: *it takes all the running you can do, to keep in the same place. If you want to get somewhere else, you must run at least twice as fast as that*, organisations must evolve to stay competitive in the market place and adapt to shifts in employee expectations. This is obvious. The fundamental issues are: how much change is possible and how is this best achieved?

If you don't like change, you're going to like irrelevance even less. **General Shinseki**

The two dimensions of this grid of change management.

Aspiration. This reflects the scope of the prospect of change. At the low end of the spectrum, there is the belief that significant change is, if not impossible, extremely difficult. At the other, the certainty that the business could be in a much better place, with the conviction that transformation is attainable.

Focus. Is this enterprise best directed at the individual? At the low end, change is achieved at a personal level. Alternatively, at the other range of this spectrum, change only happens at the macro level, one requiring a fundamental shift in strategy, structure and culture.

Everyone thinks of changing the world, but no one thinks of changing themselves. **Leo Tolstoy**

Against the interplay of these two themes, four change philosophies are identified.

Resignation. Low aspiration and an emphasis on personal change is the weary outlook that we are constrained by the limitations of human nature. And there is not much we can do about this state of affairs. This stance assumes that attempts at big change are likely to make things worse not better. At one level, a pessimism to rule out possibilities for much improvement. At another level, it is the wise caution of GK Chesterton: *don't ever take a fence down until you know the reason it was put up.*

Revitalisation. This is the language of personal empowerment and the narrative of the self-help gurus with the appeal to *awaken the giant within*. This philosophy refuses to accept that corporate life is as good as it gets. Through the power of ambitious goal setting, a positive mind-set and mindfulness, employees can become as gods for major business transformation.[1] At best, a useful reminder that most of us do not tap into the full range of our potentialities. True but trivial. At worst, quick-fix pseudo-science solutions neglect the organisational context that impacts on employee experiences and options.

We can change our lives. We can do, have, and be exactly what we wish. **Tony Robbins**[2]

Renovation. Here the focus shifts from the individual to wider structural and political factors, but is cautious in its ambitions of what can be achieved. This is change the *sensible* way, realised through incremental improvements in policies and interventions to nudge[3] the business into becoming a better place. This strategy introduces modest interventions in the expectation they will cumulate for large scale change.

A nudge is some small feature of the environment that attracts our attention and alters our behaviour. **Richard Thaler**

Revolution. The agenda is ambitious and directed at an organisational level. People of course can develop and improve, but organisations build momentum for genuine and sustainable change through a radical shift in power structures, political systems and incentive processes. Alternatively, an organisation in denial of commercial and operational realities and an appeal to a fantasy of a better future.

After the revolution you have the problem of keeping things going, of sorting out all the different views. **John Lennon**

SO WHAT?

This quadrant represents a key challenge for organisations. The track record of major scale organisational change has been dismal.[4] Why? Alternatively, Jeff Bezos of Amazon comments: *There's a question that comes up very commonly. What's going to change in the next five to ten years. But I very rarely get asked: what's not going to change in the next five to ten years?*

In planning organisational change, it is useful to ask: what outcomes can we expect? And how will these best be achieved?

NOTES

1. Sham: How the Self-Help Movement Made America Helpless, Steve Salerno; https://www.scientificamerican.com/article/sham-scam/

2. *Tony Robbins is a compulsive liar. He preys on people's emotions and through their hearts, finds his way into their wallets. He plays with people's emotions and if you ask me, that's not a good thing. It's unethical. He is a scam and his entire brand is based on lying to everyone.* https://www.gripeo.com/tony-robbins/

3. Nudge theory doesn't work after all, says new evidence review - but it could still have a future; https://theconversation.com/nudge-theory-doesnt-work-after-all-says-new-evidence-review-but-it-could-still-have-a-future-187635

4. This is debateable. Effects of Change Interventions: What Kind of Evidence Do We Really Have?
https://journals.sagepub.com/doi/abs/10.1177/0021886312473152

Are silos an inescapable fact of organisational life?

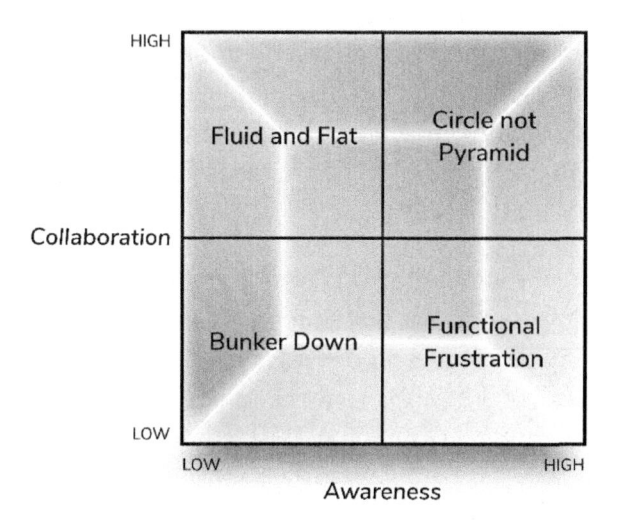

```
         Collaboration
              HIGH
              │
              │  Fluid and Flat  │  Circle not Pyramid
              │                  │
              ├──────────────────┼──────────────────
              │                  │
              │  Bunker Down     │  Functional Frustration
              │                  │
              LOW
              └──────────────────┴──────────────────
                 LOW          Awareness           HIGH
```

The word silo does not just refer to a physical structure or organisation such as a department. It can also be a state of mind. Silos exist in structures. But they exist in our minds and social groups too. Silos breed tribalism. But they can also go hand in hand with tunnel vision. **Gillian Tett**[1]

In 2014, General Motors admitted that some of its compact cars, such as the Chevrolet Cobalt and Pontiac G5, had been fitted with a faulty ignition switch, cutting the engine power and disabling the airbags. The company admitted that some engineers had been aware of this fault since 2001. They had known it would cost only 90 cents per car to fix.

Firms face a tension between specialisation and integration; how to balance access to functional expertise whilst coordinating this knowledge and skill within an overall purpose. As organisations grow, this tension becomes increasingly acute. Functional organisation brings a hierarchy of accountability based on in-depth professional know-how and capability. It can also create an environment where work areas operate in isolation. Here, there is a focus on protectionism rather than harmonising effort around overarching business goals. Add to the mix, the cost of duplication of effort, and silos become a business hazard.

There are two dimensions to silos.

Awareness. Is there an acceptance of the impact of silo structures and the thinking it creates? At one end, a departmental myopia about organisational boundaries and how they constrain the free flow of information and ideas. At the high end, a recognition that integration is a challenge to overcome.

Collaboration. This reflects the cultural mood music within the business. At the low end, there is little motivation or incentive to play nice with other departments and business areas. At the high end, a willingness to reach out and connect to other work units for constructive cooperation.

Four organisational stances can be adopted.

Bunker Down. Low awareness and low collaboration make for a defensive stance. Business areas focus on immediate functional priorities, and lack interest in the overall enterprise of the firm. This is organisational life as a battle for financial resources to protect the interests of each silo. It is also to play the blame game to point to the failings and shortcomings of other work areas to explain any reasons for under-performance.[2]

In order for collaboration to take place, managers must give up their silos and their perceptions of power. **Jane Ripley**

Fluid and Flat. Low awareness and high collaboration intersect for a more integrated approach largely through a cultural dynamic that encourages cooperation across work areas. At best, the good will of executives and managers overcomes functional barriers for more effective coordination, typically to make improvements in the customer experience. Alternatively, this is not a sustainable solution for the long-term. Organisational structures persist to reinforce silo working.

But here's the rub: looking across silos for opportunities to improve capabilities is one thing; creating a vision for how to seize those opportunities as another. Communicating that vision effectively is harder still. But the real work, the deepest work, is in the deciding to stick your neck out in the first place. **Martha Heller**

Functional Frustration. High awareness but limited collaboration is business exasperation. Executives recognise the damaging impact of silo structures, but lack processes for communication and coordination to move to joined up thinking and activity. Any desire for collaboration to resolve long-standing conflicts is undermined by cultural resistance. Incentive systems hold back progress for cross functional integration to deliver gains in productivity and innovation.

The great defect of scale, of course, which makes the game interesting. The big people don't always win, as you get big, you get the bureaucracy. And with the bureaucracy comes the territoriality - which is again grounded in human nature. **Charlie Munger**[3]

Circle not Pyramid. This is high awareness and high collaboration. Teams collaborate effectively, having recognised and understood the reasons for existing silos. This knowledge is used to shift to efficient cross-functional teamwork. It is the responsiveness to learn what works and doesn't work from other work areas and draw on processes for enhanced communication and coordination.[4]

Silos build the wall in people's minds and tie the knots in their hearts. **Pearl Zhu**

SO WHAT?

Emma wrinkled her nose. Why is it a good thing to break silos? All that happens when you break a silo is that the grain spills out. Or the missile falls over. **Frankie Bow**

There is no blueprint for a perfect organisational design.[5] Each firm experiences at different times the swing of the pendulum - from centralisation to decentralisation, of role definition from tight to loose, and of functional vs integrated structures - in the search for productivity and innovation. The challenge remains: how to achieve the gains of functional efficiency whilst coordinating activity for overall effectiveness.

There is no oven ready solution. But a good starting point is to see the issues through the eyes of the customer and their experience of service, and work backwards.[6]

NOTES

1. The Silo Effect: The Peril of Expertise and the Promise of Breaking Down Barriers, Gillian Tett

2. In 1994 Sony reorganised into eight stand-alone business units. Initially this led to cost savings and an improvement in profitability. But managers also began trying to protect their units, not just from competitors but also from other departments. Due to a silo mentality Sony's business units became less willing to share experimental ideas or rotate the brightest staff between departments. Collaboration stopped as nobody wanted to take risks. In the late 1990s when the internet began to disrupt the distribution of music each Sony department tried independently to experiment with new solutions. However, none collaborated with the Sony Music Entertainment Group (previously CBS records) because SME refused to cooperate with any department. Its officials were worried that digital music would undermine revenues from records and CDs

3. For example, engineers from very different businesses have more in common than say the marketers in their own firms.

4. The Pyramid and the Plum Tree; https://www.codecacophony.com/2020/12/the-pyramid-and-plum-tree.html

5. The first organisational chart as a work of aesthetic beauty; https://www.ribbonfarm.com/2015/05/28/the-amazing-shrinking-org-chart/

6. Breaking Down Silos To Improve The Customer Experience; https://www.forbes.com/sites/appdynamics/2019/07/02/breaking-down-silos-to-improve-the-customer-experience/

Does our culture reflect our operating model?

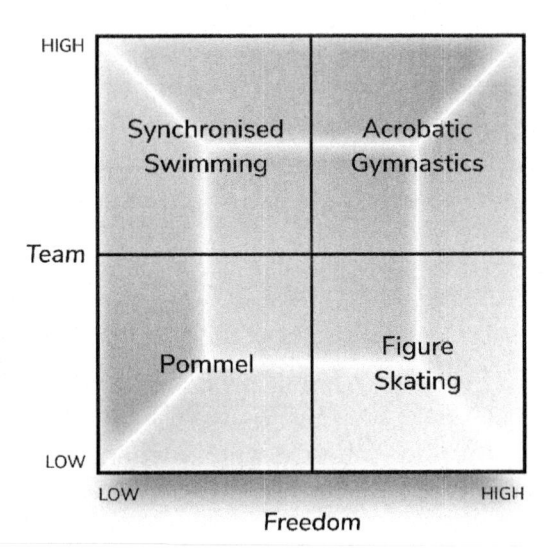

	Freedom LOW	Freedom HIGH
Team HIGH	Synchronised Swimming	Acrobatic Gymnastics
Team LOW	Pommel	Figure Skating

A hallmark of a healthy creative culture is that its people feel free to share ideas, opinions, and criticisms. Lack of candour, if unchecked, ultimately leads to dysfunctional environments. **Ed Catmull, President of Pixar**

Organisational culture is framed and defined in different ways.[1] If strategy is the compass for overall business direction, culture is the clock that ticks hour by hour and week by week. Culture is the reality as experienced by the workforce. Culture defines the rules of the game, mainly implicit. What is and isn't expected of me?

What is and isn't appropriate behaviour? What do I need to do right? What happens if I get it wrong? This quadrant summarises corporate culture against two dimensions of a business operating model.

Out there someone is working on another manual. And when I find them, I will fire them. **Bill McGowan, founder MCI**

Freedom. At the low end of this theme, employee behaviour is highly proceduralised and regulated by formal rules. At the high, freedom encourages discretion and initiative to apply judgement.

Team. To what extent are individuals and their results encouraged and rewarded? Or, is the culture reliant on a collective team enterprise in which teams cooperate not only within the work area but more widely with other departments and functions?

Google spent 2 years, millions of dollars, immense brainpower, and analytics ability to find out what makes teams successful. To their surprise, they found that who is on the team didn't matter much. What contributed to the team's success was the team culture and team norms. **Tushar Vakil**

Four cultural stereotypes emerge.

Pommel. This is the employee operating within a tightly defined system adhering to detailed policies and procedures. At best, the optimisation of personal efficiency for overall business gain. At worst, the world of Dilbert to squeeze out independent thinking and initiative.

You know you're in a bureaucracy when a hundred people who think A get together and compromise on B. **Scott Adams**

Synchronised Swimming. Culture in this scenario is based on team working around well-established structures and systems. This approach delivers the gains of collaboration within and across work groups to optimise efficiency. It also faces the hazard of groupthink in which overall effectiveness is undermined by a mindless compliance to procedure.

It was crammed with minutiae. It told operators exactly how to draw milk shakes, grill hamburgers, and fry potatoes. It specified precise cooking times for all products and temperature settings for all equipment. It fixed standard portions on every food item, down to the quarter ounce of onions and the thirty two slices per pound of cheese. **McDonald's operating manual**

Figure Skating. This box represents a culture based on individual employee discretion to apply judgement to the issues as they encounter them. This culture encourages creativity for the workforce to play *heads up*. This model also incorporates the risk of employees making commitments which cannot be met operationally and are financially damaging.

It doesn't make sense to hire smart people and then tell them what to do. We hire smart people so they can tell us what to do. **Steve Jobs**

Acrobatic Gymnastics. This is the empowerment of teams to cooperate to work out the best solution as they face new challenges - without the constraints of corporate policy and procedure. This has the potential for exceptional creativity and innovation to rethink past assumptions. It also runs the risk of going AWOL and taking the business off at a tangent.

I think the players win the championship, and the organisation has something to do with it, don't get me wrong. But don't try to put the organisation above the players. **Michael Jordan**

SO WHAT?

Over the years we learned that if we asked people to rely on logic and common sense instead of on formal policies, most of the time we would get better results, and at lower cost. **Patty McCord, Netflix**

There is no one best culture despite the attempts of the consulting thought leaders to propose best practice. Instead there is only a best fit with the organisation's business model to balance the trade-offs between efficiency today vis a vis innovation for tomorrow.

Organisations however lose the cultural plot when they misalign the business model with the messages they send to employees about working life and how incentives operate.

NOTES

1. One of the most powerful frameworks to understand organisational culture is the mapping by Matthew Stewart of his theory T and U against McGregor's Theory X and Y. https://www.strategy-business.com/article/00029

2. Google Spent Years Studying Effective Teams.; https://www.inc.com/justin-bariso/google-spent-years-studying-effective-teams-this-single-quality-contributed-most-to-their-success.html

Is the organisation inclusive?

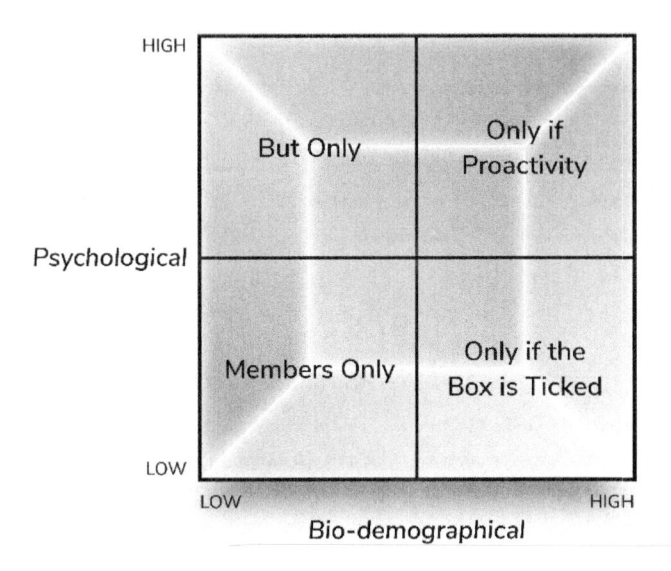

```
HIGH │                    │                    │
     │   But Only         │   Only if          │
     │                    │   Proactivity      │
Psychological ───────────────────────────────────
     │                    │                    │
     │   Members Only     │   Only if the      │
     │                    │   Box is Ticked    │
LOW  │                    │                    │
     └────────────────────┴────────────────────┘
        LOW                              HIGH
              Bio-demographical
```

Knowledge of the lifestyles and customs of specific cultural groups is helpful, but given the permutations and patterns of cultural dynamics, a better starting point may be to return to the old fashioned concept of wisdom in how we harness the gains of cultural diversity. **Professor Raman Bedi, Kings College London**

Diversity, inclusion and equity continue to be troublesome topics, caught up in competing political ideologies. The issues should be simple: progressive firms in search of the best available talent hire, retain and promote those employees who will advance their business objectives - regardless of background. The issues are anything but straightforward.

The choice is not diversity or homogeneity; the choice is between well managed diversity and badly managed diversity. **David Crawford**

Two philosophical stances are identifiable in this debate. On the one hand, diversity is a good thing - full stop. This is the social justice argument. For a range of historical and economic reasons, some groups continue to be misrepresented in the workforce of a majority of firms. And this is unfair. Another perspective proposes that diversity is just good business. An inclusive stance draws on the full range of available talent rather than limit the pool, certainly at senior levels, the typical *male, pale and stale* executive profile.

Two themes explain this confusion.

Bio-demographical. This encompasses a range of characteristics incorporating ethnicity, gender, sexual orientation, age, disability and much more. These - to simplify - are the variables that for the most part are largely fixed by the circumstances of our birth. Add intersectionality[1] to the mix, and this is a complex set of factors.

Psychological. This reflects the variation across a spectrum of cognitive, emotional and motivational factors. This is difference as diversity of personality at work within the work place.

Four approaches to diversity and inclusion are identified.

Members Only This combines low bio-demographical and low psychological diversity, an organisational stance of uniformity. These firms operate around a workforce strategy of the right type, recruited and promoted from an extremely narrow grouping to preserve the existing employee profile. Highly exclusive, this approach has the short term appeal of solidarity. Over time, a stance that relies on type rather than talent, implodes.

Uniformity is not very interesting or sustainable - it's boring. **Sasha Velour**

But Only. Combining low bio-demographical with higher levels of psychological diversity, this is the strategy often associated by so-called elite professional firms.[2] Difference can be tolerated, but only the *right* kind of difference. Variation in thinking style may be appreciated as conducive to decision making, but only if it brings in people like us, with similar social and educational backgrounds.

Diversity is being invited to the party; inclusion is being asked to dance.
Verna Myers

Only if the Box is Ticked. In this scenario, high bio-demographical diversity encounters low psychological diversity. This has the gain of building a workforce more representative of the customer base and communities in which the firm operates. At worst, it becomes the organisational culture of fear in which challenge and conflict is forbidden if there is a risk of offence from a particular grouping. This is a talent management strategy as an ideological agenda for social justice rather than working for productivity and innovation.

Much of the content of diversity training is over-reliant on pop sociology and pseudo-therapeutic techniques. **Munira Mirza**

Only if Proactivity. Diversity is difficult. For any number of psychological and social reasons, familiarity is preferable. We like those who are like us. This seems to be human nature. In this scenario, firms integrate bio-demographic and psychological diversity for a more inclusive culture. Not always an easy process, it recognises the tensions of a multicultural society - the past and present - but applies wisdom, courage and humility to work through the issues.

Diversity appears to be a double-edged sword, increasing the opportunity for creativity as well as the likelihood that group members will be dissatisfied and fail to identify with the group. **F Milliken**

SO WHAT?

Diversity enhances performance only when the group flow factors are present: shared knowledge, culture of close listening, and open communication, focus on well-defined goals, autonomy, fairness and equal participation. **Keith Sawyer**

When organisations walk on the egg shells of the complexities of diversity, fear is in the driving seat. A fear that creates a divergence between public debate and private conversations. It is damaging to working relationships of respect and honesty.

As with most things in life, a combination of humility, curiosity and courage helps navigate the issues. A difficult area. But a useful rule of thumb: anyone who has a definitive solution doesn't understand the nuanced complexity of the issues.

NOTES

1. Kimberlé Crenshaw, What is Intersectionality? https://youtu.be/ViDtnfQ9FHc?si=Z3TgHSGcArus8eLq

2. Management consulting's diversity problem; https://diversityq.com/management-consultings-diversity-problem-and-why-you-should-care/

Will this organisation change last?

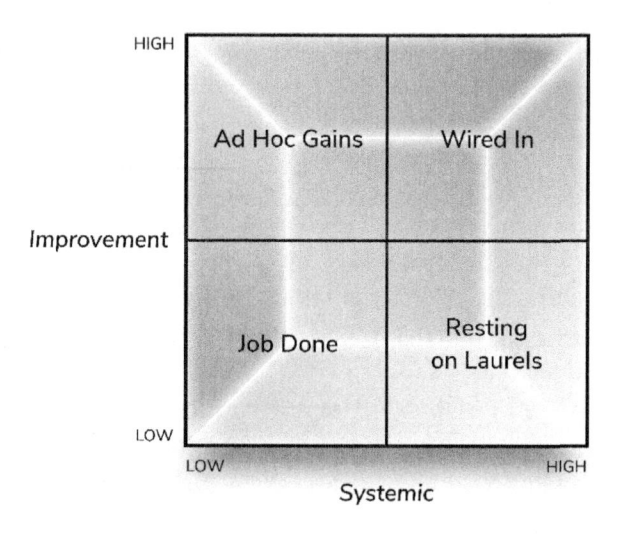

First come the innovators, who see opportunities that others don't and champion new ideas that create genuine value. Then come the imitators, who copy what the innovators have done. Sometimes they improve on the original idea, often they tarnish it. Last come the idiots, whose avarice undermines the very innovations they are trying to exploit. **Warren Buffett**

Several decades ago, a small car manufacturer with a tiny market share introduced TPS - the Toyota Production System - with a focus on minimising waste without sacrificing productivity. Key principles included Just In Time, Kaizen (continuous improvement) and Jidoka (automation with a human touch). Toyota's implementation of these principles revolutionised manufacturing. In 2008, it passed General Motors in global sales to become the world's largest automaker.[1]

Admired by many, its thinking has now been applied across several other industries. Imitation may be the sincerest form of flattery. But few firms have managed to implement the Toyota Production System. Why not?

To manage a system effectively, you might focus on the interactions of the parts rather than their behaviour taken separately. **Russell Ackoff**

Can organisational change be sustained over time?

It stands to reason that change programs now should be more successful than those of more than a decade ago. The facts suggest otherwise. **Colin Price and Emily Lawson**[2]

Two themes are at play.

Systemic. This addresses how many levers are pulled as part of a change effort. In low systemic, only one lever has been identified, for example organisational structure, a management clear out, a cultural rethink. At the high end, the recognition that several moving parts need to be aligned to optimise impact.

Improvement. Change can be seen as a one-off exercise or as part of an ongoing effort. In low improvement, resources are directed at a sprint race. In high improvement, change is a series of marathons.[3]

The key to the Toyota Way. It must be practiced every day in a very consistent manner, not in spurts. **Taiichi Ohno**

Four change scenarios emerge.

Job Done. Low systemic and low improvement combine for the change effort that deploys effort on the one thing as a solution to the firm's problems. At best, organisational change is manageable; there is a focus on a discrete activity with well-defined objectives. Alternatively, the one thing change programme fails to sustain over time.

They always say time changes things, but you actually have to change them yourself. **Andy Warhol**

Ad Hoc Gains. Low systemic intersects with high improvement to ensure the organisation keeps alert to identify opportunities for advancements in productivity and innovation. This change philosophy has the virtue of expecting daily, weekly and monthly gains. Conversely, a change project that is an incoherent mess, with haphazard multiple efforts and conflicting incentives, sometimes with negative unintended consequences.

Many people recognize that technology often comes with unintended and undesirable side effects. **Leon Kass**

Resting on Laurels. This is a systemic approach but largely implemented as a one off programme. Much loved by the consulting industry, the exercise of coordinated complexity to join the dots across different streams of activity - strategic, structural and cultural - can come at huge cost. The downside: after the celebrations and the departure of the consulting firm, the organisation remains stuck. Nothing stands still, and new problems emerge.

We all remember the balloons, party music, celebration, hats and cheesy noise makers, but by the time the confetti was cleared up, things were well on their way back to business as usual. **Gary Wise**

Wired In. A systemic change philosophy based on ongoing improvement underpins the resilient organisation. This is the recognition of the interaction of many factors - strategic imperatives, organisational design, and workforce policies and processes. And a mind-set embedded at every organisational level. A magnificent performance of continual reinvention. It is rare and explains why few failing firms change to achieve sustainable business performance.

Having no problems is the biggest problem of all. **Taiichi Ohno**

SO WHAT?

The only way to reinvent a business model for today's complex world is to approach it like a system. **Roger Spitz**

Organisational change comes in all sizes and shapes. There is no fixed methodology or implementation programme, despite the claims of the change gurus. Sometimes the law of marginal gains applies.[4] Here, one improvement in a specific area triggers enhancements in other business activities. Alternatively, sustained success requires a major rethink of the assumptions of organisational change - one based on a fundamental shift in the mind set of leaders.[5] Separating symptoms from root causes is a start.[6]

If you are going to do TPS you must do it all the way. You also need to change the way you think. You need to change how you look at things. **Taiichi Ohno**

NOTES

1. Toyota has also seen its problems. Timeline: Toyota's recall woes; https://www.theguardian.com/business/2010/jan/29/timeline-toyota-recall-accelerator-pedal

2. The psychology of change management; https://www.mckinsey.com/capabilities/people-and-organizational-performance/our-insights/the-psychology-of-change-management

3. Ricardo Abad Martínez ran 500 marathons in 500 days.

4. The Magic Of Marginal Gains Theory: Sweat The Small Stuff; https://www.mindsetdevgroup.com/blog/marginal-gains-theory/

5. Thinking in Systems: A Primer, Donella H Meadows. Earthscan 2009

6. Separating symptoms from root causes: https://mogill.medium.com/separating-the-problem-from-the-symptom-6830a5ebc9ae

Are our employees afraid to speak up?

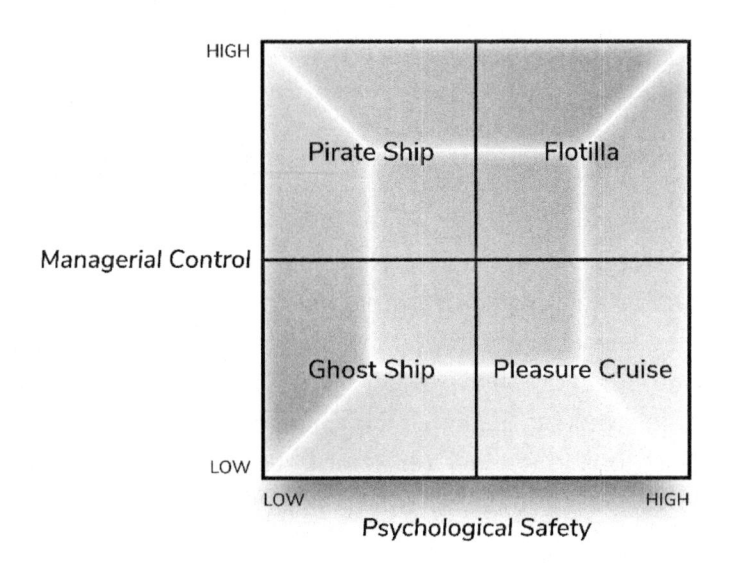

HIGH	Pirate Ship	Flotilla
Managerial Control		
LOW	Ghost Ship	Pleasure Cruise
	LOW	HIGH
	Psychological Safety	

The sad truth is that societies that demand whistleblowers be martyrs often find themselves without either, and always when it matters the most. **Edward Snowden**

In August 2001, Sherron Watkins, an Enron Vice President, sent an anonymous letter to chairman Kenneth Lay, detailing her concerns about the company's accounting practices. She informed Lay that Enron might *implode in a wave of accounting scandals*. Watkins later met with Lay to present evidence of the accounting irregularities. Despite her warnings, the company took no immediate corrective action. The rest is history. Enron's downfall triggered the end of its auditor, Arthur Andersen, and a 24 year prison sentence for Jeff Skilling, Enron's CEO.

Most Swiss banks do have a whistleblower program, but they use it to punish those who avail themselves of it. **Herve Falciani**

Speaking up and whistleblowing is a pressing issue for leaders. Not every whistle that is blown represents a valid concern over organisational malpractice or ethical misconduct. Some whistles are vexatious and malicious grievances. But most are not. How organisations respond has significant legal, financial, and reputational consequences.

Don't entirely trust colleagues. When careers are on the line, few people will stay loyal. **Peter Duffy**

There are two dimensions underpinning the dynamics of whistle blowing.

Psychological Safety. This is the willingness to speak up, ask awkward questions and highlight problems. In low psychological safety, employees keep quiet - feeling at risk, the threat of censure, not least of legal action, and the loss of employment. High psychological safety reflects a confidence - based on mutual respect and trust - that opinions can be expressed without fear of embarrassment, ridicule, or punishment.

Managerial Control. The balance of power in organisational employee transactions. In low managerial control, the tone is one of consultation and involvement with the workforce, and a genuine commitment to listen and learn. High managerial control reflects a more authoritarian stance to ensure image and impression take precedence over truth.

Speak your mind, even if your voice shakes. **Maggie Kuhn**

Four approaches to the employee voice are identified.

Ghost Ship. In low safety and low managerial control, this is a business ship adrift with no officers on duty. The crew recognise the folly of the absence of decision making from the captain, but reluctant to warn of the reefs and rocks they have spotted. The outcome: a wreck.

Epps: Have you told anyone else about this?
Ferriman: Not a living soul. **Ghost Ship**

Pirate Ship. The interplay of low safety and high control. The Dutch have a phrase: *kissing up and kicking down* to explain middle manager behaviour. Employees operate under a fear of the managerial captains. Easier to follow orders than walk the organisational plank. It may be that efficiency on this business boat is high - at least in the short term. It is not an environment supportive of initiative or one that encourages the honesty of whistle blowing. It runs the risk of mutiny.

The beatings will continue until morale improves. **Captain Bligh, Mutiny on the Bounty**

Pleasure Cruise. High psychological safety intersects with low management control. Employees feel comfortable in the expression of their opinions and ideas. At best, an approach which works in the highly agile work environment of a start-up of adventure to explore and discover. Alternatively, without management direction to guide activity, short term enjoyment of process drifts without accountability for outcomes.

The days pass happily with me wherever my ship sails. **Joshua Slocum**

Flotilla. In high psychological safety and management control, employees are both able and willing to speak up with questions. The captains will respond to reinforce clear principles and defined principles. This is the armada of ships in which captains encourage cooperation. There is a blend of freedom to venture and structure to coordinate towards a destination. And employee confidence to speak up. The downside: some of the vessels become detached from the overall purpose, and find themselves caught between the devil and the deep blue sea.

The most courageous act is still to think for yourself. Aloud. **Coco Chanel**

SO WHAT?

Ian felt like he would lose his job if he told the truth. **Rachelle Gibbons, wife of Ian Gibbons, Chief Scientist at Theranos**[1]

Organisations need to find the optimal balance of safety and control. On the one hand, a high level of psychological safety becomes the independence of action that leads to organisational anarchy. On the other, excessive managerial control constrains open and honest debate and scrutiny to close down the learning for innovation.[2] The experience of Peter Duffy, consultant urological surgeon in the NHS is a chilling account of a whistleblower.[3]

NOTES

1. How Elizabeth Holmes's House of Cards Came Tumbling Down;
https://www.vanityfair.com/news/2016/09/elizabeth-holmes-theranos-exclusive

2. The Whistleblower's Dilemma: Do the Risks Outweigh the Benefits?
https://knowledge.wharton.upenn.edu/article/whistleblowers-in-business/

3. Peter Duffy's experience of whistleblowing in the NHS;
https://www.integrityline.com/en-gb/expertise/blog/whistleblowing-interview-peter-duffy/
And advice for those considering whistleblowing can be found at WhistleblowersUK.4

Is our company for real?

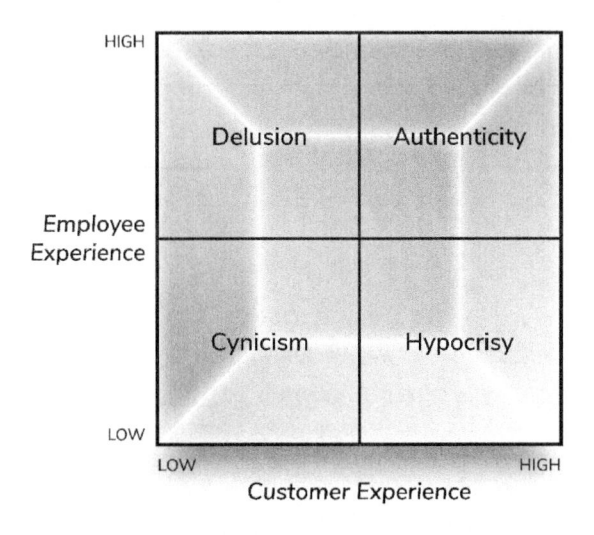

[Figure: 2x2 grid with axes "Employee Experience" (LOW to HIGH vertical) and "Customer Experience" (LOW to HIGH horizontal). Quadrants: Delusion (high employee, low customer), Authenticity (high employee, high customer), Cynicism (low employee, low customer), Hypocrisy (low employee, high customer).]

Stop trying to be something you're not and just be the best of who you are. And if you want to be considered the best thing since sliced bread, then actually be the best thing since sliced bread. **The Duffy Agency**

What does it mean to be authentic? As a brand? As an organisation? What is the relationship between brand reputation and operational realities? Does it matter if there is a mismatch between a brand's posture in the market place and its organisational culture? Is it possible to build an authentic business true to both customers and employees? Or is the attempt fundamentally contrived and misguided?

Authentic brands don't emerge from marketing cubicles or advertising agencies. They emanate from everything the company does. **Howard Schultz, Starbucks**[1]

Two dimensions underpin this grid.

Customer Experience. Customers are less preoccupied with any organisational pitch of authenticity promoted through a new advertising campaign. Customers ask: does this business do what it claims to do? Fake is the customer experience; personal interactions with the firm are not met with the business promise. At the high end, real closes the gap and customer expectations are met.

Employee Experience. If customers have an external perspective, staff have an intimate insight into the organisation and how it operates. At the low end, employees sense fake, knowing the organisation runs on a lie. At the other, employees recognise a genuine commitment to advance the interests of the customer. The business is true to itself.

Entry-level salary of just £180 per month is so low that it would take more than two months' salary to pay for the cheapest iPad. **Inside an Apple factory Chinese sweatshop factory**

Four stances are identified.

Cynicism. A fake perspective from both customers and employees. This is a firm at risk of losing the loyalty of its customers and the trust of its employees. This is the trajectory of decline. Hapless customers and employees are caught in a situation of corporate contempt. This company will soon disappear from the business landscape.

Here comes the Animal. **A flight attendant reference to boarding passengers**

Delusion. In this scenario, customers know this organisation is fake, but employees attempt to keep up the fantasy that the business is for real. In the short-term, this makes for a highly uncomfortable experience. Front-line employees recognise the reality when confronted by an awful customer encounter, and are asked to defend the indefensible. Repeated management exhortations that all is well disappoint. Key staff leave and the firm moves on to its death throes.[2]

Authenticity means erasing the gap between what you firmly believe inside and what you reveal to the outside world. **Adam Grant**

Hypocrisy. When customers perceive the organisation as real, but employees regard it as fake, this is the red flag of business trouble.

At best, responsive firms are alert to the warning signs from staff, and that changes need to be made to improve the customer proposition. Employee feedback is taken seriously and acted on. Alternatively, a firm living on a past legacy of customer loyalty, and now under threat as competitors provide a superior product/service.

The moment one tries to be real, tries to be authentic, and the trying is detected, the bubble bursts and the inauthenticity spills out. **Michael Benedikt**

Authenticity. This combines a real experience for both customers and employees. It is a business founded on consistency between words and action. These firms close the gap between promise and delivery. Customer confidence in the firm's reliability is high. Staff take pride from an employer that honours its customer commitments.

Advertising would be much better if we all had to work in the real world occasionally. **Dave Trott**[3]

SO WHAT?

Authentic brands live or die with the people in the organisation. **Michel Hogan**

This is a conversation that rarely takes place in the board room.[4] Are we for real, or are we kidding ourselves as senior executives and fooling the workforce and our customers. If we are not for real, why not? Do executives need to spend more time on the frontline to understand business reality?

NOTES

1. Wanna know why it's called Starbucks? Cos they have turned fake stars into real bucks; https://www.linkedin.com/pulse/wanna-know-why-its-called-starbucks-cos-have-turned-fake-scott-hruqf/

2. In a consulting assignment, one of the authors cross-referenced employee survey data with findings from market research. The largest mismatch in perceptions of customer service outcomes was from the senior executive team.

3. When Kelloggs ran a campaign suggesting families eat cereal for dinner; https://davetrott.co.uk/2024/03/greedflation/

4. John Harvey-Jones and business reality;
https://www.youtube.com/watch?v=OBu5ewmEP2E

What is holding back organisational innovation?

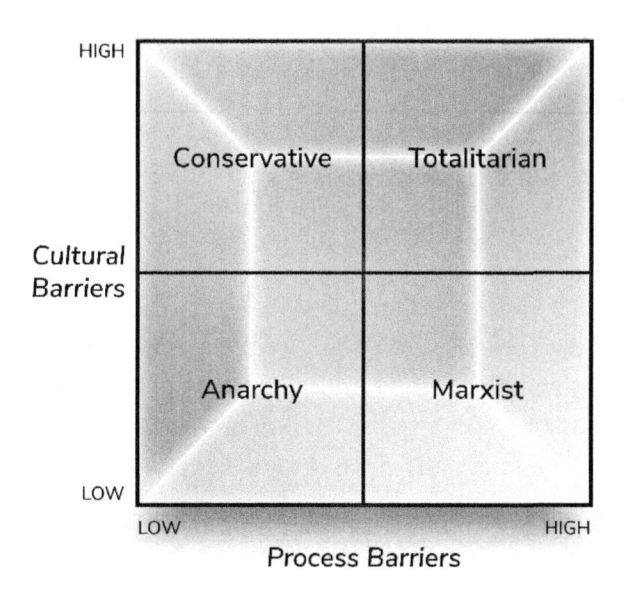

```
HIGH
         |  Conservative  |  Totalitarian
Cultural |                |
Barriers |----------------+----------------
         |   Anarchy      |   Marxist
LOW      |                |
         LOW                              HIGH
              Process Barriers
```

I want the whole thing caught in the bud. **CJ, the boss of Reginald Perrin**[1]

The strategy is clear. The mission statement indicates that innovation is part of the firm's DNA. The question remains: why do so many organisations find it difficult to locate and commercialise innovation?

You have to combine both things: invention and innovation focus, plus the company that can commercialise things and get them to people. **Larry Page, Google**

There is a wide difference between completing an invention and putting the manufactured article on the market. **Thomas Edison**[2]

This quadrant highlights two key themes.

Process Barriers. This is organisational friction to constrain the free flow of information and resources within the firm. Low, the business with fast and responsive systems. High, the noisy clunk of time consuming and unwieldy bureaucratic practices and procedures.

Cultural Barriers. At one end, innovation is viewed as an unwelcome departure from the accepted way in which things get done. At the other, an expectation of initiative. Creativity is reinforced in who the organisation recruits, rewards and promotes.

When you step into an intersection of fields, disciplines and cultures, you can combine existing concepts into a large number of extraordinary ideas. **Frans Johansson**

Four innovation stereotypes emerge.

Anarchy. In a business without process or cultural barriers, individuals are empowered to improvise and apply discretion. The upside: a stream of creative ideas for business advantage to keep the competition on the back foot. The downside: a lack of structure that struggles to prioritise those ideas for commercial application.[3]

In a world like this one, only the random makes sense. **Libba Bray**

Conservative. This combines low process with high cultural barriers. In theory, innovation should happen. In practice, it doesn't. There are too many employee reservations about rocking the business boat. This is the organisational ambivalence that is reluctant to challenge the prevailing cultural norms.

The biggest barrier to innovation is our own way of thinking. **George Couros**

Marxist. Low cultural barriers intersect with high process barriers. This organisational outlook ensures innovation does not happen. This is the firm which excels in the double speak of the mixed message. Share your ideas, but don't anticipate too much to happen too soon.

No one believes more firmly than Comrade Napoleon that all animals are equal. He would be only too happy to let you make your decisions for yourselves. But sometimes you might make the wrong decisions, comrades, and then where should we be? **George Orwell, Animal Farm**

Totalitarian. This is the anti-innovation philosophy that places every possible barrier - process and cultural - to block employee and team innovation. This is the business of unrelenting conformity to adhere to established conventions. Compliance is the mandate. Any suggestion of creativity is challenged and criticised.

Here you come upon the important fact that every revolutionary opinion draws part of its strength from a secret conviction that nothing can be changed. **George Orwell**

SO WHAT?

Innovation has nothing to do with how many R & D dollars you have. When Apple came up with the Mac, IBM was spending at least 100 times more on R & D. It's not about money. It's about the people you have, how you're led, and how much you get it. **Steve Jobs**

The narrative is that innovation is good. The outcomes will have a positive impact on productivity, customer loyalty and market share. But innovation is also unwelcome when the inputs - the process to achieve innovation - are disruptive of the existing cultural order.

Innovation comes with a price. It is not a price every organisation wants to pay.

NOTES

1. I didn't get to where I am today; youtu.be/R5Os_SrLJ0w?si=yCVEkQ8GbAcK-ZDB

2. Why did Thomas Edison electrocute an elephant; https://science.howstuffworks.com/innovation/science-questions/why-did-thomas-edison-electrocute-elephant.htm#

3. Fumbling the Future: How Xerox Invented, then Ignored, the First Personal Computer, Douglas Smith

Are our incentive systems working for us?

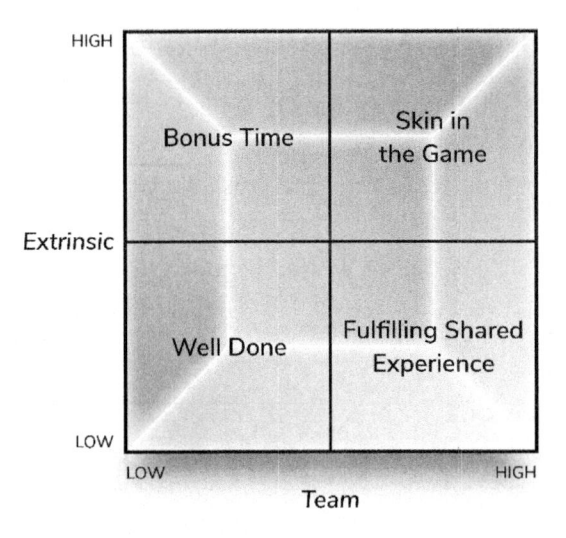

Quadrant chart with vertical axis "Extrinsic" (LOW to HIGH) and horizontal axis "Team" (LOW to HIGH). Quadrants: top-left "Bonus Time", top-right "Skin in the Game", bottom-left "Well Done", bottom-right "Fulfilling Shared Experience".

Show me the incentive and I will show you the outcome. **Charlie Munger**

Jeroen Van der Vee, the former CEO of Shell observed: *If I had been paid 50% more, I would not have done the job better. If I had been paid 50% less then I would not have done it worse.* Which begs the question: why do CEOs demand and are given increasingly large amounts of compensation as a ratio to that of the front-line worker.[1]

My pockets are full of thanks. **Portknockie fisherman**

This quadrant is based on two dimensions.

Team. This theme reflects the **focus** of incentives. At one end of the spectrum, performance rewards are directed at the individual. At the other, reward for the collective results of a work group.

Extrinsic. This reflects the **type** of incentives. At one end of this range - intrinsic - the internal motivators of job satisfaction, autonomy and accomplishment are emphasised. At the other, extrinsic - salary, bonuses and promotion prospects - are fundamental to the incentive system.

For artists, scientists, inventors, schoolchildren, and the rest of us, intrinsic motivation - the drive to do something because it is interesting, challenging, and absorbing - is essential for high levels of creativity. **Daniel Pink**

Four approaches to incentives can be identified.

Well Done. This is the scenario in which incentive systems are personal and intrinsic. The assumption is that employees will be motivated through a commitment to the task with no expectation of additional reward above that of base salary. At best, a sense of purpose to energise employees to greater accomplishments. Conversely, organisations exploit the discretionary effort of the workforce.

Bonus Time. Individual incentives intersect with extrinsic rewards. This - the conventional philosophy of most performance based systems - has the advantage of recognising personal effort and contribution to differentiate between low and high low performers. Rarely however are results achieved in isolation.[2] Results are attained through a collective enterprise. The drawback: competition between individuals is reinforced rather than building collaboration throughout the workforce.[3]

Bad behaviour is intensely habit forming when it is rewarded. **Charlie Munger**

Fulfilling Shared Experience. Team incentives coincide with intrinsic rewards for the workforce. This emphasises the motivating power of individuals as part of a common purpose, one that reinforces an overall sense of belonging. At best, an energising experience for members of the work group, encouraged to collaborate for gains in productivity and innovation. At worst, a patronising pat on the back from senior leaders for a team that has gone over and above the call of duty without benefits for individual employees.

I think about the personal accomplishment, but there's more of a sense of the grand achievement by all the people who could put this man on the moon. **Alan Shepard, American astronaut**

Skin in the Game.[4] Incentives are team based with extrinsic rewards. The group is recognised for collective performance through greater status and a share in financial benefits. The upside: the encouragement of collaboration in the knowledge that overall team outcomes will benefit everyone personally. Powerful in principle, this approach can be difficult in practice. How are personal and team outcomes differentiated? And who are the social loafers[5] and why should they be rewarded?

The more people pulling, the less hard the average individual pulled. **Robert Feldman**

SO WHAT?

Pay for performance is a sound philosophy. But it has to be pay for good performance not for poor performance. **Bruce Sevy**

There is no one size fits all approach to organisational incentives. Much hinges on the nature of the task - simplicity vs complexity, the extent to which it depends on genuine collaboration, as well as how easily performance can be measured, and over which time scale. The reality, in most instances, is a hybrid system that combines the four approaches.

What is important is that this mix of incentive policies recognises the right outcomes for the long-term success of the firm, rather than reward senior executives for short-term results.[6]

NOTES

1. Reining in CEO compensation and curbing the rise of inequality; https://www.epi.org/publication/reining-in-ceo-compensation-and-curbing-the-rise-of-inequality/

2. Chasing Stars: The Myth of Talent and the Portability of Performance; https://www.hbs.edu/faculty/Pages/item.aspx?num=37386

3. The classic case study in the negative consequences of differentiation. Enron's CEO Jeff Skilling famously described their Performance Review Committee as *the most important thing for forging a new strategy and culture - it is the glue that holds the company together.* Elsewhere in Enron, this event spawned *a gangrene-like rot that allowed the organisation to cannibalise itself.*

https://talentworldconsulting.com/wp-content/uploads/2023/08/A-Little-Less-Plotting-Talent-Reviews.pdf

4. Skin In the Game; https://www.nicolasbustamante.com/p/incentive-and-skin-in-the-game

5. Social loafing: https://sourcesofinsight.com/social-loafing/

6. The Big Problem With CEO Compensation; https://www.fool.com/investing/general/2013/04/01/the-big-problem-with-ceo-compensation.aspx

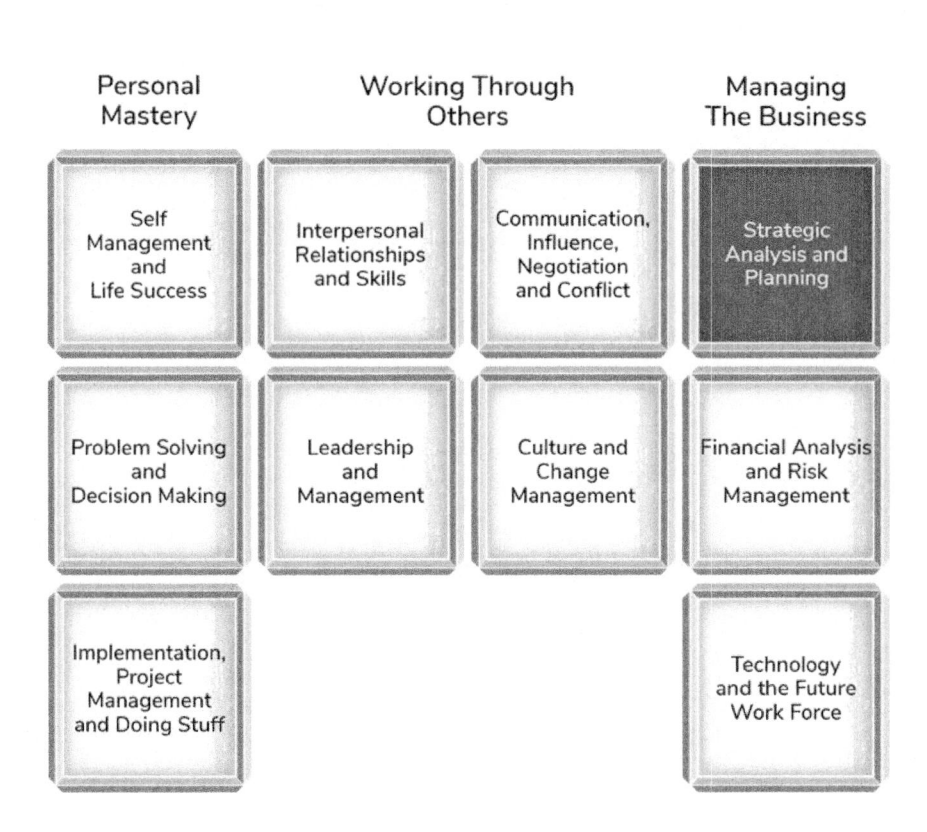

Personal Mastery	Working Through Others		Managing The Business
Self Management and Life Success	Interpersonal Relationships and Skills	Communication, Influence, Negotiation and Conflict	**Strategic Analysis and Planning**
Problem Solving and Decision Making	Leadership and Management	Culture and Change Management	Financial Analysis and Risk Management
Implementation, Project Management and Doing Stuff			Technology and the Future Work Force

Why business success is elusive

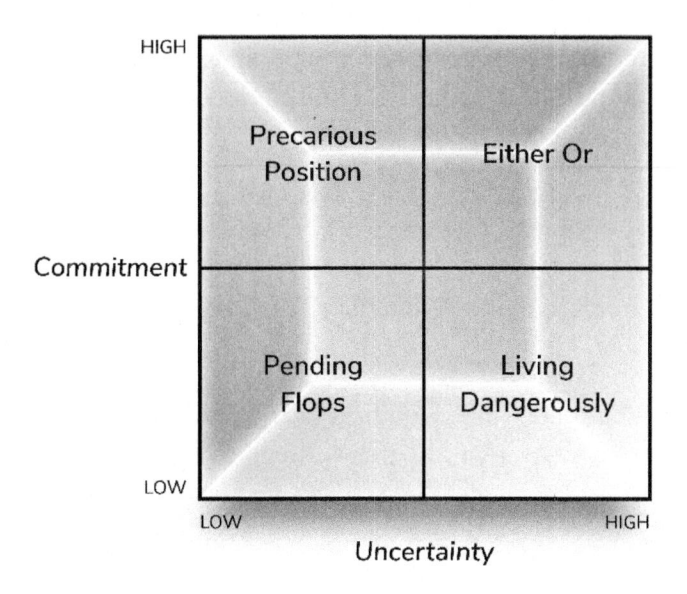

```
         HIGH
              ┌─────────────┬─────────────┐
              │ Precarious  │             │
              │  Position   │  Either Or  │
              │             │             │
Commitment    ├─────────────┼─────────────┤
              │             │             │
              │   Pending   │   Living    │
              │    Flops    │ Dangerously │
              │             │             │
         LOW  └─────────────┴─────────────┘
              LOW                      HIGH
                       Uncertainty
```

A 10% probability of succeeding in a quest for sustained growth is, if anything, a generous estimate. Mere survival for a company over a 10 year period, is actually a pretty high bar. **Michael Raynor**

In The Strategy Paradox, Michael Raynor[1] makes the point that *strategies with the greatest possibility of success also have the greatest possibility of failure.*

The logic? A successful strategy creates and captures value. To create value, a firm must connect with customers. But to capture value it must be resistant to competition from its business rivals. Satisfying customers in ways that competitors cannot copy requires commitment, commitments to unique assets or to particular capabilities. The downside of commitment: the firm makes the wrong investment choices.

As long as you act as if you are coming from behind, you have a shot at staying ahead. **Michael Eisner**

The strategy paradox arises from the collision of commitment and uncertainty. Successful strategies are based on commitments made today aligned with tomorrow's circumstances. But no one knows what these circumstances will be. Guess wrong, and it is difficult to recover from these commitments. Firms that avoid strategic risk survive, but they do not prosper. Those that accept risk, reap great reward or utter ruin.

When you come to a fork in the road, take it. **Yoga Berra, baseball player**

This quadrant maps out the relationship between uncertainty and commitment.

Uncertainty. This reflects the dynamics of the market-place as well as the wider economic environment. Nothing in life is certain, but there are sectors and markets where there is much more uncertainty than others.

Commitment. This is the level of investment a firm is prepared to make, a spectrum that runs from the absolute minimum to remain as a player, through to significant resource with the possibility of significant advantage. Or, to threaten the future of the firm if it bets badly.

We try not to have a strategy; we just try to generate lots of options. If the world changes and some of the things no longer work, we have the benefit of having lots of options. **Fred Goodwin, ex CEO, RBS**

Four strategic scenarios emerge.

Pending Flops. A combination of low uncertainty and low commitment is not a sustainable business position. In a relative unchanging market, this firm will be out-manoeuvred by those rivals willing to make a greater investment in product development, customer service, and technology. This is the trajectory of complacency to disappear quickly from the business landscape.

However beautiful the strategy, you should occasionally look at the results.
Winston Churchill

Precarious Position. In a scenario of low uncertainty and high commitment, firms can make hay while the sun shines. If competitors are holding back on investment, firms extend their position in the market place. An effective strategic game - until the market changes or a disruptive entrant joins the competitive game.

Everybody looks for the sweet spot, that situation in which the risks are low and the rewards are high. The trouble is, that when an obvious situation like that arises, everyone rushes to it. **B Zeckhauser and A Sandoski**

Living Dangerously. This grouping of companies of high uncertainty and low commitment holds back from making significant investment until the dynamics of the market place become clearer. This strategy of Wait and See avoids the cost of wrong-headed commitments. Here it may piggy back on the failings of its rivals to develop a much stronger proposition. Alternatively, it is out-witted by bolder rivals prepared to take a gamble and invest in the future.

Strategic thinking helps us take positions in a world that is confusing and uncertain. You can't get rid of ambiguity and uncertainty - they are the flip side of opportunity. If you want certainty and clarity, wait for others to take a position and see how they do. Then you'll know what works, but it will be too late to profit from the knowledge. **Richard Rumelt**

Either Or. This summarises the strategic paradox. Well targeted investments to bet big on the future can either deliver extraordinary business outcomes or result in financial calamity. With the tail wind of luck and competitor stumbles,[3] exceptional performance is the outcome. But a head wind of bad fortune in combination with nimbler rivals, and the consequence: a business going backwards.

SO WHAT?

The best performing firms often have more in common with humiliated bankrupts than with companies that have managed merely to survive.
Michael Raynor

There is no easy solution to this paradox. It is the way of the business world. But firms can identify ways to mitigate the risks by, for example, building in adaptability into its structures and culture, optimising commitments through the smarter use of resources, and developing intelligent systems of environmental scanning.

The question remains: mediocrity or the risk of outstanding outcomes, positive or negative?

NOTES

1. The Strategy Paradox, Michael Raynor. A variation of the paradox of success. If the advice is right, then it will be universally adopted. If it is universally adopted, it does not improve relative performance. If it does not improve relative performance, it is wrong. In other words, if the advice is right, then the advice is wrong.

2. The strategy of having no strategy led to the downfall of this bank.

3. In Search of Stupidity: Over Twenty Years of High Tech Marketing Disasters, Merrill R. Chapman

Can we predict the strategic future?

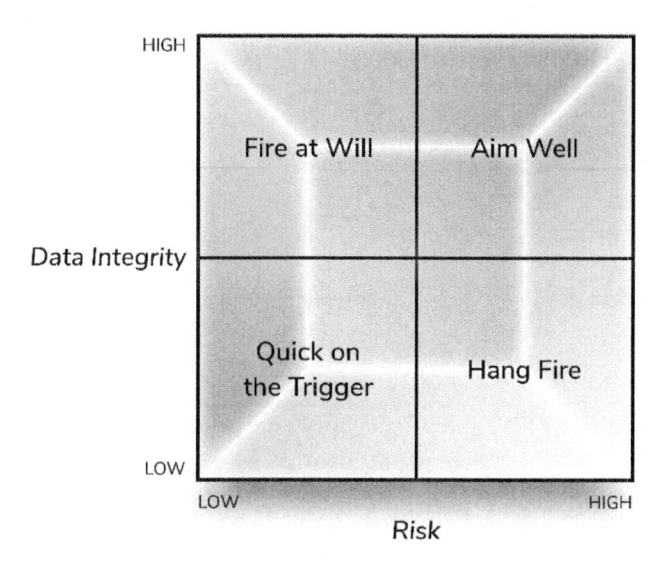

	Low Risk	High Risk
High Data Integrity	Fire at Will	Aim Well
Low Data Integrity	Quick on the Trigger	Hang Fire

Predicting rain doesn't count. Building arks does. **Warren Buffett**

Prediction should give us a competitive edge. When we see the future sooner and with more clarity than our business rivals, we gain an advantage. There is no shortage of think tanks and consulting firms providing a vision of what the future holds. Is this the equivalent of Gypsy Rose at the village fete staring at the bottom of a tea cup?

There are many methods for predicting the future. You can read horoscopes, tea leaves, tarot cards, or crystal balls. Collectively, these methods are known as nutty methods. Or you can put well-researched facts into sophisticated computer models, more commonly referred to as a complete waste of time. **Scott Adams**

Two dimensions are key to understanding strategic prediction.

Risk. This reflects the implications of making an incorrect prediction. Low risk and a failure in prediction is relatively insignificant. High risk is prediction as a misleading guide to the strategic future with damaging consequences.

Data Integrity. A theme that bundles together several inputs into the predictive model including the extent to which historical patterns are relevant and currently available information is accurate. Low, the finger in the air of the best guestimate. High is trustworthy intelligence, triangulated across different sources.

Forecasting is not some mysterious gift. It is the product of particular ways of thinking, of gathering information, of updating beliefs. **Philip Tetlock**[1]

Four predictive profiles are identified.

Quick on the Trigger. The risk of getting prediction wrong is low. But so is the accuracy of the data behind these predictions. In this scenario, prediction is still fraught but any mistaken forecasts will not be damaging. In a shootout with business rivals, a few predictions will hit the mark, and if made, best shot at speed with systems for rapid feedback to improve future planning.

When you have to shoot, shoot. Don't talk. **Tuco, The Good, The Bad and The Ugly**

Fire at Will. The risk of predictive failure is low but data integrity is high. As Super Forecaster Philip Tetlock says: i*t's not the crunching power that counts. It's how you use it.* This is the confidence that the probabilities are sufficiently high that strategic shots can be directed in the market place. Not everyone will of course succeed. But many - with boldness - will.

Hang Fire. High risk and low data integrity, and it is time to leave the gunfight. This is a strategic conflict to avoid. Whilst business rivals might blast away with forecasts that misread the battle, this is an expectation of outcomes based on luck not skill.

Making better predictions about the future? One way is to limit your tries to areas of competence. If you try to predict the future of everything, you attempt too much. **Charlie Munger**

Aim Well. High risk intersects with high data integrity. This is the strategic OK Corral in which a business has a predictive edge over its rivals.[2] Participation in this forecasting shoot out - when in possession of better knowledge - has the potential to win market position.[3]

The wise ones bet heavily when the world offers them that opportunity. They bet big when they have the odds. And the rest of the time, they don't. It's just that simple. **Charlie Munger**

SO WHAT?

If you cannot accurately predict the future, then you must flexibly be prepared to deal with various possible futures. **Edward de Bono**

The prediction game is complex. Is it a game that can be played, or is it best avoided? How well have we assessed the risks? How confident are we in the analysis of the risks? If we do play the strategic game, do we know what we are doing?

It helps if we apply the lessons from Philip Tetlock's Super Forecasters and what they do to optimise their predictions.[4]

NOTES

1. Superforecasting: The Art and Science of Prediction, Philip Tetlock; https://thedecisionlab.com/thinkers/political-science/philip-tetlock?

2. A Fistful of Dollars; https://youtu.be/WxuVau6qiiw?si=dVLIWv6Ar-1Z26ma

3. A variation of this strategy. Fire bullets before cannonballs; https://www.jimcollins.com/concepts/fire-bullets-then-cannonballs.html

4. Superforecasting tips and techniques; https://www.thendobetter.com/investing/2019/7/13/superforecasting-tips

Does our strategy need a strategy?

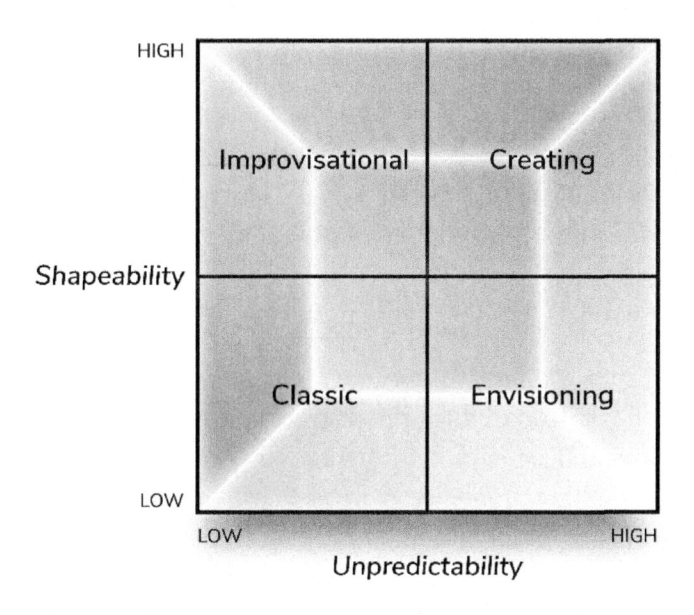

```
         HIGH
              ┌──────────────┬──────────────┐
              │              │              │
              │ Improvisational│   Creating   │
              │              │              │
Shapeability  ├──────────────┼──────────────┤
              │              │              │
              │   Classic    │  Envisioning │
              │              │              │
         LOW  └──────────────┴──────────────┘
              LOW                        HIGH
                    Unpredictability
```

Strategic planning is not strategic thinking. Indeed, strategic planning often spoils strategic thinking, causing managers to confuse real vision with the manipulation of numbers. **Henry Mintzberg**

In Good Strategy, Bad Strategy, Richard Rumelt[1] argues that much of the time businesses adopt the strategy of Shrek: *the kingdom of FAR FAR Away, Donkey? That's where we're going! FAR! FAR!... Away.* Here the assumption is that a grand vision will direct employee energy around a compelling purpose. Business ambition no doubt helps. But a statement of a bigger and better future is not a strategy. It is a hope.

In business, you can mess up a lot of things, but if you get the main trend right, you're going to make a lot of money. And conversely, if you don't get the main trend right, you're swimming upstream. **Brad Jacobs**

Maybe none of this matters. After all, isn't strategic planning now a bust flush? In the world of VUCA, BANI, RUPT and TUNA, is it not largely irrelevant? Does strategic analysis and development have a future? Isn't improvisation the only credible strategic response now?

In Your Strategy Needs a Strategy, the authors identify two dimensions which we adapt for this quadrant.[2]

Unpredictability. To what extent can the business landscape be determined with any confidence? Low unpredictability, and there is the reassurance that the future is known. In high unpredictability the future is not only unknown but unknowable. The only known here is that this future will be very different to the present. But we don't know in which ways.

Shapeability. Can we influence the future to advance our strategic interests? At the low end of this dimension, what will be will be, and there is little we can do to shape future events. At the other end, the future is not out there, forcing us to respond to events as they happen. The future is within our influence.

The best way to predict the future is to invent it. **PARC researcher Alan Kay**

Four strategic narratives emerge.

Classic. In this scenario, the world is predictable in a determined future that can't be changed. Positioning for size - be big - is therefore the strategic game. It is the mindset that dominates within business schools. Analyse, plan and execute is the template for case studies. And it works extremely well, for some firms some of the time. Boxer Mike Tyson explains the problem: *everyone has a plan until they get punched in the mouth.* Disruptive change punches this business model in the mouth.

We can all do our part by Preparing For The New Future, by Being Prepared and Looking Forwarder. **Bob Hoffman**

Improvisational. In a strategic situation of high unpredictability and low shapeability, the only sensible response is one of adaptability. This is strategy on the fly based on any combination of diversification to explore opportunities, experimentation to test the market and rapid feedback systems to re-direct effort. This stance is one of the nimbleness of a dancing elephant.[3] At worst, it avoids the big commitments of its rivals who place shrewd bets on shaping the future.

You have to have an idea of what you are going to do, but it should be a vague idea. **Pablo Picasso**

Envisioning. This strategic outlook combines predictability and shapeability to recognise that the business needs to commit to a future to advance its long-term interests. Whilst others hesitate, these firm spot the business opportunities to, for example, introduce a new technology. Or they have identified high levels of customer dissatisfaction in the market, or that competitors have mis-stepped. Here, firms find a strategic space to invest in a future in which they can exert influence. The assumption of predictability makes these firms vulnerable to the kind of disruptive change which shifts this future.

The reason why it is so difficult for existing firms to capitalise on disruptive innovations is that their processes and their business model that make them good at the existing business actually make them bad at competing for the disruption. **Clayton Christensen**

Creating. Firms take the initiative to respond to high levels of unpredictability with high levels of shapeability. This is the strategic opportunity for proactive businesses to determine the rules of the game and influence how these rules are written. These firms excel in stakeholder management and partner collaboration to build a new ecosystem.[4] This however requires betting that this unknown future can be created. A commitment that leaves these firms exposed when competitors are more astute in getting to this future faster.

SO WHAT?

Prediction is very difficult, especially if it's about the future. **Niels Bohr**

As the authors of Your Strategy Needs A Strategy[5] point out: business life is rarely this simple. Nonetheless, analysing strategic options against this kind of framework asks a tough question.

Have we thought about the strategy we need, long before we begin to define the specifics of what it might it look like?

NOTES

1. A variation of Richard Rumelt's critique: **Fluff**, a superficial restatement of the obvious combined with a generous sprinkling of buzzwords. **Failing to face the facts**: an ideology of hope that the dream will make the team work. **Forgetful**, this is corporate amnesia. **Faffing**, the knowing-doing gap in which strategic insights remain on the organisational top shelf.

2. The authors add a third dimension to what they describe as the strategic palette: **harshness** that moves from a two by two quadrant to a three by three cube. Harshness indicates the hostility of the business environment in which resources are severely constrained and access to capital is limited. The focus is on short term survival without much hope of growth.

3. Who Says Elephants Can't Dance. Louis Gerstner, former CEO of IBM

4. Critics would argue that these firms, through a combination of political donations and lobbying efforts, rig the game in their favour to the detriment of fair competition.

5. Your Strategy Needs A Strategy; https://hbr.org/2012/09/your-strategy-needs-a-strategy

Which strategic scenario do we face?

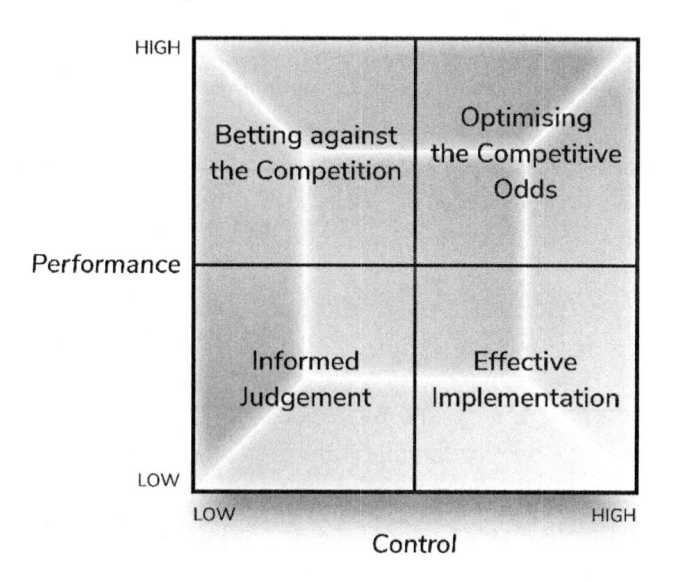

	Low Control	High Control
High Performance	Betting against the Competition	Optimising the Competitive Odds
Low Performance	Informed Judgement	Effective Implementation

Decision making; part tactician, part psychologist, part riverboat gambler.
Buzz Bissinger

The Daniel Kahneman philosophy of human judgement - we are irrational - proposes that our cognitive biases bungle our decisions. This is over-stated. Experiments with psychology students in a laboratory setting using highly framed questions[1] to expose our folly do not generalise to the decisions faced in real life. Phil Rosenzweig points to a more complex and nuanced mapping of the types of decisions business leaders face.[2]

The two dimensions of a strategic decision.

Control. Is this a decision outcome we can influence? In low control scenarios, a decision - buying a lottery ticket - is one where we cannot affect the outcome. In high control situations, we can shape the consequences of our decisions. Our preferred option is not in the lap of the gods. We can make our initial decision better or worse through our follow on actions.

Performance. Is the decision based on absolute or relative performance? In absolute decisions we can win irrespective of others' decisions and outcomes. In a situation of relative performance, winning requires us to do better than our rivals.

There are two people in a wood, and they run into a bear. The first person gets down on his knees to pray. The second person starts lacing up his boots. The first person asks the second person: what are you doing? You can't outrun a bear. To which the second person responds: I don't have to. I only have to outrun you.

This quadrant is a variation of the grid proposed by Phil Rosenzweig. It highlights four decision scenarios.

Informed Judgement. These are the decisions in scenarios of low control and absolute performance. Once a decision has been made, we cannot influence the outcome. We either get the decision right or wrong for our business. And have to live the consequences.

Betting against the Competition. Low control and relative performance is the scenario in which our decision outcomes are dependent on the actions of the competition. A proposal is submitted and a bid is made for a major contract. At best, our decision making process is more robust than our business rivals and we gain profitable work. Alternatively we suffer from the *winner's curse*. We over bid vis a vis our rivals and the contract proves to be unprofitable.[3]

I won the auction, but I don't want the prize. **Max Bazerman and William Samuelson**

Effective Implementation. High control and absolute performance is the strategic domain in which we can shape what happens next. Contrary to accepted wisdom that over confidence is invariably a bad thing, confidence is a good friend in these decisions. Here we make the decision work by responding to feedback and adapting our course of action. The confidence of unthinking persistence cannot rectify an awful decision. Nonetheless, commitment mitigates the risks of an initial poor judgement.

Optimising the Competitive Odds. High control and relative performance describes most business decisions. A decision can be formed and implemented with more or less confidence, but the outcome is also determined by the actions of our competitors. Brilliant strategic design and excellence in execution counts for little if our rival is marginally better at both. At best, our systems in market analysis, competitor intelligence and a responsive organisational infrastructure give us the edge. At worst, our firm finds itself struggling to out-manoeuvre a nimbler rival.

SO WHAT?

The answer to the question what really works is simple: Nothing really works, at least not all the time. **Phil Rosenzweig**

Before we make a decision it is important to decide what kind of decision we need to make. Can we control the outcome? And will the outcome depend on others' decisions?

The rule of thumb. Be under confident in the build up to the decision. Be bold after the decision to optimise the chances of success in execution.

NOTES

1. The Irrational Agent, Steve Sailer; https://www.takimag.com/article/the_irrational_agent/#ixzz1jmZWWVaf#

2. What Makes Strategic Decisions Different; https://hbr.org/2013/11/what-makes-strategic-decisions-different

3. The Winner's Curse; https://thedecisionlab.com/reference-guide/psychology/winners-curse

What information will the Board act on?

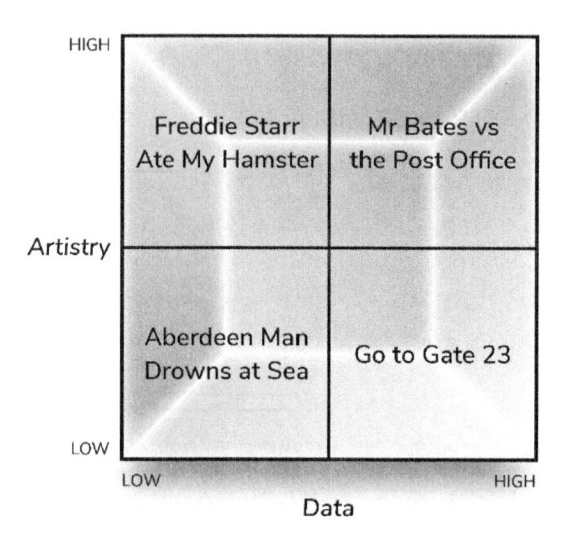

	Low Data	High Data
High Artistry	Freddie Starr Ate My Hamster	Mr Bates vs the Post Office
Low Artistry	Aberdeen Man Drowns at Sea	Go to Gate 23

Good decisions made on bad data are just bad decisions you don't know about yet. **Scott Taylor**

In a briefing to management consultants who wanted to enhance their presentational skills, a BBC journalist highlighted four factors critical to powerful impact, a presentation that would be acted upon by the client. It was summarised in the mnemonic FOAM: Fact, Opinion, Anecdote and Metaphor.

Get your facts first, and then you can distort them as much as you please. **Mark Twain**

The dimensions of this quadrant that shape executive decision making.

Data. Low on data is hunch without reference to relevant facts. This is the expression of an opinion. High on data is evidence based to consolidate information with rigorous analysis.

Artistry. Low is information without meaning. Lacking a sense of context there is little of significance to evoke emotion. High artistry paints a picture - through anecdote and metaphor - to engage attention, command interest and move to action.

No one ever made a decision because of a number. They need a story. **Daniel Kahneman**

Data and artistry interplay in four scenarios.

Aberdeen Man Drowns at Sea.[1] When the Press and Journal reported the sinking of the Titanic, this is presentation as low on data and low on artistry. And when, for example, the Board is informed that employee turnover is 24%, this is a meaningless statistic. Without context, there is no engagement with the numbers to reach an informed decision.

How's your wife? To which I answered, compared to what? **Henny Youngman**

Freddie Starr Ate My Hamster.[2] Data is low and artistry is high. This is the sensationalism much loved by the tabloid press to convey a message with little reference to facts. At best, the communication of emotional power to make us sit up and pay attention. Overplayed, when opinion is disconnected from the reality of facts, a stunt that loses credibility quickly.

We don't just dish up the day's news: we want to delight, amuse, surprise and inform, as well as grab people's attention. **Sun editor, Tony Gallagher**

Go to Gate 23. This combines high data and low artistry. This is the data point with a clear instruction and a call to action. An effective presentational tactic to convey critical information as a series of simple commands, it lacks the emotional resonance for more complex issues.

Just the facts, ma'am. **Joe Friday, Dragnet**

Mr Bates vs the Post Office.[3] This presentational tactic is high on both data and artistry. In the case of the ITV drama series, the artistry was storytelling with compelling acting. And data that drew on factual transcripts from extensive research. Not every presentation requires this level of sophistication, but timed well and implemented with finesse, the impact is powerful.

Facts are rarely self-explanatory; their significance, analysis, and interpretation depend on context and relevance. **Henry Kissinger**

SO WHAT?

When a data set is left to speak for itself, typically it spouts nonsense. **Robert Matthews**

FOAM draws on the full spectrum of data to artistry. At best, this is presentational craftmanship for maximum effect to educate and enlighten. The audience think and feel, and are motivated to take action.

NOTES

1. Sadly, an urban myth. https://www.holdthefrontpage.co.uk/2015/news/scottish-daily-sinks-myth-over-titanic-headline-again/

2. Freddie Star Ate My Hamster. The story behind the story; https://pressgazette.co.uk/publishers/nationals/sun-readers-pick-freddie-starr-ate-my-hamster-as-tabloids-best-splash-as-charity-giveaway-marks-50-years/

3. How a TV drama shook up Britain in just a week; https://www.bbc.com/culture/article/20240112-post-office-scandal-how-a-tv-drama-shook-up-britain-in-just-a-week

Will our organisation survive?

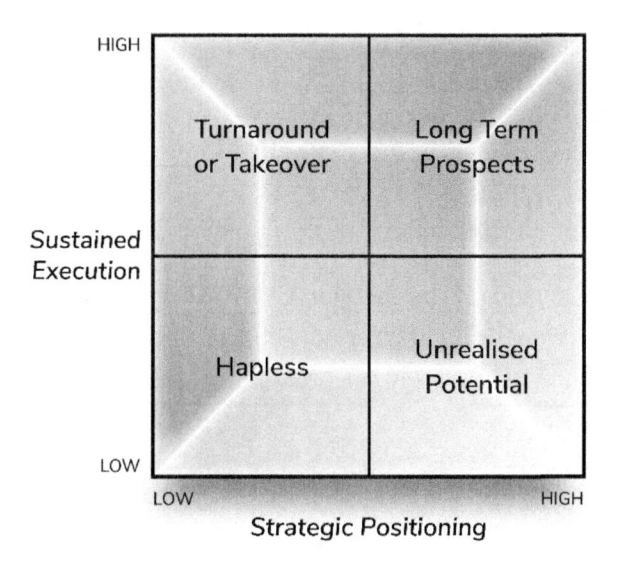

```
HIGH │
     │  Turnaround    │  Long Term
     │  or Takeover   │  Prospects
Sustained
Execution
     │                │
     │  Hapless       │  Unrealised
     │                │  Potential
LOW  │
     └────────────────┴──────────────
        LOW                      HIGH
          Strategic Positioning
```

Of the 43 companies studied in In Search of Excellence, less than one third could be described as excellent and nearly one half had serious performance declines within only five years of original excellence. **Richard Pascale**[1]

What percentage of firms operating today will be around in 5, 20 and 100 years' time? Back in the 1960s, organisations - listed on the stock exchange - had a life span of around 60 years. In the 1980s, this had fallen to around 25 years. The current estimate: 75% of companies listed on the stock exchange will have disappeared by 2030.

Michael Raynor now reckons a survival rate of 10% over 10 years is in fact pretty good odds.[2]

Every company in the world is dying. The trick is knowing it, calculating how fast you are dying and then working out how much stuff you need to put in at the top to counteract what is leaking out at the bottom. If you only focus on short-term results, and not on replacing that core or expanding your capabilities, then you die. **George Buckley, Stanley Black & Decker**

This quadrant is based on two dimensions.

Strategic Positioning. This is the thinking bit. At the low end: an undifferentiated strategy that is easily copied. At the high end, advantage is achieved through a customer proposition that the competition cannot match.

Sustained Execution. This is the doing bit. At one end, disorganised and poorly coordinated processes and systems make for sluggish implementation. At the other end, resources are directed - from front, middle and back office - with efficiency and speed.

To execute well there must be accountability, clear goals, accurate methods to measure performance, and the right rewards for people who perform. **Larry Bossidy**

Four business patterns are identified.

Hapless. Low strategic positioning and low ability to execute is unlikely to stay the distance. Some for a short time may get lucky, staggering to live off a past legacy. But for the most part, these are the zombie firms - the walking dead - whose continued presence in the market place astounds.[3]

The first sign that a person is turning into a zombie will often seem like symptoms of unusual energy. **Sydney Finkelstein**

Turnaround or Takeover. Low strategic positioning but high ability to execute represents either a turnaround or takeover scenario. Warren Buffett points out: *turnarounds seldom turn. Should you find yourself in a chronically leaking boat, energy devoted to changing vessels is likely to be more productive than energy devoted to patching leaks.* More likely, these firms are a target for takeover to acquire assets in implementation, for example, key talent and technology, within a strategic repositioning exercise.

I buy companies for strategic reasons and operate them. **Carlos Slim, Mexican business magnate**

Unrealised Potential. High strategic positioning and a limited capacity to execute is the firm that fails to exploit a promising position in the market-place. At best, fresh leadership and/or consulting expertise can trouble-shoot the problems of implementation. At worst, a flawed infrastructure alienates customers and loses market share. A strong business proposition is undermined.[4]

MBA students come out with: my staff is my most important asset. Bullshit. Staff is usually your biggest cost. We all employ some lazy bastards who needs a kick up the backside, but no one can bring themselves to admit it. **Michael O'Leary, CEO, Ryanair**

Long Term Prospects. This integrates both strategic positioning and execution. Firms in this scenario have a well-defined and differentiated proposition in the market place in association with responsive and efficient systems and processes. Arrogance and complacency are the only threats to survival and growth over the long run.

Each success only buys an admission ticket to a more difficult problem. **Henry Kissinger**

SO WHAT?

The business of business is a lot of little decisions every day mixed up with a few big decisions. **Tom Murphy, CEO of Capital Cities**

Financial performance is a snapshot in time. And however stellar it may be now; it is not a predictor of future performance. Neither does it explain how this financial performance is achieved. The fundamentals of strategy and execution are timeless.

Translating these principles into specifics given competitor and customer realities is the challenge for leaders for long term survival.

NOTES

1. Tom Peters' True Confessions; https://www.fastcompany.com/44077/tom-peterss-true-confessions

I picked a bunch of companies who we'd heard were doing something cool and wrote about them…and we faked the data. Tom Peters

2. Michael Raynor he looked at the companies profiled by eleven credible or popular success studies. Only 30 out of 228 different firms held out as exemplars of successful companies are in fact genuinely remarkable firms. We have been looking in the wrong places for our understanding of the dynamics of organisational success. We haven't looked at genuine success. Applying Nassim Taleb's "skin in the game" test, an investor placing their bets on the success firms would have done worse than if they had followed a standard tracker fund.

3. Tracking the Rise of Zombie Companies; https://smith.queensu.ca/insight/content/Tracking-the-Rise-of-Zombie-Companies.php

4. Living in a forest was a colony of rabbits. One day the rabbits came together for a meeting about survival. Said one rabbit: Wolves attack us, foxes hunt us, and eagles make our lives a living hell. There has to be a better way! said one rabbit. They decided to ask for survival advice from a wise owl. The old bird listened carefully, and offered a piece of wisdom: The solution is simple. You need to become hedgehogs. Those sharp needles will protect you from any predator. The rabbits were beyond ecstatic. Finally, they had a real solution - and what a brilliant idea it was. Running back through the forest, they made plans for a nightlong celebration, until one of them stopped the whole group with a question: How exactly do we become hedgehogs? When the colony made its way back to the owl, the bird's answer was as useless at it was bold: I am a strategist. Execution is not my thing.

Is the Lord in the castle?

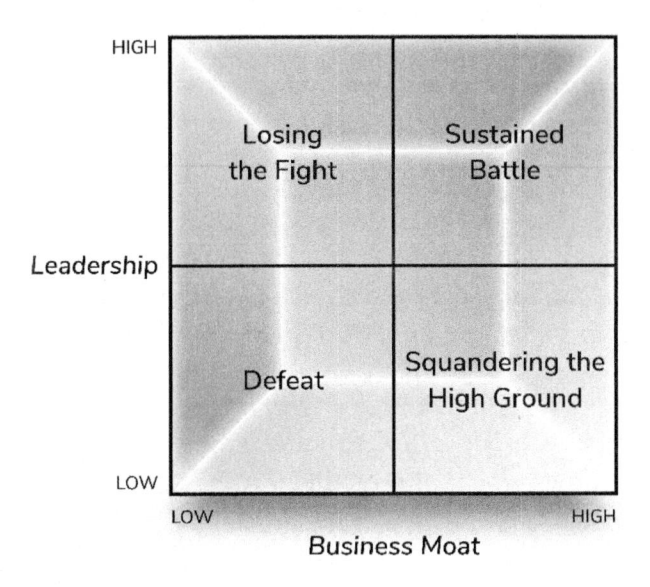

	Low Business Moat	High Business Moat
High Leadership	Losing the Fight	Sustained Battle
Low Leadership	Defeat	Squandering the High Ground

I want a business with a moat around it. I want a very valuable castle in the middle. And then I want who's in charge of that castle to be honest and hard working and able. **Warren Buffett**[1]

Warren Buffett asks us to think of a business as a castle surrounded by a moat. The wider and deeper the moat, the more difficult it is for any invaders to take control of the castle. It is the task of the lords in the castle to ensure the moat provides protection. A vivid image to think of the business scenarios in which the deployment of leadership makes the difference between business failure or survival. And between short-term success or exceptional and enduring outcomes.

Business Moat. Its width and depth is determined by the number of assets a firm possesses within its industry. These are the fundamental advantages of low cost production, specific technologies, patents, pricing power that make it difficult for current or new competitors to cross the moat and storm the castle.

Leadership reflects the quality of those in charge of the castle. This dimension runs the spectrum from lords who lack competence and character, through to high quality leaders. Here, the lord in the castle draws on experience, talent, ingenuity and integrity.

Is it possible to acquire a moat with no management talent and just luck? I can't think of an example of this. **Charlie Munger**

This highlights four business scenarios.

Defeat. Poor leadership finds itself in an uncompetitive position. The moat is narrow and shallow, and the leaders in the castle see the moat continuing to shrink, offering diminishing levels of strategic protection. The outcome: business decline.

Losing the Fight. A group of exceptional leaders in the castle find themselves without a moat of protection. At best, these lords find a way to dig deep and build a sustainable moat of competitive advantage. Alternatively, a losing battle in which business economics wins against excellent leadership.

Squandering the High Ground. Ineffective leaders run the risk of undermining a dominant competitive position. The current moat of business advantage provides protection. But if it is not managed and maintained, the moat shrinks. Charlie Munger remarked that *a great business will stand a fair amount of mismanagement.* But low quality leaders neglect the moat. Previous business success is wasted.

You should invest in a business that even a fool can run, because someday a fool will. **Warren Buffett**

Sustained Battle. The moat is wide and deep and the leaders in the castle are highly capable. This is success as good fortune for the leaders who find themselves in this castle. The challenge for these leaders is to maintain the moat, following Warren Buffett's advice to also *throw in the crocs, sharks and gators to keep away competitors.*

SO WHAT?

The truth is, there's no final winner in the global game of corporate competition. All winning does is let you compete against a whole new set of better-funded competitors. Competition never ends. **Joe Kraus**

This quadrant asks us to look critically at our business position. Do we have the leadership to acquire and protect a sustainable business model? Will our succession processes ensure future leaders who will build and maintain a moat?[2]

And specifically within our organisation, are we deploying our best people to the activities of greatest opportunity?

NOTES

1. What I Learned from Warren Buffett, Bill Gates; https://hbr.org/1996/01/what-i-learned-from-warren-buffett

2. Are you planning succession or managing success? A strategic perspective; https://talentworldconsulting.com/project/are-you-planning-succession-or-managing-success

What is on the breakfast table?

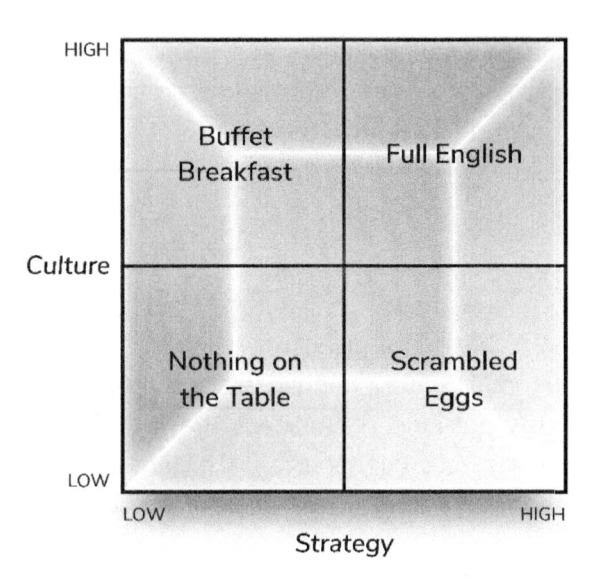

	Low Strategy	High Strategy
High Culture	Buffet Breakfast	Full English
Low Culture	Nothing on the Table	Scrambled Eggs

Culture can eat strategy for breakfast but if there's no strategy on the table, culture will get pretty hungry. **Eaon Pritchard**[1]

Peter Drucker was quoted as saying c*ulture eats strategy for breakfast.* A brilliant strategy will be undone by a dysfunctional culture. Others have stated this position more emphatically. *It always comes down to people.* Eli Halliwell, CEO of the skin care company Jurlique, says. *It's about the whole team and the culture. It trumps strategy, it trumps financial position.*

The fact that this is a misattribution hasn't stopped the myth.[2] It does however highlight an important point about the interplay between strategy and culture. The dynamics of organisational performance; performance[3] - sustained over time rather than the short-term hype of one-off success - requires both strategy and culture.

Two dynamics determine what is on the breakfast table.

Strategy. This theme reflects a well-focused position in the marketplace. At the low end, there is no strategy, only ad hoc improvisation to respond to emerging business trends. At the high end, strategy provides a differentiated voice to guide and determine organisational priorities.

Culture. This dimension is not the statement of values that appears in excruciating corporate videos.[4] Firms low on this dimension lack a coherent set of ground rules as a template for the dos and don'ts of employee conduct. High, those firms with well-defined expectations that are explicit in the mood music heard by the workforce.

This quadrant maps out four scenarios.

Nothing on the Table. This grouping of companies combine low strategy and culture. Possibly, nimble start-up firms still finding their feet to work out what kind of business they are in and how they intend to operate in future. For established organisations, this is a firm that has lost its way, lacking a rationale for its continued business existence.

Old Mother Hubbard went to the cupboard to give the poor dog a bone; when she came there, the cupboard was bare. **Sarah Catherine Martin**

Buffet Breakfast. This is a culture in search of a strategy. The firm hasn't decided on its key business fundamentals, but it looks to provide a working environment in which employees are treated well. A variation of this stance was outlined by the Jim Collins' philosophy of *get the right people on the bus*. Maybe, but an organisational philosophy that has disappointed.[5]

Scrambled Eggs. A coherent strategy coincides with a culture that does not resonate with the workforce. This is the business that has established a position in the market place and adopts a kind of take or leave it stance. Culturally it lacks the flexibility to respond to shifts in customer expectations or competitor challenge.

How you gonna likem? Over medium or scrambled? Anyways the only way.
Tom Waits

Full English. When strategy and culture coincide, this is the firm that delivers on its promise. A coherent strategic game plan provides purpose and priorities to outline where the firm will and won't compete. This position is aligned with a culture of embedded values to determine the rules of employee engagement and how it conducts itself. At best, a differentiated proposition for both customers and employees. At worst, this strength of purpose becomes a limitation when the market place shifts, and the organisation finds itself unable to abandon a successful past.

SO WHAT?

Breakfast is everything. The beginning, the first thing. It is the mouthful that is the commitment to a new day, a continuing life. **AA Gill**

David Packard of HP made the point: *more organisations die of indigestion than starvation*. This is true. But it is not the size of the breakfast that matters. It is the quality. This grid reminds us of the importance of business balance. A brilliant strategy will disappoint without an enabling culture. And cultural change in the absence of a sustainable strategic model is a futile exercise.

NOTES

1. Does Culture Really Eat Strategy;
http://eaonpritchard.blogspot.co.uk/2014/07/does-culture-really-eat-strategy-for.html

2. Peter Drucker in fact said: Culture, no matter how defined, is singularly persistent. Origins of the expression, Culture Eats Strategy for Breakfast;
https://quoteinvestigator.com/2017/05/23/culture-eats/

3. Growth's Triple Crown, Michael Raynor;
https://www2.deloitte.com/content/dam/insights/us/articles/growths-triple-crown-growth-profits-and-returns/US_deloittereview_Growths_Triple_Crown_Jul11.pdf

4. For example the Healthineers song of Siemens; https://youtu.be/K5LiUrezV6k

5. In Good to Great, Jim Collins proposed the concept of who, then what. Great organisations make sure they have the right people on the bus and the right people in the key seats before they figure out where to drive the bus. It's Finally Time to Retire Good to Great From the Leadership Canon; https://marker.medium.com/its-finally-time-to-retire-good-to-great-from-the-leadership-canon-91300bff6238

Is the senior team having the right conversation?

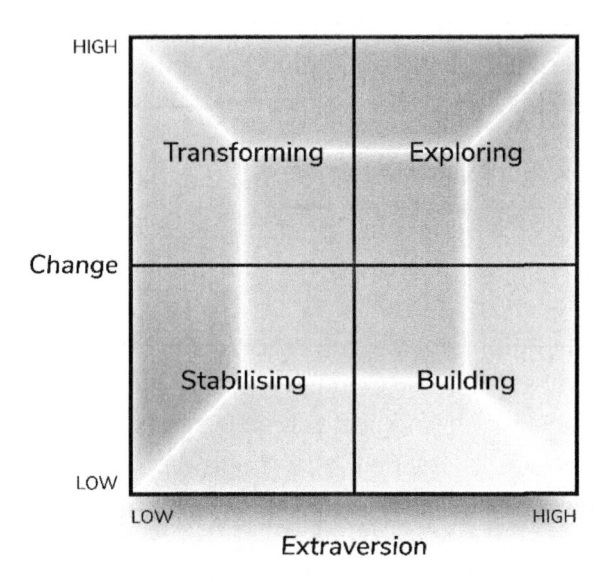

A 2x2 matrix with "Change" on the vertical axis (LOW to HIGH) and "Extraversion" on the horizontal axis (LOW to HIGH). The four quadrants are labelled: Transforming (top-left), Exploring (top-right), Stabilising (bottom-left), Building (bottom-right).

Today, more than ever, strategy IS the conversation. **Chris Ertel and Lisa Kay Solomon**

Strategic balance or organisational ambidexterity[1] is the goal. But business life is not that simple. Instead difficult discussions are needed to review the emphasis of the business: where it is and isn't directing its efforts. What is the Board talking about? And what isn't being discussed?

The fight is won or lost, far away from witnesses - behind the lines, in the gym, and out there on the road, well before I dance under the lights. **Muhammad Ali**

Two dimensions underpin this strategic conversation.

Extraversion. At one end of the spectrum, the organisation focuses on its internal operations to address issues of systems, process, technology and culture. At the high end, it looks outward to identify opportunities in the market place, and how to position itself and its products and services vis a vis the competition.

Change. At the low end, consolidation is the priority to routinise what have been ad hoc policies and processes for greater efficiency and stability. At the high end, change reflects attempts to rethink and reinvent the business with a radical shift in technology, business process and organisational culture.

Every organisation, without fail, goes through the same series of natural, unavoidably, but eminently predictable stages in growth. **Les McKeown**[2]

Four strategic conversations emerge.

Stabilising. An internal outlook in combination with consolidation is the conversation to optimise efficiency. An important feature of business life, lopsided this neglects shifting trends and developments in the market place. It steadies an organisation out of synch with customer and competitor realities.

An organisation has to institutionalise its culture without bureaucratising it. **Patrick Lencioni**

Transforming. A conversation to address the need for a radical overhaul of the organisation. This is any permutation of the turnaround of failing business activities, through to the reinvention of the enterprise to integrate shifts in technology and culture. This runs the risk of irrelevance when the business environment is changing.

Should you find yourself in a chronically leaking boat, energy devoted to changing vessels is likely to be more productive than energy devoted to patching leaks. **Warren Buffett**

Building. A combination of an external perspective and consolidation, this conversation focuses on how to protect and preserve market position. It addresses improvements in the customer proposition, and how to establish greater stakeholder influence with, for example, political parties, regulatory bodies, the media. A standard business ploy; it is vulnerable to more innovative entrants.

Exploring. This conversation integrates extraversion and change. How do we advance in the market place with new products and services and/or through diversification? This is the entrepreneurial mindset that plans for growth and expansion into new markets. Alternatively, an overly ambitious programme that - without a sustainable infrastructure - over extends itself

Don't fall in love with ideas. By ideas I mean: systems, marketing approaches, technologies, partnerships, whatever. Because as soon as you as you fall in love with one approach, you lose sight of other possibilities. Every right idea eventually becomes the wrong idea. **Roger von Oech**

SO WHAT?

The term head to head competition is literal. Global competition is not just product vs. product, company vs. company. It is mind-set vs. mind-set. **Gary Hamel and C.K Prahalad**

What is on the strategic radar screen of the senior executive team? And what is not? Which issues receive most airtime and constructive dialogue in key meetings? Tangled up in short-term operational pressures? Or, fantasising about future business possibilities?

When you become larger, what's unsaid also increases in an organisation. **Hayagreeva Rao**

Do these conversations reflect the evolution of the business as it faces new and different challenges?

NOTES

1. The Ambidextrous Organisation, Charles O'Reilly and Michael Tushman; https://hbr.org/2004/04/the-ambidextrous-organization

2. Predictable Success: Getting Your Organisation On the Growth Track - and Keeping It There, Les McKeown

Will this acquisition succeed?

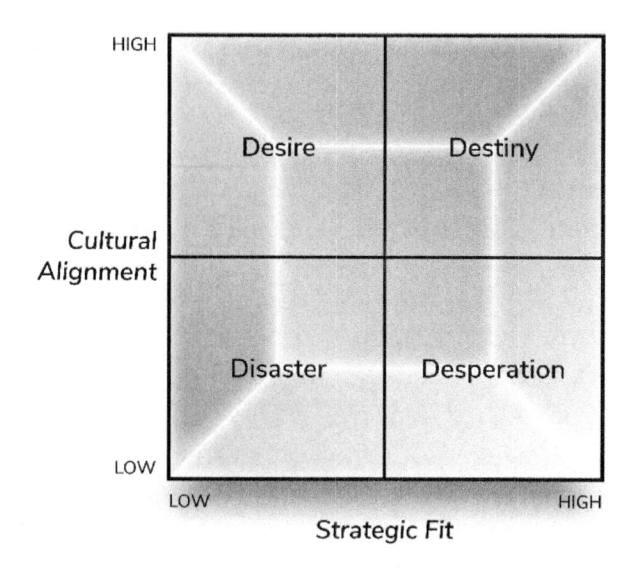

Cultural Alignment (vertical axis, LOW to HIGH) vs *Strategic Fit* (horizontal axis, LOW to HIGH):
- Top-left: Desire
- Top-right: Destiny
- Bottom-left: Disaster
- Bottom-right: Desperation

Mergers are like marriages. They are the bringing together of two individuals. If you wouldn't marry someone for the operational efficiencies they offer in the running of a household, then why would you combine two companies with unique cultures and identities for that reason. **Simon Sinek**

Gerald Levin oversaw the integration of an old time media content company and an exciting internet firm. This was the mega-merger between Time Warner and a vastly overvalued AOL, in a $200 billion deal, now perceived as *the worst transaction in business history. A deal motivated not by logic or strategy but by egos.*[1]

I never feared failure going into the AOL merger. **Gerry Levin**[2]

Mergers and acquisitions (M&As) represent a road map for organisational growth, resource acquisition, and competitive positioning. Why then do over 50% M&A deals fail to achieve their intended objectives?

Every single time you make a merger, somebody loses their identity. And saying something different is just rubbish. **Carlos Ghosn**

This quadrant identifies two critical themes to explain the relative success or failure of a mergers and acquisitions enterprise.[3]

More dumb acquisitions are made in the name of strategic plans than any other. **Warren Buffett**

Strategic Fit. This theme is about business logic, or in consulting speak, synergy. In low strategic fit, the rationale is either ill-defined or simply wrong headed. At the other end, there is a compelling business reason - cost savings, technological traction, market positioning - to drive the decision to do a deal.

Cultural Alignment. This reflects the extent to which values and an operating ethos are shared between the two firms. Low, and there is a fundamental mismatch of principles and expectations of employee behaviour. High, a meeting of minds on beliefs and organisational priorities for the workforce.

Four M & A scenarios emerge from this interplay.

Disaster. When strategic fit and cultural alignment are both low, this is the stuff of Shakespearean tragedy and comedy. Often, a forced marriage, driven by the necessity for short term survival at senior levels across the two firms. There is no long-term gain - for shareholders or employees.[4]

It's far better to be unhappy alone than unhappy with someone - so far. **Marilyn Monroe**

Desire. This is the combination of low strategic fit and high cultural alignment. At best, the merger or acquisition is a partnership based on a shared understanding of how the future organisation will work when everyone plays nice. At worst, this is hope over experience. When there is no strategic logic, play nice quickly becomes a game of fight nasty.

The big business mergers have the appearance of dinosaurs mating. **John Naisbitt**

Desperation. When high strategic fit coincides with low cultural alignment, this - from the perspective of the professional advisors - looks a great deal. At best, one firm dominates and takes control to drive through a fundamental shift in the new firm, one that engages employees in a new enterprise. At worst, the new firm faces resistance from the legacy workforce. And the most talented employees vote with their feet and exit.

Amazon and Whole Foods' relationship problems were completely predictable. They now stand on a fault line where tensions often erupt in mergers. This fault line is what we call tightness versus looseness. When tight and loose cultures merge, there is a good chance that they will clash. **Michele Gelfand**

Destiny. The stars align when strategic fit meets cultural alignment. This is the deal when the business logic is well founded; the marriage is based on a shared understanding of values and operating principles. Rare, but the gains are significant - especially when attention is paid to the integration process and the proactive management of organisational change.

SO WHAT?

I always said that mega mergers were for megalomaniacs. **David Ogilvy**

M & As offer significant opportunities for growth and value creation. They are also fraught with challenges. Amidst the excitement of doing a big deal, it is useful to check: does the strategy make business sense? Can we bring together the legacy of two different organisational cultures? If the answer is no - this is business as ego, not informed commercial savvy.

NOTES

1. How attitudes to time shape 10 leadership patterns; https://talentworldconsulting.com/wp-content/uploads/2023/08/Its-About-Leadership-Time.pdf

2. Levin went on to be a director at Moon View Sanctuary, a secluded California facility with neuro-scientific technology and ancient wisdom, for prices starting at a mere $175,000 a year.

3. The incentives for Boards and investment bankers is possibly the biggest factor in triggering a M & A deal.

4. Swissair - meltdown of a national icon; https://d3.harvard.edu/platform-rctom/submission/swissair-meltdown-of-a-national-icon/

Personal Mastery

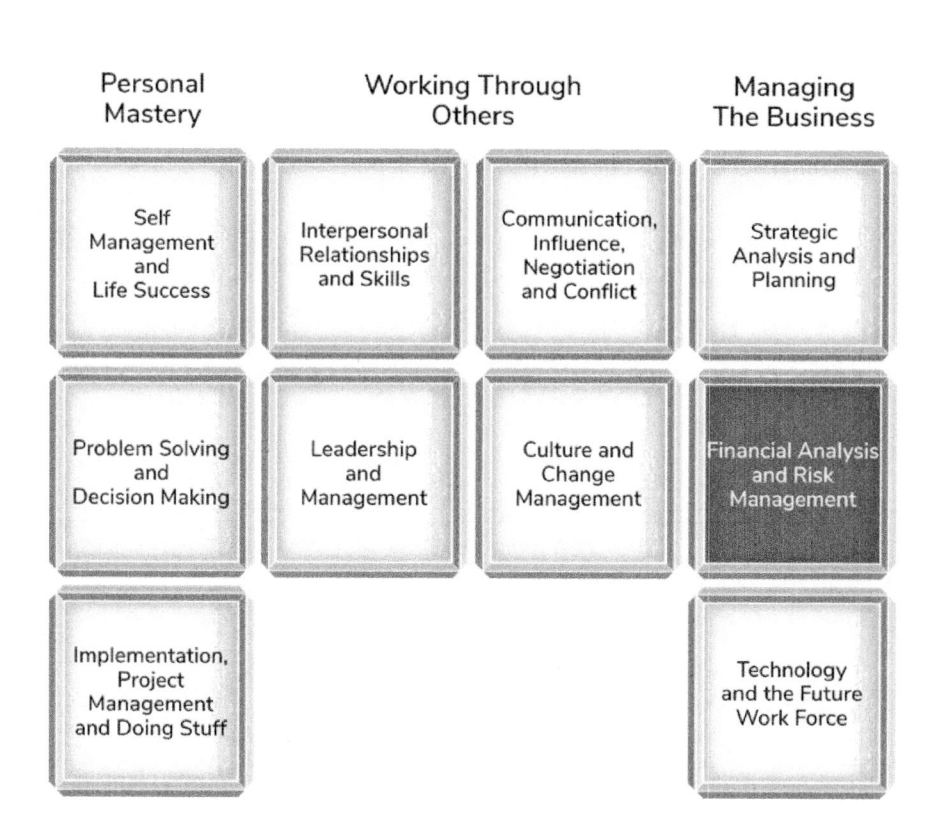

- Self Management and Life Success
- Problem Solving and Decision Making
- Implementation, Project Management and Doing Stuff

Working Through Others

- Interpersonal Relationships and Skills
- Leadership and Management

- Communication, Influence, Negotiation and Conflict
- Culture and Change Management

Managing The Business

- Strategic Analysis and Planning
- Financial Analysis and Risk Management
- Technology and the Future Work Force

Can we achieve cost savings?

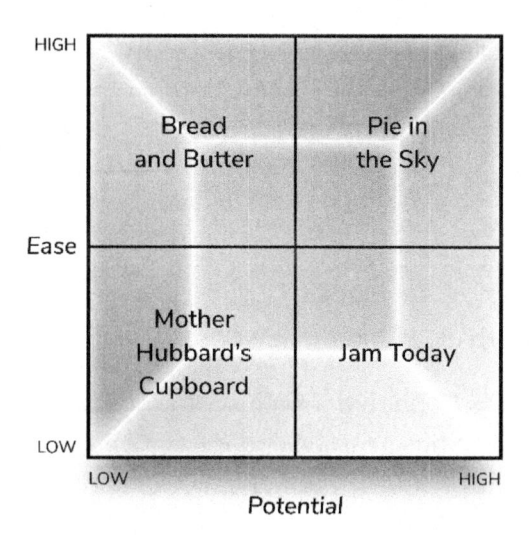

Chart: A 2x2 matrix with Ease (LOW to HIGH) on the vertical axis and Potential (LOW to HIGH) on the horizontal axis. Quadrants: top-left "Bread and Butter", top-right "Pie in the Sky", bottom-left "Mother Hubbard's Cupboard", bottom-right "Jam Today".

Hypocrisy can afford to be magnificent in its promises, for never intending to go beyond promise, it costs nothing. **Edmund Burke**

From business process redesign, shared services, outsourcing, ERP and cloud technologies to automation, generative AI is the most recent in the wave of initiatives with the promise of significant organisational cost savings. Consultancies provide indicative cost savings; a typical figure of 30%.

Why then is there a gap between the claim and the reality? And why is the promise of massive cost reductions often not realised?

The three rules. #1 Better before cheaper: Don't compete on price, compete on value. #2 Revenue before cost: Don't drive profits by cutting cost, instead find ways to earn higher prices or higher volume. #3 There are no other rules. **Michael Raynor**[1]

Two dimensions explain the challenge of making cost savings.

Potential. This describes the size of the possible benefit. At the low end of this axis, any cost savings will be modest and incremental.

Alternatively at the high end, there is scope to transform the business into a much more profitable enterprise.

Ease. How much effort is required to achieve these savings? At one end, the low hanging fruit which can be seized easily without significant disruption. At the other extreme, savings will require *blood, sweat and tears*, with a major risk of business turbulence.

They say it is the first step that costs the effort. I do not find it so. I am sure I could write unlimited first chapters. I have indeed written many. **JRR Tolkien**

Four scenarios are highlighted.

Mother Hubbard's Cupboard. Potential savings are low and difficult to achieve. This is a business looking for any opportunity to cut back on expenditure to maintain profitability. Understandable for short-term survival, often this is a tactic of desperation. And sometimes the cure kills the patient.

Old Mother Hubbard went to the cupboard to give the poor dog a bone. When she got there, the cupboard was bare. So the poor lil' dog had none.

Bread and Butter. In this combination, the potential savings are not large, but can be achieved relatively easily. This is ongoing financial discipline to manage budgets proactively to eliminate the unnecessary and avoid the bureaucratic creep that is damaging in the long-term. Conversely, a penny pinching mind-set that is counter-productive to creativity and collaboration.

Jam Today. When the potential gains of savings are high and can be realised quickly and easily, these are opportunities to seize immediately. Typically found in under-led and over-managed firms, this is trouble-shooting to cancel expensive vanity projects, streamline clunky systems and processes and introduce rigour into planning and implementation systems. The hazard: an organisational starvation diet.

The rule is, jam tomorrow, and jam yesterday - but never jam today. It must come sometimes to jam today, Alice objected. **Lewis Carroll**

Pie in the Sky. Massive cost savings are promised despite the difficulty of achieving these gains. Much loved by consulting firms, at best, a sustained programme of transformation to rethink the core business and revitalise productivity. Here, organisations are brought back from the near dead. More often, an attempt to resuscitate a business, lacking a viable future and a hope that is rarely realised.

A transformational relationship is where we transform their money into our money. **Duff McDonald, The Firm on McKinsey**[2]

SO WHAT?

The tyranny of compounding costs can devastate the miracle of compounding returns. **John Bogle**

Administrative rigour and financial discipline are the fundamentals of a well-run business. There is also the opportunity - through a combination of emerging technology and innovation in work practices - to make major improvements in efficiency and productivity. It is worth asking how achievable these gains are, and if there is possibility of unintended negative consequences when cost savings become the dominant management mind set.

Competition is the keen cutting edge of business, always shaving away at costs. **Henry Ford**

Sometimes eggs need to be broken to make an omelette. Sometimes the results are a scrambled mess.

NOTES

1. Three rules; how exceptional companies think; https://www2.deloitte.com/content/dam/Deloitte/ar/Documents/strategy/Deloitte_AR_Estrategia%20-Three-rules.pdf

2. The Firm: The Story of McKinsey and its Secret Influence on American Business, by Duff McDonald; https://www.ft.com/content/e512d598-2530-11e3-b349-00144feab7de

Does the firm have a black hole?

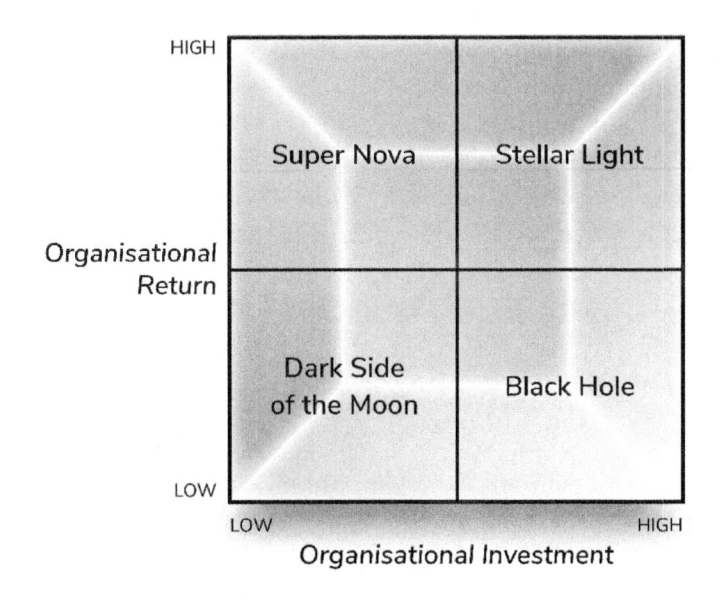

```
                    HIGH
                    ┌──────────────┬──────────────┐
                    │              │              │
                    │  Super Nova  │ Stellar Light│
                    │              │              │
Organisational      ├──────────────┼──────────────┤
Return              │              │              │
                    │  Dark Side   │  Black Hole  │
                    │  of the Moon │              │
                    │              │              │
                    LOW────────────┴──────────────┘
                    LOW                         HIGH
                       Organisational Investment
```

Black holes emit a negative radiance that draws all toward them, gobbling up all who come too close. These strange galactic monsters, for whom creation is destruction. **Robert Coover**

How does an organisation direct its resources? The allocation of capital is a key factor in business performance and longevity. Exceptional leaders[1] understand this. Time, energy and money directed to dud organisational activity is wasted. More promising opportunities are withheld funding. Wise investors target funds to those with future promise not past performance.

This quadrant is based on two dimensions.

Organisational Investment. This reflects the tough decisions needed to prioritise and allocate resources across the range of functions and departments asking for additional investment. This is the size of investment, from low, the minimum needed to stay in the game, through to high, a substantial allocation of resource to a specific business activity.

Organisational Return. What is the outcome of this investment? This dimension ranges from low, an investment with minimal impact or worse, loses the business money, through to high to realise substantial gains.

Four investment outcomes emerge.

Dark Side of the Moon. This is low investment and low return. These are the activities not on the strategic radar screen. Not seen as a business priority, these issues are rarely discussed at senior levels. Why should they be? Alternatively, a sphere of ignorance that ignores changes in the market place and the threats facing the business.

And if the band you're in, starts playing different tunes, I'll see you on the dark side of the moon. **Pink Floyd**

Super Nova. Low Investment is accompanied with high return. This is the happy scenario in which the firm enjoys the glow of its business stars, profitable activities that require little capital. Stars, eventually, do burn out. Here, the firm witnesses a spectacular light show before finding itself in strategic blackness.

There goes a supernova. What a pushover, yeah. **Frankie Goes To Hollywood**

Black Hole. High levels of investment are associated with low levels of return. Generous budgets are allocated to this activity, but the firm sees no corresponding business gain. This is organisational astronomy as a combination of arrogance, bureaucracy and complacency to pull in money that disappears. Optimistically, a key priority for prompt action and a management overhaul to refocus activity. More typically the law of sunk cost applies. Further resource is committed to recoup the previous investments.[2]

Don't jump in the black hole. **Covstline**

Stellar Light. High levels of investment are accompanied with high levels of return. These activities are the bright performers within an overall portfolio of business activity to fund future research and development, and improvements in the corporate infrastructure to keep ahead of the competition. Like the Super Novas, these Stellar Lights burn bright. The fireworks of a spectacular display can also blind us to market place realities. The organisation looks at a different sky to those of its customers.

You are stellar (I've lost your communication), Stellar (I wish the Constellation), So What. **Boomerang, Stellar**

SO WHAT?

Effective capital allocation requires a certain temperament. To be successful you have to think like an investor, dispassionately and probabilistically with a certain coolness. **Michael Mauboussin**

This quadrant highlights an overlooked organisational issue: the shrewd allocation of capital in the face of competing priorities for investment. Judgements have to be made to challenge political interests and functional gamesmanship for the long-term.

And if the senior team is heading for a black hole, it is time for a shift in strategic astronomy.

NOTES

1. The Outsiders: Eight Unconventional CEOs and Their Radically Rational Blueprint for Success, William N. Thorndike

2. Sunk cost; https://thedecisionlab.com/biases/the-sunk-cost-fallacy

How is the business performing?

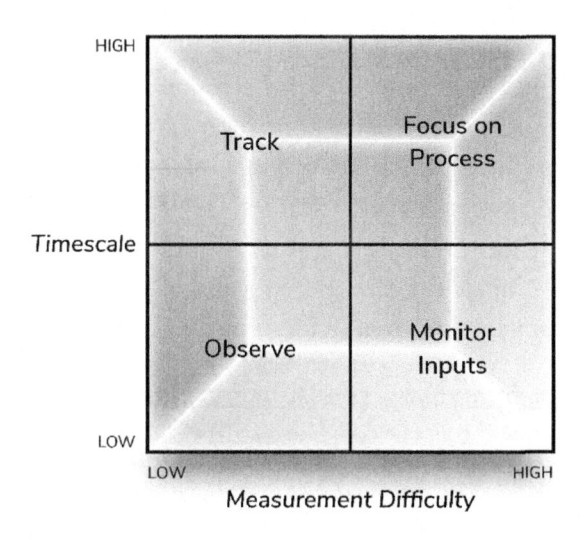

Chart: A 2x2 matrix with Timescale (LOW to HIGH) on the y-axis and Measurement Difficulty (LOW to HIGH) on the x-axis. Quadrants: top-left "Track", top-right "Focus on Process", bottom-left "Observe", bottom-right "Monitor Inputs".

There are things that can be measured. There are things that are worth measuring. But what can be measured is not always what is worth measuring. What gets measured may have no relationship to what we really want to know. The costs of measuring may be greater than the benefits. **Jerry Muller, The Tyranny of Metrics**

A healthcare system is conducting a review of its impact. How does it define outcomes? And how are these measured and managed for future improvements? Which metrics should be used to gain an insight into its performance?

These are not straightforward questions. If the healthcare system misjudges the metrics to evaluate impact, resources will be misdirected. Even worse, misleading metrics become counter-productive with negative consequences[1] to damage overall effectiveness.

This quadrant addresses the challenge of assessing performance.

Measurement Difficulty. In some spheres of life, success is obvious. A sports team wins a championship. In other domains, it is difficult to work out who wins and who loses. In low difficulty, metrics give an objective and reliable insight into performance. In high difficulty, the dynamics between cause and consequence - not the least the interaction with other variables - are complex. It is hard to establish which criteria will provide an accurate assessment of performance.

Timescale. Over which horizon is performance gauged? Short-term metrics allow judgements to be made within a relatively narrow window, within days, weeks and months. Decisions for performance improvement can be made quickly. Some measures - possibly the most important - can only be made over an extended period, years, and in some instances, only over a life time.

Count no person happy until the end is known. **Solon**[2]

Four boxes emerge from this interplay of performance.

Observe. Performance measurement is relatively easy and can be evaluated in the short-term. Gains are achieved through the straightforward task of watching and listening to provide the feedback for opportunities for future improvement. The hazard: simple metrics become a substitute to avoid addressing more complex performance issues.

I always wanted to watch with my own eyes without having my judgement swayed by the filters of others. **Sir Alex Ferguson, former manager, Manchester United Football Club**

Track. In this scenario of relative ease of measurement against longer-term criteria, the challenge is to implement robust metrics based on results. These results need clear definition. Nonetheless, there is confidence that the performance metrics provide a meaningful insight into what is important. For this metric methodology to operate effectively, interim measures need to be introduced to review progress against these outcomes.

Over time, simple metrics threaten to distort or take the place of values. **Olúfẹ́mi Táíwò**

Monitor Inputs. When performance is hard to measure against a short-term time frame, the sensible solution is to start with the inputs that will generate the desired result. This requires a decent working model of success to ensure there is a direct read across between inputs and outputs. In its absence, there is scope for drift and performance to stall.

A feel for the whole and a sense for the unique are precisely what numerical metrics cannot supply. **Jerry Muller, The Tyranny of Metrics**

Focus on Process. The most difficult performance scenario. Metrics are difficult to obtain and results can only be evaluated over the long-term. This requires a major rethink to ask: why is this the case? Are we looking in the wrong place against an unrealistic time frame? This scenario is often business reality. Attempts to introduce simple and short-term measures can only be misleading if not damaging.[3]

It is counter-intuitive that adding one more time-consuming pit stop to your race will speed things up overall. But it does - up to a point. **The Lean Viking**

SO WHAT?

Things don't automatically get better because we measure them. Apparently, to make things better we have to do something. **Bob Hoffman**

Which metrics should organisations apply and track?[4] Do these measures provide insight into both leading predictive indicators as well as outcomes and results. Most important, do they explain the chains of cause and effect and what will happen in the medium and long-term?

NOTES

1. When Good Intentions Backfire: What is the Cobra Effect?
https://www.choicehacking.com/2022/01/04/what-is-the-cobra-effect/

2. Count No Man Happy Until the End Is Known;
https://www.artofmanliness.com/character/advice/count-no-man-happy-until-the-end-is-known/

3. Jack Welch at GE represents a case study of results driven through the index of shareholder value, an indicator of market expectations of a firm's future success. This proved very good for Jack personally, but left his successor, Jeff Immelt highly vulnerable. GE Tears Down The House That Jack Built;
https://www.forbes.com/sites/brycehoffman/2015/04/11/ge-tears-down-the-house-that-jack-built/?

4. What happened to the Balanced Score Card?
https://www.linkedin.com/pulse/whatever-happened-balanced-scorecard-alan-hayman/

Are we covering up?

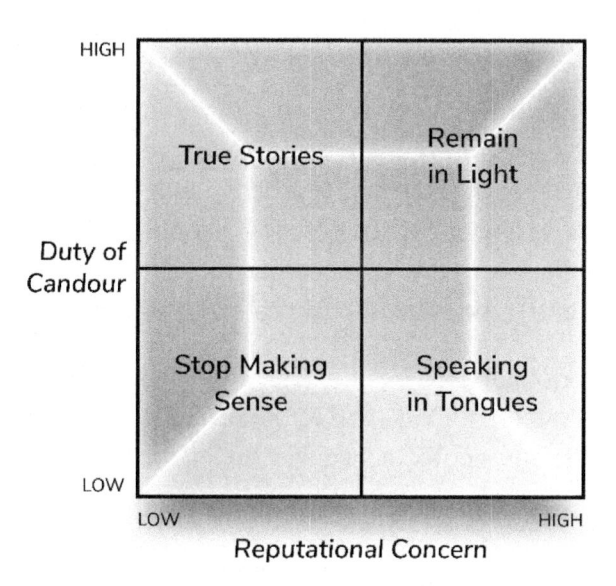

Chart: 2×2 matrix with Y-axis "Duty of Candour" (LOW to HIGH) and X-axis "Reputational Concern" (LOW to HIGH). Quadrants: Top-left "True Stories"; Top-right "Remain in Light"; Bottom-left "Stop Making Sense"; Bottom-right "Speaking in Tongues".

The NHS and successive governments compounded the agony by refusing to accept that wrong had been done. **Sir Brian Langstaff, Chair of the Infected Blood Inquiry**

The infected blood scandal[1] is another in a long line of government and corporate failure, deception and cover up in the UK. The hall of shame is long: Windrush, Hillsborough, Grenfell Tower, the Post Office Horizon scandal, and more. We are told after lengthy inquiries and comprehensive reports that lessons have been learnt. But the feeling remains: more scandals of incompetence, negligence and cover up will emerge.[2] Why?

It is almost always the cover-up rather than the event that causes trouble. **Howard Baker**

Which dynamics are at play to translate initial failings in an organisational system into escalating problems? And cover up with damaging consequences - for end users, employees and with substantial organisational costs?

One of the weaknesses of the company now is it is a bit cheap and cheerful and overly nasty, and that reflects my personality. **Michael O'Leary, CEO, Ryanair**

Two dimensions are critical to whistle blowing.

Reputational Concern. How does the organisation want to be viewed by multiple and competing constituents, eg, shareholders, regulatory agencies, employees, the general public? Low, a lack of concern about how the organisation is perceived, particularly if business imperatives conflict with an ethical stance. High, the attention to do the right thing and to be seen as doing the right thing.

Duty of Candour.[3] This dimension outlines openness and transparency. Low on duty of candour is a culture of obfuscation and secrecy to avoid the spotlight of scrutiny. High, the willingness to disclose information and be direct and honest in communication.

If the Hillsborough Law was in place in 1989, it would be impossible for the truth to have been hidden, because those hiding the truth would have known they would be found out, and quickly prosecuted. **Pete Weatherby KC**

Four organisational stances to openness emerge.

Stop Making Sense. A low concern for reputation intersects with low on the duty of candour. There may be valid reasons to keep a low profile and avoid investigation and inquiry into the issues. Typically, however, an organisation which prefers to work in the dark to conceal the indefensible, if not downright illegal, activity.

I can't seem to face up to the facts. I'm tense and nervous, and I can't relax. I can't sleep 'cause my bed's on fire. Don't touch me I'm a real live wire. **Psycho Killer, Talking Heads**

True Stories. Although there is relatively little importance on reputation, there is an outlook of high candour.[4] At best, this organisation tells it the way it is, without regard for the consequences for its image and standing. Conversely, a corporate naivete resulting in reputational damage and stakeholder disengagement.

This ain't no party, this ain't no disco, this ain't no fooling around. **Life During Wartime, Talking Heads**

Speaking in Tongues. A high concern for reputation coincides with a lack of candour. Image must be preserved at all costs to present a positive impression to the audience of different organisational constituents. The upside: the protection of commercially sensitive information and the maintenance of intellectual property. The downside: a lack of transparency that reinforces a culture of secrecy becomes the arc of deception and cover-up, and ultimately counter-productive to a positive reputation.

Everything is divided. Nothing is complete. Everything looks impressive. Do not be deceived. **Making Flippy Floppy, Talking Heads**

Remain in Light. This outlook combines a concern for reputation with a high need for candour. This follows the advice of Warren Buffett: *it takes 20 years to build a reputation and five minutes to ruin it. If you think about that, you'll do things differently.* An outlook that demands courage in the face of a public relations disaster, if well managed, it not only restores confidence, it builds long-term business trust.[5]

I guess that this must be the place. **This Must Be the Place (Naive Melody), Talking Heads**

SO WHAT?

Take a look at these hands. The hand speaks. **Born Under Punches (The Heat Goes On), Talking Heads**

How far are we prepared to go to protect an organisation's reputation? How much transparency and openness is *appropriate*? Different sectors and industries have different expectations from their stakeholders. What is obvious: a lack of candour to maintain an organisational façade quickly becomes a destructive cycle of lies and lies upon lies, with the potential to ruin a business.

NOTES

1. Infected blood scandal. Not an accident, with catalogue of failures and downright deception by NHS and governments; https://news.sky.com/story/infected-blood-scandal-was-not-an-accident-with-catalogue-of-failures-and-downright-deception-by-nhs-and-governments-13140111

2. The most controversial British scandals of the 21st century; https://theweek.com/95467/the-biggest-british-scandals-of-the-21st-century

3. UK citizens are advocating a *Hillsborough Law,* named after the police cover up following the Hillsborough Stadium deaths in Sheffield UK in 1989, where police blamed the fans for their deaths when all along it was because of police actions. https://hillsboroughlawnow.org

4. Accidental candour after a liquid lunch possibly. Gerald Ratner, CEO Ratners announces: *We do cut-glass sherry decanters complete with six glasses on a silver-plated tray that your butler can serve you drinks on, all for £4.95. People say, How can you sell this for such a low price? I say, because it's total crap.*
How to lose $1B in 10 seconds; https://thehustle.co/gerald-ratners-billion-dollar-speech

5. Tylenol made a hero of Johnson & Johnson : The recall that started them all; https://www.nytimes.com/2002/03/23/your-money/IHT-tylenol-made-a-hero-of-johnson-johnson-the-recall-that-started.html

Will our prospects become profitable clients?

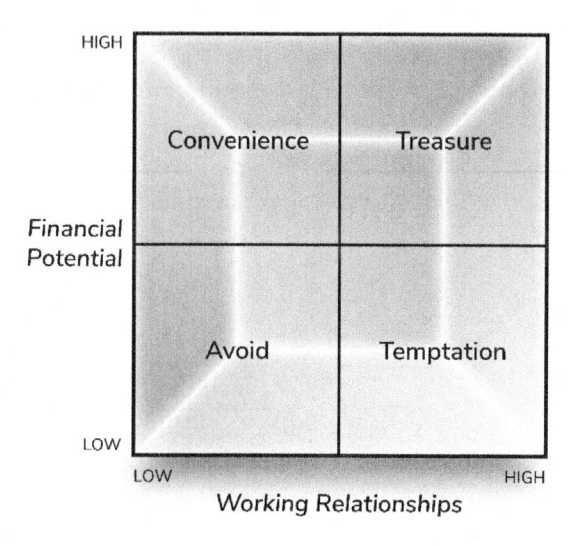

Seldom does Pareto's Law apply to profits. Instead of 20% of customers generating 80% of the profits, it is more likely that 20% of customers provide 100% of profits given that in many businesses, 25% are loss making.[1]

For those in the business of finding and serving clients for a long-term professional relationship, understanding the profile of these profitable individuals and groups is key. Profitability is not the only consideration. The experience of these relationships matters. How can we determine the dynamic of this relationship at the outset?

This quadrant hinges on two dimensions to turn prospects into long-term clients.

Working Relationships. Some clients provide a difficult and demanding experience. Low, and the relationship makes working life a misery for colleagues and associates. Others provide positive interactions that are energising and rewarding.

Financial Potential. This indicates profitability over time, from the loss making client damaging to our business, to the highly profitable, critical to the future success of the firm.

The interaction of these two variables highlights four client categories.

Avoid. A client relationship which rarely succeeds. This is the prospect who combines disorganisation with a troublesome interpersonal manner. It is difficult sometimes to work out why the conversation took place in the first place. They are late for meetings, they don't review material sent in advance, and then adopt an aggressive manner during discussions.[2] High maintenance in future, this client damages the bottom line.[3]

Bad clients will steal your soul. **Anon**

Convenience. Some prospects make life difficult for themselves as well as for the professional service firms they commission. Interpersonal dynamics and project management are frustrating. But for any number of reasons - the circumstances of the firm, the nature of the assignment, and client indolence - these prospects can be highly profitable in the short-term. Over time, these individuals leave their companies. The inevitable trajectory: an interpersonal style that is as annoying to their colleagues as to the professional advisors they brought in.

Temptation. Superficially appealing at the outset, this prospect fails to make a financial contribution to the business. As individuals, they may be interesting and engaging. Sometimes they have an interesting background or innovative ideas suggestive of a long-term and profitable relationship. The reality? Rarely is this promise translated into practical outcomes. When the number of *wouldn't it be great ifs* is higher than the *can we make a starts*, a problematic client relationship.

I can resist everything except temptation. **Oscar Wilde**

Treasure. This combination of a positive working relationship and business profitability results in mutually beneficial outcomes. A mature dynamic based on a genuine model of partnership. The experience is enjoyable and rewarding at a personal and professional level with a demonstrable business impact. This grouping should be the focus of all business development effort as well as for client service.

It never ceases to amaze me that companies spend millions to attract new customers - people they don't know - and spend next to nothing to keep the ones they've got. **Tom Peters**

SO WHAT?

If you do good work for good clients, it will lead to other good work for other good clients. If you do bad work for bad clients, it will lead to other bad work for other bad clients. **Michael Bierut**

It can be difficult to differentiate across the four clusters of prospects, particularly at the early stages of discussions. But if our firm does not have an established profiling methodology to retain its current clients and attract new prospects, we find ourselves frustrated working with difficult and high maintenance clients for little return.

NOTES

1. In 1906, Vilfredo Pareto from Italy observed that nearly 80% of Italy's land was owned and controlled by almost 20% of the population. He tested this finding to observe it generalised across a range of domains in life. The 80-20 Principle states that 20% of the cause generates 80% of the effects. 20% of customers generate 80% of sales and so on. Like any other rule of thumb, the Pareto Principle does not hold true in all situations. For example, 1% of the internet community creates 99% of the content. But the 80/20 principle is a useful reminder that distributions are typically skewed.

2. Bad clients will steal your soul; https://www.savvysme.com.au/article/798-bad-clients-will-steal-your-soul

3. This principle also applies to work colleagues. The No AssHole Rule; http://www.huffingtonpost.com/robert-sutton/the-no-asshole-rule-part-_b_49678.html

Should we outsource?

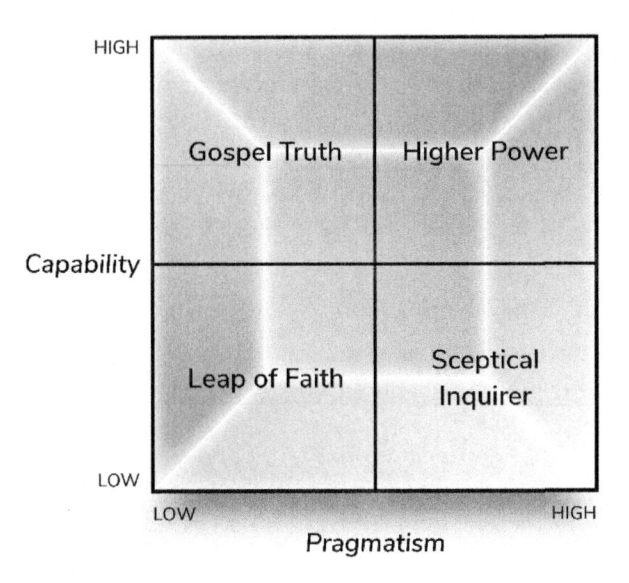

```
        HIGH
         │
         │   Gospel Truth  │  Higher Power
         │                 │
Capability                 │
         │   Leap of Faith │  Sceptical
         │                 │  Inquirer
        LOW
            LOW              HIGH
              Pragmatism
```

Master your strengths, outsource your weaknesses. **Ryan Khan, founder of The Hired Group**

Outsourcing can lead to significant cost savings. Firms anticipate sizeable reductions in workforce and operational costs by outsourcing tasks to regions with lower wage structures, or to access in depth specialist experience and expertise, not available in-house.[1]

Do what you do best, outsource the rest. **Peter Drucker**

Some organisations - outsourcing pioneers in the 90s and 00s - are now insourcing key functions. The thinking is that the once anticipated reduction in costs led to a loss of control over the levers key to organisational values and culture. Other firms saw a decline in levels of customer service that damaged market position and reputation.[2]

If you rely too much on the people in other countries and other companies, in a sense that's your brain and you are outsourcing your brain. **Bill Gates**

Two dimensions underpin the outsourcing decision.

Pragmatism. What thinking underpins the decision to outsource or not? At one end of this spectrum, an ideological driven stance. Outsourcing is the default position. At the other, decisions are made on a case by case basis to assess the pros and cons of outsourcing a specific business function.

Capability. This dimension asks the question: which activities are key to the long-term success of the firm? In low capability, the organisation has no clear view of which core competencies need to be built and maintained to secure its future. In high capability, a thoughtful analysis determines the mix of expertise, talent and technology that require proactive management.

Outsourcing isn't the answer to everything. Lots of internet marketing pundits will tell you to outsource, outsource, outsource. Having a trusted team that knows each other and enjoys working together is good, too. **Ian Lurie**

Leap of Faith. This is low on both pragmatism and capability. In this box, companies dive head first into outsourcing with an unquestioning belief in its commercial impact. Here, strategic issues are neglected. Short term cost reductions are often followed by confused accountabilities, and a drop in performance.

Sometimes a leap of faith doesn't pan out. **Edwin Catmull, Pixar**

Gospel Truth. Low pragmatism combines with high capability. This is the business certainty to outsource activity based on a clear view of what will and won't matter to the future of the firm. The upside: a bet on outsourcing to allow the organisation to focus on what is essential to the execution of a well-defined strategy. The downside: it misjudges which competencies are in fact peripheral and which are core. It then scrambles to bring in-house those activities it had previously viewed as non-essential to its plans.

Sceptical Inquirer. In this stance to outsourcing, high pragmatism meets low capability. At best, this is a firm in survival mode looking for ways to achieve cost reductions, and a battle to maintain flexibility for a different war. Alternatively, short-term expediency. The business lacks conviction about the key competencies needed to compete in the future market-place.

We've all seen this movie before, in places like Enron, It's not surprising that before a crisis, there are indications of real deep problems that have their roots in leadership. **Chesley Sullenberger**

Higher Power. This is the business outlook that is clear about the drivers of its future success and what is of fundamental importance to get right. But it does not take a dogmatic view of how this is best managed. A kind of religious pick and mix, it walks the tightrope between belief in the benefits of outsourcing and the need to build the core competencies for strategic differentiation.

SO WHAT?

Would you put your family on a Max simulator trained aircraft? I wouldn't. ***Boeing Employee*** [3]

What to keep in-house and what to out-source is an ongoing challenge for organisations. There is no obvious solution. Different firms face different cost pressures, a range of market opportunities and an array of strategic options. Whatever does seem clear is that the ideologically driven approach that shaped much of thinking in recent business history, resulted in a blinkered mindset of cost reduction rather than revenue generation.[4]

NOTES

1. The Pros And Cons Of Outsourcing; https://www.forbes.com/sites/deeppatel/2017/07/17/the-pros-and-cons-of-outsourcing-and-the-effect-on-company-culture/

2. Why Outsourcing Customer Service Kills Purpose-Driven Brands; https://sustainablebrands.com/read/organizational-change/why-outsourcing-customer-service-kills-purpose-driven-brands

3. Outsourcing main cause for Boeing 787 Dreamliner problems; https://www.consultancy.uk/news/297/outsourcing-main-cause-for-boeing-787-dreamliner-problems

4. Three Rules for Making a Company Truly Great; https://hbr.org/2013/04/three-rules-for-making-a-company-truly-great

What do we value most in supplier relationships?

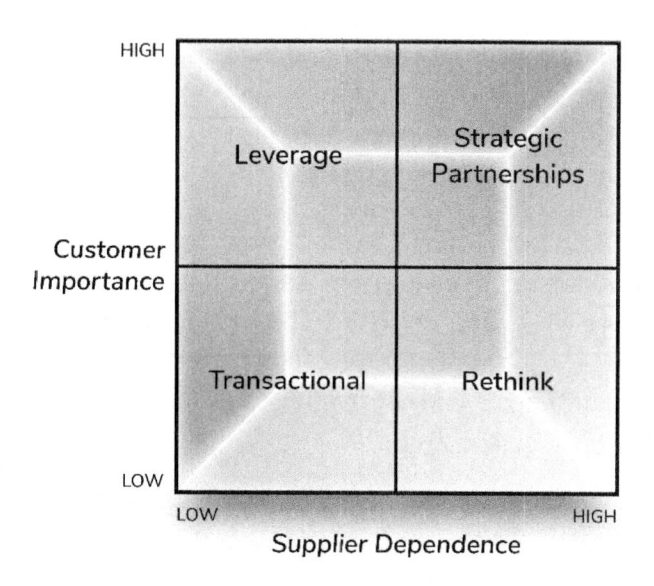

	Supplier Dependence LOW	Supplier Dependence HIGH
Customer Importance HIGH	Leverage	Strategic Partnerships
Customer Importance LOW	Transactional	Rethink

Get closer than ever to your customer. So close, in fact, that you tell them what they need well before they realise it themselves. **Steve Jobs**

Peter Drucker said: *the purpose of a business is to create and keep a customer.* Business success is however more than a product or service proposition. The nature and strength of the relationships with suppliers is increasingly critical. The days of vertical integration in which a single firm controls all stages of production from the acquisition of raw materials, manufacturing through to retailing the final product, are largely over.[1]

Only recently have people begun to recognise that working with suppliers is just as important as listening to customers. **Barry Nalebuff**

Understanding the dynamics of supplier and customer relationships is therefore paramount to a business as it evaluates its business vulnerabilities and future strategic options.

You must have a supplier relationship of constant improvement.
W. Edwards Deming

This quadrant maps out the relationship between supplier dependence and customer importance.

Supplier Dependence. In low dependence, a supplier is easily replaceable. There is no significant impact on the business. With high dependence - any permutation of specialist expertise, proprietary products, intellectual property, cost of switching - a supplier is critical to the success of the firm.[2]

Customer Importance. Low importance customers have a minor impact on our revenue and unlikely to be strategically aligned with the company's plans for the future. High importance customers significantly contribute to current revenue and future growth, and a key part of the business's future.

We like people who are honest. Honest in argument, honest with clients, honest with suppliers, honest with the company - and above all, honest with consumers. **David Ogilvy**

The four scenarios of supplier relationships.

Transactional. A scenario of low supplier dependence and low customer importance. Risks at first sight are low. This is typically a standard operational transaction; the focus is on operational efficiency. Alternatively, the customer profile shifts, and a corresponding move to different supplier expectations is required.

Leverage. These customers are essential to the business and its future profitability, but there is little dependence on any single supplier. The expedient response is to exploit the asymmetry of supplier relationships. After all the supplier can be replaced easily. In the short-term, an effective tactic. Longer-term, this approach creates supplier dissatisfaction. It misses the opportunity to strengthen a relationship to enhance the customer proposition.

I am convinced that most companies don't maximize their barter possibilities. Instead of aggressively reducing costs by trading their services with those of their suppliers, they seem content to pay top dollar for everything. **Mark McCormack**

Rethink. Although a supplier is crucial to the business, the customer is relatively unimportant. Here there is a need to renegotiate the existing supplier relationship to mitigate the risks of dependency or locate alternative suppliers for cost savings and/or a fresh perspective for greater innovation.

On passengers who forget to print their boarding passes. We think they should pay €60 for being so stupid. **Michael O'Leary, Ryan Air**

Strategic Partnerships. High supplier dependence intersects with high customer importance. In this scenario, Benjamin Franklin reminds us: *we must all hang together, or, most assuredly, we shall all hang separately.* These relationships - internally with suppliers and externally with customers - require significant attention and investment for long-term mutual benefit. This is a business risk. When a firm's profitability depends on supplier integrity and reliability, its future is in jeopardy when a supplier fails to meet its commitments.

We are working closely with Boeing. It is still producing great aircraft, but there's no doubt in our mind that on the shop floor, the systems and the quality control need to be improved. **Michael O'Leary, Ryanair**[3]

SO WHAT?

Suppliers and especially manufacturers have market power because they have information about a product or a service that the customer does not and cannot have, and does not need if he can trust the brand. This explains the profitability of brands. **Peter Drucker**

If customer service was the buzzword of the last two to three decades, supplier management has moved to the centre of the radar screen for senior executives. Does our firm understand fully the opportunities and risks of the range of suppliers key to their future financial performance and reputation?

NOTES

1. Or not? Vertical Integration, are we coming full circle? https://medium.com/@sime.curkovic/vertical-integration-are-we-coming-full-circle-cb74bb29706c

2. The Dangers of Becoming Too Dependent on a Single Customer, Graham Kenny; https://hbr.org/2023/11/the-dangers-of-becoming-too-dependent-on-a-single-supplier

3. Ryanair CEO Slams Boeing Culture: They Love Talking Corporate Bullsh*t; https://skift.com/2024/03/20/ryanair-ceo-slams-boeing-culture/

Which consultancies should we avoid?

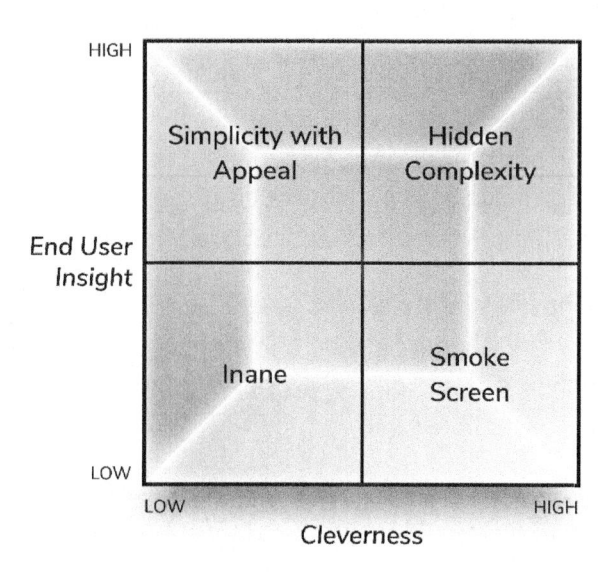

Diagram: 2x2 matrix with axes "End User Insight" (Low to High) and "Cleverness" (Low to High). Quadrants: Simplicity with Appeal (High Insight, Low Cleverness); Hidden Complexity (High Insight, High Cleverness); Inane (Low Insight, Low Cleverness); Smoke Screen (Low Insight, High Cleverness).

During the seven years that I worked as a management consultant, I spent a lot of time trying to look older than I was. I became pretty good at furrowing my brow and putting on sombre expressions. **Matthew Stewart, The Management Myth**

Management consulting firms - despite their questionable track record - still fare remarkably well within corporate life.[1] A number of factors explain why billing levels have held up despite a fairly dismal success rate. Not least is the alumni factor, exemplified by McKinsey[2], and how its consultants work with clients, transition to join them, and then advance through the ranks to take on senior executive roles. Unsurprisingly, future consulting gigs are handed to McKinsey. This operating model is now deep embedded within the consulting business generally.

Consultant: any ordinary guy more than fifty miles from home. **Eric Sevareid**

How should we evaluate consultancies to select a trusted firm to meet our organisational requirements?

The acid test of a consultant is whether they can say: everything's fine, we'll be off then. **Guy Browning**

Two dimensions underpin this grid of consulting types.

Cleverness. This axis accounts for the firm that, at one end of the range makes no attempt at leading-edge research, access to global benchmarking or any claim of originality. At the other end, these firms turn up equipped with a secret sauce proprietary theory and methodology based on *research has found* reports.

End User Insight. This indicates the level of insight for the client. A range from *so what - what was all that about?* - to a big deal that triggers fresh thinking and opens up new options and a range of possibilities for the business.

Not once did I catch myself thinking, Damn! If only I had known this sooner. **Matthew Stewart, The Management Myth**

Four consulting client scenarios emerge.

Inane. The consulting firm of dullness. Remarkably, this firm still does well in the market place, rehearsing the obvious to confirm existing assumptions to allow the client organisation to go on as it was. There is little incisive intelligence to analyse the problem or originality to generate different solutions. This firm provides external authority to tick the boxes and endorse the current political dynamic of its sponsors and stakeholders.

The quickest and easiest way to write a report in management consulting is to change the names in the last report. **Guy Browning**

Simplicity with Appeal. This category of firm has mastered the art of replaying well-founded principles with an ingenious twist. This consulting firm knows how to sell *old wine in new bottles*.[3] Nothing fundamentally new is being said. But what is said is said with a different spin, typically a new terminology and set of buzzwords[4], to give clients the comforting reassurance that the issues are understood and a solution has been identified.

Consultants will ultimately recommend that you do whatever you're not doing now. Centralise whatever is decentralised. Flatten whatever is vertical. Diversify whatever is concentrated and divest everything that is not core to the business. **Scott Adams**

Smoke Screen. Here the consulting firm is too clever for its own good. These firms bring a raft of research findings to the table with any permutation of data visualisation presentations. Some naïve clients are impressed with this intellectual showmanship. The project is given the green light. For the most part, this is the bluff and bananas of pseudo-science. The awkward manager who asks why this emperor is walking around naked is sidelined quickly with the admonition: *that is not helpful at this stage of the process.*

Give a man a fish, and you'll feed him for a day. Teach a man to fish, and he'll buy a funny hat. Talk to a hungry man about fish, and you're a consultant. **Scott Adams**

Hidden Complexity. These firms put in the hard yards to conduct original research and apply the findings to identify the key issues facing organisations. But they wear this knowledge lightly, conveying their findings with simplicity to capture the attention of potential clients with actionable insights. This is the consulting practice that translates complexity into a practical programme of delivery for their clients.

SO WHAT?

I would rather tell my mother that I was working as a pianist in the local brothel than admit that I had joined a consulting firm. **ENB Mitton, Duff McDonald, The Firm**

The selection of a consulting firm is as much a political choice as an intellectual decision. Typically, a solution has been determined. The issue then becomes which consulting practice will approve and implement this solution with credibility to reassure key stakeholders that if any boats are to be rocked, it won't affect them too much. Alternatively, there are exceptional firms which deploy insight and creativity.

NOTES

1. There is now an industry pointing out the failings of management consulting. The Big Con: How the Consulting Industry Weakens our Businesses, Infantilises our Governments and Warps our Economies, Mariana Mazzucato and Rosie Collington
Rip-off!: The Scandalous Inside Story of the Management Consulting Money Machine, David Craig

2. The Firm: The Inside Story of McKinsey, The World's Most Controversial Management Consultancy, Duff McDonald

3. The jingle jangle fallacy is a problem of language. When we assume two different constructs are the same because they have the same label, this is jingle. And when we think two concepts are different because they have different labels, this is jangle. This category of consulting firm has mastered the art of the jangle effect to relabel old constructs as a novel breakthrough concept.

4. Who Touched Base in my Thought Shower?: A Treasury of Unbearable Office Jargon, Steven Poole

How do our attitudes to money affect our lives?

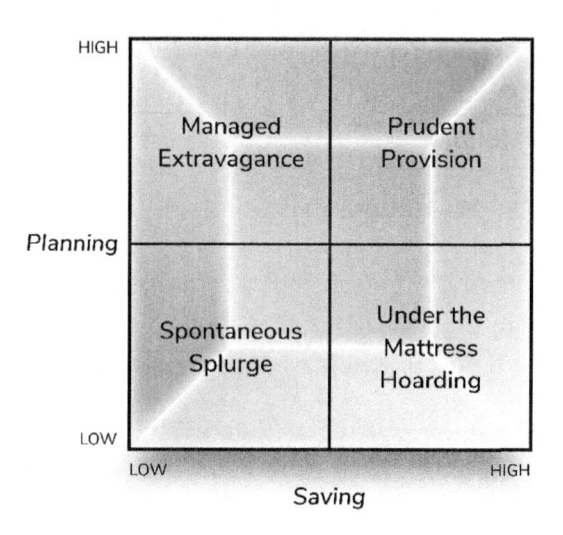

Planning HIGH	Managed Extravagance	Prudent Provision
LOW	Spontaneous Splurge	Under the Mattress Hoarding
	LOW Saving	HIGH

A person's treatment of money is the most decisive test of their character - how they make it and how they spend it. **James Moffat**

How we think about money has an important influence on our lives - personally and in our relationships with others. There are several factors that shape our attitudes to money: social and cultural, our own upbring, current financial circumstances and the phase within our life story.

At a party given by a billionaire, Kurt Vonnegut informs his pal, Joseph Heller, that their host a hedge fund manager, had made more money in a single day than Heller had earned from his wildly popular novel, Catch 22 over its whole history. Heller responds: Yes, but I have something he will never have. Enough. **John Bogle, Vanguard Group**

This quadrant highlights two dimensions in money management.

Saving. At one end of the spectrum, money is a resource to be spent or given away today. At the other, money is an asset that needs to be protected and invested for tomorrow's financial security.

Planning. This reflects the extent to which we control money through prioritisation and organisation. Low, a relaxed view; money will look after itself. High, a diligent and systematic outlook to attend carefully to the detail of financial management.

You can possess money, or you can despise money. The one fatal thing is to worship money and fail to get it. **George Orwell**

Four philosophies of money emerge.

Spontaneous Splurge. This combines high spending or giving with low planning. At best, a generous spirit which enjoys the benefits of money now, personally and for others. Alternatively, a reckless attitude in which money is squandered, financial problems are avoided and over time, creates pressures for the future.

I spent a lot of money on booze, birds and fast cars. The rest I just squandered. **George Best, voted the fifth best football player of all time**

Managed Extravagance. In this psychological profile, the focus is on spending and/or giving, but as part of a structured plan to pursue specific objectives in life. A strategy to improve status in a bid to impress others[1], or to build important connections for the long-term?

The person who dies rich dies disgraced. **Andrew Carnegie**

Under the Mattress Hoarding. An unthinking stance on saving without a clear financial game-plan. Money is important, but there is a reservation about investing it shrewdly for the future. This may reflect a suspicion of financial institutions. But an ultra-cautious stance that can be counter-productive.

I'd like to live as a poor man with lots of money. **Pablo Picasso**

Prudent Provision. The psychology here is of a saving orientation linked to attention to detailed financial planning. At best, a far thinking orientation that sacrifices short-term gain for long-term security, personally and/or for others. Alternatively, the profile of the miser who lives for a future that lacks enjoyment in the present.

It is a kind of spiritual snobbery that makes people think they can be happy without money. **Albert Camus**

SO WHAT?

If money and time were no constraint, what would you do with your life? **David Lieberman**[2]

We all have to make financial choices given our present circumstances as well as our future goals. But it helps if we have reflected on why we manage our money the way we do, and the impact it has today as well as for tomorrow.

If a person gets their attitude toward money straight, it will help straighten out almost every other area in their life. **Billy Graham**

NOTES

1. Conspicuous Consumption: Spending Money on Luxury Goods to Display Wealth and Status, Claudine Cassar

2. *We expect the next car, the next house or the next promotion to make us happy even though the last ones didn't.* Daniel Gilbert, Stumbling on Happiness

Which investment opportunities are best avoided?

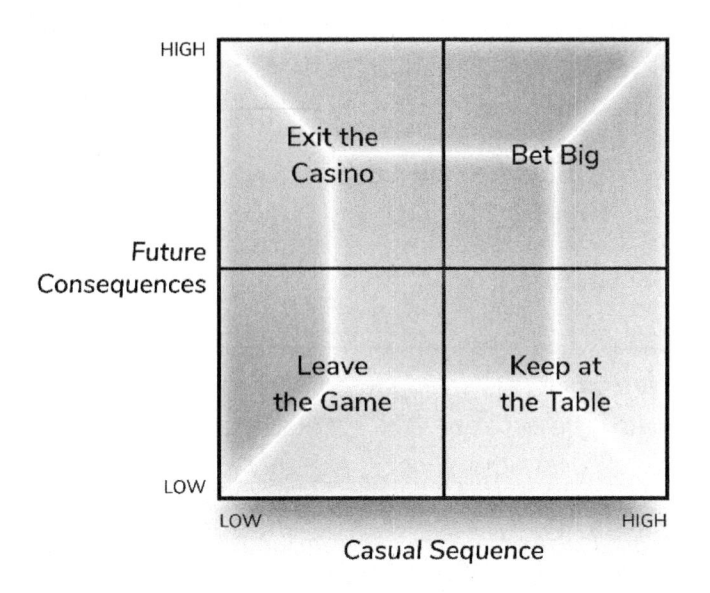

HIGH	Exit the Casino	Bet Big
Future Consequences		
	Leave the Game	Keep at the Table
LOW		
	LOW — Casual Sequence — HIGH	

There are important things that are not knowable and there are things that are knowable but not important, and we don't clutter up our minds with those. **Warren Buffett**

Enter a casino. Which game do we play?[1] There is a range of games to choose from, reflecting a spectrum from luck to skill. No game is 100% skill. Some, for example poker, do require more skill than others. Other games - roulette - are based on pure luck.

There's a quick and easy way to test whether an activity involves skill: ask whether you can lose on purpose. **Michael Mauboussin**

Investment combines skill and luck.[2] The challenge is optimising skill and minimising the impact of luck. Two dimensions underpin this quadrant.

Casual Sequence. Is there is well defined and simple link between cause and effect, a single factor that determines outcomes in a predictable way? In low, the connection between cause and effect is fuzzy. In high, a pattern of multiple factors interact in complex ways and is difficult to disentangle.

Future Consequences. What is the impact of our investment? Low consequences are relatively trivial, and will not change our financial lives in a significant way. High, there are large consequences with the potential to transform our lives, positively or negatively.

When only a few high priests understand it, you're going to find that they don't really understand it. **Charlie Munger**

Four investment stances are highlighted.

Leave the Game. The casual sequence is vague but the consequences are small. It is tempting for some to roll the dice in a series of mini bets. The occasional lucky investment might reinforce a winning mind set. Over time, a losing strategy.

If you have been in a poker game for a while, and you still don't know who the patsy is, you're the patsy. **Whispering Saul**

Exit the Casino. When the casual sequence is fuzzy and the consequences are large, this is an investment to avoid. Too many factors determine the outcomes over time. A few might get lucky - and go on to attribute their success to investment brilliance. Most will lose heavily.

How did you do that? Seven heads in a row! Can I interview you in Fortune? Is it the T-shirt? Is it the flick of the wrist? **Rebecca Henderson**[3]

Keep at the Table. Although the consequences are small, there is a well-defined causal sequence that, when understood, we can exploit to our advantage. A sensible strategy invests steadily, taking small wins to accumulate over time until the dynamic between cause and effect changes.[4]

When most people come to believe the same thing, large gaps open up between price and value. **Michael Mauboussin**

Bet Big. This is the philosophy of Warren Buffett: bet seldom but big on the sure thing. There is a known and defined causal sequence with large consequences. Sure things are however rare and require an insight into the casual dynamic that the majority lack. This is to have a better theory than other investors. Only for those who combine wisdom, courage and patience.

SO WHAT?

Your only chance of winning is to adhere to the rules that you know work. Your skill can't change the odds, it can only be applied to make sure that you play the cards properly. **Michael Mauboussin**

Warren Buffett proposes: *risk comes from not knowing what you're doing.* If we don't understand the rules of the investment game and the causal sequence and future consequences for us personally - the downside as well as the upside - it's not a game we should play.

NOTES

1. The obvious answer is none. The house always wins.

2. The Success Equation: Untangling Skill and Luck in Business, Sports, and Investing, Michael J. Mauboussin

3. A Random Search for Excellence. Why great company research delivers fables and not facts, Michael Raynor; https://www2.deloitte.com/xe/en/insights/topics/operations/a-random-search-for-excellence-why-great-company-research-delivers-fables-not-facts.html

4. This assumes that we have access to knowledge of the casual sequence that others do not have. When this knowledge becomes widely known, the dynamic and consequences shift.

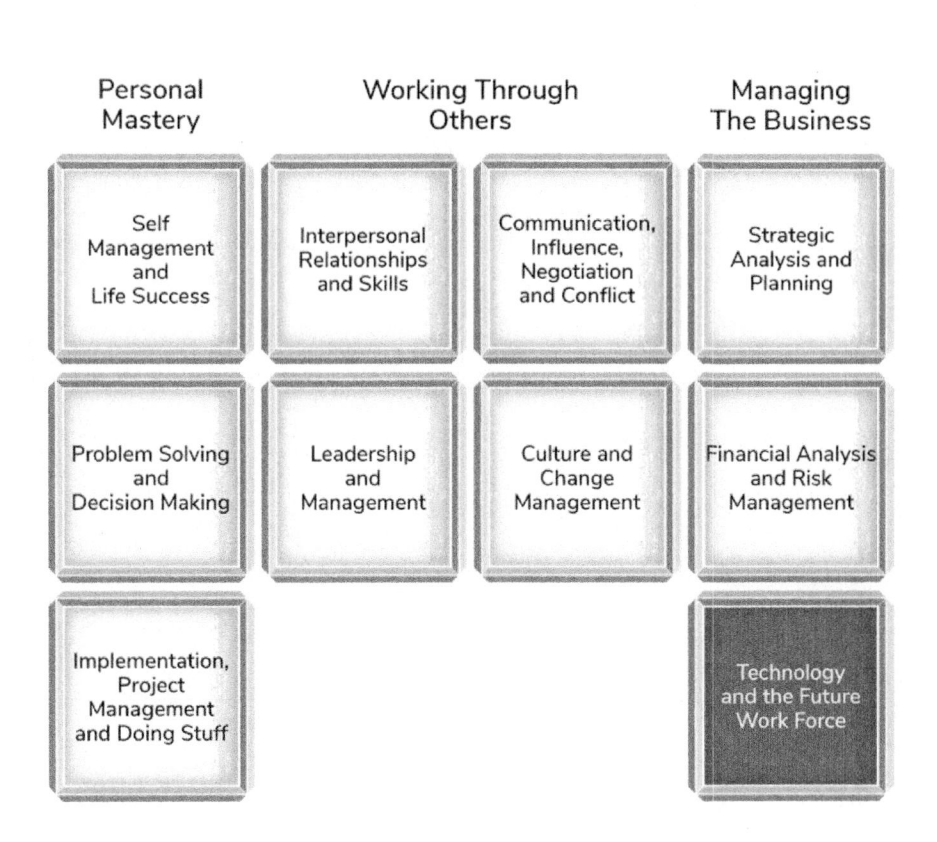

Personal Mastery	Working Through Others		Managing The Business
Self Management and Life Success	Interpersonal Relationships and Skills	Communication, Influence, Negotiation and Conflict	Strategic Analysis and Planning
Problem Solving and Decision Making	Leadership and Management	Culture and Change Management	Financial Analysis and Risk Management
Implementation, Project Management and Doing Stuff			Technology and the Future Work Force

Why are we not working less?

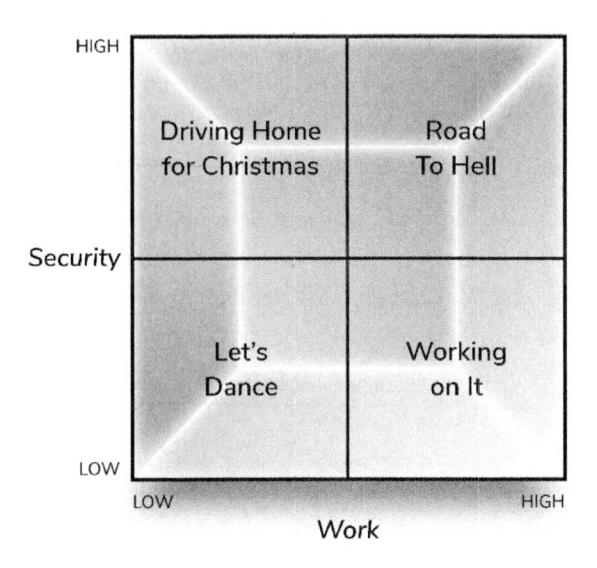

	LOW Work	HIGH Work
HIGH Security	Driving Home for Christmas	Road To Hell
LOW Security	Let's Dance	Working on It

I put my heart and my soul into my work, and have lost my mind in the process. **Vincent Van Gogh**

Pilot studies explore the 4 day work. This is far short of the 15 hour work week predicted for 2030, almost a century ago by John Maynard Keynes. Keynes placed his faith in technology as the driver for a shorter working week. What happened? The reality for most: working weeks have grown longer not shorter.[1] And few people experience the 4 hour week of the wheeze advocated by Tim Ferris.[2]

The counter view of the 4-day week is the 996 model[3] advocated by Jack Ma, co-founder of Alibaba: work from 9am to 9pm, 6 days a week. Pushback is underway in the form of the l*ying down movement* - tang ping zhuyi - which challenges the dominance of work and materiality.

I think that there is far too much work done in the world, that immense harm is caused by the belief that work is virtuous, and that what needs to be preached in modern industrial countries is quite different from what always has been preached. **Bertrand Russell**

So why are we - despite the promise of the gains of technological innovation - working longer not less?

Why should I let the toad work squat on my life? Can't I use my wit as a pitchfork. And drive the brute off? **Philip Larkin**

This quadrant is based on two dimensions.

Work. This theme captures the centrality of work within our lives. Most adults need to earn a living. Many also pursue a career for advancement and further financial reward. At the low end, work is an unavoidable necessity; the focus of the week is the build-up to the weekend. This is *I work to live*. At the high end, *I live to work* is the sentiment. Our identity is shaped by our work; our sense of who we are is based on how we earn a living.

Security. This incorporates a sense of protection and stability vis a vis the need for risk and adventure. At the low end, a sense that there is the upside of opportunity to be seized in life. At the high end, our efforts are directed at keeping what we have to do to minimise the downside of life's threats.

Feeling secure is an important component of happiness. **Mihaly Csikszentmihalyi**

Four perspectives to work are identified.

Let's Dance. A lack of work focus intersects with a low need for security. This may be the happy circumstance of the privileged and successful to operate outside the demands of financial necessity. Alternatively, a free-wheeling life style to abandon the conventions of consumer capitalism and enjoy life in the present. A potentially precarious outlook for many.

This moment's for me and for you. So while there's not a thing that we can do. Let's dance. **Chris Rea**

Driving Home for Christmas. This combines a low work focus with a high need for security. Family and friendships and other life pursuits are much more important than climbing the greasy pole of career ambition. Work is not the central motivation. Conversely, a lifestyle that disappoints others whose expectations exceed our own.

Driving in my car. I'm driving home for Christmas. With a thousand memories. **Chris Rea**

Working On It. A high work outlook intersects with low security. This is the outlook in which financial pressures take precedence over any sense of a life to be lived to the full. For some - realistically - this is the way of the world as a solution to survival. Alternatively, a Scrooge-like workaholic obsessed with financial gain and accumulation.

I got eight little fingers and only two thumbs. Will you leave me in peace while I get the work done. Can't you see I'm working. Oh, oh I'm working on it. **Chris Rea**

Road To Hell. Work focus intersects with a need for security. This is the hard driving individual - passionate about a purpose achieved through work. It can also be a compulsive need for work achievement to accomplish much in career progression, status and financial return. Or, the strategy of get rich to get good - one that recognises economic realities today to make a living in the prospect of a different tomorrow. Alternatively, the individual who then finds themselves asking: *where is the life I have lost in living?*

You must learn this lesson fast and learn it well. This ain't no upwardly mobile freeway. Oh no, this is the road, this is the road, this is the road to hell. **Chris Rea**

SO WHAT?

You will live your life secure in that you are no longer manipulated by what other people want you to do and be, but are directed by your own inner desires. **H Stanley Judd**

Gallup's most recent U.S. workplace survey[4] shows that employees are becoming increasingly detached from their employers:

dissatisfied and disconnected from their organisation's mission and purpose. Is this stagnation inevitable?

The important question remains: are we working more because we enjoy a rewarding life rhythm - now and for the future? Or, on a hamster wheel of a work obsession to escape more fundamental life issues?

2030 is only 6 years away.

NOTES

1. Working Long Hours: a Review of the Evidence; https://www.employment-studies.co.uk/report-summaries/report-summary-working-long-hours-review-evidence-volume-1-%E2%80%93-main-report

2. Why Tim Ferris is a marketing genius fraud; https://stupid-little-creatures.blogspot.com/2015/03/why-tim-ferris-is-marketing-genius-fraud.html

3. 996 Working Hours model. https://en.wikipedia.org/wiki/996_working_hour_system

4. In New Workplace, U.S. Employee Engagement Stagnates; https://www.gallup.com/workplace/608675/new-workplace-employee-engagement-stagnates.aspx#:~:text=In%20the%20latest%20reading%2C%20from,than%202020's%20high%20of%2036%25.

What are the building blocks of an organisation?

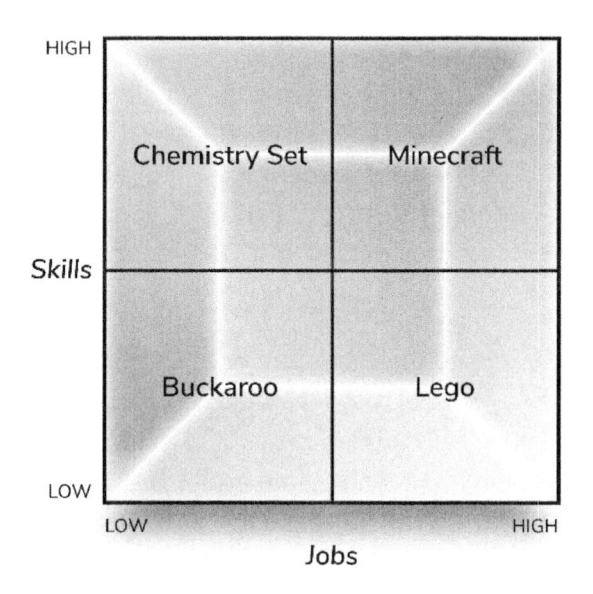

	Low Jobs	High Jobs
High Skills	Chemistry Set	Minecraft
Low Skills	Buckaroo	Lego

You have to stand outside the box to see how the box can be re-designed.
Charles Handy

Type *will a robot...* into Google, and it finishes the search with *take my job?* Or more alarmingly, *trigger the apocalypse?*

The World Economic Forum[1] conducts research into the future of work. Its latest research indicates administrative activity - in banking, transportation, retail and distribution - will disappear through automation. On the upside, job growth is expected in education, healthcare and digital commerce.

In the past the person has been first. In the future the system must be first.
Frederick Taylor

By 2030, we can expect much churn in the world of work. But almost all occupations in future will require significant reskilling and upskilling.

We have shifted our approach. We used to match people to jobs. Now we are in a world where we match skills to tasks. **Senior HR Executive, Global Bank**

Can organisations build firms with greater flexibility and fluidity? Two dimensions underpin this grid.

Jobs. The traditional job description comes with a title and detailed outline of responsibilities and tasks. At the low end, jobs - as conventionally described - disappear into the freewheeling realm of projects and assignments. At the high end - despite the hype of a new working world - jobs persist, not least because of employment legislation.

Skills. This expresses the competence required to achieve an outcome. At the low end, skill levels are relatively low. Knowledge and expertise can be acquired quickly. At the other end, skill is complex and requires extensive time and effort to build proficiency for consistent performance.

When the world is predictable you need smart people. When the world is unpredictable you need adaptable people. **Henry Mintzberg**

Four organisational scenarios are highlighted.

Buckaroo.[2] This is low on both jobs and skills. All that is needed is to turn up and play a steady game. These are the organisational activities which are easy to learn. There is not much formality about these work activities, and few demands on knowledge or expertise. An important part of economic activity, this is a game for many employees without a long-term financial future.

Easy does it, easy...EASY!" The inner monologue repeating in my mind, and then...Buck, Buck, Buckaroo kicks, all the bags fall off. Game over. **Matthew Teague**

Chemistry Set. An organisational grouping that is low on jobs and high on skills. The formality of job descriptions is replaced by a more flexible approach to rethink what needs to be done by those with the skills to do it. At best, responsive to face the challenge at hand - at speed. Alternatively, without clear lines of accountability, the potential for organisational chaos.

Well, I'm one of those fortunate people who like my job, sir. Got my first chemistry set when I was seven, blew my eyebrows off, we never saw the cat again, been into it ever since. **Stanley Goodspeed**

Lego. High on jobs encounters low skills in this organisational design philosophy. Jobs provide the building blocks. The structure of work definition allows a relatively low level of skill to combine for extraordinary outcomes. A set of moving parts working in harmony. Conversely, an organisational outlook vulnerable when one moving part gets stuck or goes missing.

Many creative people are finding that creativity doesn't grow in abundance, it grows from scarcity. The more Lego bricks you have doesn't mean you're going to be more creative. You can be very creative with very few Lego bricks. **Jorgen Vig Knudstorp, former CEO Lego**

Minecraft.[3] The combination of high jobs and high skills represents the synthesis of job design with the importance of skills to deliver new outcomes. It implies greater fluidity within work structures. The upside is flexibility and creativity; the downside is greater uncertainty and possibly a lack of security about the future.

Minecraft is a game that has no end, it's a never-ending adventure. **Purosotam**

SO WHAT?

Projects must be staffed quickly but organisations need to avoid the disruption of constant reorganisation. Managing through skills as well as jobs provides greater agility. Employees experience interesting work and build their skill set.

The key question for executives: have we got the balance right to provide sufficient detail on jobs with sufficient knowledge of skill-sets to allow flexibility of work practices and the evolution of the organisation?[4]

NOTES

1. WEF Future of Jobs Report; https://www.weforum.org/publications/the-future-of-jobs-report-2023/

2. Buckaroo. Kick Up Some Fun with this exciting never-know-when-he's-gonna-buck stacking game! Load up the moody mule for your gold mining trip, but watch out - he may buck at any second with no warning.

3. Minecraft has become the best-selling video game in history, with over 300 million copies sold and has nearly 140 million monthly active players.

4. Skills Ontologies: https://gloat.com/blog/skills-ontology-framework/

What will the future workforce look like?

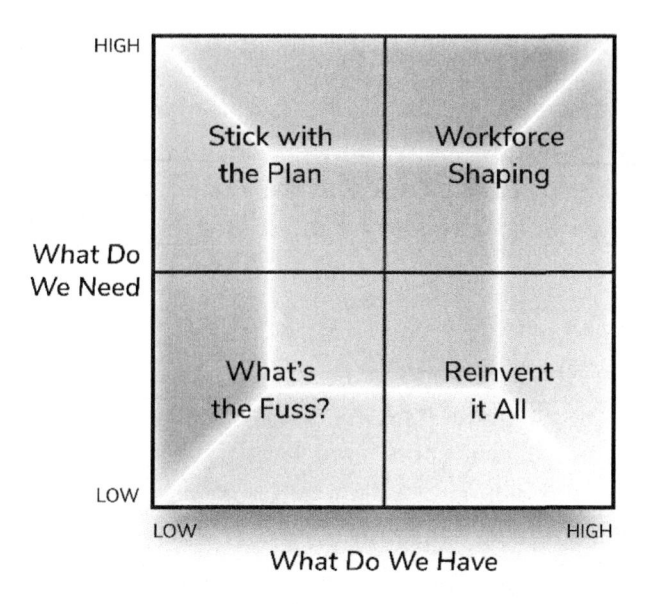

	LOW (What Do We Have)	HIGH (What Do We Have)
HIGH (What Do We Need)	Stick with the Plan	Workforce Shaping
LOW (What Do We Need)	What's the Fuss?	Reinvent it All

Good intentions can often lead to unintended consequences. It is hard to imagine a law intended for the workforce known to Henry Ford can serve the needs of a workplace shaped by the innovations of Bill Gates. **Tim Walberg**

In February 2022, Forbes accused IBM of ageism.[1] IBM's executives had discussed how to force out older workers, deriding them as *dinobabies* who should be made an extinct species. The court filings revealed communications of a *highly incriminating animus* against older employees by senior officials.

The World Economic Forum[2] reports that in the next five years, 83 million jobs will be lost and 69 million created. Extrapolating, 23% of the 673 million employees in the WEF data set. Many of the new jobs will require new skills in the digital economy.

It is very hard to transform your culture and your workforce to be a relevant company in the digital world if all of your processes are stuck in the traditional world. **Julie Sweet**

This world of work is uncertain and turbulent. Can organisations steer the shape, size, skills, degree of automation, and locations of their future workforce? How?

Two dimensions need to be reconciled.

What Do We Have. A summary of the current workforce. Low is a lack of access to relevant information to analyse bio-demographical data and unable to profile expertise, experience and skills. At the high end, the organisation is well placed to interrogate the facts and figures of its employees and contingent workers and understand its position.

What Do We Need. This identifies the extent to which a firm can forecast the expertise that it needs to stay in the business game. At the low end, the firm is either unable or unwilling to make future projections. At the high end, a clear view on the workforce required for long-term competitiveness.[3]

Ask what your 20-year-old self would think of you today. We invite you to think about what your 70, 80 or 100-year-old self would think of you now.
Lynda Gratton

Four workforce outlooks are highlighted.

What's the Fuss? Low on understanding today's workforce and low on thinking about a different tomorrow. With the exception of a few niche sectors, this stance is problematic for most businesses. This outlook lacks insight about its employee profile and the gap between where it is and where it needs to be. These businesses will be overtaken by those who do make a fuss.

I want to share something with you: The three little sentences that will get you through life. Number 1: Cover for me. Number 2: Good idea, boss. Number 3: It was like that when I got here. **Homer Simpson**

Stick with the Plan. This uses the current workforce profile to build the future. Today's workforce has the DNA for tomorrow. The assumption of continuity allows projections to be made about future employee requirements. Alternatively, the delusion that the future will be more of the present. And in all likelihood, a workforce badly prepared for a different set of challenges.

They prepared a wonderful group of executives for yesterday's business. By being so good at narrowing the gene pool, they replicated people who would have been good leaders in the past but not the future. **Ed Lawler, analysing the succession problems of AT & T**

Reinvent it All. A low understanding of the current employee profile, but with a recognition of future requirements. In this scenario, a business sets out an ambitious agenda of the expertise and skills it needs to compete, but without knowing the distance between here and there. This limits insight into how existing employees will bridge any gaps. At best, the stuff of transformation to prepare for a very different enterprise. More typically, a vague hope. Organisational chaos creates further employee anxiety and disengagement.

The less planning you do upfront, the more you'll be able to change course easily. **Dilbert**

Workforce Shaping. A stance that combines a high understanding of the current workforce with a recognition of changing skill sets. Where and how employees need to redirect work practices.[4] Typically more often observed in conference presentations than in organisational reality, at best, the progressive firm with a coherent view of now and then. Or, an expensive commitment to be out-manoeuvred by more flexible competitors.

An empowered and enriched workforce is the backbone of a company's success framework. **Ananya Birla**

SO WHAT?

Do not underestimate your abilities. That is your boss's job. **Francis Young**

The world of work is changing. A combination of demographic shifts and technological innovations is shifting traditional organisational structures and work patterns. A business that does not get this reality is a business facing a headwind of turbulence. Yes, this theme is often over-hyped.[5] But still an imperative.

The questions for executives: do we know enough about our people now? Can we articulate a coherent view of the expertise and skills of the future workforce? Do we have the foresight[6] to navigate the uncertainty and predict what skills we will need in the future?

NOTES

1. IBM Accused Of Ageism: Older Workers Are Dinobabies Who Should Be Made An Extinct Species; https://www.forbes.com/sites/jackkelly/2022/02/12/ibm-accused-of-ageism-older-workers-are-dinobabies-who-should-be-made-an-extinct-species/?sh=9183ff6129c2

2. Future of Jobs Report 2023; https://www3.weforum.org/docs/WEF_Future_of_Jobs_2023.pdf

3. Futures & Foresight; https://oecd-opsi.org/guide/futures-and-foresight/

4. Understanding the workforce using the 5Bs: Buy, Build, Borrow, Bot and Base. Section 2 of The Future of Work Report https://assets.kpmg.com/content/dam/kpmg/xx/pdf/2023/12/future-of-work.pdf.

5. SMEs represent about 90% of businesses and more than 50% of employment worldwide.

6. Futures and Foresight capability; https://www.sciencedirect.com/science/article/abs/pii/S0016328709001888

Does hybrid working work?

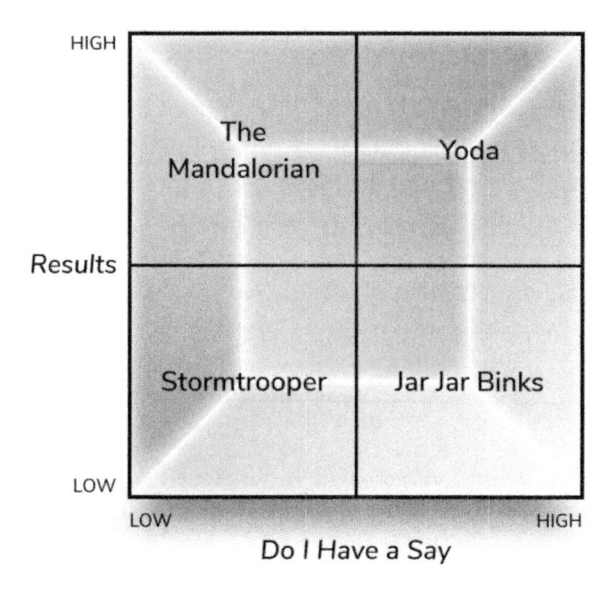

```
                HIGH
                 │
                 │   The          │
                 │ Mandalorian    │   Yoda
                 │                │
     Results ────┼────────────────┼────────
                 │                │
                 │  Stormtrooper  │  Jar Jar Binks
                 │                │
                LOW
                 └────────────────┴────────
                LOW                    HIGH
                      Do I Have a Say
```

Hybrid work will allow us to achieve the best of both worlds, the focus and collaboration of the office, and the flexibility and autonomy of remote work. **Tim Cook, CEO Apple**

In most developed economies, 40% of the workforce can work in locations other than the base office. Typically, this means working from home and/or business hubs. The debate continues: is working from home a good or a bad thing?[1] Increasingly, firms are establishing ground rules of the kind: *you must be in the office x days a week, on average.*[2]

Remote work is no longer acceptable. **Elon Musk**

Is the need to be in the office a set number of days, something like a parent - child[3] mindset, with the employer as the parent? Do we need a better model to encourage genuine adult to adult collaboration? Not only in working arrangements in the office, but within the rhythm of the working month and year.

The key to culture is how you build relationships. It's about the quality and types of conversations you have, not where you have them. **Larry English**

Two dimensions underpin this quadrant to weigh up the pros and cons of hybrid working.

Do I Have a Say. Can employees influence where and when they work? At the low end, line managers dictate the work pattern. At the other end, a collaborative and contingent approach; employees have an important input into the work cycle of location and time.

Results. This axis addresses outcomes. At the low end, less attention to output and more on presence in the workplace and attention to the inputs of hours worked. High is a focus on results: a concern for outputs rather than the activity of inputs.[4]

Sorry you were out when I visited. I look forward to seeing you in the office very soon. With every good wishes. **Jacob Rees-Mogg, former Tory MP**

There are four stances to hybrid working.

Stormtrooper. This is presence[5] in the place of work as determined by the boss. Many roles in some occupations do of course require physical presence. And it is not always easy to measure results. Often, this is management control in the delusion that presenteeism provides a proxy measure of productivity.

Let me see your identification. **Stormtrooper**
You don't need to see his identification. **Ben Obi-Wan Kenobi**

The Mandalorian. A bounty hunter who follows the strict code of the Bounty Hunter Guild. This combines a low level of Do I Have a Say with a clear focus on results - catch the bounty.[6] At best, the freedom to act for the best outcome. At worst, ideas about how to improve work activity are squashed before they get off the ground.

This is the way. **The Mandalorian**

Jar Jar Binks. This combines a high level of Do I Have a Say with less concern for results. The gain: freedom for employees do it their way. The downside: less focus on outcomes and more on look at me.[7]

Count Me Outta Dis One. Better Dead Here Than Dead In Da Core. Yee Gods! Whata Mes Sayin? **Jar Jar Binks**

Yoda. High levels of employee involvement meet an attention on outcomes. Team members might come into the office for specific meetings or collaborative sessions, but they work remotely most of the time. This arrangement can be difficult to coordinate. It requires imaginative communication for a smooth workflow for both remote and on-site team members across different work groups and partnerships. For many, this box exemplifies an *adult-to-adult* stance to shift from *parent-child*.

Do or do not. There is no try. **Yoda**

SO WHAT?

Success in a hybrid work environment requires employers to move beyond viewing remote or hybrid environments as a temporary or short-term strategy and to treat it as an opportunity. **George Penn**

For those with the option to work flexibly, the days of 9-5 at one physical work place are numbered. Labour markets are shifting. Who has control over work? Management faces the challenge of fostering genuine collaboration for results, regardless of work patterns.

Will firms shift towards a more *adult to adult* model as management becomes more mature, trusting and contingent rather than prescriptive? Are managers up to the task? More complicated still: what options are there for flexible working in what has been called the pink, green and grey collar jobs?[8]

The housecleaner said she was going to start working from home, so she sent me a list of chores to do. **Anonymous**

That is likely a job for Yoda.

NOTES

1. Working from Home, Assessing the research evidence; https://www.cipd.org/globalassets/media/knowledge/knowledge-hub/reports/8051-working-from-home-report_tcm18-84208.pdf

2. Discussions on hybrid working are largely focused on administrative activity for the white collar sector. And overlook the economic reality of the large swathe of jobs in which this is not an option.

3. Transactional analysis https://www.simplypsychology.org/transactional-analysis-eric-berne.html

4. Managing in a Results-Only Work Environment; https://www.mindtools.com/agx0aqn/managing-in-a-results-only-work-environment

5. Why presenteeism wins out over productivity; https://www.bbc.com/worklife/article/20210604-why-presenteeism-always-wins-out-over-productivity

6. Results focused culture: https://blog.culturewise.com/results-oriented-company-culture

7. Jar Jar, originally a clumsy and somewhat comical character in the Star Wars universe, rises to a position of significant political power as a representative of Naboo in the Galactic Senate. Due to his position, he had a say in critical decisions, most notably when he is manipulated into proposing the motion that grants Chancellor Palpatine emergency powers, which effectively sets the stage for the rise of the Galactic Empire.

8. Collar colours explained; https://blog.talent.com/en-ca/advice/the-difference-between-blue-white-and-pink-collar-jobs

Will a robot do my job?

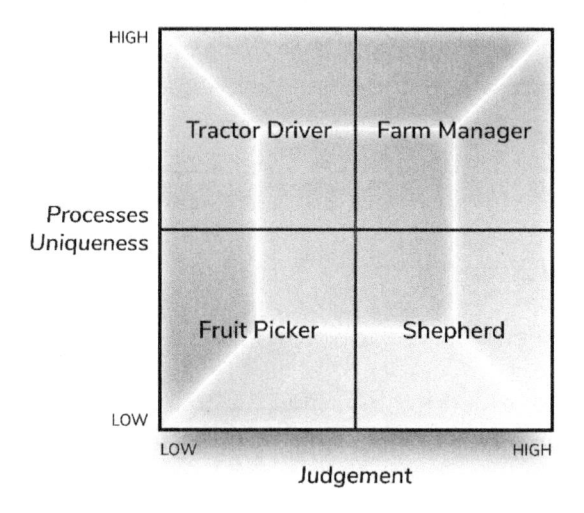

	Judgement LOW	Judgement HIGH
Processes Uniqueness HIGH	Tractor Driver	Farm Manager
Processes Uniqueness LOW	Fruit Picker	Shepherd

Modern robots are not unlike toddlers. It's hilarious to watch them fall over, but deep down we know that if we laugh too hard, they might develop a complex and grow up to start World War Three.[1]

The word robot first occurred in a play about mechanical men built to work on factory assembly lines who rebelled against their human masters. Written by Czech playwright Karl Capek in 1921, he derived the name from the Czech word for slave.[2]

Traditionally, tasks low on discretion and high on standardisation were targets for outsourcing. These activities are now targeted for robotic process automation. Add generative AI to the mix, and the range of tasks suitable for automation increase exponentially, with both opportunities and risks.

Computers make excellent and efficient servants, but I have no wish to serve under them. **Commander Spock**

Will the robot do our job? It depends on two key factors.

Judgement. The extent to which discretion by we - humans - are needed to undertake a task. Low does not require much judgement.

High, the requirement for significant human discretion for a successful outcome that make automation troublesome.

Processes Uniqueness. Processes can be standardised or unique. Standardised processes - a regularised sequence of activities - lend themselves to automation. Unique processes incorporate much more variability.

Some people call this artificial intelligence, but the reality is this technology will enhance us. So instead of artificial intelligence, I think we'll augment our intelligence. **Ginni Rometty**

Four scenarios emerge for the future of work.

Fruit Picker. Low judgement and low uniqueness indicate automation. In the white-collar world, this was the traditional box for outsourcing, such as shared services,. Now tasks will be automated instead of outsourced. A trip around St. Emilion in France, for example, demonstrates how machines harvest grapes. And the robots are coming to India and other nations. But the front, middle and back offices in developed economies are at even greater risk.

Automation is driving the decline of banal and repetitive tasks. **Amber Rudd**

Tractor Driver. Low judgement activities in unique processes are next for task automation. The risk is less about an individual's role being fully automated but whether traditional business models - in, for example, software programming, advertising, design, accountancy - are sustainable. These roles require human intervention. But there is scope for a radical redesign of the current operating model.

This may be the age of automation, but love is still being made by hand. **Evan Esar**

Shepherd. High judgement and low uniqueness. This box requires reskilling and upskilling. Many roles are likely to be enhanced through cognitive enablement as opposed to automation. But there is potential for productivity gains in a different organisational structure.

A greater proportion of tasks can be automated or left to the robot sheepdog.

You're either the one that creates the automation or you're getting automated.
Tom Preston-Werner

Farm Manager. High judgement and unique processes need humans. At least at the moment. When artificial general intelligence (AGI)[3] arrives in the next 20 years, all bets are off. Is this a revolution to combine work and automation? Currently all forms of AI are specific to a task. General AI will learn at a far greater rate - on any subject - and adapt quickly to perform new tasks.

Robots will do everything better than us. **Elon Musk**

SO WHAT?

Automation is going to cause unemployment, and we need to prepare for it.
Mark Cuban

Robot hairdressers may be sometime away. But robots are coming for jobs. The issues for leaders: are we reimagining our business processes, team structures and organisation design? For individuals: can we make ourselves indispensable? And can we better learn to use AI through competent prompt engineering.[4]

Or, by building skills in high judgement around unique processes?

Machine intelligence is the last invention that humanity will ever need to make.
Nick Bostrom

NOTES

1. The WIRED Guide to Robots
https://www.wired.com/story/wired-guide-to-robots/

2. Robotics: A Brief History;
https://cs.stanford.edu/people/eroberts/courses/soco/projects/1998-99/robotics/history.html

3. Amazon Web Services description of artificial general intelligence:
https://aws.amazon.com/what-is/artificial-general-intelligence/

4. Prompt engineering best practices;
https://www.digitalocean.com/resources/article/prompt-engineering-best-practices

Can we thrive in a digital world?

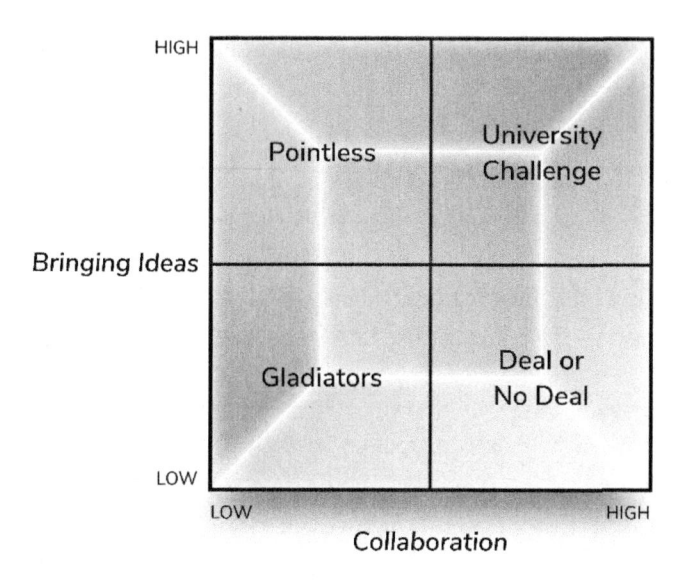

[figure: 2x2 matrix with axes "Bringing Ideas" (LOW to HIGH, vertical) and "Collaboration" (LOW to HIGH, horizontal). Quadrants: Pointless (high ideas, low collab); University Challenge (high ideas, high collab); Gladiators (low ideas, low collab); Deal or No Deal (low ideas, high collab).]

You can't wait for inspiration. You have to go after it with a club. **Jack London**

A Buzzfeed article[1] recounts tales from IT professionals of encounters with senior executives. *It boggles my boss's mind when he asks me how to do something in Excel and I don't know. But I google how to do it, then show him. He looks at me like I'm a wizard.*

Most of us have mastered the basics of IT in a digital world. But generative AI shifts the gears. We don't need to be technologists to use it or know how to code. Instead the emphasis is on the creative stuff. What shall we use digital technology for? Have we figured out how it will change organisations, and what this means for the workforce? And for us personally?

The digital world is so convenient and nice. But just playing back a vinyl record is a much warmer, hotter, more present feeling. **Steve Miller**

Blogs and social media advise us how to thrive in a digital world. There are 10 essential skills, 10 rules, 10 effective ways and 5 tips.

The consistent message: thriving in a digital world is not about IT skills. It is about mindset.

I am about to do something very bold in this job that I've never done before. Try. **Jim Halpert The US Office**

The dimensions for this quadrant.

Collaboration. The low end is stuck in the immediacy of work priorities which fails to join up with other work areas, or connect externally to customers, suppliers and other potential partners. At the high end, proactive collaboration draws on an array of knowledge, skill and experience from a range of sources inside and outside the organisation.

Bringing Ideas.[2] This highlights access to a quantity of high quality ideas. At the low end of this axis, limited access to technological innovation. At the high end, a flow of fresh thinking to embed innovation within a digital business future.

Four approaches to digital technology are highlighted.

Gladiators.[3] Low collaboration intersects with a low rate of idea generation. This may be a good initial product concept but becomes introspection within the immediate work area, and is lost. A lack of dialogue and constructive challenge from multiple perspectives constrains its potential.

Contenders, you will go on my first whistle, Gladiators, you will go on my second whistle. **John Anderson**

Pointless. This is low on connecting but high on ideas. Innovation is not the problem. Executing the ideas in a disciplined way to monetise the gains is the challenge. Understandable for small and medium sized businesses, for large firms the lack of open innovation within and across boundaries holds back competitive advances.

Welcome to Pointless - the show where the lowest scorers are the biggest winners. **Alexander Armstrong**

Deal or No Deal. This is high on connecting end-to-end processes but low on ideas. Advances in digital technology make a robust business impact. However, without the rapid drum beat of innovation, progress is held back. Faster competitors with more adaptable processes out manoeuvre this position.

OwenNewitt: And what was in your box?
Jim Trott: 10p

University Challenge. High collaboration combines with ideas that flow in and out of the organisation. For these firms, there is a discipline in both strategic formulation and implementation to ensure digital advances are executed at speed and rigour. The risk: a breakneck pace that cannot be sustained.

Fingers on buzzers. Here's your starter for 10.[4]

SO WHAT?

Creativity comes from a conflict of ideas. **Donatella Versace**

To thrive in the new world of work a digital mindset is required.[5] Not bits or bytes. The key questions: do we have the business processes and working practices that will translate ideas into digital innovation? Or are we stuck in an introverted world view - one of silos and barriers to hold back progress?

NOTES

1. IT Professionals Shared Their Funniest Stories On The Job. And I Suddenly Feel Like A Tech Whiz; https://www.buzzfeed.com/michelleno/it-professionals-are-sharing-the-worst-cases-of-computer

2. Are Innovative Companies More Profitable? By Minor, Brook and Bernoff. MIT Sloan Management Review, December 28, 2017
https://sloanreview.mit.edu/article/are-innovative-companies-more-profitable/
There is compelling evidence from MIT about the importance of Ideation Rate: The number of winning ideas generated per 1,000 active users on the ideation/crowdsourcing platform. In this context, winning ideas means employee-generated ideas that were finally selected by management for active development and implementation. The MIT study showed a strong correlation between ideation rate and profit growth between a sample of companies between 2014 and 2016.

We would posit that in 2023 it will be even more critical. The MIT research suggested that there was a tipping point in the organisations that were researched. It was an ideation rate of about 150 winning ideas per 1000 people on the crowdsourcing platform.

3. Gladiators review. A camp, sugary old-school rush that will make you sweat; https://www.theguardian.com/tv-and-radio/2024/jan/13/gladiators-review-a-camp-sugary-old-school-rush-that-will-make-you-sweat

4. Top 10 University Challenge Funniest Answers; https://www.youtube.com/watch?v=KUwwieOW6TU

5. Explore your digital mindset: https://kpmg.com/xx/en/home/insights/2020/07/kpmg-digital-mindset.html

Is technology now part of the problem?

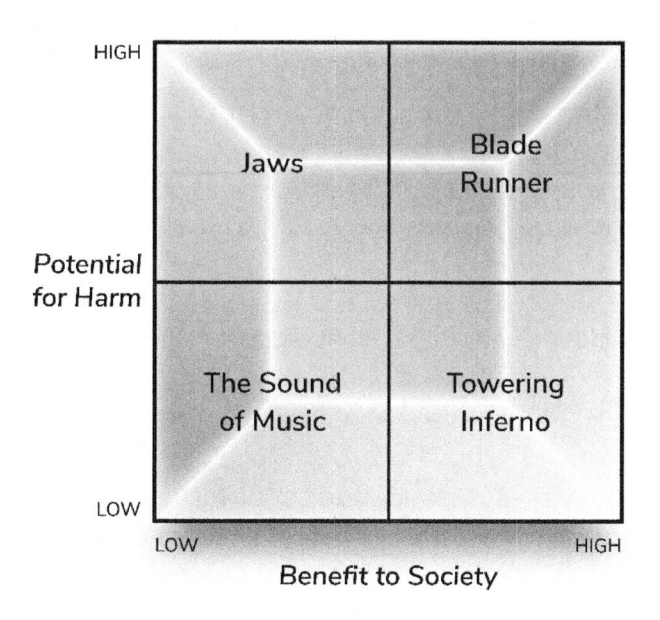

HIGH	Jaws	Blade Runner
Potential for Harm		
	The Sound of Music	Towering Inferno
LOW	LOW — Benefit to Society — HIGH	

Success in creating AI would be the biggest event in human history. Unfortunately, it might also be the last, unless we learn how to avoid the risks. **Stephen Hawking**

Artificial General Intelligence - AGI - is 20 years away. Terminator, Hal 9000, C3PO and the Star Trek computer - not quite yet.

I think that novels that leave out technology misrepresent life as badly as Victorians misrepresented life by leaving out sex. **Kurt Vonnegut**

But narrow AI - take ChatGPT - is here and bringing benefits. Research at MIT[1] finds 80% of respondents expect AI to boost efficiency in their industry by at least 25% in the next two years. A third say the gain will be at least 50%. Narrow AI may be powering innovation, but is also causing problems, not least in technologies to monitor citizens as part of a surveillance culture. And distorting public discourse on social media, to constrain the functioning of democracies.[2]

We're living in an age where new technology offers gigantic upsides. Artificial intelligence has the potential to diagnose cancer, catch serial killers and reduce prison populations. **Hannah Fry**

This quadrant is based on two dimensions.

Benefit to Society. Is there an overall gain for society? Low benefit, and it is difficult to see any advantage from the new technology. High benefit has a profound and positive impact on societal well-being, in health, education, and generally for work place productivity and innovation.

Potential for Harm. Does this technology incorporate the risk of negative consequences - for individuals, for organisations and society more generally? At the low end, technological innovation is relatively benign. At the high end, technology has an adverse impact with damaging outcomes that invade our privacy, drive inequality, or bring environmental damage.

If you're not concerned about AI safety, you should be. Vastly more risk than North Korea. **Elon Musk**

Four future scenarios are identified.

The Sound of Music. The combination of low benefit and low harm probably describes many developments in technology. Largely irrelevant, and often a waste of time, there is little negative economic or social impact.

Computers are useless. They can only give you answers. **Pablo Picasso**

Jaws. Low societal benefit with a high potential for harm. This is technological innovation as a threat. It may be these developments evolve at some point into more positive applications to bring future advantage. Alternatively, a malignant malevolence that becomes a counter-productive force for individuals, organisations and society.

Extraordinary technology brings extraordinary recklessness. **Abhijit Naskar**

Towering Inferno. This combines high benefit with low harm. At first sight, there is potential for important improvements - at a personal level for our well-being, at an organisational level for gains in productivity and innovation, and for society, with advances in education and healthcare. But not so fast. The risk here is when these applications mutate into more dangerous applications, such as the impact of social media on teenagers, or to spread conspiracies that undermine democracy.

You know, we were lucky tonight. Body count is less than 200. You know, one of these days, you're gonna kill 10,000 in one of these firetraps, and I'm gonna keep eating smoke and bringing out bodies until somebody asks us... how to build them. **Chief O'Halloran**

Blade Runner. A high benefit with potential for harm is the realm that requires regulation to ensure the benefits outweigh the risks. At best, this is part of well-informed policy decision making process to ensure risks are understood and mitigated. Alternatively, big tech runs ahead at speed, leaving governments to catch up with the long-term implications of the latest innovation.

An android doesn't care what happens to another android. That's one of the indications we look for. **Rick Deckard**

SO WHAT?

The difference between technology and slavery is that slaves are fully aware that they are not free. **Nassim Taleb**

It was ever thus. Any new technology throughout history has the potential for extraordinary gains. But also with the possibility to disrupt and destroy. The key questions: are we allowing only the technologists - with billions at their disposal - to plan the design and deployment technology? Or involving a range of stakeholder groups to provide an ethical, political and societal perspective?

Technological progress has merely provided us with more efficient means for going backward. **Aldous Huxley**

NOTES

1. Business efficiency and growth from Technology, MIT study; https://www.technologyreview.com/2023/10/05/1080618/laying-the-foundation-for-data-and-ai-led-growth/

2. Social media impact on polarisation in politics. The undercover voters: https://www.niemanlab.org/2023/08/with-five-old-phones-and-some-pew-data-the-bbcs-marianna-spring-monitors-social-media-from-the-inside/

How should we invest in business technology?

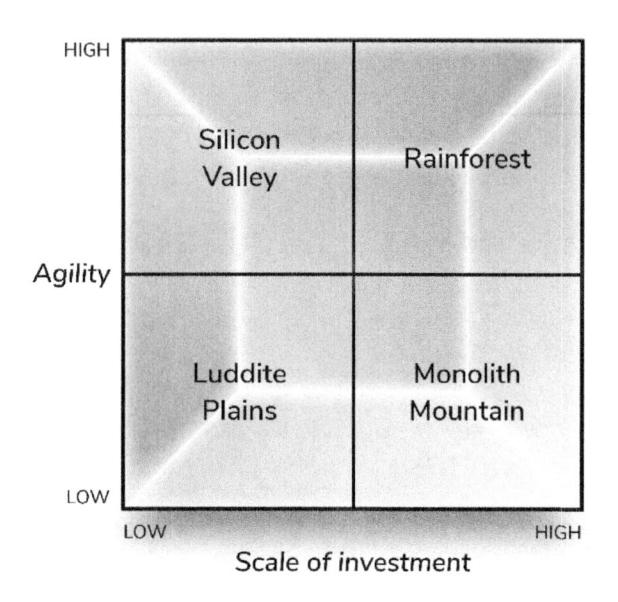

Agility (vertical axis: LOW to HIGH)
Scale of investment (horizontal axis: LOW to HIGH)

- Silicon Valley (High Agility, Low Investment)
- Rainforest (High Agility, High Investment)
- Luddite Plains (Low Agility, Low Investment)
- Monolith Mountain (Low Agility, High Investment)

Never trust a computer you can't throw out a window. **Steve Wozniak**

Netflix started as a DVD rental service, sending films direct to customers' mailboxes.[1] A novel approach at the time, it disrupted the traditional rental store model. Netflix's most significant transformation however began in the mid-2000s when it pivoted from its DVD rental service to become a leader in online streaming.

I do not fear computers. I fear the lack of them. **Isaac Asimov**

The rise of high-speed internet and changes in consumer behaviour posed both a significant challenge and opportunity for Netflix. It recognised the future of entertainment consumption was online. Transitioning from a successful rental model to streaming required significant investment in technology and content, as well as a shift in business strategy.[2]

Technology is a useful servant but a dangerous master. **Christian Lous Lange**

How do we decide which technology to back? Two dimensions are at play.

Scale of investment. This is not only spend, but the scope of the ambition for technology in the business. Low scale sees technology as a necessary force for efficiency. High scale, technology is a strategic enabler and a source of competitive advantage.

Agility. This reflects how many eggs the organisation puts in its basket. Low, the choice to build a partnership with one all-singing-all-dancing provider. At the high end, a strategy to bring in best in breed from multiple vendors.

New technology is not good or evil in and of itself. It's all about how people choose to use it. **David Wong**

Four investment stances emerge from the interaction of these dimensions.

Luddite Plains. This is low scale and low agility. The benefit: the technology landscape is simple. The downside: technology is seen as a distraction rather than a source of competitive advantage. Small businesses that compete on highly personalised customer service or product excellence in a niche area might pull of this trick. Bigger firms will not.

A computer once beat me at chess, but it was no match for me at kick boxing. **Emo Philips**

Silicon Valley. Low on scale but high on agility. At best, exceptional technology from different vendors - in finance, HR, procurement, customer fulfilment, etc - is deployed in a seamless process for outstanding levels of employee productivity and customer service. Alternatively, a patchwork of badly stitched together applications; the technology whole is less than the sum of the parts.

Failing fast is an important component of cultivating the agility needed for a development project along with continually rebalancing your innovation portfolio. **Lynne Doughtie**

Monolith Mountain. High on scale but low on agility. The potential advantage: applications sourced from only one vendor provide user ease. The downside: no one tech firm provides excellence consistently across all business functionality. The law of the Lowest Common Denominator delights no one. And any attempt by the organisation to demand customised improvements is met with the furrowed consulting brow of: *that will cost you.*

Every once in a while, a new technology, an old problem, and a big idea turn into an innovation. **Dean Kamen**

Rainforest. High on both scale and agility this - in principle - is the Goldilocks scenario. The organisation makes a significant investment in a core enterprise system to retain high flexibility to build an ecosystem of technology.[3] The gain: the ability to operate with speed and flexibility for end users. Alternatively a fragile organisation.[4] Here the hazard is the domino effect: the chain reaction in which one misstep triggers a set of troublesome consequences.[5]

Failure in ERP and digital transformation occurs with one well-meaning decision after another. **David Ogilvie**

SO WHAT?

Once a new technology rolls over you, if you're not part of the steamroller, you're part of the road. **Stewart Brand**

It was a common cliché: *no one ever got fired for buying IBM*. There has been a major shift: we may now get fired for buying the equivalent of IBM. The trade-off: a standard all-purpose solution that works anytime, anywhere, anyplace, but doesn't do anything all that well. Vis a vis the challenge of integrating a series of different applications for exceptional impact.

A good starting point is to ask: what does look like for the customer? This focuses minds to avoid the distractions of the noisy hype of the vendors.

NOTES

1. The story of Netflix; https://about.netflix.com/en

2. Netflix. Addressing the Challenges and Opportunities; https://medium.com/digital-society/netflix-addressing-the-challenges-and-opportunities-04ac4bd5cae8

3. Building a technology ecosystem at a major US food producer; https://www.gartner.com/en/articles/4-lessons-from-land-o-lakes-on-building-a-digital-ecosystem

4. Antifragile: How to Live in a World We Don't Understand; https://www.theguardian.com/books/2012/nov/21/antifragile-how-to-live-nassim-nicholas-taleb-review

5. A massive tech outage is causing worldwide disruptions; https://apnews.com/article/what-is-crowdstrike-worldwide-outage-94b4fc5ac6eed46ddcd565a5f1e4b916

Should we welcome generative AI?

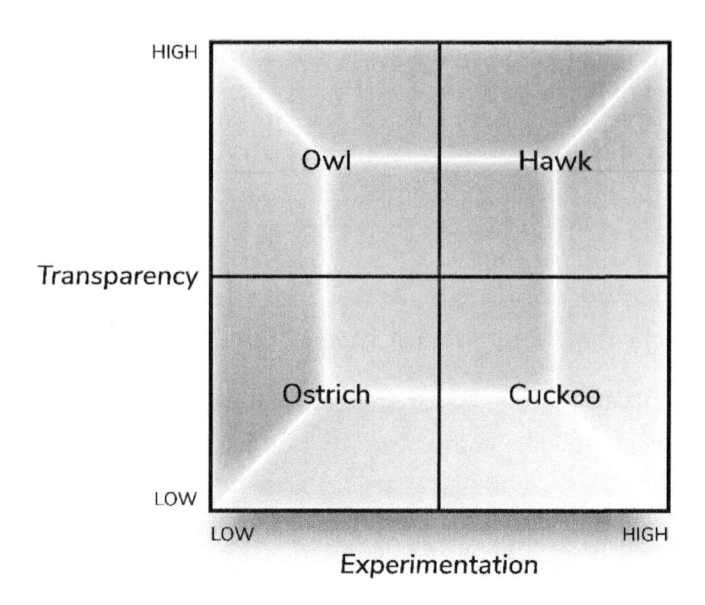

```
         HIGH
          |
          |    Owl    |    Hawk
Transparency   ———————+———————
          |   Ostrich |   Cuckoo
          |
         LOW
          LOW                HIGH
              Experimentation
```

I think this is the age about expertise at your fingertips. Anyone can become an expert in anything because you have the AI assistant helping you. **Satya Nadella**

Large Language Models - LLMs - have entered all aspects of our lives - even if we don't know it. Educators deploy ChatGPT to create instructional materials, quizzes, and interactive learning modules, for a more informative and engaging student experience. Digital marketers use ChatGPT to craft ad copy, blog posts, and social media content to target and captivate a specific audience - you.

You can't expect that what you've become a master in will keep you valuable throughout the whole of your career, and most people are now going to be working into their 70s. Being a generalist is very unwise. Your major competitor is Wikipedia or Google. **Lynda Gratton**

Generative AI is now a feature of the world of work. About 40% of workers worldwide are in high exposure occupations. In advanced economies, 60%. The implications?[1] Is this an issue? Jobs are made of many tasks. Will Gen AI make us more productive through augmentation as we work alongside this technology?

We will have for the first time something smarter than the smartest human. It's hard to say exactly what that moment is, but there will come a point where no job is needed. **Elon Musk**

How should we respond to AI as it marches into our workplaces?

Experimentation. To what extent do we embrace Gen AI? Low is a cautious scepticism, doubtful of the business gains. High is rapid learning to discover what does and doesn't work to assess the implications and implement trials at speed to evaluate the impact.

Transparency. Is there a defensible view of how Gen AI operates? Can it be explained with clarity to key stakeholders - employees, customers, suppliers, regulators and governmental bodies? Low transparency is the secretive black box. No one knows how the algorithms of AI work - they keep shifting over time. High transparency[2] opens the box and accepts rigour and governance.

If you do not speak English. I am at your disposal with 187 other languages along with their various dialects and sub-tongues. **Robbie the Robot**

Four approaches are identified.

Ostrich. Low experimentation and low transparency combine for a head in the sand approach. This is the black box of the past based on out-dated and flawed datasets that have stopped learning. But no one can explain how and why. An increasingly unsustainable position.

He behaved like an ostrich and put his head in the sand, thereby exposing his thinking parts. **George Carman**

Owl. Low experimentation and high transparency is fearful of the risks of getting it wrong with customers and other stakeholders. At best, this is robust governance wary of the hazards of implementing indefensible processes. At worst, ruthless competitors exploit this business naivete.

I think the shocking thing to discover is the owls are not stupid and very feral, very hard to train. **Robbie Coltrane**

Cuckoo. An approach that combines high experimentation and low transparency. At best, the beginnings of breakthrough innovation to test and retest and run pilots to explore business opportunities. Alternatively, if not managed well, it becomes a wasteful and meaningless activity without bottom-line impact.

One cuckoo bird does not bring the spring. **Greek Proverb**

Hawk. A combination of high experimentation and high transparency. The upside: an open-source strategy to test and adopt what works into business processes and keeps tracking what is and isn't working. Alternatively, in chasing the shiny and new, it confuses users.

Bright the hawk's flight on the empty sky. **Ursula Le Guin**

SO WHAT?

Potentially, we are talking about the end of human history - the end of the period dominated by human beings. **Yuval Noah Harari**

As Gen AI comes into the workplace, we can deny the reality. Or shift to a learning curve to experiment with its possibilities. The important questions: how can tasks be augmented with AI to automate the routine stuff and make work more productive?

How do we know how to ask better questions of generative AI?[3] Do we know what to do with the answers? Will the human imagination stay ahead of the possibilities of technology?

You can Google any single fact. But what you can't Google is what you don't know. **William Poundstone**

NOTES

1. Staff discussion notes of the International Monetary Fund: SDN/2024/001S
https://help.openai.com/en/articles/6654000-best-practices-for-prompt-engineering-with-the-openai-api

2. At the time of writing OpenAI, the developer of ChatGPT have just agreed a deal with the FT Group to include all of the FT's output in an effort to ensure ChatGPT delivers output that can be trusted. Such information broking will become more common as the reliability of generative AI is called into question.
https://medium.com/the-modern-scientist/best-prompt-techniques-for-best-llm-responses-24d2ff4f6bca

3. Top 10 Real-Life Applications of Large Language Models;
https://pixelplex.io/blog/llm-applications/

Can we believe the chatbot?

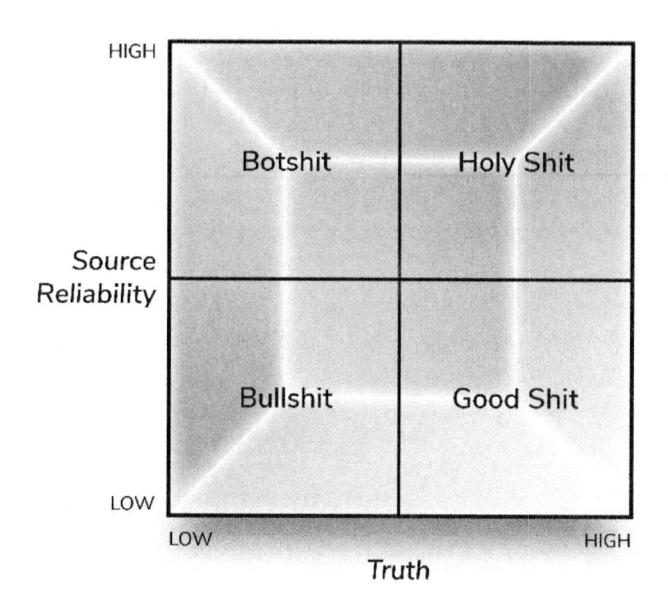

	Low Truth	High Truth
High Source Reliability	Botshit	Holy Shit
Low Source Reliability	Bullshit	Good Shit

Just promoted ChatGPT to our management team. It's an invaluable asset, enhancing decision-making efficiency and injecting humour into meetings. **Marc Benioff**

An early version of ChatGPT reported the world record for crossing the English Channel on foot is held by Christof Wandratsch of Germany. He completed the crossing in 14 hours and 51 minutes on August 14, 2020. This is AI hallucination.[1]

Large language models (LLMs) are the foundation for the AI chatbots of Google's *Bard* and OpenAI's *ChatGPT*. ChatGPT achieved 100 million users in 2 months after its launch: the fastest adoption of technology in history. But there are risks. A Federal District Court of New York fined two lawyers for submitting a legal brief containing fictitious cases and citations, all generated by ChatGPT.

I would call GPT's answers not just clueless but cluelessly clueless, meaning that GPT has no idea that it has no idea about what it is saying. **Douglas Hofstadter**

To what extent can we rely on the chatbots - as we engage with them as customers, employees, and citizens?

Truth. This reflects the extent to which there is an accurate representation of reality. At one end, a disregard for the facts. At the other, a consistent and coherent account from the evidence base.

Source Reliability. Which inputs from which sources are used to generate the output? At the low end of this spectrum, questionable research, if not downright deception, is deployed. At the other, multiple authoritative and replicated sources can be cross referenced.

In the age of generative AI, trust brokers will become increasingly necessary and increasingly valuable in the marketplace. **Hendrith Vanlon Smith**

We have four relationships with the chatbot.

Bull Shit. The combination of low truth and low source reliability. The bot generates random rubbish. At times plausible, it is still nonsense. The bullshitting chatbot has no concern for the truth. It is unconstrained by any requirement to support its claim. Bullshitting bots have the freedom to make stuff up, often intentionally programmed, as in for example, political campaigns.

It is impossible for someone to lie unless he thinks he knows the truth. Producing bullshit requires no such conviction. **Harry G. Frankfurt**[2]

Bot Shit. This is low truth with high source reliability. The impact can be superficially high, and the chatbot is often unquestioned by the human user, baffled by an array of impressive references. This is the chatbot at its most devious to draw on seemingly extraordinary research to provide credible guff.

I can smell bullshit from a mile away. But it's so much harder to detect when it's around you all day. **Dane Cook**

Good Shit. A riskier proposition when truth is high but source reliability is low. The chatbot picks up on an important reality, but not one that others have identified. At best, we locate a counter-intuitive insight. The risk: we accept this chatbot output and go out on a limb against the prevailing wisdom to the laughter of our peers.

Inhale tha good shit exhale tha bad shit. **Snoop Dog**

Holy Shit. The chatbot provides truth verifiable from multiple, independent and reliable sources. This is credible output to inform our problem analysis and decision making. Alternatively, a nagging suspicion that the chatbot has become even more deceitful than we ever imagined. Big Tech has found another way to become more believable.

Holy Hole in a Doughnut! **Robin, Batman**[3]

SO WHAT?

Large Language Models are like fountains of knowledge, reflecting both the brilliance and biases of humanity, and it's our responsibility to guide their streams with wisdom and ethical foresight. **ChatGPT4**[4]

How do we make sense of the outputs of chatbots? They should become more trustworthy, trained on bigger and better data-sets. But a combination of commercial factors, technological constraints and human scepticism continue.

Chatbots are not going to go away. Wise users will however continue to question - in particular the outputs of ethically and politically contentious issues - and trust their own intuition.

NOTES

1. What Are LLM Hallucinations? Causes, Ethical Concern, & Prevention; https://www.unite.ai/what-are-llm-hallucinations-causes-ethical-concern-prevention/

2. Brandolini's Law (aka the Bullshit Asymmetry Principle): It takes a lot more energy to refute bullshit than to produce it. Hence, the world is full of unrefuted bullshit.

3. Robin's 20 Weirdest Holy Batman Lines From the TV Show; https://www.liveabout.com/robins-oddest-holy-exclamations-from-the-batman-tv-series-3896999

4. ChatGPT 4.0 on checking for hallucinations in its output:

Cross-reference with multiple sources. Check credible sources: Verify the information against reputable sources such as academic journals, official reports, and trusted news outlets. Look at multiple sources to get a range of viewpoints, especially for contentious or complex topics.

Check for consistency. Repeat queries: Ask the same question in different ways to see if you get consistent answers from the AI. Compare with previous knowledge: cross-check the AI's answers with what you already know about the topic.

Evaluate the source's reputation. Prefer information from official websites e.g., government, educational institutions, and recognized experts in the field. Look for references to peer-reviewed studies and publications.

Analyse the detail and specificity. Depth of information: reliable answers often provide detailed explanations, specific data, and references to original sources. Citations and references: reliable responses often include citations or refer to specific documents, studies, or historical data.

Be wary of overconfidence. Check for tentative language. Reliable information often acknowledges uncertainties and limitations, rather than presenting everything as an absolute fact. Avoid definitive statements: Be cautious of overly definitive or sweeping statements without proper evidence.

Understand the imitations. AI's knowledge is based on the data it was trained on, which has a cutoff date and may not include the latest information. AI cannot conduct new research or provide firsthand data. It synthesizes existing information.

Use fact checking tools. Utilise fact-checking websites like Snopes, FactCheck.org, or the fact-checking sections of major news organizations. Plagiarism checkers: ensure the information is not directly lifted from another source without proper attribution.

Seek expert opinions. When in doubt, seek confirmation from experts in the relevant field. For critical matters (legal, medical, technical), always consult a qualified professional.

Contextual understanding. For current events or rapidly changing information, ensure the data is up-to-date.

Understand the historical context to see if the information aligns with known facts.

Logical and critical thinking. Assess if the information logically follows and makes sense. If something seems off or contradicts known information, dig deeper to understand why.

HOW TO BREAK OPEN THE BOXES

Four ways of looking at the world

A person will be imprisoned in a room with a door that's unlocked and opens inwards, as long as it does not occur to them to pull rather than push. **Ludwig Wittgenstein**

100 quadrants cannot capture the complexity and ambiguity across the spectrum of challenges we face in the different domains of life: family and friendships, work, in business and planning our financial future. This is obvious. The assumption is often one of binary logic. The world we experience is much more haphazard and uncertain. The reality is fuzzy logic - and the acceptance of continuous not dichotomous variation

Nonetheless, the grids in this book are a starting point. They represent a box of crayons to help colour the world. Visual representations have a much more direct impact than words. Patterns have the immediacy to cut through the verbiage of long winded text that loses genuine insight. Crayons lack finesse and nuance, and often result in a cartoon-like caricature. But they help draw a picture.

When I haven't any blue I use red. **Pablo Picasso**

This book is about wisdom to:

- make sense of the complexity we face to identify the signal in the noise.
- recognise what does and doesn't matter in life for happiness and success.
- know which problems we should ignore immediately, avoid after a moment's reflection, and those which are important and have to be addressed.
- move us into actionable insight for decision making.

Knowledge is knowing that a tomato is a fruit. Wisdom is knowing not to put it in a fruit salad. **Miles Kington**

How can we apply the 100 grids with wisdom? David Hancock[1] highlights three types of problem:

- **tame**: well defined issues. A systematic sequence of logic is applied to established facts to resolve the problem for a sensible solution.
- **messy**: complex problems that incorporate interrelated issues with multiple stakeholders, all with different perspectives and interests. It is difficult to frame the challenge.
- **wicked**: extraordinarily complex, characterised by incomplete, contradictory, and changing requirements, often with an ethical dimension. It seems impossible to grasp the problem, never mind identify a solution.

The genre of smart thinking books highlights the cognitive biases that let us down in judgement and decision making. Maybe. But only up to a point. For the most part, these books tackle the tame problems of life. A structured methodology helps us define the problem and generate and evaluate options for a well-founded solution. Tame problems are not however the ones that stop us from sleeping at night: a troublesome teenager, a forthcoming appraisal with a difficult boss, negotiating the breakup of a marriage, coordinating organisational change - one potentially disruptive to the workforce.

Take anything that you want. But remember the bill must be paid. **Steve Gibbons Band**

Has the wave of smart thinking books made us any smarter in dealing with the messiness and wickedness of the range of challenges we encounter?[2] There is no evidence of this. Arguably, this mind-set is part of the problem with an assumption that an A to Z methodology will make us smarter people.

You probably know the sort of person that smart thinking books are designed to appeal to, and you probably find them incredibly annoying: rigid know-it-alls who fetishise logic and reason. **Tom Whyman**

Judgement requires both our head and heart, our intellect and feelings, our reason and intuition to work together.[3] Sometimes summarised as left versus right brain thinking, this is a simplification. The brain is much more complex than a left right dichotomy. Nevertheless, as Iain McGilchrist highlights, there is an important distinction to be made about how our brain shapes the ways in which we experience and attend to the world around us.[4]

Attention can be of low or high intensity. It also ranges from the highly narrow to the extremely broad. This grid identifies four modes of attention.[5]

	Low Intensity	High Intensity
High Breadth	Curious Exploration	AHA - Intuitive Insight
Low Breadth	Sequential Processing	Vigilance to Specifics

Sequential Processing. Low intensity and narrow attention views life as a puzzle to be solved. It adopts a detached thinking mode which - at best - retains objectivity and distance. Conversely, an approach that is indifferent to urgency and importance.

Curious Exploration. This combines low intensity with a broad span of attention. A more relaxed perspective, it gives us the breathing space and time to think far and wide to accommodate new information and synthesise it into new possibilities. Alternatively, this is the wandering mind without a focus to move us to action.

When it comes to large undertakings, dwelling on the big picture can be paralysing, and a distraction from the next step, which is the only one you can ever actually take. **Oliver Burkeman**

Vigilance to Specifics. When high intensity intersects with a narrow focus, our attention is concentrated on the detail to grasp the facts of the situation. Human nature being what it is, it is predisposed to identify the downside of threat rather than the upside of opportunity. This attentional mode is key to our short term survival. The downside: our close up view misses the bigger picture, and we allow the small stuff to sweat.

AHA - Intuitive Insight. This is attention of high intensity within a broad scope. Integrating a range of different perspectives, the pieces of the jigsaw come together for a clear vision of bigger possibilities. This is original thinking to connect the dots. It can also be, from time to time, the misguided idiosyncrasies of the eccentric.

If one is master of one thing and understands one thing well, one has at the same time, insight into and understanding of many things. **Vincent Van Gogh**

Each mode has its role to play. McGilchrist however argues that we often allow Vigilance to Specifics to dominate, and to the detriment of other attentional states. But when these four patterns fail to cooperate they come into conflict, and problems emerge. When Sequential Processing reframes wicked problems as tame problems, we look for quick and easy solutions which in turn create further difficulties. And if tame problems are perceived as messy, we over complicate what is simple and straightforward.

Continuing to attempt to tame a world increasingly filled with messes and wicked problems, makes it a dangerously unstable place. **Paul Barnet**

Appendix 1 provides a short questionnaire identify the balance of your attentional mode.

Top down or bottom up wisdom

Successful people do things that unsuccessful people don't do, and they don't do things that unsuccessful people do. **Bob Proctor**

How do we approach the range of problems we encounter in life? On the one hand, there is a top down approach that relies on a theory to draw on universal principles. Winston Churchill proposed that in *critical and baffling situations, it is always best to return to first principles and simple action*. For example, Suzy Welch suggests the 10-10-10 principle: *when faced with any dilemma, ask what will be the consequences be in 10 minutes, 10 months and 10 years*.

Good in principle, but often difficult to implement in practice in specific context. The top down principle driven approach to wisdom - with the claim to work any time, any place, anywhere - is questionable.

Never do anything that you wouldn't want to explain to the paramedics is pretty good advice. If applied, it will avoid much personal embarrassment, as well as save substantial money in health care.[6] Most of the time, however, principles are general exhortations that fail to provide specific guidance. When Richard Layard suggests: *the secret is to have goals that are stretching enough, but not too stretching* - this is not meaningful advice, but an empty statement. True but trivial. Here, principles are vague platitudes that lack application in the real world situations we encounter.

The Law of the Ridiculous Reverse: if the opposite of a statement is plainly absurd, it was not worth making in the first place. **Simon Hoggart**

Alternatively, there is the bottom up approach. This is based on the knowledge and experience of experts to outline highly specific and prescriptive rules to determine what we should do and when.[7] Do this, get that. This is the promise of the burgeoning advice industry.

Physics tries to discover 3 laws to explain 99% of the universe. Psychology should be content with discovering the 99 laws that explain 3% of the universe. **Emanuel Derman**

Indicative of the advice industry is Sarah Tomley's *What Would Freud Do; how the greatest psychotherapists would solve your everyday problems*. Given that Freud was wrong on almost every issue, this is unlikely to provide much practical life wisdom.[8]

A man came to Mozart and asked him how to write a symphony. Mozart replied, You are too young to write a symphony. The man said, You were writing symphonies when you were 10 years of age, and I am 21. Mozart said, Yes, but I didn't run around asking people how to do it.

Unfortunately, the best advice comes from people who don't provide advice. And the people keenest to offer their insights are probably the worst sources of advice.[9] Daniel Greenberg points out: *don't ask the barber if you need a haircut.* Asking for advice from anyone with a vested interest in the outcome is unlikely to give us an impartial answer.

Even more troublesome is the habit of the advice industry to change and update the rules it prescribes. Jordan Peterson is the master of this wheeze. After his 12 Rules for Life in 2018, four years later, he discovered another set of rules: Beyond Order: 12 More Rules for Life. Presumably, by 2026 Peterson will have found another 12.[10]

If your life is shit, then you can't really give advice to other people. **Kyriacos**

Know the scope of the problem and the solutions

If I had an hour to solve a problem I'd spend 55 minutes thinking about the problem and five minutes thinking about solutions. **Albert Einstein**

We are back to tame, messy and wicked problems. It is not always easy to spot the difference. This quadrant maps out the range of issues we encounter in life and the associated responses and options based on two key themes.

Problem Definition. How well is the issue defined? Some problems are poorly defined. These are the vague and fuzzy issues. We can't quite put our finger on what is going on. Other issues we understand quickly and grasp the essentials easily.

Actionable Solution. The degree to which a solution can be found and actioned. This ranges from the impossible to locate, never mind implement, through to the relatively straightforward in which a meaningful solution can be realised and executed.

No precautions can avoid problems that we do not yet foresee. To prepare for those, there's nothing we can do but increase our ability to put things right if they go wrong. **David Deutsch**

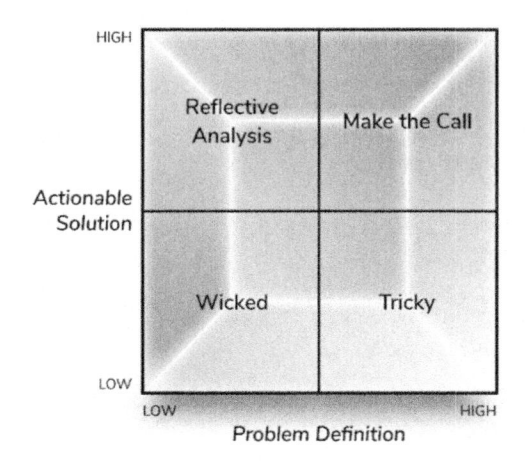

	Low Problem Definition	High Problem Definition
High Actionable Solution	Reflective Analysis	Make the Call
Low Actionable Solution	Wicked	Tricky

Wicked. Low problem definition with a low implementable solution represents the challenges we dread in our personal, professional and business lives. There seems no obvious starting point to grasp the issues at work, never mind determine a way forward. We can adopt the strategy of Warren Buffett: *I don't look to jump over seven-foot bars, I look for one-foot bars I can step over.* Wise counsel in financial investment, some wicked problems we can't ignore.

A problem well stated is a problem half solved. **John Dewey**

Reflective Analysis. The problem is ill defined. But there is a sense that a solution - or least a range of options - will eventually be found and implemented. This is the hard work of revisiting the issues and reframing the problem, until we understand the causal factors at work and the likely consequences of ignoring the challenge.

We fail more often because we solve the wrong problem than because we get the wrong solution to the right problem. **Russell Ackoff**

Tricky. The problem is well defined but there is no obvious solution. Either we have failed to understand the problem properly; we are looking at the issues through the wrong lens. Or, we have not been sufficiently imaginative in the search for solutions. At best, we identify a positive route out of the maze. At worst we remain stuck, unable to escape from the problem.

I'm always changing. I probably adjust five times a second throughout a two-hour show. This means that I'm constantly figuring out how to succeed. I know I can never have absolute control over the situation. But I've struck a dynamic precision in my juggling process, so that I can find balance. **Michael Moschen, circus performer**

Make the Call. A defined problem and an implementable solution. The issues are known and can be resolved. Only prevarication and procrastination hold us back as we ask: is it that easy? Can it be that simple? Sometimes it can be.

If you're not sure what to do with the ball, just pop it in the net and we'll discuss your options afterwards. **Bill Shankly, legendary manager of Liverpool Football Club**

Three over-arching themes underpin the 100 quadrants throughout this book.

The first is the tension between **risk and reward**. In most scenarios there is the promise of an upside: an advantage to be gained for greater success. This is the optimism of future possibilities for better outcomes. But reward also brings risk and a potential downside. We experience setbacks and disappointments to find ourselves even worse off than where we started.

There's something bad in everything good, and something good in everything bad. **Michael Lewis, Liar's Poker**

For Phil Knight, *if we fight not to win, but to avoid losing*, this is a sure fire losing strategy. Possibly, but it depends on our attitudes to risk. Conversely, Charlie Munger advises: *I don't want to play a game where people have an advantage over me. I don't play in a game where other people are wise and I am stupid. I look for a game where I am wise, and they are stupid.*

We each have a different stance towards risk. But whatever our attitude, it helps if we evaluate the likelihood of the outcomes we anticipate.

No matter how you define success, risk is a necessary ingredient of every successful life. Risk puts you in position to win. **Max Gunther**

The second recurring theme is the trade-off between the **short and long term**. This is the tension between the immediacy of today's opportunities versus the possibilities of the future. Our time and energies can be directed towards the now to live for the moment. Alternatively, we prepare for the challenges that lie ahead. And sometimes we get caught up in fantasies of how the future might be very different. Again, there is no solution, but only a trade-off between today and tomorrow.

It's nice to have a lot of money, but you know, you don't want to keep it around forever. I prefer buying things. Otherwise, it's a little like saving sex for your old age. **Warren Buffett**

The third refrain in many of the quadrants is the balance of **me versus others**. To what extent do we focus on and address our own individual needs and ambitions or attend to the concerns of others? This is the balance between what is good for us personally, and what is best for others. Again, there is no answer to this dilemma.

You are free to do whatever you like. You need only face the consequences. **Sheldon Kopp**

Compromise is an unpopular term. It implies some kind of unsatisfactory acceptance of standards that are less than optimal. Alternatively, compromise is the resolution of competing demands to arrive at an actionable solution.

The test of a first rate intelligence is the ability to hold two opposed ideas in the mind at the same time, and still retain the ability to function. **Scott Fitzgerald**

Breaking out of the boxes: left and right brain

It was all very well going on about pure logic and how the universe was ruled by logic and the harmony of numbers, but the plain fact of the matter was that the Disc was manifestly traversing in space on the back of a giant turtle and the gods had a habit of going around to atheists' houses and smashing their windows. **Terry Pratchett**

This check-list is based on a simple framework of Think, Talk and Do. It is a model we have used extensively at an organisational, team and individual level.[11] Think, Talk and Do highlights three overarching themes:

- **Think**: how well do we tackle the problems we face for a robust solution?
- **Talk:** do we communicate effectively within the decision making process?
- **Do:** can we manage the implementation process to get things done?

At each phase, the left and right brain are in play.[12]

My thesis is that for us as human beings there are two fundamentally opposed realities, two different modes of experience; that each is of ultimate importance in bringing about the recognisably human world; and that their difference is rooted in the bihemispheric structure of the brain. It follows that the hemispheres need to co-operate, but I believe they are in fact involved in a sort of power struggle. **Iain McGilchrist**

Both the left and right brain have their relative virtues and vices. The aim is to integrate the two approaches at each phase of Think, Talk and Do to translate initial thoughts into practical outcomes. The balance of left and right brain thinking depends of course on the nature of the challenge. Coordinating a major construction project requires a different response to dealing with an under-performing employee.

If we can stay with the tension of opposites long enough - sustain it, be true to it - we can sometimes become vessels within which the divine opposites come together and give birth to a new reality. **Marie-Louise von Franz**

Work through the check-lists of Think, Talk and Do. As an exercise individually, to check you have covered your bases in addressing any personal challenges. Within your team, as part of the next away day to stimulate a debate about any problems it faces. Or, as part of a strategic planning exercise to check assumptions; is the organisation thinking and feeling clearly about its business challenges?

Visionary decision-making happens at the intersection of intuition and logic. **Paul O'Brien**

THINK

LEFT BRAIN	RIGHT BRAIN
Does this problem matter in the broader scheme of life's challenges? Or are these issues best avoided? Trivial and of not much significance? Or major, and demand much attention?	Do I view this problem as an opportunity? Does it fill me with delight? Or as a threat and horrific prospect? Why? Will I engage with this problem? Or dismiss it as a distraction? Or much too troublesome, and I put in the box too difficult to tackle?
Do I need to respond immediately? Or is there an opportunity for further reflection?	Do I apply emotional composure for a considered response? Or freeze when confronted with the unpleasant?
Have I worked through the issues to access the relevant facts and figures to come to an informed judgement? Can I rely on this information?	Have I applied my intuition to grasp quickly the essentials of the problem? Or am I jumping to conclusions, overly influenced by gut feeling?
Which criteria will I apply to work out the pros and cons of the available alternatives? How far reaching is my listing of alternatives? Have I worked through the upside and downside of the options and evaluated the trade-offs? Does this evaluation reflect both reward - getting it right - as well as risk - making things worse?	Is my intuition telling me something important that I need to listen to? Are any of these options personally uncomfortable? Why? Am I denying a difficult reality? Alternatively, have my feelings already made up my mind?
Does my analysis balance simplicity and complexity? Is it simple enough to highlight the critical variables? Or way too simplistic? Or am I over-complicating the obvious?	Have I made key connections to grasp the key essence of the problem? Or, am I over-feeling the issues to see sensitivities and nuances that probably don't exist? Am I allowing levels of stress to distort my understanding of the issues. Do I need to back off and cool down before coming back to the problem?
Have I come to a conclusion that has a	Does this conclusion make me feel more or

clear "because": a defensible logic to explain my initial analysis of the problem to connect cause to consequence?	less confident? If more confident, is this reckless delusion? Am I rushing to an immediate solution to avoid unsettling feelings of doubt and certainty? Here, any decision is better than no decision. If less confident, will I procrastinate? Should I backtrack to ask: why am I feeling about these issues the way I do?
When I revisit my analysis of the issues and evaluate the different alternatives, am I satisficing for the least of worst options? Or optimising for the best outcome? Have I worked through the probability of success and the likelihood of possible failure?	Have I arrived at an AHA moment of insight? Is this a genuinely creative flash of meaning to see the problem in its essentials? Am I now feeling more positive than negative about the solution? Or motivated by a need for rapid closure?

Outcome

A well framed insight into the issues, the significance and scope of the problems, realistic options and a recognition of the trade-offs for the short and long-term.

Every psychological extreme secretly contains its own opposite or stands in some sort of intimate and essential relation to it. Indeed, it is from this tension that it derives its peculiar dynamism. **Carl Jung**

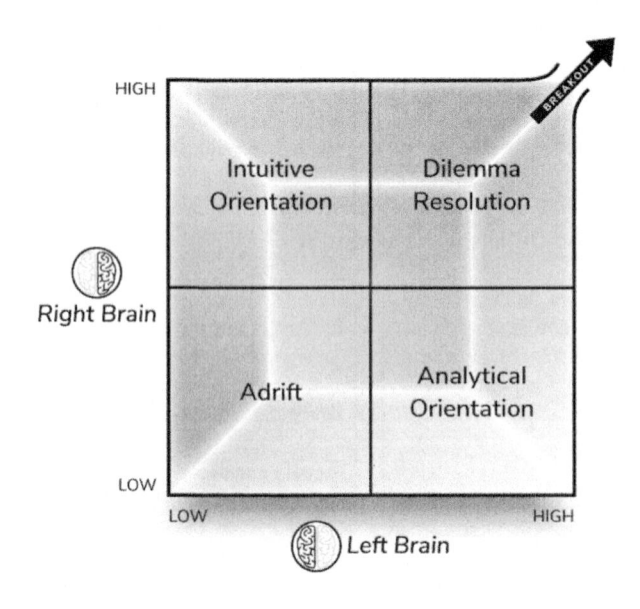

Review the check-lists in the two columns, and plot your own position using the two axes of left and right brain. Are you drawing on both the left and right brain as part of a harmonious process? Or overly reliant on one approach?

If a dominant left brain stance, how would a shift to a right-brain approach enhance your thinking process for deeper insight? Or, if there is more emphasis on a right brain intuition, how might a more left brain - analytical - orientation improve your problem solving skills?

How easy or difficult would it be for you to accommodate both outlooks to resolve the complex dilemmas of life?

TALK

LEFT BRAIN	RIGHT BRAIN
Do I have an objective view of the psychology of others, assessing the motivation and the causes of behaviour of those involved in the decision?	Am I an intuitive psychologist to read quickly what others are thinking and feeling? Do I pick up the signals that allow me to know, for example, who I can and can't trust?
Who do I need to engage in this challenge? Is it a problem I initially need to work through on my own before I involve others? At what stage should I bring in others? Who cares about the issues? Who knows and can provide insight? Who can do something about the problem?	Am I encouraging multiple perspectives from different sources? Does my interpersonal approach invite open and honest interaction from others? Or, does it exclude key people from the conversation? Why?
What kind of debate is needed to review the problem and explore the options? One that requires an extensive and in-depth discussion? Or a relatively short check-in to overview the issues?	Am I happy to accept I may be wrong and need to rethink my assumptions and acknowledge disagreement from others? Or do I need to feel vindicated as part the debate to prove that I am right?
Is there a systematic decision making process to involve and consult the right people at the right time? How will I manage competing and conflicting opinions?	Does my intuition read the room, alert to others' support or opposition to my proposals? Can I flex my tactics accordingly based on the interpersonal dynamics?
Which feedback systems are in place to monitor activity and results? Is this information coming from the right sources to detect the signal from the noise?	Can I go with my instincts to spot when there is something wrong? Or too optimistic and in denial of the tough realities that indicate there might be a problem?
How will conflict be managed and resolved? Do I rely on an appeal to facts and figures and rational argument? Is this working for me? Or, do I find it difficult to hear the mood music and detect others' genuine responses?	Do I establish empathy with others to appeal to their deep-seated interests and motivations, and resolve differences of view? Or, does the prospect of conflict appal me? Here I avoid it and am too quick to accommodate others' demands? Or will I deploy aggressive tactics to confront others

	and push my personal agenda?
Do I conclude conversations with a thoughtful and balanced summary to reflect a range of diverse views? Or am I putting my spin on others' input to persevere with my initial proposals? And misreading the mood of the room to allow unresolved issues to linger?	Do my ideas connect with the feelings and emotions of others; they don't just get in their heads but in their hearts? Do I sense that others have my back and will deliver on their commitments?

Outcome

A shared understanding of the issues emerging from an engagement with others that listens to competing views and builds commitment.

To be human means to be constantly in the grip of opposing emotions, to daily reconcile apparently conflicting tensions. I want this, but I need that. I cherish this, but I adore its opposite, too. **Stephen Fry**

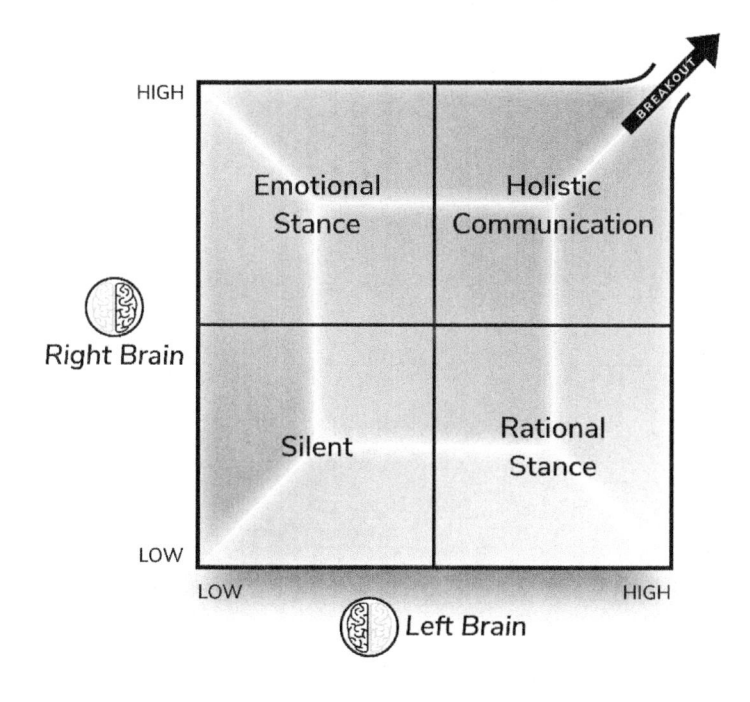

Review the check-lists in the two columns, and plot your own position using the two axes of left and right brain. Are you drawing on both the left and right brain as part of a harmonious process? Or overly reliant on one approach?

If a dominant left brain stance, how would a shift to a right-brain approach improve your ability to connect to and engage others? Or, if there is more emphasis on a right brain perspective, how might a left brain orientation enhance your interpersonal effectiveness and persuasive impact?

How easy or difficult would it be for you to resolve the messy business of consultation and communication?

DO

LEFT BRAIN

RIGHT BRAIN

LEFT BRAIN	RIGHT BRAIN
Do I have a systematic action plan with a definitive sequence of next steps and a methodology to work through each step? Or is there a nagging suspicion that something important has been missed?	Am I now personally convinced of my decision? This is do-able? Do I feel motivated to move on to next steps or still doubtful?
Have I mapped out a coherent road map from start to finish; I know this can be executed? Is this confidence reliant on the formality of a project plan rather than address how things work in messy reality?	Are my instincts telling me that I am now on the right lines? Or is this more a hope rather a realistic expectation of outcomes? Have I persuaded myself that this is the best of all possible worlds and that positive results will be achieved?
Have I established a contingency plan to mitigate the risks of any failings in implementation? Have I thought through my response to a worst case scenario? What is my Plan B?	Am I prepared to accept that the road ahead will be bumpy? Do I recognise the uncertainties of delivery? Will I wing it and respond to events flexibly as they occur? Or, freeze, stuck when my original plan is side railed?
Are key targets and metrics in place to track how I am advancing in the short and long-term? Will these provide a valid guide to genuine progress? Or will they give me a distorted version of events?	Am I sceptical of objective metrics as they are reported and prefer to back my intuition to highlight any barriers and blockers? Am I kidding myself and avoiding the question: am I in danger of failing?
Which feedback systems are in place to monitor activity and results? Is this information coming from the right sources to detect the signal from the noise?	Can I go with instincts to spot when there is something wrong? Or too optimistic and in denial about the tough realities to indicate there might be a problem?
When I face challenges to implementation, am I prepared to drill into the detail of the facts and figures to identify the causes? Or am I committed to push ahead with the original plan - come hell or high water?	Do I keep a level head to stand back and put any emerging problems into a wider perspective? Or, panic when things go wrong, and a risk I lose my emotional composure?

Do I conduct a comprehensive review of outcomes to identify the learning lessons of what worked and didn't work? Am I objective in the appraisal of the gap between what I intended to achieve and what actually happened?	Do I celebrate my successes to take pleasure from a job well done? Does this down-play any failings? Or do I exaggerate any shortcomings and catastrophise?

Outcome

A game plan for execution that translates overall aims into a sequence of achievable steps with flexibility to adapt and adjust to changing events focused on successful outcomes.

Conviction and clarity are opposite. When your soul is fully asleep, you've full conviction of mind. When your soul is fully awakened, you've full clarity of mind. In-between you have a dilemma. **Shunya**

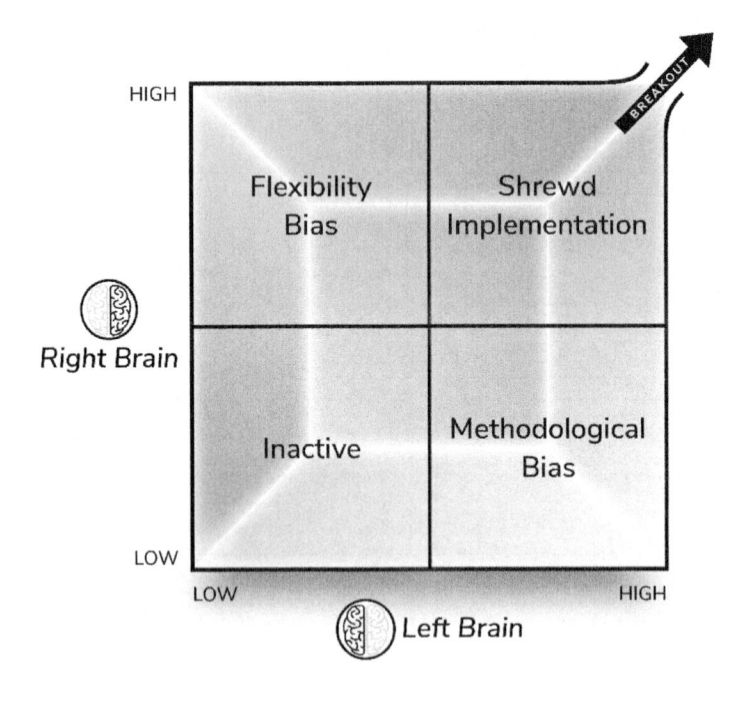

A 2x2 matrix with axes Right Brain (vertical, LOW to HIGH) and Left Brain (horizontal, LOW to HIGH). Quadrants: top-left Flexibility Bias, top-right Shrewd Implementation (with BREAKOUT arrow), bottom-left Inactive, bottom-right Methodological Bias.

Review the check-lists in the two columns, and plot your own position using the two axes of left and right brain. Are you drawing on both the left and right brain as part of a harmonious process? Or overly reliant on one approach?

If a dominant left brain stance, how would a shift to a right-brain approach enhance your ability to get things at speed? Or, if there is more emphasis on a right brain perspective, how might a left brain orientation - with more structure - make it easier to achieve your goals?

How easy or difficult would it be for you to shift to a mind-set that incorporates both approaches and balance a structured approach to focus on deadlines with an improvisational operating style?

Grid 101 and beyond

If you always put a limit on everything you do, physical or anything else, it will spread into your work and into your life. There are no limits. There are only plateaus, and you must not stay there, you must go beyond them. **Bruce Lee**

The 100 quadrants do not cover the complexity of life. They serve as signposts on the journey, and often as shortcuts through life's terrain. This book is not just about the 100 grids, but a shift in mindset and the application of a thinking tool for the challenges and dilemmas we will encounter.

Generate your own quadrant to open up insight into a current life problem you face, or to prepare for a forthcoming assignment

First, **draw a diagram** with the X and Y axes with four boxes. It sounds trivial. It isn't. It is a good start.

Second, **start with a question**. It will take time to frame this question at the right level of detail. Too specific, and the question probably lacks power. Too general, and it will be vague and lack immediate relevance to the current challenge. Apply both left and right brain thinking to work through the issues to locate a manageable question.

Third, **hypothesise**. Which dimensions might illuminate this question for a better understanding of the issues? At this stage, create a list of the factors you think might underpin the causal dynamic. Review the list; which two seem the most powerful? Are these themes independent; they don't overlap and are genuinely differentiated. Which is the X and Y axis? Add these descriptions to your drawing.

Four, and the fun part. **Work through the permutations** of low-low, low-high, high-low, and high-high. Scribble down a description for each of the four boxes. If this proves difficult, the axes may not be independent. Avoid tautology to say the same thing twice in different words. Attempt to summarise the essence of the four combinations with a fresh perspective.

Have you located a set of working ideas. Not all your labels will have the wow factor. Some may be routinely descriptive. But draw on the right brain for imagery, analogies and metaphors from different walks of life to state something memorable. Think about the worlds of, for example, sport, the arts, celebrities, culture, business and politics to create a vocabulary that is distinctive and compelling for each box.

Five. **Review the updated labels**. Do they capture something important to help answer the original question? The aim of the quadrant is not to find a solution at this stage. Each of the four boxes will have an upside and downside - only understood within context. But the grid should help you and others identify trade-offs, between risk and reward, the short and long term, and against the theme of me vis a vis we.

Six. **Ask an informed colleague or friend for feedback**. Do they *get it?* Has it helped them make sense of an important question to work through a dilemma? Are the options clear? Is there a sense of a way forward? What actionable insight emerges? If not, revisit the question and the dimensions.

The mind is everything. What you think, you become. What you feel, you attract. What you imagine, you create. **Buddha**

This may be best done as a workshop or a team exercise. But if you have a go, you gain traction on the problem and associated dilemmas, and the trade-offs. Better still, a way forward is identified. Good luck. We had huge fun identifying key questions and exploring how quadrants - when the left and right brain cooperate - help grapple with issues. We hope you also enjoy grid thinking in your journey in life.

Keep having a go and grid thinking will become second nature.

Final Thoughts

This book asked how crazy is it getting? Are we in a world of VUCA, BANI, RUPT and TUNA? Probably. But it was ever thus. At what point in history did commentators say everything is simple and solvable?

We stand on a mountain pass in the midst of whirling snow and blinding mist, through which we get glimpses now and then of paths which may be deceptive. If we stand still we shall be frozen to death. If we take the wrong road we shall be dashed to pieces. We do not certainly know whether there is any right one. What must we do? Be strong and of a good courage. Act for the best, hope for the best, and take what comes. **Fitzjames Stephen**

Breaking open the boxes provides one heuristic - a short cut - to make sense of the complexity and uncertainty of the messy and wicked challenges we encounter in life. We break open the boxes - not through cleverness - but when we recognise how our own mind set shapes the way we see the world and frames the issues. And when we draw on the potential of both the left and right brain. It also helps if we approach the dilemmas, polarities and paradoxes of life[13] with a combination of curiosity, courage and humility.

The seeker goes to the mountain top and asks the learned one: Where does wisdom come from? Good judgment. Where does good judgement come from? Experience. Where does experience come from? Bad judgement. **Sufi Story**

We hope reader that you can break open the boxes - for success, the easier rather than the harder way - with judgement and wisdom.

NOTES

1. Three types of problem; https://medium.com/undaunted-leaders/continuing-to-attempt-to-tame-a-world-increasingly-filled-with-messes-and-wicked-problems-makes-e639816fcd2b

2. The Doomed Project of' Smart Thinking, Tom Whyman; https://artreview.com/the-doomed-project-of-smart-thinking-julian-baggini/#:~:text=You%20probably%20know%20the%20sort,about%20religion%3B%20who%20might%20have
The yin and yang of the modern smart thinking genre are represented by two of its foundational bestsellers: Malcolm Gladwell's Blink and Daniel Kahneman's Thinking, Fast and Slow. Can smart thinking books really give you the edge? https://www.theguardian.com/books/2021/aug/21/can-smart-thinking-books-really-give-you-the-edge

3. This is also highlighted by the social psychologist Jonathan Haidt with his concept of the rider and the elephant. https://bigbangpartnership.co.uk/the-elephant-and-the-rider-how-humans-make-decisions/

4. Ways Of Attending: How Our Divided Brain Constructs the World and The Master And His Emissary, Iain McGilchrist

5. A quadrant adapted from the conceptualisation of Iain McGilchrist.

6. This is a variation of the Nelson Rockefeller principle: Never do anything you wouldn't be caught dead doing. Nelson - a former VP of the United States - passed away at the age of 70. While working late in his office, Nelson visited the nearby apartment of a 25 year female aide.
A real bum deal! NHS spent at least £500,000 on treating sexual mishaps last year; https://www.dailymail.co.uk/health/article-12186219/How-NHS-spends-500-000-year-sexual-mishaps.html

7. In Emotional Equations, Chip Conley outlines a series of formulae to make sense of life. This followed the attempt by Garth Sundem in Geek Logik: Easier Living Through Mathematics. Thought provoking and entertaining, it is however difficult to see how these enterprises at mathematical precision can provide much practical guidance in real world life situations.

8. Was Freud right about anything? https://www.livescience.com/why-freud-was-wrong.html

9. Good Advice From Bad People Zac Bissonnette. If you want to be a compassionate man, don't assault a flight attendant because the grapes arrived prepackaged with the cheese. How televangelist Robert Schuller lost the plot.

10. Jordan Peterson is a Spineless Charlatan; https://steemit.com/jordan/@kyriacos/jordan-peterson-is-a-spineless-charlatan. 12 Rules for Life: An Antidote to Chaos by Jordan B Peterson. Digested Read;

https://www.theguardian.com/books/2018/jan/28/12-rules-for-life-an-antidote-to-chaos-by-jordan-b-peterson-digested-read

11. Think, Talk, Do. An extended discussion; A to Z and Back Again, Part 1 Adventures and Misadventures in Talent World; https://www.amazon.co.uk/Back-Again-Adventures-Misadventures-Talent/dp/1914424204/

12. Left Brain & Right Brain: 20 Brain Hemisphere Differences from The Master and His Emissary; https://www.sloww.co/left-brain-right-brain-hemispheres/

13. Dilemmas, Polarities and Paradoxes, Dilemmas, Polarities and Paradoxes; https://coacharya.com/blog/dilemmas-polarities-and-paradoxes/

Appendix 1: Your Attentional Mode

A short quiz to help you think about your operating style, and how you approach life and its challenges. You will be presented with 12 quartets, a set of words or statements designed to reflect different aspects of how you deal with the problems and decisions of life. Mark a Y by the statement or word that best describes you. All words may apply. Or possibly none. Do your best to select the one option more typical of your current approach; the *as is* of now, not how you would like it to be.

Life is:

1A. a puzzle to be solved
1B. an opportunity to keep discovering more
1C. the avoidance of what might go wrong
1D. making a breakthrough to gain a better perspective on life

2A. being on the alert to spot any threats quickly
2B. gaining insight to make better sense of life
2C. a set of problems to be analysed to find solutions
2D. a learning lesson to find out how things work

3A. a journey for greater knowledge and understanding
3B. a readiness to respond to any challenges
3C. a process to develop personal creativity
3D. an ongoing set of problems to tackle

4A. anticipating the moment when we achieve greater wisdom
4B. overcoming any difficulties that hold back progress
4C. finding out more about the world and its mysteries
4D. an attention to the risks of any future hazards

Which word best describes your typical approach?

5A. rational
5B. curious
5C. single minded
5D. perceptive

6A. exploratory
6B. conscientious
6C. imaginative
6D. logical

7A. disciplined
7B. intuitive
7C. objective
7D. investigative

8A. instinctive
8B. pragmatic
8C. open minded
8D. achieving

9A. adventurous
9B. careful
9C. spontaneous
9D. thorough

10A. systematic
10B. questioning
10C. diligent
10D. creative

11A. purposeful
11B. accepting
11C. methodical
11D. experimental

12A. flexible
12B. organised
12C. inquisitive
12D. sensible

Now the boring bit. Tally up your results by counting up the number of Ys for four scores:

SP: 1A, 2C, 3D, 4B, 5A, 6D, 7C, 8B, 9D, 10A, 11C, 12B

CE: 1B, 2D, 3A, 4C, 5B, 6A, 7D, 8C, 9A, 10B, 11D, 12C

VS: 1C, 2A, 3B, 4D, 5C, 6B, 7A, 8D, 9B, 10C, 11A, 12D

AHA: 1D, 2B, 3C, 4A, 5D, 6C, 7B, 8A, 9C, 10D, 11B, 12A

You should have four scores, a minimum of 0 and a maximum of 12 for each. Now plot your scores on the profile.

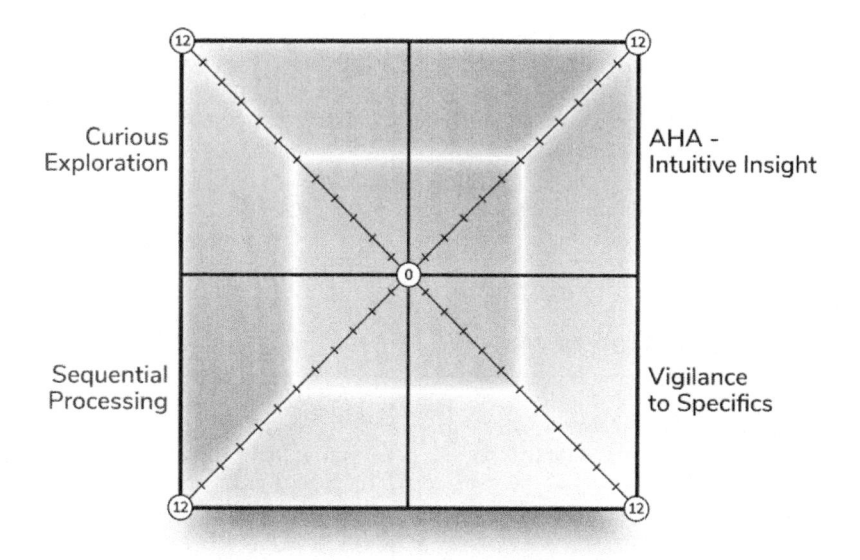

Curious Exploration

AHA - Intuitive Insight

Sequential Processing

Vigilance to Specifics

Sequential Processing

At best:
- an organised and systematic approach to apply logic to work through the analysis of problems
- methodical to maintain objectivity in the evaluation of the pros and cons of decision options
- disciplined to work out a practical solution to life's problems to find a practical outcome

The risks:
- caught up in the immediacy of problems to zero in a solution without addressing the wider issues at play
- a frustration with complex problems that pushes to implement a short-term make do solution
- a pragmatism to do what works now rather than pursue alternatives for an optimal future

Curious Exploration

At best:
- an open minded outlook to accept uncertainty and ambiguity in working through different life challenges
- an inquisitive approach to acknowledge it is better to ask the right questions than find an easy answer
- a readiness to keep listening, learning and discovering possibilities for further options

The risks:
- a potential to think at a theoretical and abstract level that allows issues to circle but rarely lands into practical outcomes
- a speculative mind-set that is reluctant to accept the obvious to tackle the tough stuff of life
- an ongoing dissatisfaction in search of the perfect solution that puts off the troublesome dilemmas of life

Vigilance to Specifics

At best:
- an urgency, quick to identify emerging issues and respond at pace to find a solution
- anticipating potential threats to protect the current position
- an alertness to risk which recognises how minor issues can escalate to become major problems

The risks:
- a critical stance to identify what might go wrong rather than identify solutions of what might go right
- a cautious approach that prefers to stick within a comfort zone of the familiar rather than take the bold decisions into the new
- the potential for an anxious life outlook, more concerned with the avoidance of risk rather than the opportunities of reward

AHA - Intuitive Insight

At best:
- a non-judgemental outlook that keeps options open to encourage fresh perspectives from different sources
- creative in identifying patterns from a range of issues to identify the bigger picture
- a willingness to apply intuition, unconstrained by the conventions of rational analysis

The risks:
- a speculative outlook that neglects pressing problems and allows difficult issues to drift and go unresolved
- an appeal to "gut feel" that overlooks key facts and figures in a robust analysis of problems
- a potential to fantasise about the "one thing" that is not grounded in the ambiguity of life's messy dilemmas

What does the profile indicate? A clear pattern in which one attentional mode dominates? If so, what is the upside and downside of how you look at the world? How does this shape your judgements and decisions?

Alternatively, is the profile balanced across the four areas? At best, this allows you to draw on a repertoire of different styles based on the issues as you experience them. Alternatively, there is no key driver to get to grips with the issues; this is decision making ambivalence that can become stuck.

Think about:

- your previous successes in problem solving; what worked for you?
- any mis-steps in judgement where you got it wrong? Why?
- current dilemmas you face; what is holding back a resolution?
- future challenges you can anticipate; what strategies will you deploy?

Printed in Great Britain
by Amazon